"The message of this highly interesting and well-edited collection is complexity and enigma, the gap between theory and practice concerning the freedom of religion. Many countries would declare their support for it, but when it comes to implementing, we many a time face nimby-not in my backyard. While legal institutions continue their more or less successful work, reality in many societies is grim. But having said that, sadly based on the gift of memory, we should never lose hope, in the spirit of prophet Malachi (2.10) – 'Have we not all one father?'"

Justice Professor Elyakim Rubinstein, *Hebrew University, Jerusalem, former Vice President of the Supreme Court of Israel and Attorney General of Israel*

"A timely and insightful collection examining two religious minorities in Europe, whose status is increasingly precarious – not only due to the growing secularization of European societies and the resulting indifference, insensitivity, or even hostility toward religious claims but also because of polarising political events that cast them as adversaries or outsiders. This book sheds new light on the diverse interpretations of state secularism, the principle of neutrality, and the practical challenges of ensuring reasonable accommodation for Jews and Muslims in Europe. A meticulously curated edited volume featuring a stellar cast of contributors".

Professor Anna Śledzińska-Simon, *University of Wrocław, member of the Cultural and Religious Diversity under State Law across Europe project at the Max Planck Institute for Social Anthropology in Halle*

Freedom of Religion, Minority Rights and the Law

This book provides an in-depth, scholarly reflection on the challenges that arise in guaranteeing religious freedom and protection of the rights of religious minorities in law and practice. Currently, the protection of religious minorities constitutes one of the foundations of the international human rights protection systems and is provided for in the constitutions of all democratic states. The volume identifies, analyses, and assesses the legal status of religious freedom and protection of religious minorities, with special focus on Jewish and Muslim minorities in the European and Israeli legal environments. It compares the discourses on the scope and boundaries of religious freedom with the actual treatment of religious freedom in legal regulations, the case law, and in practice by the general society. The book employs the resources of comparative law and national and international law, as well as legal theory. Extensive use is also made of decisions of the international courts, including the European Court of Human Rights and the Court of Justice of the European Union. The book will be a valuable resource for academics, researchers, and policymakers working in the areas of law and religion, international human rights law, comparative constitutional law, and religious studies.

Aleksandra Gliszczyńska-Grabias is Professor at the Institute of Law Studies of the Polish Academy of Sciences, Poland.

Aviad Hacohen is President of the Academic Center for Law and Science and former Dean of its Law School, former Lecturer on Constitutional Law and Jewish Law at the Hebrew University of Jerusalem, and Senior Research Fellow, Van Leer Institute Jerusalem, Israel.

Freedom of Religion, Minority Rights and the Law

The Status of Jewish and Muslim Minorities in Europe and Beyond

Edited by Aleksandra Gliszczyńska-Grabias and Aviad Hacohen

Routledge
Taylor & Francis Group
LONDON AND NEW YORK

INTERNATIONAL JEWISH LAWYERS
IJL

INSTITUTE OF LAW STUDIES POLISH ACADEMY OF SCIENCES
ILS PAS

First published 2025
by Routledge
4 Park Square, Milton Park, Abingdon, Oxon OX14 4RN

and by Routledge
605 Third Avenue, New York, NY 10158

Routledge is an imprint of the Taylor & Francis Group, an informa business

The publication was co-financed by Institute of Law Studies, Polish Academy of Sciences and the International Association of Jewish Lawyers and Jurists (IJL).

The open access version of this book has been funded by the International Association of Jewish Lawyers and Jurists (IJL).

British Library Cataloguing-in-Publication Data
A catalogue record for this book is available from the British Library

Library of Congress Cataloging-in-Publication Data
Names: Gliszczyńska-Grabias, Aleksandra editor | Hacohen, Aviad editor
Title: Freedom of religion, minority rights, and the law : the status of Jewish and Muslim minorities in Europe and beyond / edited by Aleksandra Gliszczyńska-Grabias and Aviad Hacohen.
Description: Abingdon, Oxon [UK] ; New York, NY : Routledge, 2025. | Includes bibliographical references and index.
Identifiers: LCCN 2025007952 | ISBN 9781032696911 hardback | ISBN 9781032729770 paperback | ISBN 9781003423294 ebook
Subjects: LCSH: Religious minorities--Legal status, laws, etc.--Europe | Jews--Legal status, laws, etc.--Europe | Muslims--Legal status, laws, etc.--Europe | Freedom of religion--Europe | International law and human rights--Europe
Classification: LCC KJC5144.M56 F74 2025 | DDC 342.408/5296--dc23/eng/20250306
LC record available at https://lccn.loc.gov/2025007952

ISBN: 978-1-032-69691-1 (hbk)
ISBN: 978-1-032-72977-0 (pbk)
ISBN: 978-1-003-42329-4 (ebk)

DOI: 10.4324/9781003423294

Typeset in Galliard
by SPi Technologies India Pvt Ltd (Straive)

Contents

Contributors

Grażyna Baranowska is Professor of Migration Law and Human Rights at the Friedrich-Alexander-Universität Erlangen-Nürnberg. Prior to that, she was a senior researcher at Hertie School's Centre for Fundamental Rights, leading a project on missing migrants funded by the European Union's (EU) Marie Skłodowska-Curie Actions, and worked as an Assistant Professor at the Institute of Law Studies of the Polish Academy of Sciences. In the past, she also worked for the Volkswagen Stiftung funded MEMOCRACY project (2021–2024), which scrutinises the intersection of memory laws and democracy in Central and Eastern Europe, as well as the EU-funded project on Memory Laws in European and Comparative Perspective (2016–2019). Next to her academic work, she worked as policy advisor at the German Institute for Human Rights and was involved in the process of drafting the General Comment on enforced disappearances and migration for the UN Committee on Enforced Disappearances. In 2022, she was appointed by the UN Human Rights Council as an independent expert of the UN Working Group on Enforced and Involuntary Disappearances.

Raphael Cohen-Almagor is Chair in Politics, Founding Director of the Middle East Study Centre (MESC), University of Hull; Fellow at the Israel Institute for Advanced Studies, the Hebrew University of Jerusalem; Global Fellow, Woodrow Wilson International Center for Scholars (WWICS), Washington, DC; and President of the Association for Israel Studies (AIS). Raphael was the Yitzhak Rabin-Fulbright Visiting Professor at UCLA School of Law and Department of Communication; Visiting Professor at the Krieger School of Arts and Sciences, Johns Hopkins University; Fellow at WWICS (twice); Distinguished Visiting Professor to the Faculty of Laws, University College London; and the 2023 Olof Palme Visiting Professor, Lund University, Sweden. He received his doctorate from the University of Oxford. Prof. Cohen-Almagor was the co-founder of Israel's Second Generation to the Holocaust and Heroism Remembrance Organization, and founder of the University of Haifa Center for Democratic Studies, The Van Leer Jerusalem Institute Medical Ethics Think Tank, and the MESC. He is the author of hundreds of publications, including *The Scope of*

Tolerance (2006); *Confronting the Internet's Dark Side* (2015); *Just, Reasonable Multiculturalism* (2021); and *The Republic, Secularism and Security: France versus the Burqa and the Niqab* (2022). Presently, Raphael is completing his book *Resolving the Israeli–Palestinian Conflict: A Critical Study of Peace Mediation, Facilitation and Negotiations between Israel and the PLO* (forthcoming).

François Finck is Senior academic assistant at the Natolin (Warsaw) campus of the College of Europe, author of the "The Paradoxes of Fragmentation – Does Regional Constitutionalisation Constitute a Fragmentation Threat to the International Legal Order?" in the edited volume *Fragmentation vs the Constitutionalisation of International Law: A Practical Inquiry* (A. Jakubowski, K. Wierczyńska eds., Routledge, 2016).

Aleksandra Gliszczyńska-Grabias is Professor of the Institute of Law Studies, Polish Academy of Sciences and member of the Board of Governors of the International Association of Jewish Lawyers and Jurists. She specialises in legal tools of fighting anti-Semitism and xenophobia, freedom of speech and vulnerable groups rights. Co-editor and co-author of *Constitutionalism under Stress* (2020) and *Law and Memory: Towards Legal Governance of History* (2017). She has held numerous fellowships, including at the University of Cambridge, Yale University and the European University Institute. Principal Investigator in international research consortiums: "Memory Laws in European and Comparative Perspective" (2018–2021, sponsored by the EU Commission) and "The Challenge of Populist Memory Politics for Europe: Towards Effective Responses to Militant Legislation on the Past" (2021–2024, sponsored by the Volkswagen Stiftung).

Marcin Górski is Professor of the University of Łódź, Chair of the Department of European Constitutional Law, Faculty of Law and Administration; Dr. Habil. Juris; member of the Migration Law Research Centre of the Polish Academy of Sciences; visiting professor of the Chandigarh University, India; co-convener of the Freedom of Expression Research Group of the International Association of Constitutional Law; member of the European Union Studies Association, Pittsburgh, Pennsylvania (USA); author and co-author of some 200 research publications on human rights, EU law, international law and comparative constitutional law; attorney; Head of the Legal Department of the City of Łódź local government (2012–2025); CEO of the Łukasiewicz – Łódź Institute of Technology (from 2025); former member of the Human Rights Committee of the National Bar of Attorneys (2014–2021); Fulbright Senior Award 2023–2024 (Fordham University School of Law, New York); and judge ad hoc of the European Court of Human Rights (appointed by Poland).

Aviad Hacohen is Professor of law, president of The Academic Center for Law and Science; Former Dean of its law school; and a senior lecturer on Constitutional Law and Jewish Law at the Academic Center and at the

Faculty of Law of the Hebrew University of Jerusalem. He completed his BA and MA (cum laude) and PhD (magna cum laude) at the Faculty of Law, the Hebrew University of Jerusalem, and clerked for the Supreme Court vice presidents Prof. Menachem Elon and Mishael Cheshin. Prof. Hacohen's research focused on Constitutional Law, Religion and State, Human Rights and Jewish Law. Prof. Hacohen has edited and published numerous books and articles. He was Chief Editor of The Official Supreme Court Judgments of the State of Israel, has served as a consultant to the Codification Commission of the Ministry of Justice in Israel, and is a member of the committee on legal terms at the Academy of the Hebrew Language. He founded and headed Mosaica – the Institute for the Study of Religion, Society and State. Professor Hacohen is also an active lawyer and advocate, he and represented petitioners at the Israeli Supreme Court in more than 200 cases, mainly in the field of human rights, in general, and freedom of speech and freedom of religion cases, in particular.

Hans Michael Heinig is Professor of law, Dr. iur. and since 2008 has held a chair for public law and ecclesiastical law at Goettingen University; he is director of the Institute for Public Law at the law faculty; 2020/21 Fellow at the Wissenschaftskolleg Berlin, 2024/25 visiting professor at University of Toronto and York University. His main research interests are law and religion, constitutional law, and the welfare state. Selected Publications: "Verfassung im Nationalstaat: Von der Gesamtordnung zur europäischen Teilordnung?", in: VVDStRL75 (2016); Prekäre Ordnungen. Historische Prägekräfte des heutigen Religionsverfassungsrechts, 2018; Säkularer Staat – viele Religionen. Religionspolitische Herausforderungen der Gegenwart, 2018; "The concept of religious neutrality under German Constitutional Law: General problems and current debates", in: Quaderni di Diritto e Politica Ecclesiastica 2018; "Religions- und Weltanschauungsfreiheit", in: M. Germann u.a. (eds.), Handbuch des Staatskirchenrechts, 3. Auflage, 2020; "Art. 4 GG", in: P. M. Huber/A. Voßkuhle (eds.), Grundgesetz-Kommentar, 2023.

Kristin Henrard is Professor of international law and Programme Director of the BA in International and European Law programme at the Brussels School of Governance. She co-directs the Fundamental Rights Centre at the Vrije Universiteit Brussel (VUB). Previously she was professor of human rights and minorities at Erasmus University Rotterdam, where she worked between 2007 and 2020, following her transfer from Groningen University (1999–2007). Kristin obtained her PhD in September 1999 at the Catholic University of Leuven and authored "The Interrelation between Individual Human Rights, Minority Rights and the Right to Self-Determination for an Adequate Minority Protection: Theoretical Framework and Case Study on Post-Apartheid South Africa". She holds an LLM from Harvard Law School. She has more than 170 publications, a substantial part of which pertain to human rights and minorities, ranging from educational rights, linguistic rights, to the prohibition of (racial) discrimination (the various dimensions of the right to equal treatment), socio-economic and political participation, and religious fundamental rights. Several of her publications elaborate on the role of international courts and their legitimacy concerns (in this respect). She continuously expands her range to multi-disciplinary papers, particularly pertaining to integration and nationality/citizenship. From February 2005 to May 2010, she worked on her VIDI project, which was granted by the Dutch Council for Scientific Research regarding the implications for minority protection of the Race Equality Directive. Between March 2005 and March 2010, she was a member of the Young Academy of the Dutch Academy of Science.

Meir Linzen is Chairman of the Herzog Fox & Neeman, one of Israel's leading law firms, having served as its Managing Partner for over 20 years. He completed his legal studies at Tel Aviv University in 1980, summa cum laude, and has received an Honorary Doctorate in Philosophy from the Tel Aviv University in recognition of his contribution to the University and to public life in Israel. Meir has acted as Visiting Professor at the Tel Aviv, Bar Ilan, and Ben Gurion Universities. He served for approximately ten years on the Executive Board of Tel Aviv University and today sits as a member of the Board of Trustees of the University. He also sits as Chairman of the Board of Trustees of the Law Faculty at Tel Aviv University. Meir is a senior member of the Israel Bar Association and heads two of its important Committees – the Committee for International Relations and the Tax Committee. He also acts as a member of many public committees as representative of the Bar Association.

Iddo Porat is Professor of law at the College of Law and Business (CLB), Israel. He specialises in constitutional law, comparative constitutional law, and legal theory. Porat is the recipient of the Rockefeller Foundation Residency Fellowship for 2023, was a Senior Fellow at Melbourne Law School for the year 2017–2018, and a Visiting Professor at San Diego Law School for the year 2008–2009. Porat's scholarly activity has focused on comparing constitutional cultures and traditions, and on documenting and analysing cross-country and global constitutional developments. He has written and edited two books, "Towering Judges: A Comparative Analysis of Constitutional Judges" (2019 with Rehan Abeyratne) and "Proportionality and Constitutional Culture" (2013 with Moshe Cohen-Eliya), and more than 40 law review articles.

Russell Sandberg is Professor of law at Cardiff University in the United Kingdom. His work interrogates the interaction between law and the humanities, with particular focuses on how law interacts with religion and history. He is the author of *Law and Religion* (2011), *Religion, Law and Society* (2014), *Religion and Marriage Law: The Need for Reform* (2021), *Subversive Legal History: A Manifesto for the Future of Legal Education* (Routledge, 2021), *Religion in Schools: Learning Lessons from Wales* (2022) and *A Historical Introduction to English Law: Genesis of the Common Law* (2023).

Rhona Schuz is Professor of law at the Academic College of Law and Science Israel and Adjunct Professor at the Faculty of Law, Bar Ilan University. Before moving to Israel, she was a lecturer in law at the London School of Economics. She has an MA in law and an LLM from the University of Cambridge and a PhD from the University of London. Rhona has written extensively in the areas of child law and private international law, with particular emphasis on children's rights and international child abduction. In addition to numerous articles, she has published two books, *A Modern Approach to the Incidental Question in the Conflict of Laws* (1997) and *The Hague Child Abduction Convention: A Critical Analysis* (2013). The latter has been widely cited in the literature and by appellate courts in a number of jurisdictions.

Gerhard van der Schyff is Associate Professor in the Department of Public Law and Governance at the Law School of Tilburg University in The Netherlands. His research interests cover questions regarding constitutional identity in the relationship between the EU and its Member States, comparative constitutional law topics, and fundamental rights, with a particular interest in the right to freedom of religion. In 2015, he held a Humboldt Fellowship for Experienced Researchers at the chair of Professor Christian Calliess at the Free University of Berlin in Germany. He is a member of the editorial boards of the European Constitutional Law Review and the European Yearbook of Constitutional Law.

Ioanna Tourkochoriti is Associate Professor of Law and Associate Director of Center for International and Comparative Law, University of Baltimore. Tourkochoriti is a leading scholar on comparative law, jurisprudence and human rights. She has published numerous articles on comparative constitutional law, freedom of expression, and anti-discrimination law with leading journals all around the world. Her well-received book Freedom of Speech: the Revolutionary Roots of American and French Legal Thought was published by Cambridge University Press in 2022. Tourkochoriti was formerly Lecturer above the Bar at the University of Galway School of Law. For eight years she held research and faculty appointments at Harvard University. She was a Wertheim Fellow with the Labor and Worklife Program at Harvard Law School and a lecturer on Law and Social Studies at the Committee on Degrees in Social Studies at Harvard University. She also taught at Carleton University (Canada) and has held numerous fellowships with several institutions, including the London School of Economics' (LSE) Law Department.

Stéphanie Wattier is Professor at the Faculty of Law of the University of Namur in Belgium. She holds a Ph.D. from the Catholic University of Louvain (2015). She mainly teaches constitutional law, human rights, and law and gender. Her research focuses on fundamental rights and more particularly on the relationship between law and religions (state funding of religions, regulation of the wearing of religious signs, ritual slaughter, etc.) and between law and gender (abortion, gender violence, gender equality, etc.). She is co-director of the Centre 'Vulnérabilités et Sociétés'. She carried out several research stays abroad (Universidad Complutense Madrid, Durham Law School, American University). She is co-editor of the Collection 'Droit et religion' (Bruylant, Larcier).

Joseph H. H. Weiler is University Professor at the NYU School of Law and Senior Fellow at the Centre for European Studies, Harvard. He formally served as President of the European University Institute, Florence. He is Co-Editor-in-Chief of ICON, the International Journal of Constitutional Law. He works in the fields of public law and theory, and law and religion. In 2022 he was the first Jewish recipient of the Ratzinger Prize awarded by Pope Francis.

Acknowledgments

This book is the result of our long-standing interest in the issues of religious freedom and its protection of religious minorities, and our deep conviction that there is still a need to strengthen both this freedom and its protection. We wanted those problems that we ourselves consider the most pressing and relevant to be reflected in the top-quality scientific analysis.

This project would not have been possible without the support of the International Association of Jewish Lawyers and Jurists (IJL), for which we are very grateful. Established in 1969, IJL is an international non-governmental organisation, comprising legal practitioners and academic jurists in more than 50 countries. Among its founders were Supreme Court Justice Haim Cohn of Israel, US Supreme Court Justice and US Ambassador to the United Nations Arthur Goldberg, and Nobel Peace Prize laureate René Cassin of France, the co-author of the Universal Declaration of Human Rights. In its current activities, IJL focuses on legal methods to counter anti-Semitism and other forms of xenophobia, protect minorities, and strengthen guarantees of respect for human rights.

We would like to extend special thanks to IJL's President, Meir Linzen, who supported and believed in this book project from the very beginning, and to Avraham Yishai, the head of the IJL's Legal Center for Combating Antisemitism, who provided us with all the help we needed throughout its creation.

We are much obliged to a number of scholars who have shared their precious advice and remarks on this book and whose research on various aspects of vulnerability inspired us, including Wojciech Sadurski (Sydney and Warszawa), Anna Śledzińska-Simon (Wrocław), Marta Bucholc (Warszawa), Ulad Belavusau (The Hague), Mirosław Wyrzykowski (Warszawa), Aleksandra Szczerba (Gorzów Wielkopolski), Dina Porat (Tel Aviv), Alvin Rosenfeld (Bloomington), Kenneth Marcus (Washington), Michał Bilewicz (Warszawa), Agnieszka Haska (Warszawa), Przemysław Tacik (Kraków), and Yuval Shany (Jerusalem).

In addition, Aviad Hacohen extends his gratitude to his colleagues at the Academic Center for Law and Science at Hod Hasharon, Israel, and at the Van Leer Institute, Jerusalem.

Likewise, Aleksandra Gliszczyńska-Grabias would like to thank all her colleagues at the Poznań Human Rights Center of the Institute of Law Studies of the Polish Academy of Sciences for offering their unremitting academic support and advice, and true friendship that goes far beyond professional collaboration.

Our special thanks also go to Joanna Kurczab, who invaluably assisted in the preparation of this book at all stages of this process. Thanks to her professionalism and dutifulness, this endeavour could succeed.

Finally, enormous thanks to everyone at Routledge for their friendly and patient editorship. Last but not least, many thanks to our authors for their thoughtful contributions, advice, and endurance.

Aleksandra Gliszczyńska-Grabias and *Aviad Hacohen*
January 2025

Foreword

Meir Linzen

President of the International Association of Jewish Lawyers and Jurists

The International Association of Jewish Lawyers and Jurists (IJL) is honoured to support the scholarly project that resulted in the publication of *Freedom of Religion, Minority Rights and the Law: The Status of Jewish and Muslim Minorities in Europe and Beyond*, edited by Aleksandra Gliszczyńska-Grabias and Aviad Hacohen. This collaboration stems from several core reasons. First, it reflects IJL's long-standing commitment to protecting human rights and combating discrimination and hatred, including religious-based intolerance. Second, it addresses the urgent need for an in-depth analysis of legal bans on ritual slaughter. Finally, it aligns with our mission to promote the shared cause of Jewish and Muslim minorities worldwide.

The legal bans on ritual slaughter enacted in some European countries-issues that have also reached the Court of Justice of the European Union (CJEU) and the European Court of Human Rights (ECtHR) – remain one of the most critical challenges in the discussion on religious minority rights. IJL actively engaged in this debate by submitting an opinion to the CJEU in June 2020 in case C-336/19 *Centraal Israëlitisch Consistorie van België and Others*, authored by Professor Joseph H. H. Weiler and myself. Although the Grand Chamber of the CJEU did not adopt the arguments presented, we believe these perspectives warrant serious consideration by legislatures contemplating similar legal measures. The chapters in this book provide an important analysis of the topic, including the implications of these European courts' rulings.

I sincerely hope that this publication, which features contributions from leading experts in minority rights and religious freedom, will become a significant reference for scholars, legislators, and members of the judiciary. It is particularly crucial that decision-makers in matters of religious freedom understand the broader context in which religious minorities operate today.

Since its founding in 1969 by prominent figures including Israeli Supreme Court Justice Haim Cohn, U.S. Ambassador Arthur Goldberg, and Nobel laureate René Cassin, IJL has been committed to fighting anti-Semitism, racism, xenophobia, and other human rights violations. Honouring this legacy, IJL will continue to advance human rights through projects like this publication and beyond.

Preface

The Boundaries of Religious Freedom in Democracies

Raphael Cohen-Almagor

Abstract

In this Prologue, I discuss the power of religion by observing the teachings of John Locke and John Stuart Mill, aiming to learn from their wise counsel. I discuss the boundaries of religious freedom and the concept of toleration, explaining that toleration needs to be proscribed to avoid self-defeat. I also advocate a separation between state and religion. Such separation is required to enable coexistence between religion and liberal democracy. Lack of separation between state and religion will inevitably lead to coercive theocracy.

Keywords

coercion; freedom; liberal democracy; John Locke; John Stuart Mill; religion; toleration

1 Introduction

Religion is powerful. It cannot be underestimated or dismissed. In the name of religion, countries went to war; people were and are willing to sacrifice their lives and kill others. There are not many powerful motivations that drive people to engage in violence. Why is religion so powerful?

Several reasons come to mind. Religion satisfies human needs. Life presents many challenges. Life can be confusing, disappointing, and even brutal, facing wars, terror, natural disasters, and diseases. Religion provides a framework and organisation. Religions provide comfort and a sense of community, hope for a better future, and an answer to phenomena that we are unable to explain via rational faculties. Human frailty leads people to believe in some things that are beyond their comprehension. While non-believers doubt, believers do not doubt. They believe. Thus, religion is not always rational. Whatever believers do not understand, they attribute their limited understanding to their human weaknesses and limitations. Humanity is imperfect, whereas God is omnipotent and flawless.

To sustain themselves and attract adherents, religions distinguish themselves from each other. While we can discern many commonalities between religions, there are also accentuated differences. If all religions were the same, there would have been one universal religion. Many prefer a distinctive religion that creates a notion of us and them. At the same time, religions invite non-believers to join and do not close their gates completely to those who wish to appreciate some aspects of religion.

Religion brings about doctrinal cohesiveness. It provides answers to questions, indisputable directives, and guidance as to how believers should spend their time, things they should do, and things they should refrain from doing. Religion satisfies human needs for structure.

Some people need a guru, a guide who they approach for advice, for absolution, or for a good word. By having a sage who instructs them on what to do, they relieve themselves of the need for thinking, which for some people is quite taxing. They prefer to be led, to be told what to do, to walk the same paths that millions of people walked before them. If so many people have done this before, they cannot be wrong.

Some people use religion as a delete button and a conscience redeemer. They are aware of their frailties, of their inability to withstand temptations. In their own minds, they sin. And they seek redemption. Religion provides them solace, hope, remedy, and forgiveness. Religion judges them, but it also offers solutions. Religion enables these people to live with their weaknesses and sins.

Religion sustains humility, a quality that all people appreciate, even if they cannot find humility in themselves. Religion makes people humble because believers pray every day to God, whom they cannot touch, sense, see, or hear, who is believed to be so powerful that it is incomprehensible to us humans.

2 Religions Appreciate Tradition

They provide a sense of connectivity and continuation. Religions provide a chain of past, present, and future that is meaningful to people even if they do not believe in God, even if they are unwilling to abide by the many dictates and demands of religion. Religions appeal to the common denominator. All religions value family, a very important aspect of human life. Fortunate is the person who has a loving family. Family is the *summum bonum*. All religions provide opportunities for families to get together and celebrate religion. Many religious holidays and festivals include celebrations of food, which is an existential need but for many is not only a means to survival. It is also a means to enjoy life, bringing families and friends together to enjoy the festivities.

Religion keeps people together for generations. Some religions are thousands of years old. They sustain many challenges. With time, many phenomena have passed from the world. Religions are resilient. No student of history would ever underestimate the influence and authority of religion.

Furthermore, religion provides a sense of identity. Some people define themselves first by their religion. For them, religion comes before their nationality, race, ethnic group, class, profession, gender, sexual orientation, family status, or any other attribute. It is *that* powerful.

Religions are a source of pride. Believers are proud to declare their belonging to this or that religion and are happy to talk about and explain their affinity and belief, how religion influences their lives, their families, and their sense of humanhood.

Moreover, religion provides a sense of affinity. It connects people. Some people are more comfortable in the company of fellow believers than in the company of others. Religion provides, in their minds, a common denominator that is more important than common interests, educational or professional qualifications, hobbies, or other factors that bring people together. These people are more comfortable living with fellow believers of the same religion, speaking their minds with them, hiring people who belong to the same religion, studying with such people, and spending quality time with them.

Religion is deeply appreciated because it demands sacrifice. People appreciate things that are demanding more than things that are easily received or practiced. Believers practice their religion daily, dedicating their time and energy, both can be quite consuming. Religion is inward and outward. It is all-encompassing and unrelenting.

Religion is self- and other-regarding. As long as self-sacrifice is in action, no major problems are presented. But when it is other-regarding, involving coercion, then it becomes problematic. Generally speaking, people shirk coercion.[1] People want to do things voluntarily. When they are told that they must do something in which they do not believe, there is a tendency to resist. A case in point is France, where Muslim girls and women are instructed on how to dress in the name of keeping the public space secular.[2] Then friction and schism appear, and communities become disintegrated. When religion advocates and practices violence against non-believers, or against believers of other religions, then challenges are further compounded and might erupt into wars, wars between nations, as well as civil wars.

3 Boundaries of Religious Freedom

Religion should be a matter of personal choice, faith, and belief. Because religion provides a comprehensive framework that relates to all matters, large and small, people may opt to accept some directives and reject others. Consequently, "freedom of religion" and "freedom from religion" are both important. These

1 See R. Cohen-Almagor, "Coercion", *Open Journal of Philosophy* vol. 11, no. 3 (2021): 386–409.
2 R. Cohen-Almagor, *The Republic, Secularism and Security: France versus the Burqa and the Niqab* (Cham: Springer, 2022).

freedoms are matters of personal choice. People should be able to choose their conceptions of the good, as they see appropriate for themselves, as long as they do not harm others (discussed below). By "conception of the good", it is meant that each person has a mixture of moral, philosophical, ideological, and religious notions, together with personal values which contain some picture of a life that is worth living.

The conception of the good comprises a basic part of our overall moral scheme. It is public in that it is something we advance as good for others, as well as ourselves. Consequently, we would want others to hold a conception for their sake. But when that desire is based on coercion, it might no longer be moral because people are no longer autonomous in deciding on their way of life. They are then coerced to follow a dogma that might be very unappealing to them. I argue that nobody ought to be compelled in matters of religion either by law or force. Therefore, religion should be divorced from politics.

Classical Liberal tradition from John Locke onwards was concerned above all with the preservation of individual rights, and with the emancipation of the individual from public control and authoritarian order. It had set the individual on legal equality in opposition to feudalism and challenged the right of the monarch to govern except in the interests of the citizens. Liberalism appeared at first as a criticism of coercive modes of governance, attempting to remove obstacles that block human progress. Liberalism has found humanity oppressed and has aimed to set it free.

John Locke's (1632–1704) political philosophy was guided by his deeply held religious commitments. He accepted the existence of God and the notion that all humans are God's servants. According to Locke, God created humans for a certain purpose – namely, to live a life according to his laws and thus to inherit eternal salvation. A church is, according to Locke, "a voluntary society of men, joining themselves together of their own accord" to worship God in such a manner "as they judge acceptable to Him and effectual to the salvation of their souls".[3] Humans, through reason, discover that God exists, identify his laws and the duties they entail, and acquire sufficient knowledge to perform their duties and thereby lead a happy and successful life.

The issue of religious toleration preoccupied the minds of 17th-century European thinkers. The Reformation provoked civil wars and religious persecution. As a reaction to the Catholic persecution of Protestants, the Dutch Republic tolerated religious differences and attracted people like Locke. However, once the Calvinist Church gained power, it also grew intolerant of other denominations.

In 1685 in France, under Louis the 14th's reign, the Huguenots (French Protestants, largely Calvinists), suffered severe persecution at the hands of the

3 See J. Locke, [W. Popple (trans.)], *A Letter Concerning Toleration* (1689): 9. https://historyofeconomicthought.mcmaster.ca/locke/toleration.pdf. Accessed October 25, 2024.

Catholic Church and were forced to emigrate on mass.[4] In England, religious conflict dominated the 17th century, contributing in important respects to the eruption of the English Civil War and the abolishing of the Anglican Church during the Protectorate, the English government from 1653 to 1659. This was the reign of Oliver Cromwell and his son Richard, until the latter's resignation in May 1659. After the restoration of King Charles II, the parliament enacted laws that repressed Catholics and Protestants.[5] Locke had been reflecting on these developments. He wrote, "[N]either Pagan nor Mahometan, nor Jew, ought to be excluded from the civil rights of the commonwealth because of his religion. The Gospel commands no such thing".[6] However, Locke did not extend toleration to Catholics or atheists because Catholics have a primary obligation to Rome, and atheists have no foundations for their promises and thus constitute a danger to the state. The Catholics have seditious articles of faith that include the pope's power to dissolve oaths, to legislate infallibly, and to depose foreign rulers as excommunicates or heretics.[7] As for atheists, Locke wrote,

> Promises, covenants, and oaths, which are the bonds of human society, can have no hold upon an atheist. The taking away of God, though but even in thought, dissolves all; besides also, those that by their atheism undermine and destroy all religion can have no pretence of religion whereupon to challenge the privilege of toleration.[8]

In 1689, the English Parliament passed the Toleration Act.[9] It had provisions for the freedom of worship for nonconformists (dissenting Protestants who did not abide by the Church of England such as Baptists and Congregationalists). The Act, along with other measures after the Glorious Revolution in England between 1688 and 1689, when Protestant William of Orange invaded England and took the throne of Catholic James II, exempted nonconformists from the punitive laws that were enacted. Under the Act that was aimed to unite Protestants, Protestants estranged from the Church of England were allowed to conduct worship and have teachers in academies that provided more liberal

4 W. Uzgalis, "John Locke". In: *Stanford Encyclopaedia of Philosophy*. https://plato.stanford.edu/entries/locke/. Accessed October 25, 2024.

5 W. Uzgalis, "John Locke".

6 J. Locke, *A Letter Concerning Toleration* 40.

7 J.C. Walmsley, F. Waldmann, "John Locke and Toleration of Catholics: A New Manuscript" *Historical Journal* vol. 62, no. 4 (2019): 1093–1115.

8 J. Locke, *A Letter Concerning Toleration* 36.

9 William and Mary, 1688: An Act for Exempting their Majestyes Protestant Subjects dissenting from the Church of England from the Penalties of certaine Lawes. [Chapter XVIII. Rot. Parl. pt. 5. nu. 15.], Great Britain Record Commission, s.l, 1819.

education. Political and social restrictions, however, remained. The Act did not apply to Roman Catholics and Unitarians who did not endorse the Christian Trinity.[10]

Another great liberal thinker, John Stuart Mill (1806–1873) saw religion as a private matter. When asked about his own religious beliefs, Mill replied that he hoped people would respect his desire to keep his relationship with his God a private and personal matter. Mill understood religion to be a legitimate aspiration and a basic human need. Religion contains elements of mystery and hope that are appealing to us, humans. In *On Liberty*, Mill described religion as the most powerful of the elements that have contributed to forming moral feelings. Religion was largely governed by the ambition to seek control or by Puritanism.[11] Mill observed that religious freedom has hardly existed in practice, except where religious indifference has added its weight to the scale on the side of tolerance. But in almost all religions, even in the most tolerant countries, toleration was practiced with some reservations. Some excluded Roman Catholics, whereas others would tolerate "everyone who believes in revealed religion but not those whose religious beliefs are based on arguments and evidence rather than on revelation".[12] A few "extend their charity a little further, but stop at the belief in a God and a future state".[13]

In *Three Essays on Religion*, which was published posthumously in 1874, Mill elaborated his views on religion and invoked a secular, humanist, and godless religion, which he labelled Religion of Humanity. In *Usefulness of Religion* Mill wrote, "The essence of religion is the strong and earnest direction of the emotions and desires towards an ideal objective which is recognized as being of the highest excellence and as rightly superior to all selfish objects of desire".[14] Mill thought the Religion of Humanity satisfies this condition to a great extent. It satisfies the functions of religion better than religions that believe in the supernatural. This is because of two reasons. First, the Religion of Humanity carries the believer's thoughts and feelings "out of himself and fixes them on an objective that he loves and pursues not selfishly but as an end for its own sake".[15] Second, the Religion of Humanity respects the intellectual integrity of its believers, whereas the value of the old religions as a means of elevating and improving human character "is enormously reduced by the fact that it is nearly (if not entirely) impossible for them to produce their best moral effects unless the intellectual faculties are sluggish if

10 "Toleration Act". In: *Britannica*. https://www.britannica.com/event/Toleration-Act-Great-Britain-1689. Accessed October 25, 2024.

11 J.S. Mill, *Utilitarianism, Liberty, and Representative Government*. (London: J.M. Dent, 1948).

12 J.S. Mill, *Utilitarianism, Liberty, and Representative Government*.

13 J.S. Mill, *On Liberty* (London: The Walter Scott Publishing Co., Ltd., [1901]). https://www.gutenberg.org/files/34901/34901-h/34901-h.htm. Accessed October 25, 2024.

14 J.S. Mill [J. Bennett (ed.)], *Usefulness of Religion*. https://www.earlymoderntexts.com/assets/pdfs/mill1873c.pdf. Accessed October 25, 2008.

15 J.S. Mill [J. Bennett (ed.)], *Usefulness of Religion*.

not downright twisted".[16] Mill still acknowledged that old religions always have one advantage over the Religion of Humanity, "namely the prospect they hold out to the individual of a life after death".[17] The Religion of Humanity is logical and therefore does not entertain supernatural beliefs. But Mill provided assurances that even that advantage – belief in the supernatural – is not overwhelmingly attractive to the extent that it will make us reconsider our preference for the Religion of Humanity. Mill argued that if the Religion of Humanity were "as diligently taught and maintained as the supernatural religions are", all who had received sufficient moral education would, "right up to the hour of their own death", live imaginatively in the life of those who are to follow them. And while undoubtedly many people would like to survive as individuals in the afterlife, Mill thought it is likely that people would "sooner or later have had enough of existence and would gladly lie down" and take eternal rest.[18]

Two important ideas stem from the thinking of these two great liberal philosophers. The first is toleration, within boundaries; the second is the idea of separation between state and religion. I will now discuss these two ideas.

4 Toleration

The root of the terms "tolerance" and "toleration" is found in the Latin word *tolerabilis*, meaning that which can be endured. In its earlier history, the expression implied the general notion of enduring beliefs (say religious beliefs) as well as forms of behaviour. Tolerance arose, to a great extent, because it was viewed as a suitable alternative to endless religious rivalry. The notion was not enunciated as an ideal one, but more as a necessary evil. It became a necessity in Europe once Europeans saw that neither side in the religious controversy was going to gain the upper hand decisively. The notion was that law ought to be obeyed because it was right; hence, a common moral authority that would determine what was right had to be established. In general, it was assumed that tolerance had to prevail to make living together possible.[19]

Tolerance, of course, is not to be equated with apathy or indifference. Tolerance is composed of three main components: (1) a strong disapproving attitude toward certain conduct, action, or speech; (2) power or authority to

16 J.S. Mill [J. Bennett (ed.)], *Usefulness of Religion*.

17 J.S. Mill [J. Bennett (ed.)], *Usefulness of Religion*.

18 J.S. Mill [J. Bennett (ed.)], *Usefulness of Religion*. For further discussion, see R. Carr, "The Religious Thought of John Stuart Mill: A Study in Reluctant Scepticism", *Journal of the History of Ideas* vol. 23, no. 4 (1962): 475–495; R. Lopez, "John Stuart Mill on Religion, Utility, and Morality". In: M. Ruse, S. Bullivant (eds.), *The Cambridge History of Atheism* (Cambridge: Cambridge University Press, 2021): 346–365.

19 R. Cohen-Almagor, *The Boundaries of Liberty and Tolerance* (Gainesville: The University Press of Florida, 1994); R. Forst, "Toleration". In: *Stanford Encyclopedia of Philosophy*. https://plato.stanford.edu/entries/toleration/. Accessed October 25, 2024.

curtail the disturbing conduct; and (3) moral overriding principles which sway the doer not to exert her power or authority to curtail the said conduct. From this, it is clear that tolerance is distinguished from indifference, for the doer *does* have formidable objections regarding the conduct. The tolerators care greatly about the issue but nevertheless apply self-restraint. Tolerance could not also be equated with neutrality because, in this respect, its meaning is akin to that of impartiality. As stated, tolerance assumes that the agents are partial regarding the issue they consider.[20]

Locke instructed us that religious tolerance should be proscribed within certain boundaries. We need not tolerate everything. Boundaries must be introduced; otherwise, intolerant beliefs and religions would undermine our very existence and coerce us to lead *their* lives, not the life of *our* choosing. We need to protect against coercion and intolerant compulsion. Indeed, we need to recognise the inherent tension between religion and liberty. Some religions are all-encompassing, instructing followers on the most intimate matters of life that concern all humans, including food, dress, and sexual conduct. Religion restricts liberty to maintain cohesiveness and to demarcate boundaries. Those who practice "our" religion belong to "us". Others are suspect or excluded. Thus, liberalism and "old religions", to be distinguished from the universal Religion of Humanity, are inherently at odds.

John Stuart Mill also recognised the necessity of putting boundaries to human action, invoking the Harm Principle according to which people are free to do as they please provided that they do not harm others. The Millian Harm Principle holds that something is eligible for restriction only if it causes harm to others. People may interfere with the other's liberty of action to protect themselves and to prevent injury to themselves or others. In *On Liberty*, Mill wrote: "Acts of whatever kind, which, without justifiable cause, do harm to others, may be, and in the more important cases absolutely require to be, controlled by the unfavourable sentiments, and, when needful, by the active interference of mankind."[21] A similar idea was pronounced by Rabbi Hillel in his dictum: "What is hateful to you do not do unto your fellow people".[22]

Mill was particularly concerned that the government might overstep its authority and abuse its power to advance partisan, narrow interests. Mill wrote, "[T]he question is not about restraining the actions of individuals, but about helping them; it is asked whether the government should do, or cause to be

20 R. Cohen-Almagor, *The Scope of Tolerance: Studies on the Costs of Free Expression and Freedom of the Press* (New York: Routledge, 2006).

21 J.S. Mill, *On Liberty*. In: J.S. Mill, *Utilitarianism, Liberty and Representative Government* (London: J. M. Dent, 1948): 72–73, 114, see also p. 138.

22 M. MacLachlan, *The Golden Rule*. https://www.thinkhumanism.com/the-golden-rule/. Accessed October 29, 2024. For further discussion, see R. Cohen-Almagor, *Speech, Media, and Ethics: The Limits of Free Expression* (Cham: Palgrave Macmillan, 2005); P. Gisbertz, "Overcoming Doctrinal School Thought: A Unifying Approach to Human Dignity" *Ratio Juris* vol. 31, no. 2 (2018): 196–207. https://doi.org/10.1111/raju.12204.

done, something for their benefit, instead of leaving it to be done by themselves, individually or in voluntary combination".[23]

We should be concerned about the "evil" of adding unnecessarily to the power of government. Mill insisted on the idea of preventing evil and harm to others, resorting to different phrases: "affects prejudicially the interests of others,"[24] and "damage, or the probability of damage, to the interests of others."[25] Citizens and governments can and should prevent harm to others.[26]

To enable and promote individual freedoms, liberal democracies keep religions out of the political sphere, ensuring separation between state and religion, and promoting tolerance of all religions. When religion becomes political, coercion is unavoidable.[27] Political religion encroaches on liberty and restricts freedom from religion.

5 Separation between State and Religion

Religion can inflict tremendous harm. In the name of religion, people's rights and liberties have been restricted. Stokes Paulsen rightly observed, "All theories of religious liberty must wrestle with the problem of extraordinary harm perpetrated in the name of religion".[28] Indeed, liberalism and theocracy are mutually exclusive. There cannot be a liberal theocracy or liberal-democratic religious system. In *A Letter Concerning Toleration*, Locke's basic position is that the state has no business in the realm of religious belief, in part because the tools of government are ineffective in this matter (belief cannot be coerced), in part because no one consenting to government would possibly think it safe to trust the magistrate with the salvation of his soul ("no man can so far abandon the care of his own salvation as blindly to leave to the choice of any other"),[29] and in part because people are not harmed by one another's religious beliefs and practices.[30] It is when people act upon their beliefs that harm might be inflicted on others.

Locke's arguments for religious toleration connect to his view of civil government. Salvation is not a matter for the state to interfere; rather, it is a personal matter. In Locke's view, the freedom to choose one's own road to

23 J.S. Mill, *On Liberty* 164.
24 J.S. Mill, *On Liberty* 164. 132.
25 J.S. Mill, *On Liberty* 164. 150.
26 R. Cohen-Almagor, "Between Autonomy and State Regulation: J.S. Mill's Elastic Paternalism" *Philosophy* vol. 87, no. 4 (2012): 557–582; R. Cohen-Almagor, "JS Mill's Boundaries of Freedom of Expression: A Critique" *Philosophy* vol. 92, no. 362 (2017): 565–596.
27 R. Cohen-Almagor, "Why Separate State and Religion?", *Israel Studies* vol. 27, no. 2 (2022): 76–91.
28 M. Stokes Paulsen, "Freedom for Religion", *The Yale Law Journal Forum* vol. 133 (2023): 416.
29 J. Locke, *A Letter Concerning Toleration*.
30 D. Boucher, P. Kelly (eds.), *Political Thinkers: From Socrates to the Present* (Oxford: Oxford University Press, 2003): 196.

salvation is a natural right like life, liberty, health, and property. Liberty of conscience must be protected from any government authority. Locke wrote,

> I esteem it above all things necessary to distinguish exactly the business of civil government from that of religion and to settle the just bounds that lie between the one and the other. If this is not done, there can be no end put to the controversies that will be always arise between those that have, or at least pretend to have, on the one side, a concernment for the interest of men's souls, and, on the other side, a care of the commonwealth.[31]

Locke and Mill believed that religion cannot be compelled and, certainly, it is not the role of government to compel religion on people. Whenever religion becomes intertwined with government, freedom diminishes. For the life and power of true religion consists in faith, in the inward and full persuasion of the mind. In turn, faith involves believing, and no one can just believe what someone else tells them to believe, even if they want to. Then it would become a dead dogma. Locke explained, "[I]f we are not fully satisfied in our own mind that the one is true and the other well pleasing unto God, such profession and such practice, far from being any furtherance, are indeed great obstacles to our salvation".[32] No individual, church, or commonwealth has a right to attack the civil rights and worldly goods of anyone on the pretence of religion. No common friendship, peace, and security can ever exist if people think that governments receive authority from God and that "religion is to be propagated by force of arms".[33]

6 Conclusion

Religion can live with liberalism if it provides opportunities for personal growth and is instructive rather than absolute. Granted, the Millian idea of Religion of Humanity will not be appealing to everyone. Still, while providing specific, distinctive, and instructive dictates that separate one religion from others, and providing adherents a sense of a community, religion should not be discriminatory against those who do not adhere to a specific religion. Religion should allow basic freedoms and the ability to opt-out at will. Religion is a matter of choice and tradition. People are born into a particular way of life, and most of us will find our place within that framework. But some of us won't; these people should enjoy the freedom to decide their own path of life. Religions that are flexible enough to accept pluralism and diversity, that are tolerant and humane in acknowledging the human spark, and human viability in every one of us, can coexist with liberal democracy. Coercive religions

31 J. Locke, *A Letter Concerning Toleration*.
32 J. Locke, *A Letter Concerning Toleration*.
33 J. Locke, *A Letter Concerning Toleration*.

undermine liberal democracy. I, for one, as a liberal Reform Jew, believe in Jewish humanism and that religion and liberal ideology can coexist provided that religion is excluded from the political sphere.[34] The model that separates state and religion is not only desired. It is essential. Jewish democracy as it exists in Israel is inherently illiberal as the values of Orthodox Judaism are in contradiction to the liberal values of individualism, liberty, equality, tolerance, pluralism, rule of law, and the dignity of each and every person.

34 R. Cohen-Almagor, *Just, Reasonable Multiculturalism: Liberalism, Culture and Coercion* (Cambridge: Cambridge University Press, 2021).

Introduction

Religious Freedom and Religious Minorities in Contemporary Europe and Beyond

Aleksandra Gliszczyńska-Grabias and Aviad Hacohen

> *The right of religious freedom, while self-evident, is not self-executing. It takes hard work.*
>
> Attorney Eric Treene, 2022 Free Expression Award honoree[1]

I.1 The Essence of Religious Freedom: Current Threats to Protection and Implementation

Freedom of thought, conscience and religion, as enshrined in numerous international human rights protection treaties, constitutes one of the core foundations of a democratic society.[2] Though in its religious dimension it is vital to the practice, and broader lifestyle, of believers, its essence is no less valuable for all members of society, be they atheists, agnostics, sceptics or those completely unconcerned regarding religious issues. The expression of cultural, ethnic and religious pluralism inherent in a democratic society, which has been the subject of struggles for centuries, depends on such freedom. The latter entails, amongst other things, the freedom to hold religious beliefs, or not, and to practice a religion, or not.[3]

Today, the protection of religious minorities is regarded as foundational to international human rights protection systems and is provided for in the

1 "13 Freedom of Religion Quotes You Should Know". https://www.freedomforum.org/freedom-of-religion-quotes/. Accessed January 6, 2025.

2 J. Locke, *A Letter Concerning Toleration* ([London: Black Swan at Amen Corner], 1689). https://historyofeconomicthought.mcmaster.ca/locke/toleration.pdf. Accessed January 6, 2025. – published in 1689, is a seminal philosophical text regarding the recognition of religious freedom as an individual right subject to protection by state authorities.

3 *Kokkinakis v Greece*, 14307/88 [1993], § 31, ECLI:CE:ECHR:1993:0525JUD001430788; *Buscarini and Others v San Marino*, 24645/94 [1999], § 34, ECLI:CE:ECHR:1999:0218JUD002464594.

DOI: 10.4324/9781003423294-1

constitutions of all democratic states.[4] Yet despite its strong grounding and, in a sense, its obviousness as one of the core guarantees among human rights and freedoms, its universal observance has not been guaranteed. The Special Rapporteur on freedom of religion, in her 2024 Report on "Peace and freedom of religion or belief" drew attention to areas of concern and outlined recommendations for states, which in turn revealed troubling deficits in the most basic areas of religious freedom, including, the protection of persons belonging to religious or belief minorities from being targeted on grounds of religion or belief; the need to address human rights claims from persons belonging to religious or belief minorities rapidly and robustly; counteracting discrimination on grounds of religion or belief in laws, policy and practice.[5] However, it is the Special Rapporteur's conclusions in the area of hatred on the basis of religion or belief which appear to be even more troubling, particularly regarding the phenomenon of online religious hate speech:

> religious or belief-based hatred is often mediated, facilitated and exacerbated by online platforms and social media, which can rapidly escalate tensions. […] Myths, conspiracy theories and calls for violence now spread with greater speed and reach than ever before, often meaning that local events can have global consequences.[6]

The difficulties and controversies associated with the present understanding and guarantee of religious freedom can be found in the jurisprudence of international human rights bodies. In *Lautsi v Italy*,[7] perhaps the most famous judgement of the Grand Chamber of the European Court of Human Rights (ECtHR) on religious freedom, the ECtHR ruled that the requirement in Italian law that crucifixes be displayed in classrooms of schools does not breach the European Convention on Human Rights but rather belongs to the margin of appreciation of individual states given the absence of European consensus over the importance and meaning of religious symbols in the public sphere. The complexity of the issue at stake was aptly captured by Judge Malinverni (joined by Judge Kalaydjieva) in his dissent, when he noted:

> The presence of crucifixes in schools is capable of infringing religious freedom and schoolchildren's right to education to a greater degree than

4 A. Scolnicov, *The Right to Religious Freedom in International Law Between Group Rights and Individual Rights* (New York: Routledge, 2011).

5 UNGA, Peace and freedom of religion or belief – Special Rapporteur on freedom of religion or belief, July 18, 2024. https://documents.un.org/doc/undoc/gen/n24/213/78/pdf/n2421378.pdf. Accessed January 6, 2025.

6 UNHRC, Hatred on the basis of religion or belief: Report of the Special Rapporteur on freedom of religion or belief, Nazila Ghanea, January 8, 2024, § 16. https://documents.un.org/doc/undoc/gen/g23/267/05/pdf/g2326705.pdf. Accessed January 6, 2025.

7 *Lautsi v Italy*, 30814/06 [2011] ECLI:CE:ECHR:2011:0318JUD003081406.

> religious apparel that, for example, a teacher might wear, such as the Islamic headscarf. In the latter example the teacher in question may invoke her own freedom of religion, which must also be taken into account, and which the State must also respect. The public authorities cannot, however, invoke such a right. From the point of view of the seriousness of the infringement of the principle of State denominational neutrality, this will accordingly be of a lesser degree where the public authorities tolerate the headscarf in schools than where they impose the presence of crucifixes.[8]

Undoubtedly to no one's surprise, the *Lautsi* dictum remains the subject of reflection and contentious debate.[9]

These dilemmas arise from the increasingly complex reality faced by modern society in which the effective protection of freedom of thought, conscience and religion, and guarantees for religious minorities, tend to be confronted by a range of obstacles, as well as other, often competing, rights and freedoms. Within the legal sphere, the attempts to resolve this 'competition' have included using the principle of proportionality, margin of appreciation and other methods of balancing rights. However, the tensions accompanying the process of searching for such a balance, whilst also protecting religious groups from discrimination, extend far beyond legal analysis and can risk significantly hindering the social coexistence of various groups. Also, an ongoing dilemma remains about the nature of religion in the context of social life, which was fittingly described in one study as the question of whether religion is a "social glue or rather dangerously divisive?"[10]

One of the most telling examples of this type of conflict is the legal ban of ritual slaughter (the so-called *Shechita* bans)[11] which reached the level of the Court of Justice of the European Union (CJEU) in 2020, and, subsequently, in 2024, the ECtHR.[12] Both courts decided in favour of animal protection, significantly limiting the rights and freedoms of Jewish and Muslim minorities in Europe. These decisions were accompanied by subsequent legal developments initiated by states, for example, in response to the CJEU's decision, the

8 *Lautsi v Italy*, 30814/06 [2011] ECLI:CE:ECHR:2011:0318JUD003081406 § 51.

9 L. Zucca, "Lautsi: A Commentary on a Decision by the ECtHR Grand Chamber", *International Journal of Constitutional Law*, vol. 11, no.1 (2013): 218–229. https://doi.org/10.1093/icon/mos008; A. Kent, "Laicite or Laicita: The Regulation of Religious Symbols in French and Italian Public Schools", *Emory Law Journal*, vol. 73, no. 1 (2023): 191–239. https://scholarlycommons.law.emory.edu/cgi/viewcontent.cgi?article=1513&context=elj. Accessed December 6, 2025; B. Peters, "Case Analysis – Crucifixes in Italian Classrooms: Lautsi v Italy", *European Human Rights Law Review*, no 6 (2011): 86–92.

10 P. Cane, C. Evans, Z. Robinson (eds.), *Law and Religion in Theoretical and Historical Context* (Cambridge: CUP, 2008): 13.

11 Ritual slaughter bans are statutory prohibitions against ritual slaughter practiced by Jews and Muslims, in which the animal is not stunned before slaughter.

12 *Executief van de Moslims van België and Others v. Belgium*, 16760/22 and 10 others [2024] ECLI:CE:ECHR:2024:0213JUD001676022.

Constitutional Court of Belgium issued a ruling, closing the issue of the constitutionality of the laws passed in the regions of Flanders and Wallonia that ban the slaughter of animals without prior stunning – stunning that violates ritual slaughtering rules in both the Jewish laws of *kashrut* and the Muslim laws of halal – with no religious exemptions.[13] In response, the World Union for Progressive Judaism and the European Union for Progressive Judaism issued the following statement:

> These laws and this Constitutional Court decision are clear discriminatory actions that deleteriously affect many Jewish and Muslim citizens of Belgium and make more challenging the continuation of Jewish community life in Europe, by making it increasingly difficult to obtain ritually slaughtered meat.[14]

In recent years, in many European states, other issues pertaining to religion have had profound legal, social and political implications. For example, furore has erupted over circumcision, with critics arguing that the practice is inhumane and should be banned for everyone under the age of 18.[15] Similarly, the discussion over religious clothing and symbols displayed in public, regulations on the safeguarding of religious rights in workplaces and educational institutions, the implications of secularism, the clash between religious freedom and LGBTQ+ rights, as well as challenges of customary religious law have all become topics of great importance and often trigger heated disputes.[16] Hence why the topic of religious freedom and the protection of religious minorities cannot be reduced to an obvious claim or simple application of existing laws. On the contrary, with the rise of tensions and conflicts in the world, religious issues - and differences - are becoming even more important with even more far-reaching consequences.[17]

Therefore, this edited volume aims to provide a timely, and necessary, in-depth scholarly reflection on the challenges associated with the field of law

13 S. Wattier, "Ritual slaughter case: The Court of Justice and the Belgian Constitutional Court Put Animal Welfare First", *European Constitutional Law Review* (2022): 264–285.

14 Statement in Response to September 30th Ruling of the Constitutional Court of Belgium, September 30, 2021. https://eupj.org/in-response-to-the-september-30th-ruling-of-the-constitutional-court-of-belgium/. Accessed January 6, 2025.

15 I. Porat, "The problem with Iceland's proposed ban on circumcision". https://blogs.lse.ac.uk/europpblog/2018/04/27/the-problem-with-icelands-proposed-ban-on-circumcision/. Accessed 6 January 2025.

16 See, for example, the collection of annual thematic reports submitted by the UN Special Rapporteur on freedom of religion or belief to the Human Rights Council and the General Assembly: https://www.ohchr.org/en/special-procedures/sr-religion-or-belief/annual-reports. Accessed January 6, 2025.

17 OHCHR, Report: Preliminary Analysis of Recent Protests and Unrest in Bangladesh, August 16, 2024. https://www.ohchr.org/sites/default/files/2024-08/OHCHR-Preliminary-Analysis-of-Recent-Protests-and-Unrest-in-Bangladesh-16082024_2.pdf. Accessed January 6, 2025.

devoted to guaranteeing religious freedom and facilitating the protection of the rights of religious minorities. In doing so, this reflection utilises the protection of the rights of Jewish and Muslim minorities, as a major case study. Thus, the core objective of this volume is to identify, analyse and assess the legal status of religious freedom and the protection of religious minorities, with special focus on European legal environments. To achieve this ambitious goal, it compares the discourses on the scope and boundaries of religious freedom with the actual treatment of religious minorities in legal regulations through relevant case law and by general society.

This book employs the resources of comparative law, national and international law, as well as legal theory. Each of the chapters contribute to the general topic by focusing on a carefully selected issue or a specific national/state example. The contributions also make extensive use of decisions of the international courts, including the ECtHR and the CJEU, as well as domestic constitutional courts of relevant states.

I.2 The Selection of Jewish and Muslim Religious Minorities as Case Studies

Surveys regularly conducted by the EU Agency for Fundamental Rights (FRA) indisputably show that Muslim and Jewish religious minorities remain to be most exposed to discrimination on the basis of their religion in Europe, remain Muslims and Jews. In 2024, FRA published two reports with extremely disturbing data on the scale and forms of anti-Semitism and Islamophobia in EU countries. In the case of anti-Semitism and Islamophobia, the peculiarity of these phenomena lies in the combination of various grounds of discrimination (racial, ethnic, national origin and religion), that nevertheless, collectively result in acts of exclusion, hatred and even violence against members of these minorities. Still, the element that remains inherent in such hatred and discrimination is the "religion factor". The latest survey by FRA, published in July 2024 on the "Jewish People's Experiences and Perceptions of Antisemitism in selected EU member states", [18] revealed that half of the respondents across all states under review "at least sometimes wear, carry or display things that might help people recognise them as Jewish in public". Such items include religious symbols, for example, a kippa/skullcap or a mezuzah (religious piece of parchment fixed to the main doorpost of a Jewish home). Shockingly, in Germany, France, Sweden and Denmark more than 80% of the Jewish respondents occasionally avoid displaying Jewish symbols in public and around half (48%) of those who do not wear or display any such symbols refrain from doing so due to concerns about their

18 *Jewish People's Experiences and Perceptions of Antisemitism* (Vienna: FRA, 2024): 56–57. https://fra.europa.eu/sites/default/files/fra_uploads/fra-2024-experiences-perceptions-antisemitism-survey_en.pdf. Accessed January 6, 2025.

safety. In 2024, FRA also published a report on Islamophobia and Muslim experiences in Europe and again, the results proved to be concerning: almost a third of Muslims in Europe had experienced racist harassment in the five years prior to the survey. Importantly: "A considerable proportion (79%) of those who said that they felt discriminated against because of their religion in the year before the survey also faced discrimination due to their ethnic or immigrant background. 26% of respondents who said that they felt discriminated against because of their religion also experienced discrimination due to their skin colour, 19% due to their age and 12% due to their sex/gender."[19]

In a highly interesting collective volume edited in 2017, by Janes Renton and Ben Gidley on anti-Semitism and Islamophobia in Europe, the authors interrogate how the dynamic relationship between these two phenomena and the European attitude towards Muslims and Jews has evolved over time and space.[20] One of the dimensions of this evolution is religion. Thus, building upon this, the present volume adds to existing studies addressing the current situation and status of these two religious minorities in Europe, their rights and freedoms, by trying to indicate common elements of discrimination they experience as well as the, sometimes varying, legal responses to such discrimination. Perhaps at a time of heightened polarisation and conflict, focusing on the fact that the discrimination both groups experience along religious lines, is equally painful and unacceptable, is an idea worth pursuing.[21]

I.3 Religious Freedom as a Recurring Research Subject

As noted earlier, the issues that are the subject of this book have been widely and deeply considered within the framework of scientific reflection on law. However, it is our hope that this volume stands out for its original approach towards conceptualising the most recent challenges to the protection of religious freedom and religious minorities in the context of the functioning of liberal democracies (as well as democracies being dismantled and under populist rule) in the contemporary world. While a steady flow of monographs and edited volumes on religious freedom and the protection

19 *Being Muslim in the EU – Experiences of Muslims: EU Survey on Immigrants and Descendants of Immigrants* (Vienna: FRA, 2024). https://fra.europa.eu/sites/default/files/fra_uploads/fra-2024-being-muslim-in-the-eu_en.pdf. Accessed January 6, 2025.

20 J. Renton, B. Gidley (eds.), *Antisemitism and Islamophobia in Europe: A Shared Story?* (London: Palgrave Macmillan, 2017).

21 S. Har-El, *Where Islam and Judaism Join Together a Perspective on Reconciliation* (New York: Palgrave Macmillan, 2014).

of religious minorities has been published over the past decade,[22] there remains an ongoing demand for the systematic exploration of the most recent developments in this field. This volume addresses this need for knowledge in a theoretically sustained manner. The team of editors and contributors, who are all highly recognised experts in their fields, provide the top-quality legal expertise required to provide a unique synthesis that transcends the circumscribed scope of traditional analysis. By bringing together comparative law scholars from a wide range of national and legal backgrounds this book offers an in-depth analysis and reflection on the boundaries of religious freedom and the protection of religious minorities in the contemporary world, serving as a repository of information for readers interested in these issues.

Additionally, many of the problems addressed in this book find themselves at the heart of current discussions on liberal democracies and multicultural, multiethnic and multireligious societies. The rise of illiberalism and populism in many democratic states is posing new threats to the safeguarding of religious freedom

22 For example, L. Zucca, *A secular Europe. Law and Religion in the European Constitutional Landscape* (Oxford: OUP, 2013); S. Mancini, M. Rosenfeld (eds.), *Constitutional Secularism in an Age of Religious Revival* (Oxford: OUP, 2014); F.B. Cross, *Constitutions and Religious Freedom* (Cambridge: CUP, 2015); M. Evans, P. Petkoff, J. Rivers (eds.), *The Changing Nature of Religious Rights under International Law* (Oxford: OUP, 2015); W. Gräb, L. Charbonnier (eds.), *Religion and Human Rights: Global Challenges from Intercultural Perspectives* (Berlin: De Gruyter, 2015); R. Ahdar, I. Leigh, *Religious Freedom in the Liberal State* (Oxford: OUP, 2015); F. Requejo, C. Ungureanu (eds.), *Democracy, Law and Religious Pluralism in Europe, Secularism and Post-Secularism* (New York: Routledge, 2016); W.C. Durham, D.D. Thayer (eds.), *Religion and Equality Law in Conflict* (New York: Routledge, 2016); R. Sandberg (ed.), *Religion and Legal Pluralism* (New York: Routledge, 2017); S. Strong, *Transforming Religious Liberties: A New Theory of Religious Rights for National and International Legal Systems* (Cambridge: CUP, 2017); M. Koskenniemi, M. García-Salmones Rovia, P. Amorosa (eds.), *International Law and Religion Historical and Contemporary Perspectives* (Oxford: OUP, 2017); K. O'Halloran, *Religious Discrimination and Cultural Context: A Common Law Perspective* (Cambridge: CUP, 2018); N. Bhuta (ed.), *Freedom of Religion, Secularism, and Human Rights* (Oxford: OUP, 2019); W.C. Durham, D.D. Thayer (eds.), *Religion, Pluralism, and Reconciling Difference* (New York: Routledge, 2020); M.-C. Foblets, K. Alidadi, Z. Yanasmayan (eds.), *Belief, Law and Politics. What Future for a Secular Europe?* (New York: Routledge, 2020); D. Ferrari, *Legal Code of Religious Minority Rights, Sources in International and European Law* (New York: Routledge, 2021); K. O'Halloran, *State Neutrality: The Sacred, the Secular and Equality Law* (Cambridge: CUP, 2021); H. Bernitz, V. Enkvist (eds.), *Freedom of Religion: An Ambiguous Right in the Contemporary European Legal Order* (London: Hart Publishing, 2021); E. Howard, *Law and the Wearing of Religious Symbols in Europe*, (New York: Routledge, 2021); J. Temperman, *Religious Speech, Hatred and LGBT Rights* (Brill Nijhoff, 2021); W.C. Durham Jr., J. Martínez-Torrón, D.D. Thayer (eds.), *Law, Religion, and Freedom, Conceptualizing a Common Right* (New York: Routledge, 2022); B.A. Rieffer-Flanagan, *Promoting Religious Freedom in an Age of Intolerance* (Cheltenham: Edward Elgar, 2022); J. Hossain Bhuiyan, C.M. Zoethout (eds.), *Freedom of Religion and Religious Pluralism* (Berlin: Brill 2023); R. Sandberg, *Rethinking Law and Religion* (Cheltenham: Edward Elgar, 2024); J. H. Bhuiyan, A. Black (eds.), *Freedom of Religion and Religious Diversity State Accommodation of Religious Minorities* (New York: Routledge, 2024).

and the principle of religious neutrality of states.[23] By offering comparative perspectives and proposals of solutions to existing challenges, this book explains how particular legal orders (national and international), which recognise freedom of religion and the need to protect religious minorities as fundamental values, can and should address such challenges. Because freedom of thought, conscience and religion belong to the category of the most important aspects of life, their legal implications have constituted a major topic of legal doctrine and general discussion. The case of already invoked ritual slaughter bans serves as one of the most telling examples here: increasing social, ideological and, to some extent, political tensions between the supporters of the idea of animal welfare and the religious requirements of observant Muslims and Jews have reached the highest judicial bodies in Europe. Another recent challenge that has not been properly tackled to date is that of the attitudes of illiberal, populist governments regarding issues such as offending religious sensibilities, the protection of religious symbols, and generally, the position and empowerment of institutional churches and religions within states. Therefore, there is still the need for a systemic, in-depth and comparative analysis of freedom of religion and protection of religious minorities. The aim of this book, therefore, is to fill remaining gaps, whilst simultaneously developing, and perhaps offering, a different perspective on the issues already discussed in the literature.

Lastly, as we believe, the audiences of the volume are copious. Conceived as a theoretically-driven and empirically dense collection of research, this book's primary target audience is academic – scholars of legal studies, religious studies, politics, philosophy, history, social psychology and cultural studies. The hope is that the volume will also be of interest to policymakers, representatives of religious communities and others actively involved in handling practical aspects, and consequences, of challenges related to religious freedom and its limits. Therefore, the volume is expected to have a rich appeal far beyond standard academic audiences in Europe. The discussion of cases drawn from various countries will serve as a platform for theorising the role of law in handling social tensions and conflicts of rights and freedoms arising from the challenges posed by religious issues.

I.4 Freedom of Religion, Minority Rights and the Law: A Guide to Chapters

This book proceeds from the focus on the nature, scope and limitations of religious freedom in Europe, with special attention directed towards Jewish and Muslim minorities, primarily in the context of national and European

23 One of the most telling examples of the complication of the attack on liberal and democratic values is the case of Poland in 2024, which was under the rule of populist right-wing circles. Poland witnessed the capture of human rights notions and the introduction of rules resulting in the extension of the enhanced protection not to religious minorities but to the religious majority. The most comprehensive approach towards this situation has been authored by Wojciech Sadurski and can be found in W. Sadurski, *Poland's Constitutional Breakdown* (Oxford: OUP, 2019).

anti-discrimination law. Each of the collected chapters contributes to this general focus, drawing upon various methods and theoretical frameworks. All contributions comprehensively consider the subject of this book from the standpoint of the legal implications of religious freedom and religious minorities protection. They embed their remarks in recent developments, refer deeply to historical perspective, and shed light on implications beyond Europe, namely, in Israel and the United States (US).

The book opens with a prologue by Raphael Cohen-Almagor on the boundaries of religious freedom in democracies, focusing on general reflections on the power of religion and the concept of toleration, by observing the teachings of John Locke and John Stuart Mill and delving into contemporary conditions and challenges. He starts with a just seemingly obvious statement that "Religion is powerful. It cannot be underestimated or dismissed. In the name of religion, countries went to war; people were and are willing to sacrifice their lives and kill others". Than he asks one of the core questions of this book: why religion is so powerful and what implications this powerfulness creates, also offering some convincing responses. Furthermore, Cohen-Almagor strongly advocates for a separation between state and religion, proving via convincing examples that the lack of such separation inevitably leads to coercive theocracy.

The volume comprises four sections, covering the following subjects: (1) the situation of religious minorities as vulnerable groups under international human rights law, (2) the duty of the state to remain religiously neutral and impartial, (3) *Shechita* and traditional circumcision bans, and, finally, (4) the constitutional boundaries of religious accommodation of minorities (with a focus on Jewish and Muslim minorities) in selected national perspectives. Although each of these parts (except Part III, where issues specific to the Jewish and Muslim minorities are discussed), deal with issues generally related to the subject of this book, each of the authors have taken special care to ensure that they relate the results of their analyses to the situation of the minorities that were singled out, in this case, as the most important: the situation of Jews and Muslims.

The first part of the book offers insight into the concept of vulnerability in the context of religious minorities and their legal status under international human rights law. With the concept introduced and discussed in recent years alongside the emergence of new groups aspiring to be defined as vulnerable and thus, protected by law.[24] The groups that undoubtedly fall into the category of vulnerability are religious minorities. Accordingly, this part of the book

24 On the various aspects of the concept of vulnerability in international human rights law, see, for example: T. Pagotto, J. M. Roose, G. P. Marcar, *Security, Religion, and the Rule of Law: International Perspectives* (London: Routledge, 2024). https://doi.org/10.4324/9781003453086; M.A. Fineman, S.W. Allard, "Vulnerability, the Responsive State, and the Role of Religion". In: H. Springhart, G. Thomas (eds.), *Exploring Vulnerability* (Göttingen: Vandenhoeck & Ruprecht, 2017); S.M. Stephens, "Freedom from Religion: A Vulnerability Theory Approach to Restricting Conscience Exemptions in Reproductive Healthcare", *Yale Journal of Law and Feminism* vol. 29 (2017): 93–121. http://hdl.handle.net/20.500.13051/7088. Accessed December 6, 2025.

commences with Kristin Henrard critically assessing ECtHR and CJEU case law regarding protecting religious minorities. Her conclusions are far from flattering, with Henrard urging both courts to adopt a more systematic approach to the level of scrutiny applied in such cases, in order to provide a more robust protection of the fundamental rights of religious minorities. In the next chapter Aleksandra Gliszczyńska-Grabias considers whether the long-standing idea of strengthening the protection of religious minorities by establishing a new universal human rights treaty is a necessary, or rather, a redundant effort. She focuses on the prominent advantages of such a move, whilst also highlighting potential dangers. Set in the context of the difficulties accompanying any process of creating an international treaty of universal nature, Gliszczyńska-Grabias leans towards the conclusion (though not without important caveats) that, at present, making such an effort is a decision that cannot, or should not, be made. Finally, in the concluding chapter, a general reflection on the most recent understandings of vulnerability in the context of religious minorities is offered by Grażyna Baranowska. This chapter looks at the way in which the still not strictly defined concept of vulnerability has been applied to said minorities, particularly in the context of the case law of the ECtHR and UN treaty bodies where the concept is being utilised in non-refoulement cases and cases involving discrimination or pressure from within minorities' own religious groups.

The second part of the volume deals with normative demands of religious neutrality and the impartiality of states. It consists of two chapters, both offering responses to pertinent questions: what are the main conflicts between general laws and religious norms and how these conflicts are or should be resolved; what the balancing of competing interests looks like in terms of free speech and religious sensitivity; and what the duties of employers are in terms of respecting the religious freedom of employees in the workplace. These issues have become increasingly tense as a result of multidimensional developments on both the national and global scene. In particular, the new demands of a working environment, as well as the challenges faced by free speech in general (including fake news, online hate propaganda and censorship), make the debate on these aspects of state obligations *vis-a-vis* securing the guarantees of religious freedom even more urgent. Thus, the chapter by Marcin Górski, entitled, "Free Speech and Religious Sensitivity: between Today's State-Sponsored SLAPPing and Careful Balancing of Competing Interests", deals with the issue of SLAPPs, which, while increasingly present in the public and legal space, has not often been discussed in the context of religious freedom. Górski examines how national and international courts which decide cases categorised as SLAPPs are able to balance the right to free speech against the right to protect religious sensitivity from "gratuitous and serious harm", whilst also addressing the challenge of the so-called blasphemy laws. On the other hand, the second chapter, by Ioanna Tourkochoriti, returns to subject matter inherent in the scope of religious freedom, i.e., employers' duties to respect the religious freedom of employees at the workplace, and in doing so, she focuses on the most recent developments and a very specific comparative approach: she discusses the criterion of neutrality that the CJEU has articulated in its decisions and illustrates the differences in the understanding of neutrality in Europe and the US. Tourkochoriti's general conclusion that the legal regime in Europe is more restrictive towards manifestation of religion in the public sphere than in the US is framed by extremely interesting examples of case law that allow one to trace the dynamics observed in cases involving religion in the workplace.

The next section is dedicated to two specific issues that have recently begun sparking fierce public debates which extend far beyond legal environment. To elaborate, the chapters in this part of the volume consider the right to freedom of religion and the guarantees of the rights of religious minorities in relation to (1) the ritual slaughter bans (*Shechita* bans) and (2) bans of ritual circumcision. What are the historical versus current implications of legislation banning ritual slaughter in comparative perspective? What further consequences or controversies have been caused by the CJEU 2020 ruling and the subsequent 2024 ECtHR judgement regarding the Belgian ban on ritual slaughter? Does the religious practice of male circumcision violate children's rights, or are the bans of such practices violations of religious freedom of both the children and their parents or legal guardians? These are all questions answered by three distinguished experts: Iddo Porat, Gerhard van der Schyff and Rhona Schuz. First, Porat analyses *Shechita* legal bans by adopting a comparative perspective of the past and the present, providing insight into elements of the currently debated conflict of rights and freedoms that often escape the attention of commentators - and those deciding on the form and scope of such bans. This is because it focuses on advancing not only a legal/normative argument, but also a descriptive/sociological one, proving that on the sociological level, the current debate surrounding ritual animal slaughter should be seen as linked to historical prejudiced perceptions of such practices in Europe. Porat argues that current conflicts and political tensions exploit and exacerbate this aversion, rightly pointing to links between today's controversies and the fact that the practice of ritual slaughter comes from cultures and ethnicities that are ancient and foreign to the European culture and ethnicity (Islam and Judaism), which inevitably implies the need to reflect on the motives of anti-Semitism and Islamophobia in the context of introduced or postulated bans.[25] In addition, Porat, like Tourkochoriti in the previous book part, cites, under comparative constitutional law, the example of the US

25 An extremely interesting book focused on the Jewish context, has been authored by R. Judd, cited in the chapter by Porat: R. Judd, *Contested Rituals: Circumcision, Kosher Butchering, and Jewish Political Life in Germany, 1843–1933* (Cornell: Cornell University Press, 2007).

constitutional doctrine, which he claims is better equipped doctrinally to meet the challenge of assessing proportionality in cases such as *Shechita* bans. Following this discussion, focus then shifts to the CJEU dictum in the Belgian case, as analysed by van der Schyff in the chapter entitled "Ritual Animal Welfare and the Right to Freedom of Religion Before the CJEU: The Case of Stunning and Ritual Slaughter". He considers the ruling in detail, citing the relevant ECtHR judgement, whilst also situating his comments, amongst other things, in the context of human dignity, which adds a novel and reflexive level to the current legal understanding of this matter. The last chapter, however, is devoted to the second of the issues identified earlier: ritual male circumcision and children's rights. Schuz points to two seemingly opposing resolutions of the Parliamentary Assembly of the Council of Europe concerning children's ritual male circumcision: one adopted in 2013, which expressed concern about the fact that ritual male circumcision violated children's rights and the other in 2015, on the Right to Freedom of Religion, which acknowledges the negative impact such bans may have on Jewish and Muslim communities in Europe. In her chapter, Schuz seeks to identify "reasonable accommodations" of this practice, focusing on arguments stemming from both sides of this controversial dilemma.

The fourth, and final, part offers a collection of work presenting and analysing carefully selected national case studies, including chapters on legal boundaries of religious accommodation in Israel, Germany, Belgium, France, and the United Kingdom (UK). Each of these states is governed by different legal norms and traditions (including the examination of Germany, as one of the civil law countries and the UK as a common law country), and yet, at the same time, all bound by particular international human rights protection treaties. Despite differing traditions, they often face similar challenges in terms of setting limits on religious freedom on the one hand and protecting religious minorities on the other. While, in some of the cases under review, the scope of religious freedom has been broadened as a result of, among other things, a more multireligious composition of society, in others such attempts have been limited. Against this backdrop, Israel stands out, amongst European case studies, as a distinct but interesting example of multiple dimensions intertwined with navigating religious freedom and its legal implications. With this in mind, the concluding part of this volume opens with a chapter on the constitutional boundaries of religious accommodation in Israel, in which Aviad Hacohen presents how Israeli law, and in particular Israeli courts (including the Supreme Court in its capacity as the High Court of Justice) sought to find creative solutions in order to achieve a balance between the fundamental principles of "freedom of religion" and "freedom from religion", but at the same time stressing that in Israel, from the supreme principle of freedom of religion and freedom from religion follows the rule that no religious commandments shall be imposed on those who are not observant and on those who do not wish to observe religious commandments. The second contribution in this section, by Hans Michael Heinig, sets the stage for understanding of the situation in

Germany, and the way in which the Germany state, legislators and courts collectively understand the term "neutrality" and the minority-protective aspects of fundamental rights. Integrated into his analysis is an extremely interesting element about the forms of cooperation between the German state and Muslim and Jewish religious organisations, which proves to be instrumental, and sometimes even decisive, in advancing religious minorities rights. Having dealt with this case study, in the next chapter, Stéphanie Wattier delves into the "Belgian case study", characteristic of what the author refers to as the, "Belgian laïcité". Wattier addresses the paradoxical case law of the Belgian courts in religious matters, such as, the ban on the full veil in the public space, religious and moral courses in public schools, the Covid-19 crisis and ritual slaughter, with a special focus on Islam and Judaism. accommodated. The chapters then transitions from "Belgian laïcité" case to Russell Sandberg's chapter reflecting on what he calls a "lethargy" in the UK being, according to the author, an example of how religion or belief should not be accommodated. Sandberg formulates a number of objections to the constitutional and legal protection of religion or belief in the UK, pointing out that though many of the difficulties and controversies in this area have historical explanations, they no longer correspond to the observed sociological reality. This chapter incorporates the significance of the existence of a state church, making the UK an even more interesting and distinctive case. The closing chapter gets back to the issue of the "original", French secularism which serves as a fundamental principle of the French legal order and the legal framework governing the exercise of minority religions in France. François Finck defines "French laïcité" as being based on the triad of inseparable values: freedom of conscience, legal equality of spiritual and religious options, and neutrality of political power. Analysing similar examples to the ones tackled by Wattier, from the French perspective, Finck concludes strongly in favour of this principle, that is, according to him, not an anti-religious construct, but rather a response to acute awareness of the oppressive potential of religions, hence the need to regulate their free exercise.

The book closes with the epilogue, presented in the form of a legal Amicus Curiae Opinion by Joseph H. H. Weiler and Meir Linzen, submitted by the International Association of Jewish Lawyers and Jurists (IJL) to the CJEU (*Centraal Israëlitisch Consistorie van België and others*, C-336/19[26]), arguing against ritual slaughter bans as introduced in the Belgian precedent. While Advocate General Hogan[27] shared the arguments given in the Opinion, his conclusions were later rejected by the CJEU in its final dictum. The Opinion, drafted by some of the world's greatest legal minds, is a significant contribution to the discourse associated with ritual slaughter bans in many jurisdictions, as well as a brilliant representation of a philosophical and religious reflection on the dilemma that CJEU faced.

26 *Centraal Israëlitisch Consistorie van België and others*, C-336/19 [2020]. ECLI:EU:C:2020:1031.

27 Opinion of Advocate General Hogan delivered on 10 September 2020, *Centraal Israëlitisch Consistorie van België e.a. and Others*. C-336/19 [2020] ECLI:EU:C:2020:695.

I.4.1 Concluding Remarks: Understanding the Surge of Challenges Facing Religious Freedom

The increasingly complex social and legal realities of today's world, combined with growing tensions within entire societal, religious, ethnic and national groups, make the topics tackled in this book urgent and in demand of further exploration. In such realities, in particular, the process of accommodation of religious minorities by the states and law gain significance.

What becomes clear is that despite the same international standards for the protection of human rights, the situation has unfolded differently in respective jurisdictions and thus, each requires an "insider's look" into relevant challenges and debates. Therefore, in this book, we have tried to include as many issues as possible, ranging from more universal ones to those presented in individual European countries and in Israel, where extremely important and interesting topics in the area of religious freedom are concentrated on through varied lenses.

Taken together, the contributors of this volume have tried to address the following questions, in their respective contexts:

1 What constitutes the essence of religious freedom today and how are its boundaries changing in law, relevant jurisprudence and public perception?
2 What new institutions and solutions are protecting religious minorities today, and what are the most prominent challenges faced by this protection?
3 How are the concepts of neutrality and impartiality of states presently defined, including in the context of new legal, social and political developments?
4 What factors are crucial for perceiving Jewish and Muslim minorities as vulnerable religious minority groups in Europe?
5 What, and where, are the constitutional boundaries of religious accommodation in selected, most relevant states?

Formulating answers to these questions was not only an academic challenge, but also an opportunity to attempt to identify solutions to existing problems - sometimes strongly linked to the historical and political context of a particular place and time - that are as compatible as possible with the very idea of guaranteeing religious freedom and protecting the rights of religious minorities.

However, perhaps the most important point we as editors would like to make in this introductory chapter has been poignantly left for its end. The academic and scholarly ambitions that guided the idea of this book from the beginning, however, cannot be separated from the difficult political and social reality. The drama of the war that began with the murderous Hamas attack on

Israel on October 7, 2023, is inevitably linked to the subject matter of this volume. In this context, although today's reality is painfully far removed from 1999, when the book *Comparing Religions Through Law. Judaism and Islam* by Jacob Neusner and Tamara Sonn was first published, it is still worth quoting the authors' words in the introduction: "We venture to hope that, at the dawn of peace between the State of Israel and its Arab, and mostly Muslim, neighbors, the historical interchange between the two religions, which bear so much in common, may renew itself".[28] We remain hopeful that this "dawn of peace" will come as soon as possible.

28 J. Neusner, T. Sonn, *Comparing Religions Through Law. Judaism and Islam* (New York: Routledge, 1999).

Part I

Jewish and Muslim Minorities as Vulnerable Groups under International Human Rights Law

1 The ECtHR, the CJEU, and the Protection of Religious Minorities

A Mixed Scorecard

Kristin Henrard

Abstract

The protection of human rights historically got a major impulse from measures aimed to protect particular, often religious, minorities. To what extent does the interpretation and application of human rights still reflect this minority protection rationale? In Europe, two major European courts deserve special attention in this respect. The European Court of Human Rights (ECtHR) may be the European human rights court *par excellence*, it is well known that the Court of Justice of the European Union (CJEU) has also developed an ever-growing human rights jurisprudence. The ECHR and the ECtHR jurisprudence remains a reference point for the CJEU, as was confirmed in the Charter of Fundamental Rights of the European Union. Nevertheless, the latter Charter and several equality directives also include provisions going beyond the ECHR, thus providing possibilities for distinct lines of jurisprudence. Several lines of jurisprudence of both courts reflect a minority protection rationale, going to the positive side of their scorecard. However, this chapter will show how and to what extent their respective case law gets an overall mixed scorecard regarding the protection of religious minorities. Particular attention will be had for the ECtHR's jurisprudence on the 'broad' margin of appreciation for states concerning 'church- state relations', which tends to go hand in hand with a reduced level of scrutiny, and the degree to which the CJEU has also adopted this line of reasoning. By way of conclusion, and noting that both ECtHR and CJEU have *de facto* increased their scrutiny in regard to certain religion-state matters, both Courts are urged to more systematically increase the level of scrutiny they adopt, thus providing a more robust protection of the fundamental rights of religious minorities.

Keywords

equal treatment; reasonable accommodation; ECtHR; CJEU; margin of appreciation

DOI: 10.4324/9781003423294-3

1.1 Introduction and Historical Perspectives

Considering the multiple controversies regarding ethnic, religious and/or linguistic minorities, a recent conference focused very aptly on the question of whether minority rights are still human rights.[1] To some extent, the answer seems obvious since persons belonging to minorities are human beings and as such entitled to human rights. In this respect, minorities' fundamental rights are indeed human rights.

It remains important to emphasise that in relation to religious minorities, this question is particularly relevant, in the sense that historically, in Europe, the development of the contemporary human rights paradigm, as rights that needed to be respected and protected by public authorities/states, as well as the identification of *de facto* minority-specific rights, was triggered by problems and related protection needs of religious minorities. The provisions included in peace treaties at the end of the religious wars in the middle ages, and the list of fundamental rights included in the earlier human rights declarations, focused on rights of particular relevance to religious minorities in times of persecution of such minorities – namely, the freedom of expression, of manifestation of one's religion, the right not to be expropriated arbitrarily and the prohibition of discrimination on grounds of religion.[2]

However, subsequently, both as regards developments in standard setting and related supervisory practice (including jurisprudence), a relative neglect of religious minorities and their protection needs can be noted. As regards norm development, it is striking that unlike for gender and race, the Declaration on the Elimination of All forms of Intolerance and Discrimination based on Religion and Belief[3] took two decades and was never followed by a legally binding convention. Similarly, the recognition of duties of reasonable accommodation at the United Nations (UN) and European Union (EU) level is confined to the ground 'disability', while such duties were originally conceived

1 Serbian Academy of Sciences and Arts. "Scientific Conference «Are Minority Rights (Still) Human Rights?" https://www.sanu.ac.rs/en/scientific-conference-are-minority-rights-still-human-rights. Accessed August 30, 2019.

2 D.H. Davis, "The Evolution of Religious Freedom as a Universal Human Right" *Brigham Young University Law Review* no. 2 (2002): 217, 220. https://digitalcommons.law.byu.edu/lawreview/vol2002/iss2/2/. Accessed August 30, 2019; E.F. Defeist, "Religious Liberty and Protections in Europe" *Journal of Catholic legal Studies* vol. 45, no. 1 (2006): 73, 77–78. https://scholarship.law.stjohns.edu/jcls/vol45/iss1/6/. Accessed August 30, 2019. See also J.E. Wood, "The Relationship of Religious Liberty to Civil Liberty and a Democratic State" *Brigham Young University Law Review* no. 2 (1998): 479. https://digitalcommons.law.byu.edu/lawreview/vol1998/iss2/7/. Accessed August 30, 2019.

3 General Assembly Declaration on the Elimination of All Forms of Intolerance and of Discrimination Based on Religion or Belief 36/55 (25 November 1981). https://documents.un.org/doc/resolution/gen/nr0/406/81/pdf/nr040681.pdf. Accessed August 30, 2019.

in Canada and the United States for religious minorities.[4] Last but not least, contrary to the strong presence of linguistic rights in the minority-specific rights, no similar elaboration of religious rights can be identified.[5] This contribution zooms in on the interpretation and application of human rights of special relevance to religious minorities in the jurisprudence of the European Court of Human Rights (ECtHR) and the Court of Justice of the European Union (CJEU), the two regional courts in Europe. Notwithstanding their different frame and legislative framework, striking similarities emerge, resulting in a mixed scorecard for both courts.

By way of preliminary point, the chapter reflects on what features of the supervisory practice of courts matter for an effective protection of minorities' fundamental rights. Subsequently, in the third section, the jurisprudence of the ECtHR is analysed and evaluated, having regard to promising starting positions, but also noting the tendency of the Court to grant states a broad margin of appreciation when regulating religion-states relations. While more recent developments reduce the said margin in some respects, where a sufficient level of European consensus emerges, the ongoing controversial manifestations of (the Muslim) religion (ritual slaughter and headscarves) overwhelmingly result in the Court stepping back and adopting a low level of scrutiny. The fourth section of this chapter then turns to the jurisprudence of the CJEU. That Court undoubtedly played a groundbreaking role in the recognition of the relevance of human rights for the EU, as general principles of EU law. Its human rights body of case law grew especially since 2000 given the adoption of the EU Charter of Fundamental Rights and the two equality directives on grounds other than gender. The CJEU's case law allows to identify three movements: the first judgements set a promising scene, but the second movement shows a Court that is reticent to protect controversial manifestations of (the Muslim) religion and increasingly embraces the ECtHR's line of jurisprudence on the broad margin of appreciation regarding the regulation of religion. Thirdly, and as in the case of the ECtHR, also the CJEU case law shows that in some respects the CJEU is ready to increase its

4 See Article 5.3 Convention on the Rights of Persons with Disabilities (https://www.ohchr.org/en/instruments-mechanisms/instruments/convention-rights-persons-disabilities. Accessed August 30, 2019) and Article 5 Council Directive 2000/78/EC of 27 November 2000 establishing a general framework for equal treatment in employment and occupation (OJ L 303, December 2, 2020). This can be contrasted with the original development of the notion of duties of reasonable accommodation, which took place in the USA, precisely to address concerns of religious minorities: the US Civil Rights Act of 1964 (Public Law 88–352) was amended in 1972 to include a duty on the employer to accommodate the religious practices of employees, unless this would cause undue hardship to the employer.

5 Compare in the Framework Convention for the Protection of National Minorities (Strasbourg, February 1995, H(95)10. https://rm.coe.int/16800c10cf. Accessed August 30, 2019) the succinct restatement of the "freedom of thought, conscience and religion" in Article 7 and "the right to manifest his or her religion or belief and to establish religious institutions, organisations and associations" in Article 8 FCNM on the one hand with the detailed and multiple paragraphs in Articles 10, 11, and 14 FCNM on the other.

de facto level of scrutiny, even in relation to headscarves. The conclusion then paints a mixed scorecard indeed, noting striking similarities in the jurisprudential stance of both courts, notwithstanding the different frame in which they operate. The jurisprudence of both courts reveals an interesting mix of promising and problematic lines of jurisprudence, with mutual influences going back and forth. Ultimately, the analysis identifies several cases that show avenues for more robust protection of religious minorities, leading to the recommendation to both ECtHR and CJEU to level up their protection.

1.2 An Adequate, Effective Protection of Fundamental Rights

When evaluating the jurisprudence of international courts as regards the level of protection that they are providing, it merits reflecting on the notion of what constitutes an adequate protection of fundamental rights. There seems an obvious link between an adequate and an effective protection of fundamental rights. A steady line of jurisprudence of the ECtHR, emulated by many other courts, both international and national, emphasises that human rights should not be theoretical or illusory, but practical and effective.[6] In other words, there seems a strong agreement that fundamental rights need to be protected 'effectively'. When exploring what the effectiveness of human rights implies, one often finds reference to the effectiveness of human rights regimes and, more particularly, the role and impact of supervisory, monitoring mechanisms.[7] It then merits reflecting on the potential role of these supervisory mechanisms, the interpretation principles that they adopt, and how they review the practice of contracting states.

Given the nature and underlying ratio of fundamental rights as flowing from human nature and aimed at ensuring human dignity,[8] it only seems appropriate to interpret the scope of application of fundamental rights broadly, while exceptions, in the sense of legitimate limitations, are to be interpreted narrowly.[9]

6 This line of jurisprudence was started with the ECtHR's case *Artico v. Italy*, No. 6694/74 [1980] § 33, ECLI:CE:ECHR:1980:0513JUD000669474 and has developed in a steady line of jurisprudence which is also emulated by other courts.

7 Inter alia UN Human Rights Offce of the High Commisioner, "Effective Implementation of Human Rights Instruments: Development of the Human Rights Treaty System: Treaty Bodies". https://www.ohchr.org/en/treaty-bodies/effective-implementation-international-human-rights-instruments-development-human-rights-treaty. Accessed August 30, 2019; FRA, *Strong and Effective National Human Rights Institutions. Challenges, Promising, Practices and Opportunities. Report* (Luxembourg: Publications Office of the European Union, 2020). https://doi.org/10.2811/297231.

8 As is confirmed by the Explanations to Article 1 of the Charter of Fundamental Rights of the EU ((2000/C 364/01), OJ C 364, December 18, 2020), the dignity of the human person is not only a fundamental *right in itself but constitutes the real basis of fundamental rights.*

9 This follows general principles of interpretation: see also Economic, Social and Cultural Rights: Handbook for National Human Rights Institutions (Geneva: UN, 2005): 45. https://www.ohchr.org/sites/default/files/Documents/Publications/training12en.pdf. Accessed August 4, 2024.

States may have the primary responsibility to protect the fundamental rights of persons in their jurisdiction,[10] when a case gets to the international courts (after national remedies have been exhausted), their baseline should not be to grant states a margin of appreciation, understood as discretion to determine the minimum threshold set by the human right concerned, or to determine whether a limitation is indeed proportionate to the legitimate aim pursued.[11] To be sure, human rights do not require uniformity across all contracting states, and a variety of approaches are possible and legitimate above the minimum threshold. However, international courts should provide the required guidance to national courts and authorities concerning the determination of the minimum threshold itself, since such a court is removed from political pressure, and thus less prone to bias and prejudice.[12]

The ECtHR started developing its margin of appreciation doctrine in 1976.[13] Over time, this doctrine solidified, and was ultimately in 2013 enshrined in the text of the Convention's preamble with Protocol 15 amending the ECHR.[14] While the Court has not really developed a comprehensive theory on the margin of appreciation, going beyond references to the subsidiarity principle, it did identify over time certain criteria that are used to determine the width of the margin of appreciation. An often-recurring criterion is the extent of a European consensus about the matter at hand.[15] When there is a strong European consensus, the Court only grants a narrow margin of appreciation to the states and scrutinises the case closely. The Court thus solidifies and possibly further

10 See also Protocol 15, amending the ECHR, Article 1.

11 This more searching enquiry is certainly visible in the jurisprudence of other international courts, such as the Human Rights Committee (ICCPR) and the Inter-American Court of Human Rights. See *inter alia Hebbadj v. France Communication*, No. 2807/2016 [2018], UN Doc. CCPR/C/123/D/2807/2016 (in comparison with *S.A.S. v. France [GC]*, No. 43835/11 [2014], ECLI:CE:ECHR:2014:0701JUD004383511). See also IACHR in *Artavia Murillo et al v. Costa Rica* ([2012]. https://www.corteidh.or.cr/docs/casos/articulos/seriec_257_ing.pdf. Accessed August 4, 2024), where the Court in a case pertaining to IVF proceeds with high level scrutiny to only at the end refer to the margin of appreciation invoked by the state, merely stating that it did not consider it pertinent to rule on this argument (§ 316).

12 J. Raz, "The problem of authority: revisiting the service conception" *Minnesota Law Review*, no 90 (2006): 1003, 1014.

13 *Handyside v. UK*, No. 5493/72 [1976] § 48–49.

14 Protocol No. 15 amending the Convention for the Protection of Human Rights and Fundamental Freedoms, Strasbourg, June 24, 2013, CETS no. 213.

15 For an extensive and wide ranging analysis of the European consensus criterion used by the European Court of Human Rights, see P. Kapotas, V. Tzevelekos (eds.) *Building Consensus on European Consensus: Judicial Interpretation of Human Rights in Europe and Beyond* (Cambridge: Cambridge University Press, 2019). https://doi.org/10.1017/9781108564779.

develops the standards itself.[16] If the Court notes the absence of a European consensus on a particular human rights matter, though, it chooses to grant the contracting states a wide margin of appreciation, steps back, and does not provide any guidance to the contracting states.[17] However, one could also argue that exactly in such moments of uncertainty, the international court should step in and provide the outer framework that needs to be respected by states.[18] This framework would still leave some discretion to states to take into account the local circumstances. Relatedly, in a context of sustained prejudice against a particular group, as is visible in the growing level of Islamophobia in the West, international courts should be especially vigilant in relation to (hidden) prejudice against Muslim minorities.

1.3 ECtHR and Religious Minorities

When zooming in on the ECtHR case law of relevance to religious minorities, not only the freedom of religion but also the prohibition of discrimination on grounds of religion and parental rights to respect for their religious convictions in public education need to be considered.

There are undeniable signs of an ambivalent approach of the ECtHR towards religious minorities not only in relation to questions concerning the scope of application of the freedom of religion but also the delimitation of both negative and positive state obligations.

1.3.1 Promising Lines in the Jurisprudence of the ECtHR

Promisingly, the freedom of religion is steadily framed as being inherently related to religious pluralism, the latter being one of the foundations of a democratic society. This means that the state can neither dictate what a person believes[19] nor has any power to assess the legitimacy of religious beliefs or the way in which these are expressed.[20] Furthermore, in case of tension between

16 A good example of a line of case law where the ECtHR where the Court has over time added further criteria and sub-criteria to evaluate the proportionality of an interference concerned the conflicts of rights between a journalist' freedom of expression and the right to respect for privacy of a famous person (see inter alia *Von Hannover v. Germany*, No. 59320/00 [2004], ECLI:CE:ECHR:2004:0624JUD005932000) and *Axel Springer AG v. Germany*, No. 39954/08 [2012], ECLI:CE:ECHR:2012:0207JUD003995408.

17 See inter alia A. Jain, "In Critique of the European Court of Human Rights' Views of Secularism: Can Religious Freedom be Restricted in the Name of Promoting Democracy?", November 27, 2022, https://www.humanrightspulse.com/mastercontentblog. Accessed August 4, 2024.

18 After all, all contracting states accept that the ECtHR is the official supervisor of state compliance with the power to pronounce legally binding judgements.

19 *Nolan and K. v. Russia*. No. 2512/04 [2009] § 73. ECLI:CE:ECHR:2009:0212JUD000251204.

20 Inter alia *İzzettin Doğan et al v. Turkey*, No. 62649/10 [2016] § 69, ECLI:CE:ECHR:2016:0426JUD006264910.

religions or between different strands of the same religion, the state is not to choose sides but to aim for the opposing groups to tolerate one another.[21] Also, in order to receive the protection of the freedom to manifest one's religion, claimants do not need to prove that they are acting on a religious duty.[22] Another promising feature of the ECtHR's case law is the acknowledgement and protection of the community aspect of the manifestation of religion.[23]

1.3.2 More Ambiguous Lines of Jurisprudence of the ECtHR

Turning to more ambiguous, or even restrictive stances of the ECtHR, the Court does not systematically adopt a broad interpretation of the scope of application of the freedom of religion,[24] as would be expected for human rights. While it is acceptable to withhold protection from activities with a most slim connection to the freedom to manifest one's religion,[25] this should be done at the level of the non-binary limitation analysis and not at the level of the scope of application.[26]

As regards the evaluation of limitations imposed by states on the effective enjoyment of the freedom of religion, it seems promising that the Court considers the freedom of religion as one of the foundations of a 'democratic society' within the meaning of the Convention, while constituting for the believers one of the most vital elements that go to make up their identity.[27] Nevertheless, the Court has developed a prominent line of jurisprudence following which states have a broad margin of appreciation when it concerns decisions affecting relations between religions and states. Such choices would concern choices of society about which states should get a broad margin of

21 Inter alia *Agga v. Greece* (no. 4), No. 33331/02 [2006], ECLI:CE:ECHR:2005:0526DEC003333102.

22 *Eweida et al v. UK*, Nos. 48420/10, 59842/10, 51671/10 and 36516/10 [2013] § 82, ECLI:CE:ECHR:2013:0115JUD004842010; *S.A.S. v. France*, No. 43835/11 [2014] § 55, ECLI:CE:ECHR:2014:0701JUD004383511.

23 *The Church of Jesus Christ of Latter-Day Saints v. the United Kingdom*, No. 7552/09 [2014], ECLI:CE:ECHR:2014:0304JUD000755209.

24 The ECtHR maintains that not every act which is in any way inspired, motivated or influenced by that belief constitutes a "manifestation" of it, the latter requiring an intimate link. See inter alia for the ECtHR's stance in relation to *the Church of Scientology of Moscow v Russia*, No. 18147/02 [2007] § 64, ECLI:CE:ECHR:2007:0405JUD001814702. See also ECtHR, Guide on Article 9: Freedom of Thought, Conscience and Religion, updated on February 29, 2024, § 20, https://www.echr.coe.int/documents/d/echr/guide_art_9_eng. Accessed August 30, 2024.

25 *V. v. the Netherlands*, No. 2988/66 ([1967] https://www.strasbourgconsortium.org/common/document.view.php?docId=4843. Accessed August 4, 2024) concerning a doctor's refusal to subscribe to a professional old-age insurance scheme.

26 See also *Eweida et al v. UK*, Nos. 48420/10, 59842/10, 51671/10 and 36516/10, § 83. See also L. Peroni, "Eweida and other *v.* the United Kingdom: Taking Freedom of Religion more Seriously". https://strasbourgobservers.com/2013/01/17/eweida-and-others-v-the-united-kingdom-part-i-taking-freedom-of-religion-more-seriously/. Accessed August 4, 2024.

27 *Kokkinakis v. Greece*, No. 14307/88 [1993] § 31, ECLI:CE:ECHR:1993:0525JUD001430788.

appreciation, as there is no European consensus.[28] Importantly, the Court used to adopt the wide margin of appreciation for a broad category of topics, going well beyond questions of state registrations and recognition schemes.[29]

Clearly, granting states a broad margin of appreciation implies that the Court adopts very low scrutiny, which is difficult to reconcile with the understanding that exceptions to fundamental rights should be interpreted narrowly.[30] Similarly, regarding states' positive obligations, states tend to get a broad margin of appreciation, as the Court is careful not to impose an impossible or disproportionate burden,[31] and also leaves states the choice of means how to fulfil their positive state obligations. Whereas the Court has become more critical, reducing the margin of appreciation, when assessing the lack of police intervention to stop and investigate religious violence and ill-treatment,[32] the margin remains particularly broad for the accommodation of religious diversity, inter alia at work, in public education and in the public sector more generally, as is discussed in more detail in this chapter.[33]

A similar ambiguous approach becomes visible in relation to the Court's jurisprudence on religious discrimination. Also, here the level of scrutiny adopted by the Court is important to gauge the effectiveness of the protection against discrimination. Strikingly, the ECtHR has not recognised 'religion' as suspect ground in its analysis under Article 14 junctio 9,[34] which would trigger heightened scrutiny and thus also higher levels of protection. As was already hinted at earlier, *de facto* the Court does seem to scrutinise cases of invidious

28 See also ECtHR, Guide on Article 9 § 47.

29 Topics that are also included in this notion concern prohibitions on private persons to wear religious gear, state obligations to protect religious communities against discriminatory violence. The ECtHR could conceive almost any religious matter as concerning state-church relations.

30 See also M. T. Parker, "The Freedom to Manifest Religious Belief: An Analysis of the Necessity Clauses of the ICCPR and the ECHR" *Duke Journal of Comparative and International Law*, vol. 17 (2006): 91, 95–96.

31 Inter alia *Karaahmed v. Bulgaria*, No. 30587/13 [2015] §§ 91–96, ECLI:CE:ECHR:2015:0224JUD003058713.

32 Inter alia Members of the *Gldani Congregation of Jehovah's Witnesses and Others v. Georgia*, No. 71156/01 [2007], ECLI:CE:ECHR:2007:0503JUD007115601; *Begheluri v. Georgia*, No. 28490/02 [2014], ECLI:CE:ECHR:2014:1007JUD000334413; and *Tsartsidze et al v. Georgia*, No. 18766/04 [2017], ECLI:CE:ECHR:2017:0117JUD001876604.

33 See the analysis below and for a more detailed analysis: K. Henrard, "The European Court of Human Rights, ethnic and religious minorities and the two dimensions of the right to equal treatment: a jurisprudence at different speeds?" *Nordic Journal on Human Rights*, vol. 34 (2016): 157.

34 The Court was explicitly invited by one of the applicants in the *Eweida et al.* case to recognize religion as suspect ground (*Eweida et al v. UK*, Nos. 48420/10, 59842/10, 51671/10 and 36516/10 [2013] § 71), but the Court chose not to respond at all to this argument, thus revealing its disinclination to do so. Interestingly, the Court has a few times recognized that religion was a suspect ground of differentiation in terms of Article 8 junctio 14, more particularly when the religious affiliation of one of the parents played a role in custody decisions: *Hoffmann v. Austria*, No. 12875/87 [1993], ECLI:CE:ECHR:1993:0623JUD001287587; *Vojnity v. Hungary*, No. 29617/07 [2013], ECLI:CE:ECHR:2013:0212JUD002961707.

discrimination strictly. However, when the differentiation or the lack of differentiation concerns more controversial questions of accommodation of religious diversity, the non-discrimination analysis is avoided or dismissed for the same reasons it has developed in relation to the freedom of religion.[35]

1.3.3 European Consensus Modulating the Actual Level of Scrutiny: From Strong to Weak

As demonstrated in more depth in an article for the *Oxford Journal on Law and Religion* (2015),[36] when the Court identifies a sufficient degree of European consensus about a particular matter, it does feel 'secure' to increase the level of scrutiny, thus leading to an overall more positive, while still 'mixed', balance sheet. The following paragraphs will first discuss two areas where this development can be identified – namely, the recognition and registration schemes of religions, and religion in educational curricula. Subsequently, the case law in three other areas will be analysed where this is not yet in sight, exactly because of their controversial nature, going hand in hand with a lack of European consensus, more particularly religious symbols in public classrooms, the wearing of headscarves in the public sphere, and ritual slaughter.

1.3.3.1 A Strong European Consensus and a Low Level of Scrutiny

The strongest example of a steady line of jurisprudence that clearly restricts the margin of appreciation of states concerns systems pertaining to registration and especially co-operation schemes with recognised religions, having a special status and rights. Over time, the ECtHR has become increasingly demanding as regards the non-discriminatory content of the conditions/criteria for such registration and co-operation and about the transparency of the process.[37] The context in which this line of jurisprudence developed is an ever-reinforcing practice of the overwhelming majority of European states, thus pointing to a convincing European consensus. A particularly interesting case in this regard

35 See, for example, the Court's reasoning in the judgements discussed below of *Cha'are Sjalom ve Tsedek v. France*, No. 27417/95 [2000], ECLI:CE:ECHR:2000:0627JUD002741795; *v. France [GC]*, No. 43835/11 [2014].

36 K. Henrard, "How the European Court of Human Rights' Concern Regarding European Consensus Tempers the Effective Protection of Freedom of Religion" *Oxford Journal of Law and Religion*, vol. 4, no. 3 (2015): 398–420.

37 Inter alia *Savez crkava and others v. Croatia*, No. 7798/08 [2010] § 88, ECLI:CE:ECHR:2010:1209JUD000779808; *Religionsgemeinschaft der Zeugen Jehovas v. Austria*, No. *40825/98* [2008] § 92, ECLI:CE:ECHR:2008:0731JUD004082598; *Genov v. Bulgaria*, No. 40524/08 [2017] § 37, ECLI:CE:ECHR:2017:0323JUD004052408. See also *Anderlecht Christian Assembly of Jehovah's Witnesses and others v. Belgium*, No. 20165/20 [2022], ECLI:CE:ECHR:2022:0405JUD002016520.

is *Magyar Kereszteny Mennonita Egyhaz*[38] since the Court finally seems ready to send clear signals that state churches are potentially problematic in view of state duties of neutrality and impartiality under Article 9. Again, this shift in the Court's jurisprudence aligns with the decline of state churches. Clearly, this heightened scrutiny by the Court in relation to states' registration and recognition schemes constitutes a positive score regarding the proper protection of religious minorities.

Similarly, a strong line of jurisprudence developed relatively early on about public authorities' duty to make reasonable efforts to provide prisoners with meals conforming to their religious prescripts (Hindu, Muslim, etc.). In this respect, the Court actually scrutinises critically whether accommodating the request would be unreasonable. As in the other examples in the preceding analysis where the Court does scrutinise strictly and thus provides adequate protection to religious minorities, the Court's confidence in doing so in relation to meals in prison can be explained by the strong European consensus on the matter, which is reflected in the European Prison Rules. [39]

The ECtHR's case law also reveals a positive development towards higher protection of minorities in relation to the content of the public curriculum, as the ECtHR case law developed from light review of the prohibition of indoctrination to stricter scrutiny, both quantitatively and qualitatively.

Traditionally, the ECtHR used to adopt a rather light standard for its review of public curricula. The Court demanded that states ensure that the information or knowledge included in the curriculum is conveyed in an objective, critical and pluralistic manner.[40] Nevertheless, it reduced the latter requirement to a prohibition of indoctrination, with a very narrow understanding of indoctrination, glossing over instances of risks of indoctrination. The ECtHR thus allowed a course about religions, to focus on a particular religion and pay scant attention to others, owing to the traditional importance of that particular religion in the country. Furthermore, and more generally, states were granted a broad margin of appreciation regarding curriculum choices.

Nevertheless, in 2007, the Grand Chamber changed the equilibrium when it proceeded with a deep review of a course on religions in Norway. Indeed, in *Folgero et al.*,[41] the Court pursues a detailed evaluation of all aspect of the

38 *Magyar Kereszteny Mennonita Egyhaz and others v. Hungary*, Nos. 70945/11, 23611/12, 26998/12, 41150/12, 41155/12, 41463/12, 41553/12, 54977/12 and 56581/12 [2014], ECLI:CE:ECHR:2014:0408JUD007094511.

39 The European Prison Rules were adopted by the Committee of Ministers in 1973 (Resolution 73.5) and several times revised since then. Rule 22.1 of the European Prison Rules identifies unambiguous state obligations to provide prisoners with a diet that takes into account their religious beliefs. See also UN Standard Minimum Rules for the Treatment of Prisoners (the Nelson Mandela Rules). https://www.unodc.org/documents/justice-and-prison-reform/Nelson_Mandela_Rules-E-ebook.pdf. Accessed August 4, 2024.

40 *Osmanoglu and Koçabas v. Switserland*, No. 29086/12 [2017] § 95, ECLI:CE:ECHR:2017:0110JUD002908612.

41 *Folgero et al v. Norway*, No. 15472/02 [2007], ECLI:CE:ECHR:2007:0629JUD001547202.

course concerned, leaving *de facto* only a very narrow margin of appreciation to the state. Taking into account the quantitative and qualitative differences between Christianity and other religions in the course, the Court established a failure to provide the requisite objective, critical, and pluralistic information in public education. Since the exemption scheme did not sufficiently remedy this problem, the Court concluded to a violation.[42] Since then, the Court has followed this line of reasoning in subsequent cases – for example, in *Hasan and Eylem Zengin v. Turkey*[43] regarding a course in which priority was given to one particular version of Islam, again combined with a flawed exemption scheme.

Whereas the Court in most of these cases[44] does not refer explicitly to a European consensus, it is striking that around the time of the *Folgero case*, the OSCE's *Toledo Guiding Principles on Teaching about Religions and Beliefs in Public Schools* were finalised, thus reflecting a certain consensus regarding the place of religion in the public curriculum.

1.3.3.2 A Weak European Consensus, Controversy, and a Low Level of Scrutiny

However, the picture in relation to religious symbols in public classrooms reveals a Court reluctant to intrude on a domain that states consider closely intertwined with their sovereignty. *Lautsi and others v. Italy*[45] dealt with whether having a crucifix in classrooms of state schools violates state duties to respect parents' religious and philosophical convictions. This is an example where the Chamber and Grand Chamber come to opposite conclusions. The Chamber had concluded to a violation of the convention, relying on the principles of duties of state neutrality and impartiality enshrined in Article 9 ECHR. When the case was referred to Grand Chamber there were over 30 intervening parties, many of which states, being 'outraged' about the intrusion into their sovereignty. The Grand Chamber then 'reverted' to a broad margin of appreciation for the state, while arguing that there is no European consensus about the place of religious symbols in public schools.[46] The crucifix would merely be a passive symbol that did not trigger teaching practices that

42 *Folgero et al v. Norway*, No. 15472/02 [2007] §§ 100 and 102.

43 *Hasan and Eylem Zengin v. Turkey*, No. 1448/04 [2007], ECLI:CE:ECHR:2007:1009JUD000144804.

44 But see *Mansur Yalcin et al v. Turkey*, No. 21163/11 [2014], ECLI:CE:ECHR:2014:0916JUD002116311 with the reference to "almost all of the Council of Europe's member states".
Almost all of the Council of Europe's member states offer at least some possibility of dispensation to pupils who do not want to follow religious education, thus pointing again to European consensus.

45 *Lautsi et al v. Italy*, No. 30814/06 [2011], ECLI:CE:ECHR:2011:0318JUD003081406.

46 *Lautsi et al v. Italy*, No. 30814/06 [2011] § 70.

are proselytising.[47] It is hard to read this judgement otherwise than a conscious choice to 'step back' and 'follow' the state's argumentation, *de facto* sacrificing the adequate protection of religious minorities in the process.

The sensitivity of states surrounding the regulation of religious symbols in the public sphere, and the ECtHR's preference to 'step back', is confirmed in the case law concerning headscarves in public at large, and headscarves in public sector employment. While the respective landmark cases concern France, a country with laicité as a constitutional principle, the confirmation of the Court's reasoning in later cases against countries without such a constitutional principle, demonstrate the solidification of the lines of jurisprudence.

The French legislation prohibiting and criminalising the wearing of face covering clothes in public provided the ECtHR with the opportunity to define its position about *de facto* burqa bans. Admittedly, in several respects, the Court's reasoning reflects a critical attitude and high level of scrutiny, particularly by not accepting several legitimate aims invoked by the state. The Court is justifiably firm about 'gender equality', which cannot be invoked "to ban a practice that is defended by women".[48] Similarly, it does not accept 'human dignity' as a legitimate aim for this legislation since it considers wearing the full-face veil in public space to be "an expression of a cultural identity which contributes to the pluralism that is inherent in democracy".[49] Furthermore, the Court's acceptance of the public safety argument goes hand in hand with a strict scrutiny of and finding of a lack of proportionality, because "a blanket ban can only be regarded as proportionate in a context where there is a general threat to public safety".[50]

Unfortunately, the judgement takes a 'grim' turn when the Court does accept France's 'living together' argument as one that contributes to "the protection of the rights of others", more particularly "the rights of others to live in a space of socialization which makes living together easier".[51] The fundamental problem with this argument is that 'the others' are the (non-Muslim) majority. The Court thus accepts and reinforces a majoritarian argument, in stark contraposition of the countermajoritarian core of human rights, as well as the Court's own steady line of jurisprudence on the importance of pluralism and the protection of minorities against undue majority pressure.

The acceptance of this inherently problematic 'legitimate aim' sets the scene for equally problematic and inconsistent reasoning in relation to the proportionality requirement. The Court had actually recognised that the inherent flexibility of the notion of living together carried a risk of abuse and thus requires a careful examination of its necessity. Contrary to the strong level of

47 *Lautsi et al v. Italy*, No. 30814/06 [2011] §§ 72, 74.
48 *S.A.S. v. France*, No. 43835/11 [2014] § 119.
49 *S.A.S. v. France*, No. 43835/11 [2014] § 120.
50 *S.A.S. v. France*, No. 43835/11 [2014] § 139.
51 *S.A.S. v. France*, No. 43835/11 [2014] §§ 121–122.

scrutiny thus announced, the Court resolutely steers towards a broad margin of appreciation because "the question whether or not it should be permitted to wear the full-face veil in public" as a "choice of society", which is a matter of general policy, going hand in hand with the granting of a wide margin of appreciation.[52] While the Court acknowledges that France may be "very much in a minority position in Europe" by adopting such a ban, it goes on to identify a lack of European consensus because the question of wearing the full-face veil in public is a subject of public debate in a number of member states.[53] Clearly, 'measuring' European consensus all depends on the way one wants to frame the consensus, in casu seemingly to further strengthen the Court's choice for a broad margin of appreciation.

In the meantime, the ECtHR has solidified its lines of reasoning in two follow up cases against Belgium, more particularly ***Dakir v. Belgium*** and ***Belcami and Oussar v. Belgium***.[54] Strikingly, the jurisprudence of the ICCPR's Human Rights Committee has gone a diametrically opposite direction, in cases on the same French legislation, establishing both a violation of the freedom to manifest one's religion and of the prohibition of indirect discrimination on grounds of religion. Importantly, the HRC does not accept the living together argument put forward by France and underscores that there are no "rights of others" in play, thus denying the existence of a legitimate aim.[55]

In line with the strong emphasis on laicité in France, a strict neutrality requirement has been applied in the entire French public service. Concretely, this led to the non-renewal of a contract of a social assistant because she refused to put off her headscarf during work time. She contested this decision, ultimately before the ECtHR. The Court acknowledges in *Ebrahimian v. France*[56] that this constitutes an interference with the freedom to manifest her religion but considers that this has a sufficient legal basis in the combination of Article 1 of the French Constitution establishing France as Laic Republic and the jurisprudence of the Council of State of May 3, 2000, in which it established

52 *S.A.S. v. France*, No. 43835/11 [2014] §§ 153–154 as compared to § 122.

53 *S.A.S. v. France*, No. 43835/11 [2014] § 156.

54 See *Dakir v. Belgium*, No. 4619/12 [2017], ECLI:CE:ECHR:2017:0711JUD000461912, and *Belçami and Oussar v. Belgium*, No. 37798/13 [2017], ECLI:CE:ECHR:2017:0711JUD003779813. See also similar lines of reasoning in relation to the obligation of children in a public school to engage in mixed swimming, also when this conflicts with one's religious beliefs: *Osmanoglu and Koçabas v. Switserland*, No. 29086/12 [2017].

55 *Hebbadj v. France*, No. 2807/2016 [2022] § 8.10 CCPR/C/123/D/2807/2016 and *Yaker v. France*, No. 2747/2016 [2018] § 8.13, CCPR/C/123/D/2747/201.

56 *Ebrahimian v. France*, No. 64846/11 [2016], ECLI:CE:ECHR:2015:1126JUD006484611. See also CJEU's preliminary ruling regarding *OP v. Commune d'Ans*, C-148/22 [2023], ECLI:EU:C:2023:924.

that the principle of neutrality applies to the entire public service.[57] Also in this case, the "rights and freedoms of others" are invoked and accepted by the Court as legitimate aims, more particularly the right of patients, to respect their religion and their right to equal treatment without distinction on grounds of religion.[58] While the Court spends about seven pages on the evaluation of the proportionality of the measure, in the end, it is all about the importance of laicité in France as constitutional principle, a lack of European consensus on the place of religion in societies, resulting in France's broad margin of appreciation.[59] Turning to the facts of the case, the Court agrees with the national courts about the particular vulnerability of patients in a psychiatric hospital, which make respecting the principle of neutrality even more important.[60]

As in previous cases, the Court seems set on granting France a broad margin of appreciation, notwithstanding the fact that it acknowledges that the majority of states do NOT prohibit showing religious convictions to public servants.[61] The constitutional principle of laicité, in combination with the hospital setting would still justify a broad margin for French administration and courts.[62] In a somewhat circular argument, the Court underscores that the claimant had been warned several times and that she thus had triggered the disciplinary procedure by refusing to comply.[63] Overall, adopting a very light scrutiny, the Court concludes that there would not be a disproportionate interference, so no violation of Article 9 ECHR.[64]

Ritual slaughter is obviously particularly important for adherents of the Jewish and Muslim religion. The ECtHR case law does not have many cases on this topic yet but so far offers a rather ambiguous protection. *Cha'are Shalom Ve Tsedek v. France*[65] concerned the refusal to grant an exemption for ritual slaughter for a group of orthodox Jews to obtain glatt meat, while France had granted such an exemption for *kosher* meat to the national

57 *Ebrahimian v. France*, No. 64846/11 [2016] §§ 47, 50–51. Note, however, the dissenting opinion of O'Leary, who underscores that this opinion of the Council of State concerning teachers in a public school concerned only one sentence in that opinion, that furthermore was adopted only a few months before the facts of the case: Can this really be considered to be sufficiently accessible and foreseeable as basis in national law?

58 *Ebrahimian v. France*, No. 64846/11 [2016] § 53.

59 *Ebrahimian v. France*, No. 64846/11 [2016] §§ 55–57.

60 *Ebrahimian v. France*, No. 64846/11 [2016] §§ 60–61.

61 *Ebrahimian v. France*, No. 64846/11 [2016] § 65.

62 *Ebrahimian v. France*, No. 64846/11 [2016] §§ 65–67.

63 *Ebrahimian v. France*, No. 64846/11 [2016] § 70.

64 *Ebrahimian v. France*, No. 64846/11 [2016] § 72. See also E. Brems, "Ebrahimian *v.* France: Headscarf Ban Upheld for Entire Public Sector", November, 27 2015, https://strasbourgobservers.com/2015/11/27/ebrahimian-v-france-headscarf-ban-upheld-for-entire-public-sector/. Accessed August 4, 2024.

65 *Cha'are Sjalom ve Tsedek v. France*, No. 27417/95 [2000].

organisation representing the Jews in France. It is nevertheless striking that already at that time, the ECtHR made several pronouncements pointing to a low level of protection in relation to ritual slaughter. The Court recognises that eating ritually slaughtered meat is an essential aspect of practice in the Jewish religion, but Article 9 would not guarantee the right to be involved in ritual slaughter. As long as one has access to such meat, there would not even be an interference with one's freedom to manifest one's religion. In *casu*, the French orthodox Jews could import glatt *kosher* meat from Belgium, and thus there would not be an interference with their Article 9 rights.[66] The Court could have dismissed the case at this stage but still proceeds with a summary subsidiary argument that Article 9 was in any event not violated: "regard being had to the [broad] margin of appreciation left to Contracting States, particularly with regard to the establishment of the delicate relations between the Churches and the State, [the interference] can not be considered excessive or disproportionate".[67]

In the meantime, in line with the increasing controversies surrounding ritual slaughter, the Court appears willing to accept even more far-reaching restrictions on ritual slaughter, while at the same time sending some protective signals. In a judgement of February 13, 2024, *Executive of the Muslims of Belgium and others v. Belgium*,[68] the Court had to decide on the legitimacy of legislative prohibitions of slaughter without reversible stunning, which would not allow certain forms of ritual slaughter. Importantly, and in line with the *Eweida* line of jurisprudence to shift the focus of the analysis away from the 'interference' stage to the proportionality review,[69] in this judgement, the Court does accept that the prohibitions constituted an interference with the freedom of religion of those groups that consider that any form of stunning, even reversible, would go counter to their religious precepts.[70] The Court furthermore emphasised that from the moment that a particular religious conviction is sufficiently serious and coherent, there is no further room for the government to challenge or for the Court to evaluate the legitimacy of the religious convictions concerned.[71] Continuing a promising line of reasoning, the Court recognises that the legitimate aims in Article 9 need to be interpreted restrictively and also that, unlike EU law, the ECHR does not aim to protect animal welfare.[72] Nevertheless, the Court does accept that the

66 *Cha'are Sjalom ve Tsedek v. France*, No. 27417/95 [2000] §§ 80–83.

67 *Cha'are Sjalom ve Tsedek v. France*, No. 27417/95 [2000] § 84.

68 *Executive of the Muslims of Belgium and others v. Belgium*, No. 16760/22 [2024], ECLI:CE:ECHR:2024:0213JUD001676022.

69 *Eweida et al v. UK*, Nos. 48420/10, 59842/10, 51671/10 and 36516/10 [2013] § 83.

70 *Executive of the Muslims of Belgium and others v. Belgium*, No. 16760/22 [2024] § 88.

71 *Executive of the Muslims of Belgium and others v. Belgium*, No. 16760/22 [2024] §§ 85–86.

72 *Executive of the Muslims of Belgium and others v. Belgium*, No. 16760/22 [2024] §§ 91 and 93, respectively.

protection of animal welfare can be linked to 'public morals' as legitimate aim in Article 9, § 2.[73] The Court relies in this regard on the living instrument doctrine and developing understandings about morals, as well as developing practice in other member states of the Council of Europe and jurisprudence of the CJEU.[74]

Subsequently, the reasoning of the ECtHR shows it has taken note of the criticisms in relation to the preceding CJEU judgement in the case while still steering towards a broad margin of appreciation for the state, mimicking its reasoning in *SAS*. The former is clearly visible in its acknowledgement in the proportionality review that animal rights and human rights do not have the same value.[75] For the latter, it builds on its "lack of European consensus about relations between church and religions" argument, and the importance of showing respect for a thorough democratic process resulting in a "choice of society".[76] In line with its "turn to procedural reasoning",[77] the Court attaches also a lot of weight to the very careful parliamentary process, as well as the preliminary ruling of the CJEU, that had revealed a concern for respecting the freedom of religion by the addition of reversible stunning in relation to ritual slaughter.[78] It is exactly also the latter modification, making the stunning reversible, for ritual slaughter, that leads the Court to conclude that the prohibition of discrimination is not violated.[79]

While the Court's reasoning seems very careful and balanced, what message is being sent though? On the one hand, the Court says that it does not claim that animal welfare and fundamental rights can be considered as two rights with equal value in terms of the ECHR. However, in the end, it does allow Belgium's prohibition, which is based on the understanding that the most optimal way to realise animal welfare outweighs the freedom to manifest one's religion.[80] Should the Court's review not have specified that ultimately the freedom of religion should not be sacrificed on the altar of animal welfare, also

73 *Executive of the Muslims of Belgium and others v. Belgium*, No. 16760/22 [2024] § 101.

74 *Executive of the Muslims of Belgium and others v. Belgium*, No. 16760/22 [2024] § 99.

75 *Executive of the Muslims of Belgium and others v. Belgium*, No. 16760/22 [2024] § 107.

76 *Executive of the Muslims of Belgium and others v. Belgium*, No. 16760/22 [2024] §§ 105–106.

77 There is extensive literature on this 'turn'; several authors welcome this turn, with others being more critical. Compare the edited volume by E. Brems, J. Gerards, *Procedural Review in European Human Rights Cases* (Cambridge: CUP. 2017) with M. Jackson, "Judicial Avoidance at the European Court of Human Rights: Institutional Authority, the Procedural Turn, and Docket Control" *International Journal of Constitutional Law vol. 20, nr 1* (2022): 112. https://doi.org/10.1093/icon/moac003.

78 *Executive of the Muslims of Belgium and others v. Belgium*, No. 16760/22 [2024] §§ 109–118.

79 *Executive of the Muslims of Belgium and others v. Belgium*, No. 16760/22 [2024] § 148. Note that there was also a complaint comparing with hunters and fishermen but the ECtHR did not consider the respective positions comparable as the latter concern animals in the wild (§ 146).

80 See also *Executive of the Muslims of Belgium and others v. Belgium*, No. 16760/22 [2024]. Concurrent Opinion of judge Yüksel § 7.

taking into consideration that ritual slaughter can sufficiently minimise animal suffering? Put differently, would it not be more appropriate for the Court to acknowledge the state's margin of appreciation when approving the compromise of reversible stunning for most instances of ritual slaughter while requiring narrow exceptions for those orthodox believers for which the reversible stunning would not be acceptable? This line of reasoning would embrace states' choices to take animal welfare seriously, while still ultimately giving more weight to the freedom of religion. In the current Islamophobic and also growing anti-Semitic climate, this seems a particularly important message to send. Furthermore, returning to the practical argument: if all Council of Europe states are going to prohibit ritual slaughter, it will become increasingly difficult to obtain such meat, and thus eat it, while this is an essential element of Jewish faith, as recognised by the ECtHR itself (see the earlier discussion). The Court seems to acknowledge that this could weigh in the balance over time, where it notes that there is indeed this trend to prohibit slaughter without stunning among Council of Europe countries[81] but not yet sufficient proof about a lack of such meat.[82]

1.3.3.3 Limits to Neutrality Rules and Headscarf Bans on Private Citizens in Judicial Proceedings

Notwithstanding the Court's acceptance of a *de facto* burqa ban in the entire public space, thus also for private citizens, and its allowance of a strict neutrality requirement to the entire public sector, the ECtHR does not accept states imposing strict neutrality requirements on private citizens present in judicial proceedings. In *Hamidovic v. Bosnia Herzegovina*, the Court underscored the difference between private citizens on the one hand and public officials while exercising official authority on the other. [83] The former could only be punished with contempt of court for being disrespectful during trial. A witness in a criminal trial could not be so punished simply for refusing to remove his skullcap, a religious symbol.[84] Similarly, in *Lachiri v. Belgium* (2018), the Court concluded to a violation of Article 9 ECHR because the applicant, a private citizen, had been excluded from a courtroom on account of her refusal to remove her hijab.[85] While this interference had the legitimate aim to protect public order, in the form of respect for the judiciary and not disrupting the

81 *Executive of the Muslims of Belgium and others v. Belgium*, No. 16760/22 [2024] § 99.

82 *Executive of the Muslims of Belgium and others v. Belgium*, No. 16760/22 [2024] § 122.

83 *Hamidovic v. Bosnia Herzegovina*, No. 57792/15 [2017] § 40, ECLI:CE:ECHR:2017:1205JUD005779215.

84 *Hamidovic v. Bosnia Herzegovina*, No. 57792/15 [2017] §§ 41–43.

85 *Lachiri v. Belgium*, No. 3413/09 [2018] § 47–48, ECLI:CE:ECHR:2018:0918JUD000341309.

proper conduct of a hearing, it had not been appropriate in casu, since wearing a hijab as such does not disrupt the proper conduct of a hearing.[86]

A similar 'mixed scorecard' emerges from the analysis of the CJEU case law, as the following analysis will demonstrate. Increasing similarities between the two Court's jurisprudence regarding religious minorities flows from the CJEU's adoption of the ECtHR's jurisprudence on the wide margin of appreciation for states regarding church-state relations.

1.4 The CJEU and Religious Minorities

The EU may not be an international organisation that is primarily concerned with human rights, as is the Council of Europe, but the former does like to depict itself as an organisation that has human rights high on its agenda.[87] The adoption of the EU Charter of Fundamental Rights surely was an important signpost.[88] When zooming in on the case law of the CJEU, it is important to mark that it was actually the CJEU that introduced human rights in EU law, more particularly as general principles of EU law, and this already from the early beginnings.[89] As is well known, Article 2 TEU explicitly refers to "respect for human rights, including the rights of persons belonging to minorities". While the latter are still an important parameter in accession negotiations, further references to minorities rights in the treaties and the Charter of Fundamental Rights of the European Union (CFR) are scarce, leading to allegations of 'double standards'. [90] The lack of minority-specific internal standards makes the contribution to minority protection of general human rights particularly relevant.

The following analysis' focus on religious minorities and zooms in on the CJEU jurisprudence concerning the freedom of religion (Article 10 FCR) and/or the prohibition of discrimination on grounds of religion (Directive 2000/78). Admittedly, the case law of the CJEU on religious themes was scarce prior to the adoption of the EU Charter of Fundamental Rights and Directive 2000/78. In the meantime, more than ten additional judgements have been pronounced. Three 'movements' are distinguished, albeit that these do not entirely run consecutively.

86 *Lachiri v. Belgium*, No. 3413/09 [2018] § 44.

87 This is now nicely visible in Article 2 Treaty on European Union (Consolidated version 2016 OJ C 202, June 7, 2016), identifying human rights as one of the foundational values of the EU and in Article 6 TEU.

88 See inter alia EU Charter of Fundamental Rights. https://fra.europa.eu/en/eu-charter. Accessed August 4, 2024.

89 *Stauder*, 29–69 [1969], ECLI:EU:C:1969:57; *Internationale Handelsgesellschaft*, No. 11–70 [1970], ECLI:EU:C:1970:114.

90 Inter alia K. Henrard, "'The EU, Double Standards and Minority Proteciton': A Double Redefinition and Future Prospects". In: K. Henrard (ed.), *Double Standards Pertaining to Minority Protection* (Leiden: Martinus Nijhoff, 2010): 21.

In the first movement, a promising starting position is drawn, with the 'early' *Prais* judgement[91] and the first judgements post 2000, in which the CJEU signalled it would not adopt the ECtHR's broad margin of appreciation. In the second movement, the CJEU is confronted with a range of cases concerning often controversial manifestations of religion by members of the Muslim minority in European states, more particularly ritual slaughter and the wearing of headscarves at work. In several respects, these cases belong on the negative scorecard of the CJEU, not in the least for its change of tactics, embracing explicitly the ECtHR's broad margin of appreciation for the regulation of religion in the member states. Fortunately, some more recent cases, still concerning controversial manifestations of the freedom of religion, allow us to identify a third movement in which the CJEU becomes more critical about (certain) restrictions to manifest one's religion.

1.4.1 On the Positive Side of the CJEU Scorecard: From Duties of Reasonable Accommodation to a Reticent Stance about a Broad Margin of Appreciation for States

Prior to the adoption of the Charter of Fundamental Rights and Directive 2000/78, only one case merits attention. Contrary to the ECtHR, which remains reluctant to identify duties of reasonable accommodation on grounds of religion (in the workplace),[92] the CJEU already did so in the 1976 *Prais* judgement. In response to a complaint from a Jewish candidate for a position in EU institutions concerning the timing of the tests on a Saturday, the CJEU acknowledged a duty for EU institutions akin to duties of reasonable accommodation on grounds of religion. The CJEU deduced from the freedom of religion, as general principle of EU law, enshrined in Article 9 ECHR, that EU institutions when setting a test date, should avoid dates that a candidate informs the appointing authority about as being dates that would be impossible for religious reasons. Typical reasonability constraints would imply though that the candidate would have to inform the appointing authority "in good time" of the difficulties.[93]

In a more recent case on the state recognition of religious holidays of minorities, *Achatzi*,[94] the CJEU allows states to adopt special measures of protection aimed at enabling religious minorities to respect their religion's prescripts. At the same time, the CJEU demonstrates that it adopts strict scrutiny towards differentiations on grounds of religion by emphasising that these measures should not be limited to one particular religious minority.

91 *Vivien Prais*, No. 130–75 [1976], ECLI:EU:C:1976:142.

92 See *Eweida et al v. UK*, Nos. 48420/10, 59842/10, 51671/10, and 36516/10 [2013] and related analysis.

93 Because in casu *Vivien Prais* had given a very late notice of the religious constraints she faced on the chosen date, the Court concluded that no violation of the freedom of religion took place: *Vivien Prais*, No. 130–75 [1976] § 20.

94 *Vivien Prais*, No. 130–75 [1976] §§ 16–19.

Furthermore, again in favour of religious minorities, the CJEU urges national courts to 'level up', providing similar protection to other religious minorities, while awaiting the adaptation of national legislation.[95]

While other cases may not concern religious minorities, the questions they raise typically come up in relation to minorities – namely, what can a religious employer expect from its employees? What makes these cases particularly noteworthy is the Court's position about Article 17 TFEU's prescription that the "EU respects and does not prejudice the status under national law of churches and religious associations and communities in the member states".[96] The wording of Article 17 TFEU appears to align with the often criticised jurisprudence of the ECtHR, granting states a broad margin of appreciation for the regulation of religion. Nevertheless, in the first judgements in which the Court was called upon to interpret and apply Article 17 TFEU, *IR* and *Egenberger*,[97] it actually construed its impact narrowly.

The CJEU indeed emphasised that Article 17 TFEU does not allow member states to exempt the employment related decisions of religious organisations as employers from the operation of EU non-discrimination law. [98] This position favours the protection of employees against discrimination on grounds of religion. The CJEU clarified furthermore that states need to ensure that religious employers can only impose those demands of loyalty (and related sanctions) that are proportionate to the respective function of the employee concerned.[99] The freedom of religion of employees should thus not be disproportionately limited by autonomy concerns of religious employers.

1.4.2 *On the Negative Side of the CJEU Scorecard: Cases on Ritual Slaughter and Headscarves at Work towards a Broad Margin of Appreciation of States*

The cases of the second movement belong on the CJEU's negative scorecard, as the CJEU case law becomes more restrictive towards the protection of religious minorities in favour of states, leaving states a wide margin of appreciation. Strikingly, these cases concern controversial manifestations of Muslim faith in European states, namely ritual slaughter and the wearing of headscarves (at work).

It is arguably telling that it is in one of these cases that the CJEU explicitly embraces the ECtHR's broad margin of appreciation for the regulation of

95 *Achatzi*, C-193/17 [2019] §§ 79–82, ECLI:EU:C:2019:43.

96 Consolidated version of the Treaty on the Functioning of the European Union, OJ C 326, November, 26 2012.

97 *IR v. JQ*, C-68/17 [2018], ECLI:EU:C:2018:696, § 48; *Vera Egenberger v. Evangelisches Werk für Diakonie und Entwicklung e.V.*, C-414/16 [2018] §§ 56-58, ECLI:EU:C:2018:257.

98 *IR v. JQ*, C-68/17 [2018].

99 *IR v. JQ*, C-68/17 [2018] § 50–50.

religion in the member states.[100] Subsequent cases further entrench this line of jurisprudence. This entrenched position becomes very clear when this reasoning even spreads to the CJEU case law on one of the fundamental freedoms of the internal market – namely, the freedom of establishment.[101]

Three arguments are developed through the critical discussion of the case law on headscarves and ritual slaughter. By way of first and overarching theme, it is argued that the CJEU does not adopt a sufficiently high level of scrutiny in relation to action or lack of action by the public authorities, particularly called for given the context of Islamophobia in European states. A second and closely related point concerns the lack of critical assessment of cases of possible hidden direct discrimination. The latter is especially important in EU law given the very different justification possibilities for indirect and direct discrimination respectively.[102] Thirdly, and even more problematically, are some pronouncements of the CJEU that can be considered stigmatising towards the Muslim minority.

1.4.2.1 CJEU Case Law on Ritual Slaughter

In relation to ritual slaughter, we first need to reflect on the explicit legal standards in EU law before discussing the CJEU's interpretation and application thereof. Importantly, these standards demonstrate that while considerable importance is attached to animal welfare, the freedom to manifest one's religion should not be disproportionately limited.

Indeed Article 13 TFEU combines a duty of EU and member states to "*pay full regard* to animal welfare" when formulating and implementing EU policies, "*while respecting* customs of the EU countries, relating in particular to *religious rites...*", with 'religious rites' referring to ritual slaughter. Regulation 1099/2009[103] underscores the importance of stunning animals prior to slaughter but allows a derogation for ritual slaughter as manifestation of the freedom of religion (Article 4(4)). The regulation continues to confirm the importance of this balancing act by allowing states to protect animal welfare even more extensively, as long as they still respect the freedom of religion enshrined in

100 See also below the critical remark about the CJEU use of stigmatizing language in relation to Islam and Islamic practices.

101 See below: *Freikirche*, C-372/21 [2023], ECLI:EU:C:2023:59.

102 While the distinction between direct and indirect discrimination was first developed by the CJEU, in the mean time, equality directives contain definitions of both concepts that clearly demonstrate that direct discrimination is in principle prohibited, unless an explicit exception has been carved out in treaty or secondary legislation, whereas indirect discrimination works with the general justification formula (also found in international human rights law): inter alia Article 2(2)(a) and (b) of Directive 2000/78 and the same Article of Council Directive 2000/43/EC of 29 June 2000 implementing the principle of equal treatment between persons irrespective of racial or ethnic origin (OJ L 180, July 19, 2000).

103 Council Regulation (EC) No 1099/2009 of 24 September 2009 on the protection of animals at the time of killing (text with EEA relevance), OJ L 303, November 18, 2009.

Article 10 Charter of Fundamental Rights of the EU. The following paragraphs will critically evaluate the way in which the CJEU has reviewed the outcome of this balancing by states.

Regarding the appropriate level of scrutiny, arguably, a context of systemic discrimination and the underlying prejudice against a particular group should lead to the adoption of heightened scrutiny in relation to the proportionality requirement, similarly as is the case for so-called suspect grounds. Indeed, one of the recurring criteria to identify a suspect ground is a history of systemic discrimination on that particular ground.[104] Already since more than a decade, several reports of prominent non-governmental organisations (NGOs), the Fundamental Rights Agency of the EU and various Council of Europe bodies, have emphasised the worrying nature and the broad range of manifestations of intolerance towards the Muslim minority across Europe,[105] labelled as Islamophobia.

In *Liga van Moskeeën*,[106] the CJEU was confronted with a preliminary question from a Belgian court concerning the validity of an EU regulation that only allowed ritual slaughter (without prior stunning) in approved slaughterhouses. During the peak demands of the Feast of Sacrifice, there are too few of those slaughterhouses to meet the demand in the Flemish region, resulting in several families not being able to obtain ritually slaughtered meat during the Festival,[107] which would imply a violation of the freedom of religion.[108] Unfortunately, the CJEU combines a very narrow approach to what amounts to an interference with the freedom to manifest one's religion with a formal equality approach, which fails to acknowledge the disproportionate impact of this rule, and thus

104 See also E. Holzleithner, "Mainstreaming Equality: Disentangling Grounds of Discrimination" *Transnational Law and Contemporary Problems* no. 14 (2005): 927, 953.

105 E. Bayrakli, F. Hafez (eds.), *European Islamophobia Report 2017* (İstanbul: SETA, 2018). https://sfera.unife.it/retrieve/e309ade5-3c94-3969-e053-3a05fe0a2c94/Italy.pdf. Accessed August 31, 2024. Since 2014, the Council of Europe has a European Action Day against Islamophobia – namely, September 21, which has been actively supported by the European Commission. T. Hammarberg, *Human Rights in Europe: No Grounds for Complacency* (Brussels: Council of Europe, 2011): 36–39 and 47–48; *Living Together: Combining Diversity and Freedom in 21st-Century Europe. Report of Group of Eminent Persons of the Council of Europe* (Brussels: Council of Europe, 2011): 15–16; Resolution 1743(2010) Parliamentary Assembly of the Council of Europe (PACE) Islam, Islamism and Islamophobia in Europe (Resolution 1743). https://pace.coe.int/pdf/f39be711428626cdcb1dab77d413db67d6a3fb205d7bf6dce3bcaf03dcb7422c?title=Res.%201743.pdf. Accessed August 31, 2024.

106 *Liga van Moskeeën en Islamitische Organisaties Provincie Antwerpen VZW and Others v. Vlaams Gewest*, C-426/16 [2018], ECLI:EU:C:2018:335.

107 *Liga van Moskeeën en Islamitische Organisaties Provincie Antwerpen VZW and Others v. Vlaams Gewest*, C-426/16 [2018] §§ 17–19.

108 *Liga van Moskeeën en Islamitische Organisaties Provincie Antwerpen VZW and Others v. Vlaams Gewest*, C-426/16 [2018] § 21.

the possible indirect discrimination, requiring justification.[109] Indeed, the CJEU only had regard for the technical nature of the requirements that applied to all forms of slaughter.[110] What is entirely absent is a consideration of positive state duties to ensure the effective enjoyment of the freedom of religion. As it is well known that there is a peak demand during the Feast of Sacrifice, a very narrowly drawn exception could have been added.

In this case, the argument that comes out most clearly is the lack of attention by the CJEU for a possible case of hidden direct discrimination, in the sense that it did not even identify a case of indirect discrimination and adopted a formal equality reasoning. Indeed, the CJEU's narrow approach glossed over the context of Islamophobia and its particular manifestation in casu as the ban on ritual slaughter was also pushed by nationalists, eliciting claims of "bigotry under guise of animal welfare".[111]

In a subsequent case, *Centraal Israëlitisch Consistorie van België and Others*,[112] the CJEU was asked a preliminary question by the Belgian Constitutional Court, when the latter court had to decide on the constitutionality of a Belgian law making reversible stunning obligatory, while dispensing with any exemption for ritual slaughter. The reversible stunning was meant to respect the requirements of ritual slaughter but failed to satisfy the more orthodox groups, who took their complaint to the Belgian Constitutional Court.

This case revolves around the interplay of the Articles of the Regulation explained earlier, providing an exemption to the principle of prior stunning for ritual slaughter, while allowing states to protect animal welfare more, as long as they would not violate the freedom of religion.[113] Ultimately, this case speaks most to the argument concerning the inappropriate level of scrutiny adopted by the CJEU in relation to the freedom of religion.

It is an improvement that the CJEU recognises in this case that the Belgian law would amount to an interference with the freedom of

109 *Liga van Moskeeën en Islamitische Organisaties Provincie Antwerpen VZW and Others v. Vlaams Gewest*, C-426/16 [2018] §§ 56–68. See also A. Peters, "De-humanisation? CJEU, Liga van Moskeeën en islamitische Organisaties Provincie Antwerpen on Religious Slaughter", June 26, 2018. https://www.ejiltalk.org/de-humanisation-cjeu-liga-van-moskeeen-en-islamitische-organisaties-provincie-antwerpen-on-religious-slaughter/. Accessed August 31, 2024.

110 *Liga van Moskeeën en Islamitische Organisaties Provincie Antwerpen VZW and Others v. Vlaams Gewest*, C-426/16 [2018] §§ 56–61.

111 E. Howard, "Ritual Slaughter and Religious Freedom: Liga van Moskeeën" *Common Market Law Review* vol. 56, no. 3 (2019): 804, 816–818. See also L. Hehemann, "Religious Slaughtering and Organic Labels: Oeuvre d'Assistance aux Bêtes d'Abattoires" *European Papers* no. 4 (2019): 301–305.

112 *Centraal Israëlitisch Consistorie van België and Others*, C-336/19 [2020] ECLI:EU:C:2020:1031.

113 *Centraal Israëlitisch Consistorie van België and Others*, C-336/19 [2020] §§ 43–45 and 48–49.

religion.[114] However, the CJEU goes on to argue that the essence of the freedom of religion would be respected since "the interference… is limited to one aspect of the specific ritual act of slaughter, and that act of slaughter is not, by contrast, prohibited as such".[115] Taking this theological stance is inappropriate for a Court, particularly when taking into account that a "significant body of adherents to both the Muslim and Jewish faiths consider that any stunning prior to the killing of the animal would disregard an essential aspect of a necessary religious rite".[116]

Furthermore, and in contrast to the preceding cases in which it seemed to embrace a proper level of scrutiny also in religious matters, the CJEU in this case chooses to embrace the ECtHR line of jurisprudence about the broad margin of appreciation in matters of general policy, such as the determination of relations between the state and religions about which there is no European consensus (§ 67). The Court thus sends a signal to the Belgian Constitutional Court that the Belgian law has adopted an acceptable stance having regard to the regulation and the freedom of religion. However, is this the appropriate level of scrutiny in relation to an interference with the freedom of religion, in view of the weight attached to the freedom of religion as fundamental right (§ 57)?

A third preliminary ruling, *OABA*,[117] concerns ritual slaughter in a very different way, namely the question whether ritually slaughtered meat could obtain the organic food label, following an EU regulation on the matter. Interestingly, the regulation on organic food labelling contains an exhaustive list of conditions that need to be fulfilled for meat to be labelled as organic and does not say anything about prior stunning. [118] Let's not forget that EU Regulation 1099/2009 foresees in two regimes of animal welfare protection, one of which concerns ritual slaughter, while the regulation and Article 13 TFEU confirm that the importance attached to animal welfare should not entail a disproportionate limitation of the freedom of religion. Put differently, animal welfare does not trump the freedom of religion, which is after all a fundamental human right.[119]

However, the CJEU takes a different approach and arguably adopts reasoning that sends a stigmatising message about ritually slaughtered meat, thus playing into prejudice against Muslims (and Jews). Indeed, the CJEU adds, contra legem, a requirement of prior stunning for the organic food

114 *Centraal Israëlitisch Consistorie van België and Others*, C-336/19 [2020] §§ 53–55.
115 *Centraal Israëlitisch Consistorie van België and Others*, C-336/19 [2020] § 61.
116 Opinion A.G. Hogan in *Centraal Israëlitisch Consistorie van België et all*, C-336/19 [2020] § 47, ECLI:EU:C:2020:695.
117 *Oeuvre d'Assistance aux Bêtes d'Abattoires (OABA) v. Ministre de L'agriculture et de L'alimentation and Others*, C-497/17 [2019], ECLI:EU:C:2019:137.
118 See also Opinion of AG Wahl, *OABA*, C-497/17 [2018] §§ 74–108, ECLI:EU:C:2018:747.
119 L. Hehemann "Religious Slaughtering and Organic Labels" 301–305.

label, while arguing that ritual slaughter cannot guarantee that animal suffering is kept to a minimum.[120]

1.4.2.2 Case Law on Headscarves at Work: The First Judgements Concerning Companies and Public Authorities

The case law on headscarves at work concerns the application of the Employment Equality Directive 2000/78, prohibiting discrimination on four grounds, including religion, in the employment sphere and combining, as usual in EU law, a principled prohibition of direct discrimination with a balancing (proportionality) review regarding the prohibition of indirect discrimination. Importantly, this directive concerns both the private and the public sector and has triggered several preliminary rulings, most originating in cases concerning private companies, but also one concerning a municipality as employer. In relation to the former, companies prohibited workers from wearing visible signs of political, philosophical or religious beliefs in order to secure the company's neutrality policy. The latter case concerned municipal (public) authorities that aiming to realise an entirely (exclusively) neutral environment in their workplace prohibited all employees to wear any visible signs of political, philosophical or religious beliefs.

Also, these cases will be critically analysed in terms of three themes identified earlier in relation to the ritual slaughter case law – namely, the (rather low) level of scrutiny adopted by the CJEU (going hand in hand with the embrace of a broad margin of appreciation for states), the (lack of) attention for hidden direct discrimination, and the use of stigmatising language. While some promising developments of increasing scrutiny in the case law regarding the neutrality policy used by companies are noted and welcomed, the CJEU's acceptance of strict neutrality policies in the entire municipal public service arguably lowers the bar considerably for public authorities, with the concomitant risk of indirect and possibly even hidden direct discrimination. Promoting the relocation of employees wearing headscarves to the back office as a proportionate solution fails to take into account the stigmatising message that is thus sent to these employees.

1.4.2.2.1 LEVEL OF SCRUTINY – COMPANIES

Since the first two judgements in which it was confronted with the implications of neutrality policies adopted by companies with the effect that employees are not allowed to wear headscarves, the CJEU has adopted a steady line of jurisprudence. When the neutrality policies are put and applied in general terms – that is, when they prohibit the wearing of visible signs of all political, philosophical, or religious beliefs consistently – the resulting prohibition to

120 *Oeuvre d'Assistance aux Bêtes d'Abattoires (OABA) v. Ministre de L'agriculture et de L'alimentation and Others*, C-497/17 [2019] §§ 51–52.

wear headscarves would not amount to direct discrimination on grounds of religion.[121] The Court acknowledges that such a neutrality policy puts persons adhering to a certain religion at a particular disadvantage and could thus amount to indirect discrimination on grounds of religion. Nevertheless, the Court accepts that the company invoke their neutrality policy as a legitimate aim – namely, related to the right to conduct a business, enshrined in Article 16 Charter of Fundamental Rights of the EU.[122] In so far as the policy is applied consistently and systematically to all expressions of convictions, be them political, philosophical, or religious, the prohibition to wear headscarves would be appropriate to secure the proper application of the legitimate aim.[123] In terms of the further proportionality requirement of necessity, the Court emphasises that it should be determined (by the national court) that the prohibition is limited to what is strictly necessary. However, the Court explains this standard as being met when the company would only apply the prohibition to workers who interact with customers.[124] The Court goes on to underscore this point by instructing the national court to ascertain whether the company could have, without incurring an additional burden, offered her a non-customer-facing role instead of dismissing her.[125] While the focus on limiting the justifiable application of the prohibition is welcome, the message that allows employers to push Muslim employees with headscarves to the back office does not seem to align with the EU's embrace of diversity.[126] More generally, the CJEU's uncritical acceptance of a company's neutrality policy as legitimate aim for prohibitions of wearing headscarves has been criticised for failing to counteract hidden prejudice against particular religions.[127]

Furthermore, the Court only provided limited guidance to the national courts about how to assess the proportionality of neutrality policies.[128]

The *Bougnaoui*[129] *case* has a distinct fact pattern as here the prohibition for an employee to wear a headscarf (and the resulting dismissal) was the result of a complaint by a customer about the headscarf as such and the wish to not be helped by someone working with a headscarf. The CJEU here starts by repeating the *Achbita* ruling about general neutrality policies[130] but goes on to

121 *Achbita v. G4S Secure Solutions NV*, C-157/15 [2017] §§ 29–32, ECLI: ECLI:EU:C:2017:203.
122 *Achbita v. G4S Secure Solutions NV*, C-157/15 [2017] §§ 37–38.
123 *Achbita v. G4S Secure Solutions NV*, C-157/15 [2017] §§ 38–41.
124 *Achbita v. G4S Secure Solutions NV*, C-157/15 [2017] § 42.
125 *Achbita v. G4S Secure Solutions NV*, C-157/15 [2017] § 43.
126 See also S. Ouald-Chaib, V. David, "CJEU Keeps the Door to Religious Discrimination in the Private Workplace Opened. The ECtHR Could Close It", March 27, 2017. https://strasbourgobservers.com/2017/03/27/european-court-of-justice-keeps-the-door-to-religious-discrimination-in-the-private-workplace-opened-the-european-court-of-human-rights-could-close-it/. Accessed August 4, 2024.
127 See further below on the lack of attention for hidden direct discrimination.
128 See, however, the development in three subsequent cases, discussed below under 3.2.
129 *Bougnaoui v. Micropole SA*, C-188/15 [2017], ECLI:EU:C:2017:204.
130 *Bougnaoui v. Micropole SA*, C-188/15 [2017] §§ 32–33.

indicate that if there was no such internal neutrality policy, then it needs to be determined whether "the willingness of an employer to take account of a customer's wish no longer to have services provided by a worker who, like Ms Bougnaoui, has been assigned to that customer by the employer and who wears an Islamic headscarf constitutes a genuine and determining occupational requirement"[131] one of the few exceptions to the prohibition of direct discrimination on grounds of religion.

Put differently, the Court does not allow any form of restrictions on the manifestation of religion in the employment sphere and puts its foot down for clear cases of direct discrimination. In this respect, it is equally important that it adopts a suitably narrow understanding of what amounts to genuine, determining occupational requirement. The CJEU starts by underscoring that the recital of Directive 2000/78 clarifies that "it is only in very limited circumstances that a characteristic related, in particular, to religion may constitute a genuine and determining occupational requirement".[132] More particularly, what does not so qualify is "subjective considerations, such as the willingness of the employer to take account of the particular wishes of the customer".[133]

The three subsequent cases regarding companies are discussed next as representing a partial shift in the Court's jurisprudence. While the CJEU maintains its starting positions in relation to neutrality policies of companies, it does increase the scrutiny *de facto*, simultaneously providing more guidance to national courts.

1.4.2.2.2 LEVEL OF SCRUTINY – PUBLIC ADMINISTRATION

In a more recent case,[134] the first case concerning neutrality policies in the public service or public administration of a member state entailing a prohibition to wear a headscarf, the CJEU does not continue this line of increasing scrutiny but rather extends its embrace of the ECtHR broad margin of appreciation in relation to state-religion relations that it started to embrace in the case law on ritual slaughter (discussed earlier). In this case, the CJEU was asked preliminary questions from a Belgian court in relation to the strict neutrality policy adopted by a municipal authority (*Commune d'Ans*), requiring all its employees to abstain from wearing any visible signs which "might reveal their ideological or philosophical affiliation or political or religious beliefs".[135] Considering the uneven application of these general rules, and the toleration of modestly worn other religious signs, the national court is convinced that the decisions taken towards the applicant constitute prohibited direct

131 *Bougnaoui v. Micropole SA*, C-188/15 [2017] § 34.
132 *Bougnaoui v. Micropole SA*, C-188/15 [2017] § 39.
133 *Bougnaoui v. Micropole SA*, C-188/15 [2017] § 40.
134 *OP v. Commune d'Ans*, C-148/22 [2023], ECLI:EU:C:2023:924.
135 *OP v. Commune d'Ans*, C-148/22 [2023] § 32.

discrimination on grounds of religion.[136] The national court asks the CJEU whether a municipal administration can impose exclusive neutrality on all workers, also those in the back office, with the aim of creating an entirely neutral administrative environment, referring to the directive provisions on direct and indirect discrimination.[137]

The CJEU begins with discarding the possibility of direct discrimination, only considering the formulation of the municipal rules, following the lines it has set out since *Achbita*.[138] Nevertheless, it does return to the proviso about the rules being applied in an undifferentiated way, and thus opens the possibility for the referring court to establish direct discrimination on grounds of religion.[139] The CJEU proceeds with the alternative route of possible indirect discrimination, referring to its settled case law, if the rule leads to a particular disadvantage for persons adhering to a particular religion, it needs a reasonable and objective justification (requiring a legitimate aim and means that are appropriate and necessary).[140]

The CJEU accepts the municipality's argument that the legitimate aim of the measure imposing a neutral public service has a basis in the Belgian constitution, more particularly the principle of impartiality and the principle of neutrality of the state,[141] having regard to the margin of discretion of states and the infra-state bodies in designing the neutrality of the public service in light of its own context. The lack of European consensus and the related diversity of approaches as to the place of religion in the public sector implies that municipalities can opt for an exclusive neutrality throughout the administration, or for an inclusive neutrality, or a prohibition only when in contact with users.[142] The CJEU in this judgement thus extends the doctrine of the broad margin of appreciation from the freedom of religion to the prohibition of discrimination (on grounds of religion).

While public authorities have the choice in terms of what vision of neutrality to adopt and invoke as legitimate aim, the CJEU does highlight that this margin of discretion should go hand in hand with supervision by national and EU judiciary[143] and gives clear guidance about how to conduct the proportionality review. The CJEU starts by recalling the requirement that the general rule, in order to be considered appropriate and necessary, should be "genuinely pursued in a consistent and systematic manner, and…is limited to what is strictly necessary".[144] Nevertheless, the CJEU does take the position that when

136 *OP v. Commune d'Ans*, C-148/22 [2023] § 17. See the discussion of possible hidden direct versus indirect discrimination.
137 *OP v. Commune d'Ans*, C-148/22 [2023] §§ 20 and 24.
138 *OP v. Commune d'Ans*, C-148/22 [2023] §§ 25–26.
139 *OP v. Commune d'Ans*, C-148/22 [2023] §§ 27–28.
140 *OP v. Commune d'Ans*, C-148/22 [2023] §§ 28–30.
141 *OP v. Commune d'Ans*, C-148/22 [2023] § 32.
142 *OP v. Commune d'Ans*, C-148/22 [2023] §§ 33–35.
143 *OP v. Commune d'Ans*, C-148/22 [2023] § 34.
144 *OP v. Commune d'Ans*, C-148/22 [2023] § 37.

opting for an entirely neutral administrative environment, this can only be effectively pursued when no visible manifestation is allowed at all, also in contact with other employees: such a strict rule would thus be 'necessary'.[145] Ultimately, it would be for the national court to determine whether the requirements of consistency and overall proportionality are met.[146]

While it is commendable that the CJEU acknowledges that there are various understandings of neutrality, inclusive and exclusive, it leaves the choice entirely to the public authorities concerned, provided that the policy is applied consistently and indiscriminately and that it is ultimately necessary and proportionate. Two remarks are in order here. First, if neutrality can be conceived in an inclusive manner, allowing all kinds of religious and other expressions, would that not make the impact of an exclusive neutrality policy per definition disproportionate, particularly when considering the context of Islamophobia throughout Western Europe? In other words, has the CJEU been critical enough in its scrutiny? Second, in relation to the ultimate task of the national court to determine whether the policy has been applied in a proportionate manner, the CJEU does not seem to be aware that its understanding of requirement of consistency actually pushes authorities to apply their neutrality policy also in the 'back office', which may be questionable in terms of proportionality of the interference. It certainly does not provide further guidance to the national court about how to manage the tension between consistency and overall proportionality.

1.4.2.2.3 HIDDEN DIRECT VERSUS INDIRECT DISCRIMINATION

In this paragraph, the attention shifts to the extent to which the CJEU is willing to consider the broader context of the adoption of particular measures and identify cases of at first sight indirect discrimination as *de facto* hidden direct discrimination, and thus more difficult to justify. Even without considering the actual content of and setting in which a neutrality policy has been devised by a company, is it really so 'obvious' that companies have a neutrality policy? Can it be connected without more to the "freedom to conduct a business" enshrined in the Charter of Fundamental Rights? The freedom to conduct a business in a human rights instrument, is that not meant to be more about encouraging entrepreneurship and innovation, and thus about enabling social and economic development? Adopting a neutrality policy does not seem to be a good fit. When considering the content: a policy that prohibits wearing of any visible signs of philosophical, political, or religious beliefs, does that not actually target religions, and more particularly those religions with vestiary requirements, like the headscarf, pointing rather to hidden direct discrimination? Furthermore, having regard to the context: in *Achbita*, the company only devised its written general policy following a request to wear the

145 *OP v. Commune d'Ans*, C-148/22 [2023] § 39.
146 *OP v. Commune d'Ans*, C-148/22 [2023] §§ 38 and 40.

headscarf (by Achbita).[147] Does this not raise suspicions about targeting particular religions, and thus hidden direct discrimination, indeed?

The Court clearly signals in *Achbita* that it does not want to engage in this line of reasoning, a position it maintains also in subsequent cases. The CJEU repeats its principled acceptance of companies' general neutrality policies as not amounting to direct discrimination even in a very different case like *Bougnaoui*, where this did not seem relevant at all. In the two subsequent cases, *Wabe* and *Müller*,[148] the CJEU confirmed its reasoning in *Achbita*, even though it was explicitly invited to consider the argument about possible hidden discrimination on grounds of religion, in the sense that visible signs are typical for religions, and for certain religions in particular. To be sure, the Court does pick up on the possibility of hidden direct discrimination on grounds of religion in the *Müller* case as the company's neutrality policy only prohibited conspicuous large signs. The CJEU acknowledged that the wearing of large sized signs of beliefs is inextricably linked to a particular religion.[149] Nevertheless, in the subsequent case, *SCRL*,[150] the Belgian court asked many questions hinting at possible hidden direct discrimination having regard to the context of the adoption of the neutrality policy, it being triggered by requests to wear a headscarf at work, but these were ignored by the CJEU. This 'principled' position is also maintained in the subsequent case concerning the neutrality policies of the municipality *Commune d'Ans*. The Belgian court takes a firm stance that it considers the general neutrality rules by the municipality leading to an absolute prohibition to wear headscarves in the public service a case of hidden direct discrimination on grounds of religion because the development of these general rules was triggered by the request of an employee to wear a headscarf, while the application of the rules is inconsistent because other religious signs worn discretely are tolerated.[151] As indicated earlier, the CJEU did not go along and directed the national court towards indirect discrimination.

1.4.2.2.4 THE CJEU AND STIGMATISING LANGUAGE

Unfortunately, the CJEU does not merely fail to pick up on more subtle but still clear signals of possible hidden direct discrimination, but at times, it can be seen to engage in language that contributes to the stigmatisation of Muslims and their religious practices. In the Court's reasoning on the possible justification of the disparate impact of the neutrality rules (avoiding a finding of indirect discrimination) in *Achbita*, the CJEU emphasised the importance of

147 *Achbita v. G4S Secure Solutions NV*, C-157/15 [2017] §§ 14–15.

148 *IX v. Wabe eV and MH Müller Handels GmbH v. MJ*, C-804/18 [2021], ECLI:EU:C:2021:594.

149 *IX v. Wabe eV and MH Müller Handels GmbH v. MJ*, C-804/18 [2021] § 73.

150 *L.F. v. S.C.R.L.*, C-344/20 [2022], ECLI:EU:C:2022:774.

151 *OP v. Commune d'Ans*, C-148/22 [2023] §§ 13, 17–18.

limiting the neutrality rules to employees with customer-facing roles. While this can be considered relevant in terms of the proportionality review, the CJEU's statement that the employer should attempt to offer a non-customer-facing role to the employee was heavily criticised for allowing/inviting employers to push Muslim employees with headscarves to the back office.[152] While subsequent cases may not contain the latter statement, the CJEU still fails to acknowledge the possibly stigmatising implications for Muslim employees. In *Commune d'Ans*, in relation to public authorities' neutrality policies, the CJEU's focus on consistency actually almost pushes public authorities to apply the (strict) neutrality policy also to the back office, thus allowing consistency to trump overall proportionality considerations.

1.4.2.3 A Partial Development towards a More Positive Score Card: A Stricter Scrutiny and thus Narrower Margin of Appreciation for Headscarves in Companies

Notwithstanding the preceding overwhelmingly disappointing developments regarding the CJEU's case law in relation to controversial manifestations of the freedom of religion, it is noteworthy that in several of the later cases regarding prohibitions of wear headscarves in companies, a countermovement towards *de facto* stricter levels of scrutiny can be noted as well. Indeed, in *Wabe*[153] and *Müller*[154] and *SCRL*,[155] the CJEU did confirm the lines of jurisprudence allowing companies to limit the manifestation of religion through symbols/signs to safeguard their neutrality policy; it does provide more guidance to the national courts while *de facto* enhancing the level of scrutiny.

By way of prelude, in *Wabe* the CJEU follows the ECtHR's recognition of the freedom of religion as constituting one of the "most vital elements that go to make up the identity of believers and their conception of life", thus acknowledging its weight. In relation to neutrality policies having a disproportionate impact on persons adhering to a particular religion, the CJEU sharpened the justification formulae by requiring a strict scrutiny of the proportionality requirement.[156] In both *Wabe and Müller*, the CJEU indeed adopts a more rigorous justification test by requiring employers to prove economic harm to justify neutrality rules that would restrict employers' freedom to manifest their religion. In *Wabe*, the Court opined that it would not be sufficient for companies to simply state that they want to be neutral, they need to demonstrate that they have a genuine need to be neutral.[157] The CJEU even provides further guidance to the national court by giving as an example of a genuine need the legitimate wishes of customers and

152 *Achbita v. G4S Secure Solutions NV*, C-157/15 [2017] §§ 42–43.
153 *IX v. Wabe eV and MH Müller Handels GmbH v. MJ*, C-804/18 [2021].
154 *IX v. Wabe eV and MH Müller Handels GmbH v. MJ*, C-804/18 [2021].
155 *L.F. v. S.C.R.L.*, C-344/20 [2022].
156 *IX v. Wabe eV and MH Müller Handels GmbH v. MJ*, C-804/18 [2021] § 60.
157 *IX v. Wabe eV and MH Müller Handels GmbH v. MJ*, C-804/18 [2021] § 64.

parents (in relation to children's caretakers).[158] More generally, the company would have to demonstrate that it would suffer adverse consequences due to the nature of its activities or the context in which they are carried out if it would not have the neutrality policy.[159] Similarly, in *Müller*, the CJEU underscores that the employer needs to demonstrate that there is a real need, and there needs to be a sufficiently specific risk to its business activities that would be undermined when it would lose its neutrality policy.[160] Interestingly, the reference to the margin of appreciation in this case is in favour of higher (more protective) requirements in national constitutional law towards the freedom of religion.[161] In the *SCRL* case, the CJEU, on the one hand, confirms the obligation on the company to demonstrate a genuine need for the neutrality policy[162] while speaking out against abuse of a neutrality policy to the detriment of workers who are adhering to particular religions and embracing the acceptance of a greater degree of diversity.[163]

1.4.2.4 The Broad Margin of Appreciation 'Spreading': Announcing Overall a More Negative Score Card?

The embrace of the ECtHR's grant of a broad margin of appreciation for states in the regulation of religions also trickles through to the freedom of establishment, more particularly state funding for denominational schools. The CJEU, in its preliminary ruling in *Freikirche*,[164] was even willing to reduce the protection of the freedom of establishment, one of the four freedoms inherent in the internal market, in order to safeguard states' wide margin of appreciation following Article 17 TFEU.

The preliminary question was triggered by an Austrian law limited funding for denominational schools of religions that are recognised under Austrian law, thus not granting funding to a denominational school of a religion recognised under German law but not Austrian law. The CJEU acknowledged that the Austrain requirement is more easily satisfied by churches and religious communities established in Austria, thus affecting the freedom of establishment of Article 49 TFEU.[165] Nevertheless, the CJEU opined that reading Article 49 and 17 TFEU together implied that Article 49 was not violated.[166]

When the CJEU is even willing to reduce the protection of the four freedoms central to the internal market in order to ensure states a broad margin of appreciation in relation to religion-state affairs, it remains to be seen what further implications are to be expected for the effective

158 *IX v. Wabe eV and MH Müller Handels GmbH v. MJ*, C-804/18 [2021] § 65.
159 *IX v. Wabe eV and MH Müller Handels GmbH v. MJ*, C-804/18 [2021] § 67.
160 *IX v. Wabe eV and MH Müller Handels GmbH v. MJ*, C-804/18 [2021] §§ 76 and 85.
161 *IX v. Wabe eV and MH Müller Handels GmbH v. MJ*, C-804/18 [2021] §§ 86–89.
162 *IX v. Wabe eV and MH Müller Handels GmbH v. MJ*, C-804/18 [2021] §§ 37–41.
163 *IX v. Wabe eV and MH Müller Handels GmbH v. MJ*, C-804/18 [2021] § 41.
164 *Freikirche*, C-372/21 [2023].
165 *Freikirche*, C-372/21 [2023] §§ 30–32.
166 *Freikirche*, C-372/21 [2023] §§ 41–43.

protection of the freedom of religion and the prohibition of discrimination on grounds of religion.

1.5 Conclusion

In order to obtain an adequate protection of minorities' fundamental rights, it is essential that international courts adopt a sufficiently high level of scrutiny while being attentive to possible cases of hidden direct discrimination. The case law of the ECtHR and CJEU actually reveals extensive similarities, resulting in a mixed scorecard for both. Both Courts have lines of jurisprudence that promise a sufficiently elevated level of protection of the fundamental rights of religious minorities. The ECtHR's emphasis on duties of state neutrality and impartiality and the CJEU's *de facto* recognition of duties of reasonable accommodation are good examples indeed.

Nevertheless, both Courts have come to share problematic lines of jurisprudence related to the grant of a broad margin of appreciation for government regulations of religion in the public sphere. The ECtHR has a very long and steady line of jurisprudence in this regard, justifying the grant of a broad margin by the absence of a European consensus on the matter. Notwithstanding repeated criticisms, the Court has not wavered (fundamentally), as is visible in the (first) case on ritual slaughter (*Cha'are Shalom*), in several cases on headscarves in education, and in the public sphere at large (*Leyla Sahin, S.A.S., Ebrahimian*). Whereas the CJEU initially seemed to resist granting a broad discretion to member states, in the meantime, it has embraced the ECtHR's line on the broad margin of appreciation explicitly, both in its case law on ritual slaughter and on headscarves in the employment sphere as related to neutrality policies, not only in relation to companies but also public authorities. The most recent case on ritual slaughter before the ECtHR actually makes full circle, as here the ECtHR follows the line earlier developed by the CJEU.

Interestingly, particularly in the more recent cases, there is a striking mix of on the one hand some cases in which increasing levels of scrutiny and thus reduced discretion for states, are visible, and a trend of mutual confirmation of a broad margin of appreciation on the other. Regarding the former, several lines of jurisprudence of the ECtHR revealed that for matters about which there is a clear European consensus, the Court does reduce the margin of appreciation: food restrictions in prison, religion in the public curriculum and even for headscarves in judicial proceedings when it concerns third parties or witnesses. The latter was particularly visible in relation to ritual slaughter but also for headscarves in view of neutrality policies in the public service. Nevertheless, also, the CJEU is becoming more critical towards neutrality policies implying bans on wearing headscarves of private companies.

In light of the preceding criticism about granting states a broad margin of appreciation, both European courts are recommended to level up their scrutiny, thus providing actual supervision and guidance so that slowly European consensus grows in favour of a sufficiently robust protection of fundamental rights of religious minorities. The ECtHR's understanding of democracy that implies that there should be some space for minorities[167] arguably invites a more critical perspective to the invocation of neutrality policies, particularly when taking into account that 'neutrality' can be understood in an inclusive way as well. Similarly, even when one accepts that 'animal welfare' can be related to the legitimate aim of public morals, can one really maintain that animal welfare should outweigh the manifestation of the freedom of religion when one knows that ritual slaughter can be done in a way that takes serious animal welfare?

167 *S.A.S.* (n 22) § 128, see also *mutatis mutandis: Young, James and Webster v. the United Kingdom*, Nos. 7601/76, 7806/77 [1981] § 63, ECLI:CE:ECHR:1981:0813JUD000760176; *Chassagnou and Others v. France*, No 25088/94, 28331/95 and 28443/95 [1999] § 112, ECLI:CE:ECHR:1999:0429JUD002508894.

2 Strengthening the Protection of Religious Minorities by Establishing a New Universal Human Rights Treaty

A Necessary or Redundant Effort?*

Aleksandra Gliszczyńska-Grabias

Abstract

Calls for the adoption of an international treaty dedicated to countering discrimination and hatred on the basis of religion – an instrument analogous to the International Convention on the Elimination of All Forms of Racial Discrimination (ICERD) – have appeared regularly for several decades. They are the aftermath of an unsuccessful attempt to establish such a treaty when the ICERD was being formulated in the 1960s. Although preparations for the enactment of the "twin" conventions proceeded in parallel, works on the one with a religious dimension only concluded with the 1981 UN Declaration on the Elimination of All Forms of Intolerance and of Discrimination Based on Religion or Belief (1981 Resolution), adopted by the UN General Assembly. Since then, the question remains open of whether the standard of protection against religious discrimination and hatred is adequate, or whether it needs to be strengthened or thoroughly redefined and supplemented in the face of continuing threats to the rights and freedoms of vulnerable groups, which include religious minorities and individuals persecuted because of their religion or belief. At the same time, an important element of the ongoing discussions is the need to protect individuals who, by manifesting their opposition to certain religious practices, for example, are exposed to harassment and persecution. In the face of conflicts over the scope of protection to be granted to religions as such (including their sacred symbols, books, or prophets) and controversies relating to the contradiction between certain religious practices or dogmas and the prohibition of religious discrimination, the probability of reaching a consensus in such a sensitive area is low, and the eventual treaty

* The research conducted for this chapter has been funded by the Polish National Science Centre (Grant No. 2019/33/B/HS5/01634).

DOI: 10.4324/9781003423294-4

could even turn out to be less meaningful (in terms of its scope) than the existing 1981 Declaration. The proposed chapter is thus intended to present the most important arguments "for" and "against" establishing a new treaty on religious discrimination and hatred, though without aspiring to give exhaustive or prejudging answers.

Keywords

United Nations; right to freedom of religion; prohibition of religious discrimination; religious minorities; defamation of religion; vulnerability

2.1 Introductory Remarks

The particular importance of religious freedom and prohibiting discrimination on the basis of religion is demonstrated by the very long history and tradition of respect for these rights, although their understanding has clearly changed significantly over the centuries.[1] In a historical perspective, however, issues of religion and belief are also among the most sensitive areas of human rights. Indeed, religious freedom is one of the values in defence of which lives have been sacrificed, as well as the cause (to this day) of the most cruel oppressions, armed conflicts, and genocides.[2] Very often, moreover, religious freedom comes into serious conflict with other rights and freedoms: in the name of religion, some seek to limit or even nullify the rights of women, LGBTQ+ people, those who practice different religions, or non-believers.[3] Also, the conflict between the desire to protect animal welfare and the guarantees of religious

1 One of the landmark philosophical texts on the recognition of religious liberty as a right belonging to individuals and subject to protection by state authority was John Locke's *Letters Concerning Toleration*, published in 1689. Despite their progressive and Enlightenment character, Locke did not envisage equal protection for all by clearly indicating that, inter alia, Roman Catholics should not enjoy religious liberty on an equal footing with adherents of other churches, such as the Anglican Church, or even with adherents of Judaism or Muslims – J. Locke, *A Letter Concerning Toleration*, 1689. https://historyofeconomicthought.mcmaster.ca/locke/toleration.pdf. Accessed October 27, 2024.

2 One of the most drastic examples in recent years are the atrocities committed in 2017 against the Rohingya population by the Myanmar military. Representatives of this religious minority – they mostly follow Islam, whilst Myanmar is mainly Buddhist – were attacked, killed, raped, tortured, and thrown out of their homes. Around 200 villages were burnt down and around 13,000 people were killed. Within weeks, more than 700,000 refugees had crossed the border into Bangladesh to seek refuge there. See M. P. Hossain, "The Rohingya Refugee Crisis: Analysing the International Law Implications of Its Environmental Impacts on Bangladesh", *The International Journal of Human Rights* vol. 27, no. 2 (2022): 238–257.

3 For a number of interesting articles on these conflicts of values and principles, see S. Mancini, M. Rosenfeld (eds), *Constitutional Secularism in an Age of Religious Revival* (Oxford: Oxford University Press, 2014).

freedom – particularly of the followers of Judaism and Islam, whose religions prescribe so-called ritual slaughter rules for the consumption of meat – is increasingly visible and legally controversial.

Today, in a universal system of human rights protection, freedom of religion is among the most important individual rights, closely linked to other freedoms such as freedom of expression, association, and assembly.[4] At the same time, the prohibition of discrimination on grounds of religion and beliefs is one of the pillars of anti-discrimination law. The exercise of religious freedom and the protection against discrimination on grounds of religious beliefs (or irreligiousness) is a condition for the possibility of full, authentic, personal development of the individual in many dimensions, being fundamental and absolutely necessary for self-expression according to some individuals and groups. The essence and seriousness of this freedom is reflected, inter alia, in the guarantee of its observance in all contemporary systems of human rights protection, both universally and regionally.[5] It is also one of the fundamental constitutional freedoms in the basic laws of the vast majority of countries in the world. At the same time, it should be borne in mind that religious freedom and protection against discrimination on this basis are part of a broader construct contained in the provisions of international human rights law, in which freedom of thought, belief and conscience is also guaranteed and protected. As the UN Human Rights Committee (HR Committee) emphasises in its General Comment No. 22, the protection in question also applies to freedom of personal belief on all subjects and freedom of conscience.[6] These are protected in the same way and to the same extent as freedom of religion. The HR Committee also makes it clear that the right not to profess any religion or religious belief is also protected. With regard to the concept of religion and religious belief itself, the HR Committee prescribes a broad definition, which also includes new religious movements that lack the institutional structures or practices characteristic of traditional religions that are deeply rooted in history.[7] Importantly, this chapter follows the approach offered by Khaitan and Calderwood Norton on distinctions between the right to freedom of religion

4 For an exhaustive discussion, see A. Scolnicov, *The Right to Religious Freedom in International Law: Between Group Rights and Individual Rights* (New York: Routledge, 2011); P.M. Taylor, *Freedom of Religion: UN and European Human Rights Law and Practice* (Cambridge: Cambridge University Press, 2005).

5 Adequate guarantees are contained in the European Convention for the Protection of Human Rights and Fundamental Freedoms, the African Charter on Human and Peoples' Rights, the American Convention on Human Rights, and the Arab Charter on Human Rights, among others. Adequate provisions are also contained in the Charter of Fundamental Rights.

6 General Comment No. 22: Article 18 (Freedom of Thought, Conscience or Religion), CCPR/C/21/Rev.1/Add.4 [1993].

7 General Comment No. 22: Article 18 (Freedom of Thought, Conscience or Religion), CCPR/C/21/Rev.1/Add.4 [1993] § 5.

and the right against religious discrimination, which, whilst often conflated, should be considered distinct, separate human rights.[8]

However, various participants in the debate on the scope of protection of religious freedom and protection against religious discrimination, especially in the context of the rights and sensitivities of religious minorities, have certain demands and hopes that the scope of this protection could be complemented and strengthened. The most important of the arguments seems to be that there is no instrument with the force and consequences of a treaty instrument protecting against religious discrimination in the way that the International Convention on the Elimination of All Forms of Racial Discrimination (ICERD) protects against racial and ethnic discrimination. In recent decades, however, another issue has been put forward as being central to discussions on a new treaty: protection against insulting religion and its symbols, labelled "defamation of religions", which is often linked to incitement to religious hatred.[9] Significantly, this issue also seemed to lead to discussions on a new treaty being regarded as a risk of "opening a Pandora's box": some called for the introduction of protection against such defamation in a potential new treaty, whilst others (far more numerous among legal scholars) saw the need for a legal guarantee that the defamation of religion would not be criminalised.

This chapter approaches the debate on the necessity of establishing a new religion-orientated human rights protection treaty from two main angles: checking whether individuals and groups, including religious minorities, today can be effectively protected against religious discrimination and hatred and whether defamation of religion is still a core obstacle in the debates over the postulated legal changes. Thus, Section 2.2 identifies, in a condensed way, the existing relevant legal framework within the universal human rights protection system, also briefly analysing the historical and political implications of the lack of a major "religious" UN treaty. Section 2.3 extends this search further, concentrating on the relevant case law of the two UN treaty bodies: the HR Committee and the Committee on the Elimination of Racial Discrimination (CERD). It then moves to Section 2.4, which tackles the concept of defamation of religion – one of the most disturbing phenomena within the subject matter of this chapter. Section 2.5 concludes by summarising the major "pros" and "cons" of pushing for a new addition to the collection of UN treaties.

8 T. Khaitan, J. Calderwood Norton, "The Right to Freedom of Religion and the Right Against Religious Discrimination: Theoretical Distinctions", *International Journal of Constitutional Law*, vol. 17, no. 4 (2019): 1125–1145.

9 See generally N. Hatzis, *Blasphemy and Defamation of Religions, Offensive Speech, Religion, and the Limits of the Law* (Oxford: Oxford University Press, 2021).

2.2 Protection Against Discrimination and Religious Hatred – a Valid Universal Standard

The first question that needs to be tackled is, what guarantees of protection against discrimination and hatred on religious grounds are offered today under the universal human rights protection system to individuals and groups, including religious minorities? The binding treaty standard in this regard is essentially based on two pillars: the relevant provisions of the International Covenant on Civil and Political Rights (ICCPR) and of the ICERD. Other treaties also address the issue, but only in a complementary manner, being focussed on their respective subject matter.[10] These treaties are encased in protocols, general commentaries, and position papers. However, the 1981 Declaration,[11] even though it lacks the authority of a treaty and had a turbulent history during its creation, provides the focal point not only for considering how religious minorities are protected but also for the debate on establishing a new treaty.

2.2.1 The UN Declaration on the Elimination of All Forms of Intolerance and of Discrimination Based on Religion or Belief

The Declaration adopted by the General Assembly, Resolution 36/55 of November 21, 1981, most comprehensively covers the issues examined in this chapter. What is crucial for the understanding of the present legal framework

10 And thus, the International Covenant on Economic, Social and Cultural Rights, in its Article 2(2) states that the rights enunciated in this treaty shall be exercised without discrimination of any kind, including discrimination based on religion. Then, for example, the International Convention on the Protection of the Rights of Migrant Workers and Members of Their Families, in addition to prohibiting discrimination on the basis of religion and belief, contains guarantees of freedom of thought, conscience, and religion for all migrant workers and members of their families. These guarantees include the freedom to profess and adopt any religion or belief of one's choice, as well as the freedom to manifest one's religion or belief, individually or with others, in public and in private. Migrant workers and their family members may not be compelled to engage in practices or activities that nullify their religious freedom, which may only be subject to such restrictions as are provided for by law and which are necessary to protect security, order, health, and public morals or the freedoms and rights of others. The Convention on the Rights of the Child, on the other hand, in Art. 2(1) refers to the prohibition of discrimination against a child or his or her parents or legal guardians on the basis of, inter alia, religion. Also relevant is Article 14 of this treaty, which obliges States Parties to respect the child's right to freedom of thought, conscience, and religion and to respect the rights and duties of parents or legal guardians with respect to the guidance of the child, in terms of his or her rights, in a manner consistent with the child's development. Interestingly, the Convention on the Rights of Persons with Disabilities, the treaty regulating the rights and freedoms of vulnerable groups, does not contain provisions on the issues at hand.

11 General Assembly Resolution 36/55, Declaration on the Elimination of All Forms of Intolerance and of Discrimination Based on Religion or Belief. https://www.ohchr.org/en/instruments-mechanisms/instruments/declaration-elimination-all-forms-intolerance-and-discrimination. Accessed October 28, 2024.

in this area, however, is the difficult history of adopting this document and the abandonment of the idea of turning the 1981 Declaration into a convention instrument that twinned, as it were, the ICERD.

The struggle around the 1981 Declaration and the abandoned treaty has been thoroughly described by Ofra Friesel.[12] Among other things, she points to the strictly ideological and political reasons for the dispute over references to anti-Semitism, based on the Cold War conflict between the USA, the USSR, and the Arab states.[13] Similarly, consensus could not be reached on the wording of the Declaration's definition of religion or belief, on references to the rights of those who do not profess any religion (pressed for by the USSR), on the inclusion of the right to convert (strongly opposed by Muslim states) and on the prohibition of incitement to discrimination and the spread of hatred and acts of religious violence (fears of excessive restrictions on freedom of expression). During the preparatory works on the 1981 Declaration, however, it was proposed that all expressions of hatred likely to lead to violence and directed against a religion, belief, or practitioner thereof (and incitement to them) were to be prohibited by law by each of the states to which the 1981

12 O. Friesel, "Equating Zionism with Racism: The 1965 Precedent", *American Jewish History*, vol. 97, no. 3. (2013): 283–313.

13 For more on this subject, see also N. Lerner, *Group Rights and Discrimination in International Law*, (Dordrecht: Martinus Nijhoff, 1991): 75–80. Even more significantly, the initiative to establish proper treaty protection against racial and religious discrimination was closely linked with the wave of anti-Semitism of 1959 and 1960 in countries of the Western hemisphere. These events triggered resolutions in 1960 by the Sub-Commission on Prevention of Discrimination and Protection of Minorities (in its Resolution 3 A (XII): Report of the Twelfth Session of the Sub-Commission on Prevention of Discrimination and Protection of Minorities to the Commission On Human Rights, E/CN.4/800 [1960]) and subsequently the Commission on Human Rights (in its Resolution 6 (XVI): Manifestation of anti-Semitism and other forms of racial prejudice and religious intolerance of a similar nature, E/CN.4/804 [1960]). As referred to by H. Bielefeldt and M. Wiener: "The latter noted with deep concern the manifestations of anti-Semitism and other forms of racial prejudice and religious intolerance of a similar nature which might be once again the forerunner of other heinous acts endangering the future" – H. Bielefeldt, M. Wiener, "Declaration on the Elimination of All Forms of Intolerance and of Discrimination Based on Religion or Belief. General Assembly resolution 36/55 New York, 25 November 1981", https://legal.un.org/avl/ha/ga_36-55/ga_36-55.html. Accessed October 28, 2024. Also, as noted by Ben Greenacre from the Universal Rights Group: "Unlike the CERD, however, this draft convention suffered a failure to launch and its negotiation, lacking momentum and increasingly polarized, eventually stalled; falling victim to, amongst other things, the geopolitical aftershock of the 1967 6-Day War. As the Soviet Union maneuvered to further ally with Arab states, it secured revisions to the convention which undermined it as a whole, negotiations being subsequently deferred until they were formally halted entirely in 1972. This has caused it to become something of a 'lost covenant'. Progress was instead relegated to an eventual and relatively unknown UN declaration" – B. Greenacre, "The Arc of the Covenant: The Unfinished Business of UN Efforts to Combat Religious Intolerance", https://www.universal-rights.org/the-arc-of-the-covenant-the-unfinished-business-of-un-efforts-to-combat-religious-intolerance/. Accessed October 28, 2024.

Declaration would apply.[14] Ultimately, however, such references were missing from the final version of the document.

Since 1981, when the Declaration was finally enacted,[15] it has remained the main reference point for the reconstruction of the standard of protection in the religious dimension. Its most important provisions

- concern the obligation of states to guarantee full freedom of religion, conscience, and belief and to protect against discrimination on these grounds, with the Declaration very broadly setting out an illustrative, non-exhaustive list of manifestations that are protected under the right to freedom of thought, conscience, religion, or belief, including the freedoms (a) to maintain places for worship or assembly; (b) to establish charitable or humanitarian institutions; (c) to make, acquire, and use materials related to the rites or customs; (d) to write, issue, and disseminate publications; (e) to teach a religion or belief in suitable places; (f) to solicit and receive voluntary financial and other contributions; (g) to train, appoint, elect, or designate by succession appropriate leaders; (h) to celebrate holidays and ceremonies; and (i) to maintain communications with individuals and communities at the national and international levels;
- declare unacceptable any discrimination based on the religion or belief one professes or practises;
- define the term "intolerance and discrimination based on religion or belief" as any differentiation, exclusion, restriction, or preference based on religion or belief which is intended to prevent or restrict the exercise of all human rights and freedoms, or which has the effect of doing so;
- put in place such safeguards for their implementation at the national level as will allow them to be fully realised and enjoyed by individuals; and
- establish an obligation for states to protect against discrimination by private actors.

Some of the political and ideological turbulence surrounding the determination of the content of the 1981 Declaration has to some extent been overcome. The document stipulates that the right to freedom of thought, conscience, and religion "shall include freedom to have a religion or whatever belief of his choice", which replaced the direct and explicit right to conversion or apostasy. At the same time, Article 8 of the 1981 Declaration

14 See the contents of the draft Declaration on the Elimination of all Forms of Intolerance and of Discrimination Based on Religion or Belief. In: J.E. Wood Jr., "The Proposed United Nations Declaration on Religious Liberty", *Journal of Church and State*, vol. 23, no. 3 (1981): 420–422. https://doi.org/10.1093/jcs/23.3.413.

15 In 1986 the UN had also mandated a Special Rapporteur to monitor the implementation of the 1981 Declaration globally.

clarifies that nothing in the Declaration shall be construed as restricting or derogating from any rights defined, for example, in the Universal Declaration of Human Rights, whose Article 18 states explicitly that everyone has the right to change their religion or beliefs. As noted by Bielefeldt and Wiener, the fact that the right to change one's religion or belief, to adopt atheistic views, or to retain one's religion or belief remains fully protected has been confirmed in the interpretations of the Special Rapporteur on freedom of religion or belief and the HR Committee, who have clarified that "[f]reedom to change one's religious or belief-related orientations [...] remains an indispensable component of freedom of religion or belief."[16] However, the 1981 Declaration did not address the protection against religious hatred and violence or the issue of defamation of religions.

2.2.2 International Covenant on Civil and Political Rights

Article 18 of the ICCPR proclaims freedom of thought, conscience and religion, which includes the freedom to have or adopt a religion or belief of one's choice and the freedom, either individually or in community with others and in public or private, to manifest one's religion or belief in worship, observance, practice, and teaching religion. Article 26 in turn guarantees equality before the law and the equal protection of the law. It establishes the obligation of States Parties to prohibit any discrimination and to guarantee all persons equal and effective protection against discrimination on any grounds, including religion. Article 27 provides for the rights of members of religious minorities by ensuring their right to profess and practice their own religion.

In accordance with the Article 5(1), nothing in the ICCPR may be interpreted by anyone in such a way as to allow an action or act aimed at nullifying the rights and freedoms granted by the treaty. No act of religious hatred and discrimination can therefore be considered an exercise of, for example, the freedom of expression or assembly guaranteed in the ICCPR.

Among the provisions of the ICCPR, Article 20(2) – which the Declaration has no equivalent for – acquires particular significance. It states that "[a]ny advocacy of national, racial or religious hatred amounting to incitement to discrimination, hostility or violence should be prohibited by law". It can be thus claimed that religious hatred is addressed and that there are no shortcomings in the standard of protection offered. This could be true if not for the numerous doubts, disagreements, and misinterpretations which have sprung up around this provision – and indeed had already appeared during its drafting.[17]

16 H. Bielefeldt, M. Wiener, "Declaration on the Elimination of All Forms of Intolerance and of Discrimination".

17 For more on these difficulties in interpretation, in the context of the "defamation of religions" and with the call for all to oppose both the defamation of religion resolutions and efforts to reinterpret the ICCPR's Art. 20(2) and the ICERD's Art. 4 to encompass allegedly religiously defamatory speech, see L.A. Leo, F.D. Gaer, E.K. Cassid, "Protecting Religions From "Defamation": A Threat to Universal Human Rights Standards", *Harvard Journal of Law & Public Policy*, vol. 34, no. 2 (2011): 769–784.

Article 20(2) was not adopted unanimously. As reported, there were 50 votes in favour, 18 against, and 15 abstentions, many linked to the "incitement to hostility" language, which was considered overly broad and vague, with the potential for being used to outlaw a mere difference of views. Over the years, the controversies only grew till the adoption of the Rabat Plan of Action of 2012 on "the prohibition of advocacy of national, racial or religious hatred that constitutes incitement to hostility, discrimination or violence" was required.[18] It was developed by international experts with the support of the UN Office of the High Commissioner on Human Rights (OHCHR), with its normative and practical significance, providing clear guidance to states on implementing Article 20(2) of the ICCPR. It stresses that limitations to free speech should be applicable only to the most severe forms of hate speech, including hate speech based on religion or belief. The Rabat Plan of Action sets a high threshold for limitations on "incitement", formulating six criteria for a test intended to determine whether the speech has crossed the line allowing for its limitations.[19]

2.2.3 The International Convention on the Elimination of All Forms of Racial Discrimination

Although the definition of racial discrimination formulated in Article 1(1) of the ICERD does not encompass religion, Article 5(d) lists the right to freedom of thought, conscience, and religion, which names the rights whose enjoyment must be guaranteed "without distinction as to race, colour, or national or ethnic origin". In Article 4, States Parties to the ICERD shall condemn all propaganda and all organisations which attempt to justify or promote racial hatred and discrimination in any form and shall undertake to adopt immediate and positive measures designed to eradicate all incitement to, or acts of, such discrimination. At the same time, the close link between discrimination and/or hatred on the grounds of race, ethnicity, nationality, and religion is a widespread phenomenon, taking the form of multiple and intersectional discrimination – particularly against vulnerable groups.[20] As Patrick Thornberry rightly predicted, the interlocking elements of racial and religious discrimination will become an increasingly common consideration in relation to the protections guaranteed by the ICERD.[21]

18 "OHCHR and freedom of expression vs incitement to hatred: the Rabat Plan of Action". https://www.ohchr.org/en/freedom-of-expression. Accessed October 28, 2024.

19 These criteria are (1) the social and political context where the expression occurred; (2) the identity of the speaker, e.g., his or her status and influence over his or her audience; (3) the intent of the speaker; (4) the content and form of the expression; (5) the extent of the expression; and (6) the likelihood and imminence of violence, discrimination, or hostility occurring as a direct consequence of the expression.

20 For a detailed discussion, see N. Ghanea, "Intersectionality and the Spectrum of Racist Hate Speech: Proposals to the UN Committee on the Elimination of Racial Discrimination", *Human Rights Quarterly*, vol. 35, no. 4 (2013): 935–954.

21 See P. Thornberry, "Confronting Racial Discrimination: A CERD Perspective", *Human Rights Law Review*, vol. 5, no. 2 (2005): 259.

This also provokes the question of the obligation of States Parties to the ICERD to counter acts of religious hatred. In affirming this obligation, Nathan Lerner noted that the adoption of such an approach is supported by the historical relationship between instruments on race and on religion, as well as by the view expressed by the jurisprudence of a number of states that the specific nature of a group or the identifiable factors defining that group are secondary to the indisputable existence of the group itself, the self-perception of the group, and the fact that it is perceived as a separate group by the surrounding world.[22]

These issues have been pondered by the UN itself: in 2007, the UN Human Rights Council (HRC) established the *Ad Hoc* Committee of the Human Rights Council on the Elaboration of Complementary Standards (*Ad Hoc* Committee) through Resolution 6/21, with the mandate to issue complementary standards in the form of either a convention or additional protocol(s) to the ICERD, filling the existing gaps in the Convention and providing new normative standards aimed at combating all forms of contemporary racism, including incitement to racial and religious hatred.[23] The *Ad Hoc* Committee has produced volumes of reports and analysis since then, including on the troubling question of how to accommodate religion-related challenges. The starting point for these works was its "[r]eport on the study by the five experts on the content and scope of substantive gaps in the existing international instruments to combat racism, racial discrimination, xenophobia and related intolerance" published in 2007.[24] In the part devoted to assessment and recommendations concerning religious groups, it states that the reference to the right to freedom of religion in Article 5(d)(vii) of the ICERD should be further developed to cover the complexity of the connection between religion and race, racial discrimination, xenophobia, and related intolerance. In particular, it has been recommended that the CERD adopts a general recommendation to address concerns emerging in the area of racial and religious discrimination and that the HR Committee revise its General Comment No. 22 of 1993 on Article 18 of the ICCPR (freedom of thought, conscience, or religion) in order to address the present challenges – which has not yet happened. The recommendation has

22 N. Lerner, "Freedom of Expression and Advocacy of Group Hatred Incitement to Hate Crimes and Religious Hatred", *Religion and Human Rights*, no. 5 (2010): 141.

23 Resolution 6/21: Elaboration of international complementary standards to the International Convention on the Elimination of All Forms of Racial Discrimination, A/HRC/RES/6/21 [2007].

24 Complementary International Standards. Report on the study by the five experts on the content and scope of substantive gaps in the existing international instruments to combat racism, racial discrimination, xenophobia and related intolerance, A/HRC/4/WG.3/6 [2007]. The report was submitted pursuant to a request made by the Intergovernmental Working Group on the effective implementation of the Durban Declaration and Programme of Action at its fourth session (Geneva 16–20 January 2006). The request was endorsed by the Human RRC in its Resolution 1/5 of June 30, 2006.

not been implemented as regards the CERD either, even though some elements of its general position on racist hate speech, published in 2013, do address the question of religious hatred in a significant, albeit general and inconclusive, manner.[25] The 2007 report also touches upon one of the core controversies – religious intolerance and defamation of religious symbols – even though it avoids the core of the problem and focusses instead on the inadmissibility of equating certain religions with terrorism. Most importantly, in its concluding recommendations, the experts engaged in drafting the 2007 report offer their answer to the central question of this chapter, stating that from the perspective of their mandate, they consider the issues of religious intolerance connected with racial and xenophobic prejudices to be adequately covered under the existing international human rights instruments.[26]

As manifested by the 2022 report presented to the HRC by the *Ad Hoc* Committee[27] – 15 years after it was established – the previous approach has changed significantly, and the need for substantial progress is explicitly stated, even though it is as yet unfulfilled.[28] As stressed by Erica Howard, a world class expert on religious freedom and discrimination called by the *Ad Hoc* Committee to present on the contemporary forms of religion or belief, there is a gap in the protection against discrimination based on religion or belief at the international level because the 1981 Declaration is not legally binding. She also identified many links and overlaps between racial discrimination and

25 General recommendation No. 35: Combating racist hate speech, CERD/C/GC/35 [2013] § 6. The CERD states that "bearing in mind that 'criticism of religious leaders or commentary on religious doctrine or tenets of faith' should not be prohibited or punished, the Committee's attention has also been engaged by hate speech targeting persons belonging to certain ethnic groups who profess or practice a religion different from the majority, including expressions of Islamophobia, anti-Semitism and other similar manifestations of hatred against ethno-religious groups, as well as extreme manifestations of hatred such as incitement to genocide and to terrorism." The religious component also appears, if only a few times, in other parts of the General Recommendation, including the one directed at the media, calling on them to avoid referring unnecessarily to race, ethnicity, religion and other group characteristics in a manner that may promote intolerance.

26 General recommendation No. 35: Combating racist hate speech, CERD/C/GC/35 [2013] § 130.

27 Report of the *Ad Hoc* Committee on the Elaboration of Complementary Standards on its 12th session, A/HRC/51/57 [2022].

28 This fact seems to irritate multiple delegations voicing their concerns over the lack of progress in this regard. To quote the representative of the OIC: "The OIC strongly condemned Islamophobic acts in all their forms and manifestations and reiterated its call for the reversal and repeal of such discriminatory laws, and for the perpetrators to be held accountable and remedies to be provided to victims. He noted that the Committee had a clear mandate from the General Assembly and the Human Rights Council, and that OIC could not support any discussion aimed at diverting attention away from the core of the Committee's mandate. The OIC suggested that the Chair-Rapporteur utilize the expertise of the legal experts, who represented geographic balance and a diversity of legal systems, in the preparation of an initial draft of the additional protocol." General recommendation No. 35: Combating racist hate speech, CERD/C/GC/35 [2013] § 15.

discrimination based on religion or belief, indicating, among other things, that "discrimination based on religion or belief could be fit into the ICERD definition",[29] at the same time cautioning the Committee that "the lack of protection in international law for victims of discrimination based on religion or belief creates loopholes for perpetrators, as it enables them to claim that they were not discriminating based on race – which is punishable – but rather based on religion, which is not punishable under current international law".[30] Her conclusion was clear: the only feasible way to explicitly address religious discrimination is through an additional protocol to the ICERD.[31]

2.3 The Case Law of the HR Committee and the CERD

The case law of the HR Committee and the CERD represents the most up-to-date and progressive interpretation of the provisions of the ICCPR and the ICERD, which are all the more relevant for religious minorities, who lack a mechanism for dealing with complaints of exclusively religious discrimination or hatred. Or to put it another way, the ICCPR and HR Committee are for everyone, but the ICERD and the CERD are generally only for clearly defined groups and the individuals belonging to these groups.

2.3.1 Decisions of the HR Committee

In its jurisprudence to date, the HR Committee has investigated complaints of various aspects of religious discrimination and hatred.[32] One of the cases in which it recognised religious discrimination was *Waldman v. Canada*.[33] The applicant, a Canadian citizen, claimed to be the victim of a violation of, inter alia, Articles 26 and 18(1) of the ICCPR. Waldman was a practising religious Jew and the father of two school-age children whom he had enrolled in a private Jewish day school. In the province of Ontario, Roman Catholic schools were the only non-secular schools to be fully and directly publicly funded; other religious schools had to be funded from private sources, which

29 General recommendation No. 35: Combating racist hate speech, CERD/C/GC/35 [2013] § 41.

30 General recommendation No. 35: Combating racist hate speech, CERD/C/GC/35 [2013] § 46.

31 General recommendation No. 35: Combating racist hate speech, CERD/C/GC/35 [2013] § 54. This view was shared by another appointed expert, Professor Akande, who stated that "no better opportunity exists to design such a legal regime than in the additional protocol to the ICERD" – General recommendation No. 35: Combating racist hate speech, CERD/C/GC/35 [2013] § 69.

32 Y. Shany, "The Road Taken: ICCPR and Discriminatory Restrictions on Religious Freedom", *Harvard Human Rights Journal*, vol. 34 (2021): 305–313. https://journals.law.harvard.edu/hrj/wp-content/uploads/sites/83/2021/06/34HHRJ305-Shany.pdf. Accessed October 28, 2024.

33 *Waldman v. Canada*, 694/1996 [1999], CCPR/C/67/D/694/1996.

included tuition fees. In the complaint, it was argued that the funding of Roman Catholic schools provided for in national law violated Article 26 of the ICCPR, leading to differentiation and favouritism on the basis of religion.

The HR Committee, in examining the complaint, answered the question of whether public funding of Roman Catholic schools without funding schools teaching other religions constituted a violation of rights under the Covenant. The HR Committee held that the fact that differential treatment of different religious groups is enshrined in the Constitution does not automatically make it rational and objective. It rejected the State Party's argument that the preferential treatment of Roman Catholic schools was not discriminatory because of the State Party's constitutional obligations. It also noted that the ICCPR does not oblige states to publicly fund religious schools, but if a state chooses to do so it should provide such funding without discrimination. Consequently, there had been a violation of the applicant's right to equal and effective protection against discrimination on the basis of religion under Article 26 of the ICCPR.

However, the HR Committee has more frequently commented on the discrimination and persecution of Jehovah's Witnesses, including in the context of denying them the registration of religious association; charges of illegal assembly; arrests, fines, and bans on distributing religious publications; and confiscating publications,[34] as well as similar cases involving other religious groups[35] and on the issue of wearing religious clothing, in particular, cases involving headscarves. In addressing the French law banning face coverings in public spaces, the HR Committee found an unnecessary and disproportionate interference with the religious freedom of women wearing niqabs.[36] In addition to a violation of Article 18 of the ICCPR, it also found a violation of Article 26 in an intersectional context, as the law, although general and neutral in its wording, particularly affected Muslim women who chose to wear the full face veil. It reached similar conclusions in relation to the dismissal by a private childcare centre of an educator who wore a headscarf[37] and the denial of university admission to a Muslim woman who wore a wig substituting for a

34 See, e.g., the HRC decisions in *Suleymanova and Israfilova v. Azerbaijan*, 3061/2017 [2021], CCPR/C/133/D/3061/2017; *Dashkouski v. Belarus*, 2616/2015 [2022], CCPR/C/135/D/2616/2015; *Adyrkhayev and Others v. Tajikistan*, 2483/2014 [2022], CCPR/C/135/D/2483/2014.

35 E.g., the case of punishing the leader of the Krishna Consciousness Society for holding religious meetings for members of an unregistered religion: *Geller v. Kazakhstan*, 2417/2014 [2019], CCPR/C/126/D/2417/2014; the case of an illegal house search and confiscation of literature relating to the Indian religious movement Sathya Sai Baba: *Sabirova and Sabirov v. Uzbekistan*, 2331/2014 [2019], CCPR/C/125/D/2331/2014.

36 *Yaker v. France*, 2747/2016 [2018], CCPR/C/123/D/2747/2016; *Hebbadj v. France*, 2807/2016 [2018], CCPR/C/123/D/2807/2016.

37 *F.A. v. France*, 2662/2015 [2018], CCPR/C/123/D/2662/2015.

headscarf.[38] These cases confirmed the HR Committee's protective approach to manifestations of religion under Articles 18 and 26, particularly in relation to religious clothing.[39] Commenting on the "niqab cases" and their discrepancies with the European Court of Human Rights (ECHR) judgement,[40] Sarah Cleveland – one of the members of the HR Committee who examined the cases – pointed to the universal institutional role of the HR Committee, as opposed to the European Court of Human Rights, which operates only in the European context: "in interpreting the Covenant, the Committee must be sensitive to the implications of its doctrines for the protection of individual rights in a wide range of cultures and contexts".[41] The controversies over whether various forms of women's clothing, such as the niqab or the burqa, are obligations imposed by the Muslim religion or rather customs created by an oppressive patriarchal culture[42] are just one example of how complex and sensitive these problems are. Given the richness of the world's religions, the multiplicity of faiths and religious movements and the consequences of religious hatred and discrimination, perhaps the establishment of a treaty-based specialised body dealing solely with religious discrimination could ensure deeper insight into these nuanced issues.

The HR Committee has also dealt with the issue of religious hatred. One of the oldest and best-known cases on the conflict between freedom of expression and protection against discrimination and incitement to religious hatred is the case of *Ross v. Canada*,[43] which concerned anti-Semitic publications by a Canadian teacher. The peculiarity of this case was primarily due to the fact that the applicant, who had been sanctioned at the national level for discriminatory and hateful behaviour against the followers of a particular religion, had himself invoked his religious freedom. Mr Ross was a teacher and the author of books and pamphlets in which he wrote about the struggle that Christians must undertake against their enemies – the followers of Judaism – and an international conspiracy led by "prominent Jews".[44] He described other religions and denominations (particularly Judaism) with contempt and hostility and as being contrary to the one true Christian faith. In 1988, Attis, a Canadian citizen of Jewish origin whose children attended school in the New Brunswick

38 *Türkan v. Turkey*, 2274/2013 [2018], CCPR/C/123/D/2274/2013/REV.1.

39 S.H. Cleveland, "Banning the Full-Face Veil: Freedom of Religion and Non-Discrimination in the Human Rights Committee and the European Court of Human Rights", *Harvard Human Rights Journal*, vol. 34 (2021): 225. https://scholarship.law.columbia.edu/cgi/viewcontent.cgi?article=4059&context=faculty_scholarship . Accessed October 28, 2024.

40 *S.A.S. v. France*, Application no. 43835/11 [2014], ECLI:CE:ECHR:2014:0701JUD004383511.

41 S.H. Cleveland, "Banning the Full-Face Veil" 225.

42 See e.g. dissenting oppositions to *Yaker v. France*, 2747/2016 [2018] and *Hebbadj v. France*, 2807/2016 [2018].

43 *Ross v. Canada*, 736/1997 [2000] CCPR/C/70/D/736/1997.

44 *Ross v. Canada*, 736/1997 [2000] CCPR/C/70/D/736/1997 § 4.2.

district, filed a complaint with the New Brunswick Human Rights Commission alleging that the School Board, by failing to counter Ross's activities, condoned and justified his anti-Semitic views and publications. In accordance with the relevant regulations of Canadian law, a complaint was initiated before the Human Rights Board of Canada, which ultimately sanctioned the teacher and removed him from teaching. The case reached the Supreme Court of Canada, which ruled that the Board's decision was correct and based on proper grounds. The complaint mainly alleged that the Government of Canada had violated Articles 18 and 19 of the ICCPR by preventing him from freely expressing his religious beliefs. The complainant stressed that he had never disclosed his views in the presence of students, and there was no evidence that any of them had been influenced by his opinions and beliefs – nor had he discriminated against anyone. Turning to an examination of the merits of the complaint, the HR Committee firstly submitted that the applicant's removal from teaching did constitute a significant restriction on his right to freedom of expression but was a consequence of the nature of the views he expressed. After considering and analysing all the arguments, the HR Committee's decision found no violation of Article 19 of the ICCPR against the complainant, thus sharing the state's position. With regard to the applicant's allegation of a violation of Article 18 of the ICCPR, the HR Committee found that the decisions taken in his case did not relate to the freedom of his religious beliefs but rather to the public expression of hateful forms of these beliefs in a well-defined context and circumstances. The HR Committee consequently found no violation of Article 18 of the ICCPR.

2.3.2 CERD Decisions

The CERD's case law best demonstrates the "blurred lines" between racial/ethnic or religious discrimination and hatred. Among them, Islamophobia and anti-Semitism remain the most notable examples. However, the CERD's position to date sends a clear message: racial or ethnic discrimination or hatred must constitute the essential component and basis of a complaint; if the CERD deems it to predominantly concern religious aspects, it will not be investigated on its merits.

An exemplification of this approach is the CERD's position presented in the case of *A.W.R.A.P. v. Denmark*.[45] The complaint concerned the failure of the police and the public prosecutor's office to initiate proper proceedings against a politician's discriminatory and offensive statements against Muslims in Denmark. The politician, in a series of public statements, had maintained that it was part of the culture and tradition of Islam and the behaviour of Muslims to use brutal domestic violence against women and children.

45 *A.W.R.A.P. v. Denmark* [2007], CERD/C/71/D/37/2006. See also the decision in *P.S.N. v. Denmark* [2007], CERD/C/71/D/36/2006.

In refusing to accept the complaint for consideration on its merits, the CERD offered its interpretation of its jurisdiction over complaints on discrimination or religious hatred:

> The Committee recognises the importance of the interface between race and religion and considers that it would be competent to consider a claim of "double" discrimination on the basis of religion and another ground specifically provided for in article 1 of the Convention, including national or ethnic origin. However, this is not the case in the current petition, which exclusively relates to discrimination on religious grounds. The Committee recalls that the Convention does not cover discrimination based on religion alone, and that Islam is not a religion practised solely by a particular group, which could otherwise be identified by its "race, colour, descent, or national or ethnic origin." The Travaux Preparatoires of the Convention reveal that the Third Committee of the General Assembly rejected the proposal to include racial discrimination and religious intolerance in a single instrument, and decided in the ICERD to focus exclusively on racial discrimination. It is unquestionable therefore that discrimination based exclusively on religious grounds was not intended to fall within the purview of the Convention.[46]

This problem is directly related to the issue of intersectionality mentioned earlier. However, the CERD seems to have taken an overly conservative approach to interpreting the facts presented to it. Its additional remarks that adherents of Islam can also be native Danes who have converted to Islam, though truthful, seems to have failed to take into account the social reality that in the general public perception of Islam, Muslims are "automatically" associated with Arab and African origin, and assumed to be people of colour.[47]

Returning to the central dilemma considered in this chapter – whether we need enhanced protection for a religiously sensitive group – in terms of case law treaty bodies the answer appears to be no, despite the fact that the CERD excuses itself from taking a position in cases where there is no explicit element of racial or ethnic discrimination. These tasks are taken on by the HRC, whose jurisprudence includes cases of discrimination against religious minorities and religious hatred. There is also no impediment for the HR Committee to address the issue of defamation of religion, should such a case arise, either in the option of a complaint by an individual punished at the national level for defamation of religion or a possible complaint by a religious group feeling that the law does not adequately protect them from defamation of their sacred figures or symbols. Moreover, 18 years have passed since the CERD's position in the *A.W.R.A.P* case, and it would seem that given the enormity of the

46 *A.W.R.A.P. v. Denmark* [2007] § 6.3.
47 *A.W.R.A.P. v. Denmark* [2007] § 6.2.

changes in the perception of certain phenomena and the discussion on the CERD's jurisdiction over religion, today's conclusions might be different.

2.4 Controversial Discussion Point: "Defamation of Religion"

The most debated issue in the context of protecting religious feelings, but also one embedded in a serious legal dilemma concerning the limits of freedom of expression, is that of criminalising so-called defamation of religion, a concept analogous to blasphemy. This issue has also become the biggest bone of contention in UN debates on the need to strengthen the standard of protection against discrimination and hatred on religious grounds.[48]

Over the years, the issue of insulting religions has come up at the UN with increasing frequency, leading to the passage of successive resolutions and declarations. One of these was a resolution on "combating defamation of religions", adopted by the HRC in March 2010, with the support of a dozen Muslim countries as well as Bolivia, China, Cuba, and Russia, and with the opposition of European countries, as well as Argentina, Chile, South Korea, Mexico, the United States, Uruguay, and Zambia.[49] In its preamble, the HRC notes that defamation of religions and incitement to religious hatred can lead to conflict and human rights violations. It further expresses concern at the failure of a number of states to adequately respond to instances of insulting religions, leading to discrimination against their adherents. For this reason, it also stresses the need to effectively combat insults to all religions, and incitement to hatred against Islam and Muslims in particular.[50] The document did not define the concept of defamation of religions per se but listed examples of behaviour that constitutes such insult. These include the deliberate use of negative stereotypes, insulting religions, their followers and prophets, equating Islam with human rights abuses and terrorism, controlling, and stigmatising a Muslim minority, banning the construction of minarets and mosques and inciting violence and religious hatred. The resolution did not mention any religion other

48 S. Parmar, "Uprooting "Defamation of Religions" and Planting a New Approach to Freedom of Expression at the United Nations". In: T. McGonagle, Y. Donders, (eds.), *The United Nations and Freedom of Expression and Information: Critical Perspectives* (Cambridge: Cambridge University Press, 2015): 373–427. A telling exemplification of this controversy was the events commonly referred to as the Danish Cartoons case of 2005 – see "The Danish Cartoons", *Netherlands Quarterly of Human Rights*, vol. 24, no. 2 (2006): 185–191. https://doi.org/10.1177/016934410602400201.

49 HRC Resolution 13/16: Combating defamation of religions [2010]. https://www.right-docs.org/doc/a-hrc-res-13-16/. Accessed October 28, 2024. The countries that abstained are Bosnia and Herzegovina, Brazil, Ghana, India, Japan, Cameroon, Madagascar and Mauritius. Countries voting in favour of the resolution, in addition to those already mentioned, were Saudi Arabia, Bahrain, Bangladesh, Burkina Faso, Djibouti, Egypt, Philippines, Indonesia, Jordan, Qatar, Kyrgyzstan, Nigeria, Nicaragua, Pakistan, South Africa, and Senegal.

50 HRC Resolution 13/16: Combating defamation of religions [2010] § 2.

than Islam by name, nor did it mention forms of religious discrimination other than Islamophobia, omitting for example the increasing persecution of Christians in Muslim countries, the death penalty for conversion in Pakistan, or the vandalising of synagogues and desecration of Jewish cemeteries in Europe,[51] although it did call for a constructive dialogue between different religions and cultures that respects other beliefs, as well as states, non-governmental organisations (NGOs), religious leaders and the media to foster a "culture of tolerance and peace".[52] However, it is difficult not to see the dissonance between such a call and calls for the use of legal instruments against those who insult the dogmas of a particular faith or portray its prophets in a negative light.

Resolution 13/16, however, was not the first of its kind. As early as 1999, a resolution was adopted by the Commission on Human Rights (the predecessor of the HRC)[53] and was originally intended, according to a draft submitted by Pakistan on behalf of the Organisation of the Islamic Conference (OIC) states,[54] to be entitled "insulting Islam", though this was later changed despite the objections of some states to "insulting religions".[55] From then on, a resolution by this name and with almost identical wording was passed by the Commission on Human Rights every year until the end of that body's existence, subsequently also becoming a permanent part of the HRC's agenda.

At the same time, attempts to establish a more moderate and conciliatory position with regard to defamation of religions have long remained futile. During the debate on the adoption of HRC Resolution 6/37 in December 2007, on countering all forms of intolerance and discrimination on the grounds of religion, the majority of Muslim states voted against it. The resolution condemned all forms of discrimination on the grounds of religion and belief and incitement to hatred and violence, and it detailed the obligations of states to ensure full religious freedom. However, the document was not supported by Muslim states, and their criticisms were raised when the proposed text of the resolution was presented by its drafter, Portugal, speaking on behalf of the European Union (EU) states. The objections related to the lack of emphasis on the prohibition of insulting religions and their prophets that the OIC countries felt the text of the resolution should represent.[56] The section of

51 HRC Resolution 13/16: Combating defamation of religions [2010] § 2. Only in the Preamble of the document is there a reference to concern about incidents of hostility towards Christians and anti-Semitism.

52 HRC Resolution 13/16: Combating defamation of religions [2010] § 17–18.

53 HRC Resolution 1999/82: Defamation of religions, E/CN.4/1999/L.82 [1999].

54 The organisation currently uses the name Organisation of Islamic Cooperation.

55 Draft resolution submitted by Pakistan, E/CN.4/1999/L.40. During the discussion of the draft, representatives of, inter alia, Germany and Japan expressed concern that the content of the document would be unjustifiably narrowed to the problems of followers of only one religion: Islam. See the transcript of the deliberations of the HRC on 29 April 1999, E/CN.4/1999/SR.61.

56 Proposed amendments to HRC Draft Resolution 6/37, tabled by Pakistan on behalf of the OIC States, A/HRC/6/L.49 [2007].

the resolution referring to guaranteeing the right to religious conversion was also a subject of their criticism. Since then, EU states in particular have continued their efforts to pass resolutions under the name of "freedom of religion or belief", intended to counterbalance resolutions aimed at the "defence of religions" as such. [57]

Those states that oppose shaping the UN position in a way that pushes the legitimacy of criminalising insulting religions rightly argue that it poses a serious threat to freedom of expression and, paradoxically, religious freedom. Indeed, the possibility of freely expressing critical views on the dogmas of faith and even of engaging in polemics between representatives of different faiths is curtailed in a very significant way. There is particularly strong opposition, moreover, to the desire expressed in the resolution's text to transfer the protection owed to individuals to the very institution of religion, its symbols, and its prophets, which runs counter to the basic tenets of a universal system of human rights protection.[58]

The perception that the tenets of this concept contradicted the very idea of protecting human rights led to growing opposition at the UN. As a result, there has been a decisive shift in the proportions of votes cast during votes in the HRC and the UN General Assembly on resolutions against defamation of religion.[59] In 2008, at both of these fora, for the first time, the number of votes against and abstentions outweighed the number of votes in favour of the resolution.[60] In December 2010, at the UN General Assembly, the resolution was passed by 79 votes for, 67 votes against, and 40 abstentions.[61]

In 2011, there was a consequent shift in the previous position of mainly OIC states: HRC Resolution 16/18 was adopted by consensus, reconciling increasingly polarised positions on the preferred ways of combating religious hatred and discrimination, and replacing divisive calls to legally tackle defamation of

57 See HRC Resolution 43/12: Freedom of religion or belief, A/HRC/RES/43/12 [2020].

58 For a more extensive discussion of the controversy surrounding the insulting of religions as opposed to the insulting of individual adherents of a religion, as well as criticisms of Human Rights Council resolutions passed in this regard, see, e.g., J. Temperman, "Blasphemy, Defamation of Religions and Human Rights Law", *Netherland Quarterly of Human Rights*, vol. 26, no. 4 (2008): 517–545. https://doi.org/10.1177/016934410802600403.

59 L. B. Graham, "Defamation of Religions: The End of Pluralism?", *Emory International Law Review*, vol. 23, no. 1 (2009): 70. https://law-journals-books.vlex.com/vid/l-bennett-graham-defamation-935396571. Accessed October 28, 2024.

60 L. B. Graham, "Defamation of Religions: The End of Pluralism?", *Emory International Law Review*, vol. 23, no. 1 (2009): 72.

61 Information on voting is available: GA/11041, UN Women, 'Bangkok Rules' for Women Prisoners, Rights of the Child, Extrajudicial Executions, Death Penalty Moratorium among IssuesAddressed. http://www.un.org/News/Press/docs/2010/ga11041.doc.htm. Accessed October 22, 2011.

religion.[62] As a follow-up to the action plan on how to prevent and respond to manifestations of intolerance, discrimination, hatred, and violence based on religion or belief, set out in Resolution 16/18 (and its counterpart at the UN General Assembly, Resolution 66/167[63]), the so-called Istanbul Process was initiated, designed to monitor and drive the implementation of the action plan.[64] The action plan consists of eight action points (among them, the point on criminalising incitement to religious violence), indicating complementary measures that should be implemented holistically and comprehensively. Since its launch in Turkey in 2011, several expert-level meetings have been organised, focussing on securing the fragile consensus over most problematic issues, including blasphemy laws.[65]

Another UN mechanism, the Rabat Plan of Action, also derives significantly from the previously promoted narratives of pro-penalisation of defamation of religion present at various UN fora.[66] The Rabat Plan of Action expressly calls for the repeal of blasphemy laws at large, indicating that they violate international human rights law; they are discriminatory, as they deny already marginalised groups the opportunity to speak or be heard. They also run counter to the human rights protection rule: people are rightsholders, whilst abstract ideas or beliefs are not. At the same time, the qualification and legal reaction may be different if blasphemous expression separately constitutes "incitement" as defined by Article 20(2) of the ICCPR. Also, in opposition to the concept of criminalising insult to religion is the HR Committee's General Comment No. 34 to Article 19 of the ICCPR,[67] adopted in 2011, which guarantees freedom of expression and to which the Rabat Plan of Action refers. It is worth quoting in full this important voice in the discussion on this controversial issue:

> Prohibitions of displays of lack of respect for a religion or other belief system, including blasphemy laws, are incompatible with the Covenant, except in the specific circumstances envisaged in article 20, paragraph 2,

62 For a detailed analysis of this change in the OIC's position, see H.M. Haugen, "A Decade of Revitalizing UN Work Concerning Freedom of Religion or Belief (2010–2020)", *Journal of Human Rights*, vol. 22, no. 4 (2023): 469–486.

63 Since 2011, both the HRC and the UN General Assembly have annually adopted follow-up resolutions reiterating the same action plan, each time by consensus.

64 *UN HRC Res 16/18: Consolidating Consensus Through Implementation: Article 19 Briefing* (London: Article 19. Free Word Centre, 2016). https://www.article19.org/data/files/medialibrary/38262/16_18_briefing_EN--online-version-(hyperlinked)-.pdf. Accessed October 28, 2024.

65 See e.g. K. Telle, *UN Resolution 16/18 and the Istanbul Process: What Has Been Achieved? A Charting of Blasphemy Trends in Pakistan and Indonesia* (Bergen: Christian Michelsen Institute, 2022). https://www.cmi.no/publications/8174-un-resolution-16-18-and-the-istanbul-process-what-has-been-achieved#pdf. Accessed October 28, 2024.

66 "OHCHR and freedom of expression vs incitement to hatred".

67 CCPR General Commentary no. 34, CCPR/C/GC/34 [2011].

> of the Covenant. Such prohibitions must also comply with the strict requirements of article 19, paragraph 3, as well as such articles as 2, 5, 17, 18 and 26. Thus, for instance, it would be impermissible for any such laws to discriminate in favour of or against one or certain religions or belief systems, or their adherents over another, or religious believers over non-believers. Nor would it be permissible for such prohibitions to be used to prevent or punish criticism of religious leaders or commentary on religious doctrine and tenets of faith.[68]

General Comment No. 34 also clearly corresponds to the views presented in the work of the UN special procedures.[69] In the report by Nazila Ghanea, the Special Rapporteur on freedom of religion or belief, published in the beginning of 2024, this issue is taken up in several places, with an unambiguous message.[70] She writes that when one religion or belief is associated with statehood and government, "political projects of this kind may find legitimacy in the existence or propagation of legal provisions, such as anti-blasphemy or anti-conversion/anti-apostasy laws, which stigmatize certain religions or beliefs or their expressions as criminal".[71] Furthermore, quoting previous UN documents, she calls such anti-blasphemy laws discriminatory and stresses that they have led to numerous examples of persecution of religious minorities. Finally, citing a number of HR Committee comments on State Party reports, Ghanea points to the serious risks of anti-blasphemy provisions and their

68 CCPR General Commentary no. 34, CCPR/C/GC/34 [2011] § 48.

69 The joint position of the Special Rapporteur on racism, the Special Rapporteur on freedom of religion or belief and the Special Rapporteur on the promotion and protection of freedom of opinion and expression on the prohibition of incitement to hatred on grounds of nationality, race and religion, already formulated in February 2011, was of momentous importance. As they rightly note, "[T]he difficulty of formulating an objective definition of the concept of 'insult to religion' at the international level makes the whole concept easy to abuse, either through overly broad application or free interpretation. On the other hand, at the national level, laws against blasphemy can be counterproductive [...]. There are many examples of persecution of religious minorities [...] as well as atheists and non-theists that occur as a result of religious insult laws" – OHCHR Expert Works Hops on the Prohibition of Incitement to National, Racial or Religious Hatred, 9–10 February 2011, Vienna, Joint submission by Mr. Heiner Bielefeldt, Special Rapporteur on freedom of religion or belief; Mr. Frank La Rue, Special Rapporteur on the promotion and protection of the right to freedom of opinion and expression; and Mr Githu Muigai, Special Rapporteur on contemporary forms of racism, racial discrimination, xenophobia and related intolerance, p. 10. https://www.ohchr.org/sites/default/files/Documents/Issues/Religion/CRP3Joint_SRSubmission_for_Vienna.pdf. Accessed October 28, 2024.

70 Report of the Special Rapporteur on freedom of religion or belief, Nazila Ghanea: Hatred on the basis of religion or belief, A/HRC/55/47 [2024].

71 Report of the Special Rapporteur on freedom of religion or belief, Nazila Ghanea: Hatred on the basis of religion or belief, A/HRC/55/47 [2024] § 15.

instrumentalisation in the denial of freedom of religion or belief, stressing that "[v]ague or far-reaching laws against advocacy of hatred, or blasphemy, offence to religious feelings and similar offences are not only arbitrary, they can also lead to the direct and structural marginalisation of religious or belief communities".[72] She spoke in a similar tone in 2023 at the HRC during an event named "Urgent Debate to Discuss the Alarming Rise in Premeditated and Public Acts of Religious Hatred as Manifested by Recurrent Desecration of the Holy Quran in Some European and Other Countries".[73] Ghanea, whilst condemning the acts of publicly burning the Holy Quran as dangerous manifestations of hatred and religious intolerance, recalled the position of former Special Rapporteur Ahmed Shaheed that criticism of religious leaders or commentary on religious doctrine or tenets of faith should not be prohibited or punished. At the same time, a few days after her speech, the HRC adopted a resolution where it condemned and strongly rejected any advocacy or manifestation of religious hatred, including the recent public and premeditated acts of desecration of the Holy Quran, calling for legal accountability of those involved in such acts.[74]

It can be assumed that a kind of *status quo* prevails today: both for and against the aforementioned resolution; individual states have voted according to their ideological and political profile, sometimes closely linked to the role of religion in their legal systems, although its language is already markedly different from that recorded in the resolutions of previous years.[75] Efforts are still being made to channel the debate surrounding the notion of defamation of religions into developing new, effective ways of countering religious hatred as a form of hate speech. However, neither the Istanbul Process nor the Rabat Plan of Action call for the establishment of a new, separate human rights treaty to increase protection against religious hate speech or hate crime.

72 Report of the Special Rapporteur on freedom of religion or belief, Nazila Ghanea: Hatred on the basis of religion or belief, A/HRC/55/47 [2024] § 38.

73 "Human Rights Council to Hold Urgent Debate on Acts of Religious Hatred on 11 July", https://www.ohchr.org/en/press-releases/2023/07/human-rights-council-hold-urgent-debate-acts-religious-hatred-11-july. Accessed October 28, 2024.

74 HRC Resolution 53/1: Countering religious hatred constituting incitement to discrimination, hostility or violence, A/HRC/RES/53/1 [2023].

75 Countries that traditionally voted in favour of the resolution included Algeria, Argentina, Bangladesh, Bolivia, Cameroon, China, Cote d'Ivoire, Cuba, Eritrea, Gabon, Gambia, India, Kazakhstan, Kyrgyzstan, Malawi, Malaysia, Maldives, Morocco, Pakistan, Qatar, Senegal, Somalia, South Africa, Sudan, Ukraine, United Arab Emirates, Uzbekistan and Vietnam. Against were Belgium, Costa Rica, Czechia, Finland, France, Germany, Lithuania, Luxembourg, Montenegro, Romania, the United Kingdom, and the United States.

2.5 To Draft a New Treaty or Not to Draft? Some Concluding Remarks

To conclude this chapter, first of all the following should be stated: the establishment of a treaty instrument focused strictly on the issue of religious discrimination and hatred would certainly enhance the importance of this topic, elevating it to the status of an issue regulated by a binding international treaty and placing it among a limited number of other issues, thus positively singling it out. In this way, the vulnerable category of religious minorities would also be uplifted. The concept of vulnerability, which has been present for a long time in the practice of treaty bodies,[76] allows for the identification of individuals and groups that are particularly vulnerable to discrimination and human rights violations. In the case of religious minorities, additional attention is paid to the intersectional context since religious identity intersects with other marginalised identities that render religious minorities especially vulnerable around the world.[77] The persecution of the religiously and ethnically distinct Rohingya population or the discrimination against Muslim women on the basis of religious clothing are just some examples. Giving a possible treaty an intersectional character by including provisions that provide protection for vulnerable groups such as children or women – similar to what is done, for example, by the Convention on the Rights of Persons with Disabilities[78] – would highlight this issue, as it is hardly visible in the 1981 Declaration.[79] This would also imply further consequences that strengthen the level of protection: the establishment of a complaint mechanisms, allowing an individual (or group) to claim a violation of their rights by a State Party to a treaty, and the creation of an obligation for states to submit periodic reports on the implementation of treaty provisions, to be assessed by the treaty body. In the case of the issues addressed in this chapter, one more argument should speak for the establishment of treaty protection: the provisions of the 1981 Declaration, although

76 A. Gliszczyńska-Grabias, G. Baranowska, "The Concept of Vulnerability in the United Nations Human Rights Treaty Bodies Protection System". In: M. Półtorak, I. Topa (eds.), *Women, Children and (Other) Vulnerable Groups Standards of Protection and Challenges for International Law* (Berlin: Peter Lang Publishers, 2021): 23–40.

77 "Religious minorities are especially vulnerable: Intersectional identity and international aid", https://blogs.lse.ac.uk/religionglobalsociety/2019/01/religious-minorities-are-especially-vulnerable-intersectional-identity-and-international-aid/. Accessed October 28, 2024.

78 G. de Beco, "Intersectionality and Disability in International Human Rights Law", *The International Journal of Human Rights*, vol. 24, no. 5 (2019): 593–614.

79 It is worth noting that Art. 5 of the Declaration refers to the protection of children from religious discrimination. Its gendered language, on the other hand, is now very archaic ("The child shall be protected from any form of discrimination on the ground of religion or belief. He shall be brought up in a spirit of understanding, tolerance, friendship among peoples, peace and universal brotherhood, respect for freedom of religion or belief of others, and in full consciousness that his energy and talents should be devoted to the service of his fellow men").

referred to in a number of documents and debates at the UN, are largely absent from the awareness and practice of law application by individual states, as being non-binding and "soft law".[80]

However, the question of adopting a new treaty in an environment of such sensitivity and conflict is fraught with risks, far beyond the usual difficulties that accompany the process of formulating and enacting an international treaty. The relative "state of ceasefire" that has been achieved on the issue of defamation of religion, reinforced by the Istanbul Process and Rabat Plan of Action, is perhaps worth maintaining. By the same token, it should perhaps be emphasised that the scope of the obligations arising from the 1981 Declaration is broader than that which could be accepted today in the form of a treaty. The analysis carried out in this chapter, although limited in its scope, has nevertheless shown that the instruments of the universal human rights protection system currently in place guarantee victims of discrimination or religious hatred protection and the possibility to claim violations of their rights and freedoms regarding religion, conscience, and belief.

For all these reasons, it would seem that the most optimal solution would be to supplement the current standard with the adoption of an Additional Protocol to the ICERD, which would provide for the express competence of the CERD to investigate individual complaints of violations of the guarantees contained in the 1981 Declaration, and which would interpret the provisions of the ICERD in such a way that its coverage of discrimination and religious hatred would become a treaty-enshrined fact.

Separate issues remain, however: firstly, the general interpretative difficulties when it comes to criminalising certain statements debated by various UN bodies, and secondly, the proliferation of human rights protection in the UN due to more and more treaties being enacted and more special procedures being created in recent years.[81] This proliferation sometimes supersedes the proper use and possible reform of existing instruments, which would allow

80 D.H. Davis thinks differently and enthusiastically about the impact of the 1981 Declaration: "If the importance of a document were measured in terms of its pathbreaking qualities, the 1948 Universal Declaration would undoubtedly be most important. [...] If importance were measured in terms of an instrument's enforceability in courts, the 1966 Covenant would be the most important. But if by importance we refer to the comprehensiveness of rights addressed and the degree to which a document is looked to by the international community to define the religious rights that should be respected, then it is clearly the 1981 Declaration that deserves the 'most important' label" – D.H. Davis, "The Evolution of Religious Freedom as a Universal Human Right: Examining the Role of the 1981 United Nations Declaration on the Elimination of All Forms of Intolerance and of Discrimination Based on Religion or Belief", BYU Law Review no. 2 (2002): 228. https://digitalcommons.law.byu.edu/cgi/viewcontent.cgi?article=2109&context=lawreview. Accessed: October 28, 2024.

81 R. Freedman, J. Mchangama, "Expanding or Diluting Human Rights?: The Proliferation of United Nations Special Procedures Mandates", *Human Rights Quarterly*, vol. 38, no. 1 (2016): 164–193.

states to implement their obligations more effectively. There also remains, of course, the lack of efficiency and permeability of the system already in place – another element in the mechanism that does not work effectively can only worsen the situation of victims of human rights violations.[82]

However, irrespective of any solutions that are in force or are yet to be adopted at the level of universal, regional, or national human rights law, it is worth emphasising the fundamental issue highlighted by Theo van Boven precisely in the context of the discussion on the question of the legitimacy of establishing an additional treaty on religious discrimination. Indeed, van Boven emphasises the key role of building understanding, respect, and tolerance between people of different religions and beliefs, and the need for unwavering commitment from religious groups and communities in particular.[83] It may seem naïve to call for overcoming discrimination and religious hatred through the goodwill and cooperation of adherents of different religions and beliefs, but if agreement cannot be reached on a legal level, it should be reached through dialogue and ecumenical respect as a starting point for all other discussions.

82 For more on this subject, see J. Krommendijk, "The (In)effectiveness of UN Human Rights Treaty Body Recommendations", *Netherlands Quarterly of Human Rights*, vol. 33, no. 2 (2015): 194–223.

83 T. van Boven, "Advances and Obstacles in Building Understanding and Respect between People of Diverse Religions and Beliefs", *Human Rights Quarterly*, vol. 13, no. 4 (1991): 447.

3 The Concept of Vulnerability in the Context of Religious Minorities*

Grażyna Baranowska

Abstract

This chapter assesses the application of the concept of vulnerability to religious minorities and explores the added value of using this lens in the context of international human rights law. Specifically, it examines case law from the European Court of Human Rights and UN treaty bodies where vulnerability has been applied to cases involving religious minorities. The analysis identifies three contexts in which this occurs: the situation in the individual's country of origin, non-refoulement cases, and cases involving discrimination or pressure from within their own religious group. The added value of vulnerability is most apparent in the third category, where it aids in evaluating the individual's circumstances and offers an additional layer of protection. However, the analysis also highlights the challenges posed by the lack of a clear definition of vulnerability, which can result in contradictory applications of the concept.

Keywords

vulnerability; religious minorities; non-refoulement; discrimination; prejudice; European Court of Human Rights; UN treaty bodies; Human Rights Committee; Committee against Torture; Committee on the Rights of the Child; Afghanistan; hijab bans; Jehovah's witnesses; Hare Krishna; Muslim; Christian; Hindu; conversion

* Research for the article has been funded by the Polish National Science Centre (Grant No. 2019/33/B/HS5/01634).

DOI: 10.4324/9781003423294-5

3.1 Introduction

The concepts of both vulnerability and religious minorities are inherently linked to the protection of individuals, whilst also recognising their membership in a group and their broader social context.[1] However, there are important conceptual differences between them. The concept of religious minorities is also much older than that of vulnerability, and it has a significantly stronger presence in international law. Since vulnerability appeared in international human rights law during the 1990s, this concept has also been applied to religious minorities. I was invited to contribute to this edited collection to reflect on the relationship between these two concepts. The two main questions I have explored are how the concept of vulnerability has been applied to religious minorities and the added value of applying the vulnerability lens to the existing framework for protecting religious minorities in international human rights law.

To respond to those questions, I conducted an analysis of the case law of the European Court of Human Rights (ECtHR), the regional human rights court established within the Council of Europe, and the UN treaty bodies, that is, the quasi-judicial bodies created on the universal level through the core UN human rights treaties.[2] I selected only the two systems, as the aim of the chapter is not to comprehensively assess how the concept of vulnerability is applied to religious minorities by various bodies: I merely investigate the application of the concept to religious minorities and added value in the interaction. For this reason, I considered it sufficient to include only one of the regional human rights systems, which arguably has the most developed case law concerning vulnerability. However, a limitation of the chapter is that it only assesses one regional human rights system, without covering the Inter-American[3] or African systems.

For the analysis, I first selected cases relating to religious minorities in which vulnerability was applied. To identify them, I searched each of the systems' respective databases[4] and complemented this with cases indicated in the

1 M. Albertson Fineman, "The Vulnerable Subject: Anchoring Equality in the Human Condition", *Yale Journal Law & Feminism*, vol. 20, no 1 (2009): 13. https://openyls.law.yale.edu/bitstream/handle/20.500.13051/6993/03_20YaleJL_Feminism1_2008_2009_.pdf?sequence=2&. Accessed November 16, 2024.

2 There are nine core UN human rights bodies which issues decisions in individual cases. The analysis revealed that so far, only three have applied the vulnerability lens to religious minorities – namely, the Human Rights Committee (HRC), the Committee Against Torture (CAT), and the Committee on the Rights of the Child (CRC).

3 For vulnerability case law of the InterAmerican Court of Human Rights (IACtHR), see, e.g., IACtHR, *Fernández Ortega et al. v. Mexico*, no. 540-04 [2010]; IACtHR, *Tiu Tojín v. Guatemala* [2008] Serie C No. 190.

4 The database of the UN treaty bodies is available at https://juris.ohchr.org/SearchResult, and the database of the ECtHR is available at https://hudoc.echr.coe.int/.

literature.[5] Next, I conducted an in-depth analysis of selected judgements and views,[6] which allowed me to cluster ECtHR judgements and UN treaty bodies views into three groups, presented in this chapter. The case law was analysed to respond to the research questions, and not as a comparative exercise. However, I noted any significant differences between the ECtHR and UN treaty bodies.

The chapter begins with two sections dedicated to the key concepts under analysis: religious minorities and vulnerability. Section 3.2 outlines the origins and development of the protection of religious minorities, followed by Section 3.3, which explores the emergence and evolution of the concept of vulnerability. The subsequent three sections present an analysis of relevant case law from the ECtHR and UN treaty bodies, organised into three categories. Section 3.4 examines how the concept of vulnerability has been applied to religious minorities in their countries of origin, whilst Section 3.5 focusses on its more frequent use in non-refoulement cases. Section 3.6 uncovers a surprising application of vulnerability: protecting religious minorities from discrimination or pressure within their own religious groups. The chapter concludes with final observations in Section 3.7.

3.2 The Roots and Developments of the Protection of Religious Minorities

The protection of religious minorities has a long-standing tradition in international law, coming before the adoption of the Universal Declaration of Human Rights and the core human rights treaties. Peace treaties in the 19th century often included provisions covering group protection.[7] These regulations were followed in the interwar minorities' treaties (1919–1923), which contributed

5 See, in particular, L. Peroni, A. Timmer, "Vulnerable Groups: The Promise of an Emerging Concept in European Human Rights Convention Law", *International Journal of Constitutional Law*, vol. 11, no. 4 (2013): 1056. https://doi.org/10.1093/icon/mot042; C. Heri, *Responsive Human Rights: Vulnerability, Ill-Treatment and the ECtHR* (Oxford: Hart, 2021); O.M. Arnardóttir, "Vulnerability Under Article 14 of the European Convention on Human Rights Innovation or Business as Usual?", *Oslo Law Review*, vol. 4, no. 3 (2017): 150. https://doi.org/10.18261/issn.2387-3299-2017-03-03; A. Gliszczyńska-Grabias, G. Baranowska, "The Concept of Vulnerability in the United Nations Human Rights Treaty Bodies Protection System". In: M. Półtorak, I. Tolpa (eds.), *Women, Children and (Other) Vulnerable Groups: Standards of Protection and Challenges for International Law* (Berlin: Peter Lang, 2021): 23–40.

6 UN treaty bodies are mandated to issue decisions in individual and inter-state complaints; however, the decisions are not called "judgments" but "views".

7 L. Castellanos-Jankiewicz, "Minority Rights Petitions: League of Nations". In: H.R. Fabri (ed.), *Max Planck Encyclopedias of International Law* (Oxford: Oxford University Press, 2020): §§ 10–11.

to the development of legal standards of equality before the law.[8] Those treaties provided special protection to nationals belonging to racial, religious or linguistic minorities. Importantly, the minority protection in the interwar minorities' treaties came under two headings: firstly, achieving equality in respect of the dominant group and prohibiting state-based discrimination of minorities,[9] and secondly, providing some positive measures to protect group identity and differentiation.[10] These two aims are also reflected in later documents.

Members of religious minorities were among those singled out for additional protection under international human rights law from the very beginning. Already in 1948, the Universal Declaration of Human Rights ("Declaration") mentioned "religious groups" when dealing with education, stating that it should "promote understanding, tolerance and friendship" among all "religious groups".[11] Furthermore, according to the Declaration, everyone is entitled to all the rights and freedoms set forth in it without any distinction, including religion (Article 12).[12] Similarly, the European Convention on Human Rights (ECHR) adopted in 1950 contains the freedom to manifest one's religion, alone or in community with others, as well as a prohibition against discrimination on any grounds, including religion.[13] The rights provided to individuals as parts of religious groups were strengthened in the subsequent international human rights treaties. For example, according to Article 27 of the International Covenant on Civil and Political Rights ("Covenant") adopted in 1966, in those states in which religious minorities

8 L. Castellanos-Jankiewicz, "Negotiating Equality: Minority Protection in the Versailles Settlement". In: M. Erpelding, B. Hess, H.R. Fabri (eds.), *Peace Through Law: The Versailles Peace Treaty and Dispute Settlement After World War I* (Baden-Baden: Nomos Verlagsgesellschaft, 2019): 123.

9 Thus, it is dubbed the "assimilation thesis" – see analysis by M. Mazower, "Minorities and the League of Nations in Interwar Europe", *Daedalus*, vol. 126, no. 2 (2017): 47, 53–54.

10 L. Castellanos-Jankiewicz, "Minority Rights Petitions" § 18.

11 Universal Declaration of Human Rights, Res. 217 A(III) [1948] A/RES/217(III). Art. 26.2: "Education shall be directed to the full development of the human personality and to the strengthening of respect for human rights and fundamental freedoms. It shall promote understanding, tolerance and friendship among all nations, racial or religious groups, and shall further the activities of the United Nations for the maintenance of peace".

12 The other mentioned grounds are race, colour, sex, language, political or other opinion, national or social origin, property, birth or other status.

13 Arts. 9 and 14 Convention for the Protection of Human Rights and Fundamental Freedoms (European Convention on Human Rights, as amended) [1950] ETS No. 005. The protocol from 1952 added the right to education, including teaching in conformity with the families' religious convictions.

exist, their members "shall not be denied the right, in community with the other members of their groups" to practice their own religion.[14]

Whilst there is no internationally accepted definition of (religious) minorities, an often-used definition was proposed in 1979 by the Special Rapporteur of the UN Sub-Commission on Prevention of Discrimination and Protection of Minorities. However, this definition was drawn solely with the above-mentioned application of Article 27 of the Covenant in mind, and it reads as follows:

> A group numerically inferior to the rest of the population of a State, in a non-dominant position, whose members – being nationals of the State – possess ethnic, religious or linguistic characteristics different from those of the rest of the population and show, if only implicitly, a sense of solidarity, directed towards preserving their culture, traditions, religion or language.[15]

The creation of minority-specific international legal protections took off in the late 1980s.[16] Today minority protection – including the protection of religious minorities – is based on two pillars: general and group-specific protection. The first one concerns the protection of human rights, which applies to members of all minorities as human beings. The second aims specifically at protecting this group.[17] According to Kristin Henrard, minority rights are "actually just one of several sets of category-specific human rights, namely special rights for persons belonging to vulnerable groups",[18] thus clearly pointing to its interrelation with the second concept analysed in this chapter: vulnerability.

3.3 The Emergence and Development of the Concept of Vulnerability

From the beginning of the formation of the human rights protection system, particularly vulnerable groups were singled out as those most needing protection. The entire International Convention on the Elimination of All Forms of Racial Discrimination from 1969 concerns guarantees of protecting members of vulnerable groups from various, multiple and intense forms of undertreatment

14 International Covenant on Civil and Political Rights [1976] 999 UNTS 171 (ICCPR); this Article of the ICCPR also relates to ethnic and linguistic minorities, providing them the right to enjoy their own culture and use their own language.

15 Study on the Rights of Persons Belonging to Ethnic, Religious and Linguistic Minorities [1979] § 568, E/CN 4/Sub 2/384/Rev 1.

16 R. Hofmann, "Minorities, European Protection". In: R. Wolfrum (ed.), *Max Planck Encyclopedia of International Law*, vol. 2 (Oxford: Oxford University Press, 2012): 241, § 2.

17 K. Henrard, "Minorities, International Protection". In: R. Wolfrum (ed.), *Max Planck Encyclopedia of International Law*, vol. 7 (Oxford: Oxford University Press, 2012): 258, § 28; C. Heri, *Responsive Human Rights* 154–155.

18 K. Henrard, "Minorities, International Protection" § 27.

and discrimination.[19] A Council of Europe study published in 1973 analysed which particular categories of human beings should be protected, considering the particular situation that qualify and characterise them – an exercise we would currently relate to vulnerability. The report mentions the following categories: women, children, aliens, vagrants, nomads, detainees, mentally handicapped persons, men in uniform, and foreign press correspondents.[20]

The ECtHR and the majority of the core UN human rights treaties do not contain the word "vulnerability", as it was not used in international human rights law at the time they were created. It does appear in the UN human rights treaties that were adopted in the 1990s, where it serves mostly to stress the especially difficult situation of a given group or category within a group rather than to add any specially tailored rights or other mechanisms of protecting rights.[21] The turn towards vulnerability in the 1990s can also be illustrated by the Vienna Declaration and Programme of Action, following the World Conference on Human Rights in 1993, which stated that "[g]reat importance must be given to the promotion and protection of the human rights of persons belonging to groups which have been rendered vulnerable".[22] Since then, the notion of vulnerability has been gaining popularity in conversations about proposed changes to the international human rights protection treaties or developments in the case law of international human rights protection bodies.[23]

19 T. van Boven, "Combating Racial Discrimination in the World and in Europe", *Netherlands Quarterly of Human Rights*, vol. 11, no. 2 (1993): 163–172. https://doi.org/10.1177/016934419301100203.

20 M. Bossuyt, "Categorical Rights and Vulnerable Groups: Moving Away from the Universal Human Being", *The George Washington International Law Review*, vol. 48, no. 4 (2016): 717, 721. https://repository.uantwerpen.be/docman/iruaauth/1cfc2b/135079.pdf. Accessed November 16, 2024, citing P. Mertens, "Quel homme doit être pris en considération quant à la protection de ses droits?". In: *Parliamentary Conference on Human Right, Vienna, 18–20 October 1971* (Vienna: Council of Europe Consultative Assembly, 1972): 36–58.

21 See, e.g., the preamble of the International Convention on the Protection of the Rights of All Migrant Workers and Members of Their Families [2003] 2220 UNTS 39481; International Convention for the Protection of All Persons from Enforced Disappearance [2010] 2716 UNTS 3, 7.2(b).

22 World Conference on Human Rights, Provisional Agenda: Note by the Secretary-General [1993] § 11, A/CONF 157/1.

23 E.g., A.H.E. Morawa, "Vulnerability as a Concept of International Human Rights Law", *Journal of International Relations and Development*, vol. 6, no. 2 (2004): 139; A. Chapman, B. Carbonetti, "Human Rights Protections for Vulnerable and Disadvantaged Groups: The Contributions of the UN Committee on Economic, Social and Cultural Rights", *Human Rights Quarterly*, vol. 33, no. 3 (2011): 682. https://www.doi.org/10.1353/hrq.2011.0033; L. Peroni, A. Timmer, "Vulnerable Groups" 1056–1085; O.M. Arnardóttir, "Vulnerability Under Article 14 of the European Convention on Human Rights Innovation or Business as Usual?" 150–171; D. Estrada-Tanck, *Human Security and Human Rights Under International Law: The Protections Offered to Persons Confronting Structural Vulnerability* (Oxford: Hart, 2016).

Vulnerability is usually used without a definition and clear legal consequences, in the sense of its common meaning. However, theories have been developed explaining the meaning of the concept. Among legal scholars, there is tension between the universality-based and group-based deployments of vulnerability.[24] Whilst vulnerability is often applied to specific groups[25] – and in this understanding, it very much overlaps with religious minorities – others argue for a universal scope of vulnerability. Martha Fineman proposes to understand vulnerability as a "universal, inevitable, enduring aspect of the human condition".[26] Similarly, Bryan S. Turner approaches vulnerability as the foundation for universal human rights.[27] This seems to also be the underlying understanding among ECtHR judges. Peroni and Timmer found that the term "vulnerable groups" allows the ECtHR to address various aspects of inequality in a more substantive manner.[28] When the two scholars asked an ECtHR judge about the reasoning, he said, "All applicants are vulnerable, but some are more vulnerable than others".[29]

At the same time, *vulnerable* has also been used with regard to some specific groups. In her 2006 monograph, Elisabeth Reichert distinguished the following vulnerable groups: women, children, victims of racism, persons with disabilities, persons with HIV-AIDS, older persons, gays, and lesbians.[30] In 2014, Alexandra Timmer showed that the ECtHR identifies the following categories of persons as vulnerable: children and persons with mental disabilities, persons in detention, women in situations of domestic violence or precarious reproductive health, persons who are accused, persons who lack legal capacity, demonstrators and journalists, asylum seekers being detained or expelled, the Roma, and people with impaired health.[31] However, since the ECtHR has not developed a coherent set of indicators which would determine what makes a group vulnerable, it is not clear what ties all those groups together.[32] In 2013,

24 L. Peroni, A. Timmer, "Vulnerable Groups" 1060.

25 See, e.g., A. Chapman, B. Carbonetti, "Human Rights Protections for Vulnerable and Disadvantaged Groups" : 682–732, 922–923.

26 M. Albertson Fineman, "The Vulnerable Subject: Anchoring Equality in the Human Condition" 8.

27 B.S. Turner, *Vulnerability and Human Rights* (Pennsylvania: Pennsylvania State University Press, 2006): 6–9; for more theories, see C. Heri, *Responsive Human Rights* 26–28.

28 L. Peroni, A. Timmer, "Vulnerable Groups" 1057.

29 L. Peroni, A. Timmer, "Vulnerable Groups" 1060–1061.

30 E. Reichert, *Understanding Human Rights: An Exercise Book* (Thousand Oaks: Sage, 2006): 78–89.

31 A. Timmer, "A Quiet Revolution: Vulnerability in the European Court of Human Rights". In: M. Fineman, A. Grear (eds.), *Vulnerability: Reflections on a New Ethical Foundation for Law and Politics* (New York: Routledge, 2013): 152–61; see also M. Bossuyt, "Categorical Rights and Vulnerable Groups" 720.

32 L. Peroni, A. Timmer, "Vulnerable Groups" 1064.

Lourdes Peroni and Alexandra Timmer argued for the ECtHR to include religious minorities, national minorities and LGBT people in the ECtHR's vulnerable groups approach.[33] Oddný Mjöll Arnardóttir demonstrated in 2017 that the ECtHR has indeed subsequently broadened the application by including the LGBTI community and women who are victims of domestic violence, but not religious minorities.[34] In 2021, Aleksandra Gliszczyńska-Grabias and I found that the UN core human rights treaties and the UN treaty bodies have considered several groups to be vulnerable: pregnant women, minors, persons with disabilities, indigenous communities, victims of torture, the Roma, ethnic minorities in the context of ethnic conflict, persons of African descent, and unaccompanied child migrants.[35] At the same time, the UN treaty bodies apply the vulnerability in a way that is incidental and ambiguous in its construct and recall.[36] The categories proposed by scholars and applied by the ECtHR and UN treaty bodies differ, and the lists are not exhaustive. Whilst none of them includes religious minorities, this is one group that has been consistently mentioned in the scholarly literature which could fall under the notion of vulnerable groups.[37]

Vulnerability has already been widely applied in international human rights case law. References to "vulnerability" appear in 151 views of the UN treaty bodies. This occurs predominantly in cases concerning non-refoulement decisions, which is not surprising, as non-refoulement cases are the most common types of cases across all types of UN treaty bodies.[38] The first reference appeared in a decision issued by the Committee against Torture in 1999 and concerned attempts to prevent a person's deportation to Somalia (*S.S. Elmi v. Australia*).[39] As for the ECtHR, the word "vulnerability" appears in 640 judgements. The difference in the frequency of occurrence is inherently connected to the fact that UN treaty bodies receive significantly fewer applicants

33 L. Peroni, A. Timmer, "Vulnerable Groups" 1070.
34 O.M. Arnardóttir, "Vulnerability Under Article 14 of the European Convention on Human Rights Innovation or Business as Usual?" 168.
35 A. Gliszczyńska-Grabias, G. Baranowska, "The Concept of Vulnerability in the United Nations Human Rights Treaty Bodies Protection System" 33–34.
36 A. Gliszczyńska-Grabias, G. Baranowska, "The Concept of Vulnerability in the United Nations Human Rights Treaty Bodies Protection System" 32.
37 T. Hammarberg, *Human Rights in Europe: No Grounds for Complacency* (Strasbourg: Council of Europe Publishing, 2011): 36–43; L. Peroni, A. Timmer, "Vulnerable Groups" 1070.
38 B. Çalı, C. Costello, S. Cunningham, "Hard Protection Through Soft Courts? Non-Refoulement Before the United Nations Treaty Bodies", *German Law Journal*, vol. 21, no. 3 (2020): 355. https://doi.org/10.1017/glj.2020.28.
39 CAT, S.*S. Elmi v. Australia*, 129/1998 [1999].

than the ECtHR and thus also decide fewer cases.[40] The first[41] judgement in which the ECtHR applied the concept concerned the destruction of houses by Turkish military during military operations in the south-east (*Akdivar and others v. Turkey*).[42] The ECtHR's articulation of vulnerability was voiced in *Chapman v. The United Kingdom*:[43] belonging to a group whose vulnerability is partly created by wider societal, political, and institutional circumstances.[44] In the case law of the ECtHR, religious minorities are rarely mentioned when referencing vulnerability.[45] One of the instances when this does occur concerned cases brought by members from religious minorities who were discriminated against or attacked in their own countries of residence, which will be analysed in the next section.

3.4 Vulnerability of Members of Religious Minorities in Their Countries of Residence

Vulnerability has played a role in assessing the need to protect members of religious minorities living in their own countries of residence, from the actions of both state actors and private persons. For example, *Jaarey Suleymanova and Gulnaz Israfilova v. Azerbajian* was brought by members of Jehovah's witnesses against Azerbaijan. The applicants had been arrested, held by police, and convicted because of what the applicants argued was an informal conversation about religion and the state argued was an operation outside of the registered religious association. The Human Rights Committee found a

40 Additionally, as non-permanent bodies with fewer members and without the significant support the ECtHR judges have, the UN treaty bodies do not have the same capacities as the ECtHR. The decisions are significantly shorter than the judgements of regional human rights courts, which has been exacerbated with the adoption of the word limit within the so-called strengthening process – A. Seibert-Fohr, "Judicial Engagement in International Human Rights Comparativism". In: A. Reinisch, M.E. Footer, C. Binder (eds.), *International Law and...: Select Proceedings of the European Society of International Law* (Oxford: Hart, 2016): 175–181. https://doi.org/10.1163/26663236-bja10091.

41 The term was mentioned in several judgments before, but not in the deliberations of the court. Instead, it was citing the argumentation of the applicant (*Ashingdane v. The United Kingdom*, 8225/78 [1985] § 43, ECLI:CE:ECHR:1985:0528JUD000822578), separate opinion of a judge (*Nielsen v. Denmark*, 10929/84 [1988] ECLI:CE:ECHR:1988:1128JUD001092984), in domestic reports (*Bricmong v. Belgium*, 10857/84 [1989] § 44, ECLI:CE:ECHR:1989:0707JUD001085784) and proceedings before the Commission (*Tomasi v. France*, 12805/87 and 12850/87 [1992] ECLI:CE:ECHR:1992:0827JUD001285087; *Ribitsch v. Austria*, 18895/91 [1995] ECLI:CE:ECHR:1995:1204JUD001889691).

42 *Akdivar and others v. Turkey*, 21893/93 [1996] § 73, 105, ECLI:CE:ECHR:1996:0916JUD002189393.

43 *Chapman v. The United Kingdom*, 27238/95 [2001] ECLI:CE:ECHR:2001:0118JUD002723895.

44 L. Peroni, A. Timmer, "Vulnerable Groups" 1063.

45 See analysis by C. Heri, references to vulnerability under Article 3 ECHR as of 28 February 2019 – only 4% referenced religious minority, C. Heri, *Responsive Human Rights* 39.

violation of the Covenant and stated that the actions concerned "members of religious minorities who, by definition, were vulnerable to the majority".[46]

Religious minorities can also be vulnerable due to the actions of private actors. In *Milanović v. Serbia* (2010, ECtHR) a member of the Hare Krishna community in Serbia was assessed by the ECtHR to be a "member of a vulnerable religious minority". Milanović was one of the leading members in the Hare Krishna community and was subjected to a serious of physical attacks by unknown perpetrators. On three occasions, those attacks required hospital treatment. Although he reported the attacks to the police and insisted that they were religiously motivated hate crimes, the police carried out only a cursory investigation. The ECtHR found a violation of the ECHR and stated that it should have been obvious to the police that Milanović, "who was a member of vulnerable religious minority [...], was being systematically targeted and that future attacks were very likely to follow".[47] Similarly, in *Begheluri and Others v. Georgia*, the Court found that the applicants, who had been repeatedly attacked by private individuals due to their being Jehovah's witnesses, were in an extremely vulnerable situation and not sufficiently protected by state authorities.[48]

The analysis of case law revealed that there are relatively few instances where the concept of vulnerability has been applied to protect religious minorities in their countries of residence. When it is applied, it mostly pertains to violent attacks against members of these minorities. Traditional rights of religious minorities, such as access to education[49] or places of worship, have not triggered the application of the vulnerability lens. A likely explanation is that this has not been necessary, as human rights treaties and established case law already provide adequate protection for members of religious minorities in these areas.

46 HRC, *Jaarey Suleymanova and Gulnaz Israfilova v. Azerbajian*, 3061/2017 [2021] § 5.11, CCPR/C/133/D/3061/2017.

47 *Milanović v. Serbia*, 44614/07 [2010] § 89, ECLI:CE:ECHR:2010:1214JUD004461407.

48 *Begheluri and Others v. Georgia*, 28490/02 [2014] § 113, ECLI:CE:ECHR:2014:1007JUD002849002.

49 The only relevant case I identified, CRC, *A.B.A. and F.Z.A. and others v. Spain*, 114/2020, 116/2020, 117/2020 and 118/2020 [2022], concerned children in Melilla who, due to prolonged exclusion from the Spanish education system, had to attend a religious school and be educated in the Muslim religion. The Committee did not assess whether this violated freedom of religion because the applicants did not raise it in domestic proceedings and therefore did not exhaust domestic remedies (§ 9.3). It did find a violation of the Conventional rights based inter alia on their vulnerability and the serious consequences of their prolonged exclusion from the public education system (§ 10.9).

3.5 Vulnerability of Members of Religious Minorities in Non-refoulement Cases

Both the ECtHR and UN treaty bodies have considered belonging to a religious group in certain contexts as a factor which makes persons vulnerable if they are returned to their country of origin.[50] The ECtHR has stated that it has been its constant position that persons sought by Uzbek authorities on charges of religiously motived crimes constituted a vulnerable group who run a real risk of treatment contrary to the ECHR in the event of their transfer to Uzbekistan (e.g. *Eshonkulov v. Russia*).[51] The same has been stated with regard to transfers to Tajikistan (e.g. *B.U. and Others v. Russia*).[52] The vulnerability of the applicants did not directly stem from the fact that they are part of a religious group but from their being accused of religiously motivated crimes. The religious motivation of the crimes, however, was core in the assessment, as those sought for offences that are differently motivated are not protected as members of a vulnerable group.[53]

Additionally, in cases of conversion to another religion, which consequently renders the person a member of a vulnerable religious minority, this factor is considered in refoulment cases. *N.R. v. Sweden* was brought to the Committee against Torture by an asylum seeker of Afghani nationality and Hazara ethnicity who was raped by members of the Taliban as a child and converted to Christianity after arriving in Sweden. The applicant argued that those combined grounds created multiple vulnerability profiles.[54] The Committee against Torture assessed that the conversion – which led him to become a member of a religious minority – should have been considered by authorities when taking the decision on his return to Afghanistan.[55] In an earlier decision, *Q.A. v. Sweden*, the Human Rights Committee decided with regard to an Afghani asylum seeker who became an atheist after arriving in Sweden that he experienced "particular vulnerability related to his apostasy"[56] and highlighted his "intersection forms of vulnerability".[57] In *B.B. v. Sweden*, the asylum seeker

50 C. Heri, *Responsive Human Rights* 99 and 107.

51 *Eshonkulov v. Russia*, 68900/13 [2015] § 34, ECLI:CE:ECHR:2015:0115JUD006890013.

52 *B.U. and Others v. Russia*, 59609/17, 74677/17 and 76379/17 [2019] § 17; see also *Savriddin Dzhurayev v. Russia*, 71386/10 [2013].

53 See inadmissibility decision in *B.T. v. Russia*, 40755/16 [2017] § 28. However, persons charged for politically motivated crimes were also considered vulnerable.

54 CAT, Decision adopted by the Committee under article 22 of the Convention, concerning communication No. 1047/2021 [2023] § 3.5, CAT/C/78/D/1047/2021.

55 CAT, Decision adopted by the Committee under article 22 of the Convention, concerning communication No. 1047/2021 [2023] § 7.5.

56 HRC, Views adopted by the Committee under article 5 (4) of the Optional Protocol, concerning communication No. 3070/2017 [2020] § 9.2, CCPR/C/127/D/3070/2017.

57 HRC, Views adopted by the Committee under article 5 (4) of the Optional Protocol, concerning communication No. 3070/2017 [2020] § 9.6 and 9.7.

from Afghanistan had converted whilst in detention after his appeal to the asylum case was rejected. The state raised serious concerns as to the sincerity of his conversion. The Human Rights Committee assessed that regardless of the sincerity, "the test remains whether there are substantial grounds for believing that such a conversion may have sufficiently serious adverse consequences in the country of origin as to create a real risk of irreparable harm".[58] In another context, converting from Islam to Hinduism was also one of the factors contributing to the applicant's vulnerability, as considered by the Human Rights Committee (*M.Z.B.M. v. Denmark*).[59]

The real risk or irreparable harm, in violation of the respective human rights treaty, might also stem from private parties. In several cases concerning the return of Christians to Iraq, such as *N.A.N.S. v. Sweden*, the ECtHR had to assess whether individuals who form a vulnerable minority in the southern and central parts of Iraq can be returned to the country. The ECtHR found that the state authorities were generally unable to protect them, pointing to attacks on churches and violence towards Christians.[60] However, the ECtHR considered the return of the applicants to Iraq possible due to available internal relocation alternatives.[61]

Belonging to a vulnerable religious group does not automatically mean not being returned to one's country of origin; what needs to be assessed is the real risk or irreparable harm in violation of the respective human rights treaty. *J.I. v. Sweden* was brought by an Afghani national coming from a Christian family, who practiced their religion in secrecy at home. He found himself being able to join a Christian community in Sweden. Whilst the Human Rights Committee explicitly stated that Christian faith leads to particular vulnerability, it found that J.I. did not present sufficient grounds for demonstrating he would face a real and personal risk of treatment contrary to the Covenant when expelled to Afghanistan.[62] Human Rights Committee member Gentian Zyberi dissented from the majority and highlighted in his individual opinion the multifaced vulnerability, including belonging to the Christian faith.[63]

58 HRC, Views adopted by the Committee under the Optional Protocol, concerning communication No. 3069/2015 [2021] § 9.4.

59 HRC, *M.Z.B.M. v. Denmark*, 2593/2015 [2017] CCPR/C/119/D/2593/2015.

60 *N.A.N.S v. Sweden*, 68411/10 [2013] § 32, ECLI:CE:ECHR:2013:0627JUD006841110; *M.K.N. v. Sweden*, 72413/10 [2013] §§ 32–33, ECLI:CE:ECHR:2013:0627JUD007241310.

61 *N.A.N.S v. Sweden*, 68411/10 [2013] §§ 34–39; *M.K.N. v. Sweden*, 72413/10 [2013] §§ 35–40.

62 HRC, *J.I. v. Sweden*, 3032/2017 [2020] §§ 7.2 and 7.9, CCPR/C/128/D/3032/2017.

63 HRC, *J.I. v. Sweden*, 3032/2017 [2020] §§ 7.2 and 7.9, CCPR/C/128/D/3032/2017 – Individual Opinion of Committee Member Gentian Zyberi (dissenting), §§ 3–4.

The majority of cases in which the ECtHR and UN treaty bodies have applied the concept of vulnerability to religious minorities involve non-refoulement claims. Vulnerability can arise from the actions of both the state and private individuals. However, the focus of the assessment is not the vulnerability itself but rather the real risk of irreparable harm that would violate the relevant human rights treaty. The applicant must provide sufficient grounds to demonstrate this risk. Even when they do, if there are viable internal relocation alternatives available, the ECtHR has still permitted return.

3.6 Vulnerability to Discrimination or Pressure from One's Own Religious Group

The third identified group of cases concerns instances in which the vulnerability of the individual stemmed from discrimination or pressure from their own religious group. Those cases relate to two broader topics: discrimination and violence toward LGBTQ+ persons, as well as bans on religious clothing, particularly headscarves.

As for the first group, *O.M. v. Hungary* serves as an illustrative case.[64] O.M. was an asylum seeker who fled Iran due to criminal proceedings being instituted against him because of his homosexuality. He entered Hungary irregularly, without documents, and argued that it was the only way for him to enter the country, but he was detained for entering in this manner. In his application to the ECtHR, he argued that his detention following his arrival in Hungary was unjustified and in violation of the ECHR.[65] When assessing this, the ECtHR applied the vulnerability lens. According to the Court, the state authorities failed to consider whether vulnerable individuals – for example "LGBT people like the applicant" – were safe among other detained persons, "many of whom had come from countries with widespread cultural or religious prejudice against such persons".[66] In *M.K.H. v. Denmark*, the applicant applied a similar logic when bringing their case to the Human Rights Committee by arguing that the "vulnerability of his situation, which justifies his request for asylum, rests in his youth and the fact that homosexuality is a stigma in his society, family and *religion*" (emphasis added).[67]

In *O.M. v. Hungary*, the vulnerability was not caused by the Hungarian state authorities but by the community in which the individual was placed. The ECtHR assessed that in certain societies – in which O.M. was placed – there is a widespread cultural or religious prejudice against certain (vulnerable) persons. It further assessed that the state authorities need to consider whether such vulnerable persons are safe among people coming from such countries.

64 *O.M. v. Hungary*, 9912/15 [2016] ECLI:CE:ECHR:2016:0705JUD000991215.
65 *O.M. v. Hungary*, 9912/15 [2016] §§ 3, 8–9.
66 *O.M. v. Hungary*, 9912/15 [2016] § 53.
67 HRC, *M.K.H. v. Denmark*, 2462/2014 [2016] § 5.3, CCPR/C/117/D/2462/2014.

Of course, if a person flees their country because of their sexual orientation, placing them together with persons who might have homophobic attitudes leads to revictimisation and could expose the person to ill treatment. Thus, I agree with the ECtHR's conclusion and, more generally, the idea that states should always assess whether vulnerable individuals are safe among other detainees. At the same time, in this particular case, the assessment raises some questions. The judgement does not contain an analysis of whether the persons with whom the applicant was detained indeed came from countries "with widespread cultural or religious prejudice against" LGBT persons. I would argue that if a person fled a country because they were prosecuted for their sexuality, it can be assumed that this person should not be sheltered together with other persons from their own country. However, I would have doubts whether that can automatically be extended to persons having fled other countries as well. In *O.M. v. Hungary*, the ECtHR appears to be treating all refugee seekers in Hungary as coming from places with "widespread cultural or religious prejudice against" LGBT. This does not need to be the case. As homophobia and cultural or religious prejudice against LGBT persons are also present in Council of Europe countries,[68] such an assessment with regard to all refugee seekers is patronising.

The second group of cases concerns bans on wearing religious clothing. Before analysing how the ECtHR and UN treaty bodies have applied vulnerability in those cases, it is worth pointing out that the ECtHR and the Human Rights Committee have taken contrasting approaches to such bans. Without going into the details, the ECtHR finds that the bans do not violate the ECHR,[69] whilst the Human Rights Committee finds that they violate the Covenant.[70] Most of those cases concern persons who are a religious minority

68 For in-depth analysis of homophobia in the EU states (all of which are part of the Council of Europe system), see "Homophobia and Discrimination on Grounds of Sexual Orientation in the EU Member States Part I – Legal Analysis". https://fra.europa.eu/en/publication/2010/homophobia-and-discrimination-grounds-sexual-orientation-eu-member-states-part-i. Accessed November 16, 2024.

69 See, e.g., *Dahlab v. Switzerland*, 42393/98 [2001] ECLI:CE:ECHR:2001:0215DEC004239398; *Leyla Şahin v. Turkey*, 44774/98 [2005] ECLI:CE:ECHR:2005:1110JUD004477498; *S.A.S. v. France*, 43835/11 [2014] ECLI:CE:ECHR:2014:0701JUD004383511; see also E. Brems, "Hidden Under Headscarves? Women and Religion in the Case Law of the European Court of Human Rights", *Religion & Human Rights*, vol. 16, no. 2–3 (2021): 173. https://orcid.org/0000-0001-7712-4827; E. Brems, "Islamophobia and the ECtHR: A Test Case for Positive Subsidiarity for the Protection of Europe's Long-Term Migrants?". In: B. Çalı, L. Bianku, I. Motoc (eds.), *Migration and the European Convention on Human Rights* (Oxford: Oxford University Press, 2021): 196–216.

70 HRC, *Hudoyberganova v. Uzbekistan*, 931/2000 [2004] CCPR/C/82/D/931/2000; HRC, *Ranjit Singh v. France*, 1876/2009 [2011] CCPR/C/102/D/1876/2009; HRC, *Mann Singh v. France*, 1938/2010 [2013] CCPR/C/108/D/1928/2010; *Miriana Hebbadj v. France*, 2807/2016 [2018] CCPR/C/123/D/2807/2016.

in the country that has introduced the ban.[71] By analysing the relevant case law of the ECtHR and Human Rights Committee, one notices a striking difference in how the vulnerability is being applied in those cases. In the case of hijab bans, which the ECtHR found to not violate the ECHR, the Court considered women to be vulnerable to being pressurised into wearing hijabs.[72] By contrast, in their concurring opinion to two cases concerning bans on wearing religious clothing, *Miriana Hebbadj v. France* and *Sonia Yakar v. France*, Human Rights Committee members Ilze Brands Kehris and Sarah Cleveland raised the inherent vulnerability to negative stereotyping of members of a minority.[73] Thus, in both cases, the members of the religious minority who were affected by the ban were assessed as vulnerable, though in very different ways: in the ECtHR case, it was because of the pressure stemming from their own community, forcing them to wear the religious clothing, and in the second case, the Human Rights Committee members did so because of the inherent vulnerability as minority members. Firstly, this example shows that vulnerability can be applied in a contrasting manner, also because it is used without a definition and clear legal consequences. Secondly – and this connects the bans on wearing religious clothing back to *O.M. v. Hungary* – vulnerability can be applied in a patronising way, by assuming that all women wearing a hijab need protection from their own community. Just as it cannot be ruled out that certain asylum seekers are homophobic, it cannot be ruled out that some women are forced into wearing a hijab. However, applying this assumption to all becomes a very different approach. In my opinion, this is even more problematic when such assumptions are applied with regard to members of a religious minority, as it may strengthen existing negative stereotypes about the minority.

That being said, acknowledging that the vulnerability of a member of a religious minority can potentially stem from the group itself can be an extremely useful concept, which can eventually strengthen individual rights. Such an assessment could, for example, be applied to women being forced to wear religious clothing or to children being forced to participate in religious education that is of lower quality than secular education. In each such case, it would need to be assessed in-depth whether indeed there is such a vulnerability. For example, if the case is brought by a woman who wishes to wear the

71 See, e.g., *Dahlab v. Switzerland*, 42393/98 [2001]; HRC, *Ranjit Singh v. France*, 1876/2009 [2011]; HRC, *Mann Singh v. France*, 1938/2010 [2013]; and *Miriana Hebbadj v. France*, 2807/2016 [2018]. For cases brought with regard to states, in which the religion is a majority religion, see, e.g., *Leyla Şahin v. Turkey*, 44774/98 [2005] and HRC, *Hudoyberganova v. Uzbekistan*, 931/2000 [2004].

72 C. Heri, *Responsive Human Rights* 227.

73 *Miriana Hebbadj v. France*, 2807/2016 [2018], Annex II, Joint Opinion of Committee Members I. Brands Kehris and S. Cleveland (concurring) § 4; HRC, *Sonia Yakar v. France*, 2747/2016 [2018] CCPR/C/123/D/2747/2016, Annex II, Joint Opinion of Committee Members I.B. Kehris and S. Cleveland (concurring) § 4.

religious clothing but is banned from doing so by the state, such a vulnerability is rather less likely. Applying vulnerability could elucidate how rights granted to religious minorities (such as religious education) affect individuals and their human rights.

3.7 Conclusions

The aim of this chapter was to assess, first, how the concept of vulnerability has been applied to religious minorities, and second, what added value the vulnerability lens brings to the existing protection of religious minorities in international human rights law. Overall, I found that the concept of vulnerability is rarely applied to religious minorities. Three groups of circumstances where this occurs were identified in the chapter: in relation to their situation in their country of origin, in the context of non-refoulement cases, and when assessing discrimination or pressure from within their own religious group. The potential added value is particularly evident in the last group.

Whilst the aim of the chapter was not to compare the case law of the ECtHR and UN treaty bodies, it is worth noting that these human rights bodies largely did not differ in applying the vulnerability concept.[74] They also seem to be aware that the concept is applied in a very similar way. For example, in *G.J. v. Spain*, the Committee against Torture explicitly stated that the ECtHR carried out a detailed examination of the applicant's alleged vulnerability and decided the case to be inadmissible.[75] It follows from this statement that in the assessment of the Committee against Torture, there is no difference in its own and the ECtHR's examination of vulnerability.

Regarding the first group of cases, which concerns the protection of religious minorities in their countries of residence, vulnerability has been applied only in very rare instances. When it is applied, it mostly involves violent attacks against individuals from a religious minority. Traditional rights of religious minorities, such as access to education or places of worship, have not triggered the application of the vulnerability lens. This may be explained by the fact that human rights treaties and established case law already provide sufficient protection for religious minorities in these situations, making it unnecessary to additionally invoke the concept of vulnerability.

The second group consists of non-refoulement cases, which make up the majority of cases involving religious minorities where the concept of vulnerability has been applied. Whilst religious minorities are generally seen as vulnerable groups, this does not automatically trigger the application of the non-refoulement principle. In each case, the applicant must present sufficient evidence of a real risk or irreparable harm, in violation of the relevant human rights treaty. Being part of a vulnerable religious group increases the likelihood of such grounds, but it is important to note that in several of the cases analysed

74 The only considerable difference concerned the bans on religious clothing.

75 CAT, *G.J. v. Spain*, 839/2017 [2021] § 6.2, CAT/C/71/D/839/2017.

herein, members of persecuted religious groups were not found to be protected by the non-refoulement principle.

The third group of cases involves members of religious minorities who have been found to be vulnerable due to discrimination or pressure from their own religious groups. Whilst assessing this situation can be problematic, as I explained in Section 3.6, it can certainly provide added value for the protection of individuals. The few existing cases suggest that states may need to protect vulnerable individuals from "cultural or religious prejudice", including that which may arise from religious minorities.

Finally, it is problematic that the legal concept of vulnerability exists without definitional contours. It can lead, and has led, to the concept being used in contradictory ways: the women affected by the hijab bans were perceived to be vulnerable by both the ECtHR (finding that the ban has not violated their human rights) and the Human Rights Committee (coming to the opposite conclusion). The ECtHR considered the women vulnerable because of the pressure to wear religious clothing, whilst the Human Rights Committee did so because of their inherent vulnerability as minority members.

Part II

Duty of Religious Neutrality and Impartiality

4 Free Speech and Religious Sensitivity

Between Today's State-Sponsored SLAPPing and Careful Balancing of Competing Interests

Marcin Górski

Abstract

Religion-related expressions are a natural field for strategic lawsuits against public participation (SLAPPs) to blossom in, because religious belief is a unique emotional experience which exists beyond the sphere of rationality. The less a given state is founded upon laicism (or at least religious neutrality), the more likely are SLAPPs aimed at protecting religious sensitivity, including state-sponsored anti-blasphemy lawsuits.

In the United States, although no federal anti-SLAPP law has been adopted to date, states have passed a variety of laws aimed at preventing SLAPPs. Since the US Supreme Court held anti-blasphemy laws incompatible with the free speech clause of the First Amendment in the 1952 "Miracle" decision, there seems to be no significant threat of religiously motivated SLAPPs threatening free speech in America. In Europe, the European Court of Human Rights (ECtHR) generally accepts the so-called margin of appreciation applicable to balancing freedom of expression and religious sentiments. Nevertheless, throughout the decades, the Strasbourg case law reveals a tendency to tolerate only those justifications for interference which invoke the need to sustain social stability.

This paper analyses the case law of both the US Supreme Court and the ECtHR pertaining to the balancing of religious sensitivities and freedom of expression. This issue, which some considered to have long been buried six feet underground, seems to have been reborn with new force – for example, in the face of public emotions caused by Hamas' attack on Israel in October 2023 and the Israeli government's reaction to these atrocities. "Cancel culture" is spreading, and religious excitement has erupted with great force.

DOI: 10.4324/9781003423294-7

Keywords

freedom of speech; freedom of expression; religious sensitivity; blasphemy; LAPP; anti-blasphemy laws; ECHR; First Amendment; hate speech; fighting words

The available statistics show that approximately 40% of states worldwide have anti-blasphemy laws.[1] Their characters and interpretations of course vary. Sometimes, anti-blasphemous legislation is used to protect the objects of religious worship themselves; in other cases, its goal can be to protect the religious sentiments of believers, and at still other times, the aim is rather to preserve social order or to protect against the spread of hatred whilst protecting the sensitivity resulting from transcendental experiences.

Balancing competing interests has proved to be particularly troublesome recently, as shown by the difficulties experienced by Ivy League college presidents when confronted with the seemingly simple question of what response should be expected to anti-Semitism being spread on American universities under the guise of criticising the Israeli response to Hamas crimes. It is worth remembering that this reaction has a deeper basis resulting from the historically rooted belief among Israelis (and the international Jewish community) of a constant threat to Israel's statehood as well as to the physical existence of its citizens, which results from anti-Semitic prejudices shared by many Muslim believers. The validity of this belief is, of course, an issue that can be debated, but recent events demonstrate the relevance of balancing the protection of religious sensitivity and freedom of speech.

Invoking the protection of "religious sensitivity" is also a well-known element of argumentation employed in a strategic lawsuit against public participation (SLAPP). One can distinguish those SLAPPs which are the activity of individuals and/or their organisations from those which in fact constitute an element of state policies aimed at creating a chilling effect on free public discourse in matters concerning not even the religions themselves but rather their impact on government policies. The significance of the problem can be illustrated by legislative developments whose ambition is to address the challenge of SLAPPs. The European Union (EU) adopted[2] the anti-SLAPP Directive,[3] which represents significant progress, although somewhat delayed if compared

1 Virginia Villa, "Four-in-ten countries and territories worldwide had blasphemy laws in 2019", [https://www.pewresearch.org/short-reads/2022/01/25/four-in-ten-countries-and-territories-worldwide-had-blasphemy-laws-in-2019-2/] accessed September 5, 2023.

2 The agreement of the EU institutions needed for the adoption of the anti-SLAPP directive was reached at the end of 2023 – see L. Arato, "EU Institutions Reach Deal on Anti-SLAPP Law Protecting Journalists & Other Critical Voices", November 30, 2023. https://www.euronews.com/my-europe/2023/11/30/eu-institutions-reach-deal-on-anti-slapp-law-protecting-journalists-other-critical-voices. Accessed December 5, 2023.

3 Directive (EU) 2024/1069 of the European Parliament and of the Council of April 11, 2024, on protecting persons who engage in public participation from manifestly unfounded claims or abusive court proceedings ('Strategic lawsuits against public participation'), OJ L 1069, April 16, 2024.

to the USA, where the majority of states and the federal district have adopted anti-SLAPP laws.[4] However, it is much more troublesome to negotiate and adopt an anti-SLAPP measure at the EU level taking into account its nature as a very specific, yet still international organisation, with a complicated decision-making process and competence-related constraints. Generally, awareness of the problem of SLAPPs is also growing outside the United States and Europe, and the phenomenon is being identified and counteracted more and more often in various jurisdictions.[5]

Recent Polish practice has provided for many examples of SLAPPing, e.g. criminal charges (brought by the public prosecution led by a politician – the minister of justice) of "offending religious feelings" leading to convictions that are then challenged before the European Court of Human Rights (ECtHR),[6] and the publicly funded, religiously fundamentalist non-governmental organisation (NGO) Ordo Iuris actively engaging in or even inspiring litigation concerning – according to the plaintiffs – the protection of religious freedoms or religious (Roman Catholic) sensitivity.[7] Although officially not labelled as relating to any religious matters, a defamation lawsuit against two renowned Holocaust historians, Professors Barbara Engelking and Jan Grabowski, concerning their book *Night Without End* was aimed at proving the alleged "historical truth" about "good Catholic Poles helping the ungrateful (both

4 See Reporters Committee for Freedom of the Press, "Anti-SLAPP Legal Guide". https://www.rcfp.org/anti-slapp-legal-guide. Accessed December 5, 2023. See also E. Brander, J.L. Turk, *Global Anti-SLAPP Ratings: Assessing the Strength of Anti-SLAPP Laws*, March 23, 2023 (Toronto: Centre for Free Expression Toronto Metropolitan University, 2023). https://cfe.torontomu.ca/publications/global-anti-slapp-ratings-assessing-strength-anti-slapp-laws. Accessed December 5, 2023.

5 See, e.g., the *OOO Memo v. Russia*, No. 2840/10 [2022] § 43, ECLI:CE:ECHR:2022:0315JUD000284010 where the Strasbourg Court noted "growing awareness of the risks that court proceedings instituted with a view to limiting public participation bring for democracy", or the *Palacio Urrutia et al. v. Ecuador*, No. 13.015 [2021], I/A Court H.R. Report, Serie C, No. 446 § 95, where the San José Court held that "the recurrence of public officials resorting to judicial channels to file lawsuits for crimes of slander or insult, not with the objective of obtaining a rectification but to silence the criticisms made regarding their actions in the public sphere, constitutes a threat to freedom of expression. This type of process, known as 'SLAPP' [...] constitutes an abusive use of judicial mechanisms that must be regulated and controlled by the States, with the aim of allowing effective exercise of freedom of expression".

6 *Rabczewska v. Poland*, No. 8257/13 [2022] § 62, ECLI:CE:ECHR:2022:0915JUD000825713.

7 A. Curanović, "The International Activity of Ordo Iuris: The Central European Actor and the Global Christian Rights" *Religions*, vol. 12 (2021): 1038–1057. https://doi.org/10.3390/rel12121038.

ethnically and religiously different) Jews".[8] Such problems also occur to varying degrees in many other jurisdictions, as illustrated by the ECtHR or national courts' judgements – e.g. in Russia,[9] Azerbaijan,[10] Lithuania,[11] or Georgia[12] – as well as outside of Europe, e.g. in India,[13] Nigeria[14] or Indonesia.[15]

Courts of different jurisdictions and international judicial bodies are confronted with the extremely delicate task of balancing freedom of expression (speech) and the right to the protection of "religious sensitivity" (or rather, the public interest in maintaining social order and protecting it from religion-triggered turmoil) in such a way as to not stifle free public debate on matters concerning religion. The significant portion of risks posed by SLAPPs affects precisely the freedom of debate on matters concerning religion. Statements concerning religious matters often evoke a strong emotional reaction because experiencing the transcendent takes place on an emotional, rather than a rational, level.

Also, the very fast technological developments resulting in the emerging "culture of participation" (i.e. the environment of information and ideas where individuals not only receive but also impart content) may result in the dissemination of hate speech targeting religious groups. As the Strasbourg's Court Grand Chamber rightly remarked in *Delfi AS v. Estonia*,

8 For more on the Engelking and Grabowski SLAPP lawsuit, See, e.g., A. Wójcik, "Historians on Trial", March 11, 2021. https://verfassungsblog.de/historians-on-trial/. Accessed December 6, 2023; L. Kinstler, "The Right to a History Without Lies", March 22, 2021. https://jewishcurrents.org/the-right-to-a-history-without-lies. Accessed December 6, 2023; E.-C. Pettai, K. Stoll, R. Utz, I. Kertész, J. Kolleg, 'A Ruling Against Survivors – Aleksandra Gliszczyńska-Grabias about the Trial of Two Polish Holocaust Scholars', March 8, 2021. https://www.cultures-of-history.uni-jena.de/politics/gliszczynska-grabias-about-the-trial-of-two-polish-holocaust-scholars. Accessed December 6, 2023.

9 *Mariya Alekhina and others v. Russia*, No. 38004/12 [2018], ECLI:CE:ECHR:2018:0717JUD003800412.

10 *Tagiyev and Huseynov v. Azerbaijan*, No. 13274/08 [2019], ECLI:CE:ECHR:2019:1205JUD001327408.

11 *Sekmadienis Ltd. v. Lithuania*, No. 69317/14 [2018], ECLI:CE:ECHR:2018:0130JUD006931714.

12 *Gachechiladze v. Georgia*, No. 2591/19 [2021], ECLI:CE:ECHR:2021:0722JUD000259119.

13 Supreme Court of India, *Tuljapurkar v. State of Maharashtra & Ors.*, Criminal Appeal No. 1179/2010 [2015] https://main.sci.gov.in/judgment/judis/42692.pdf. Accessed September 1, 2024.

14 Kano State High Court of Justice (Nigeria), *State v. Muhammad Mubarak Bala*, No. K/89C/2021 [2022]. https://globalfreedomofexpression.columbia.edu/wp-content/uploads/2023/09/MUBARAK-BALAS-JUDGMENT.pdf. Accessed September 1, 2024. The defendant was sentenced (in the first instance) to 24 years' imprisonment for alleged blasphemy.

15 North Jakarta District Court (Indonesia), *Public Prosecutor v. Basuki Tjahaja Purnama aka "Ahok"* [2017]. The defendant was sentenced (in the first instance) to two years' imprisonment for blasphemy. See Global Freedom of Expression Columbia University, "Public Prosecutor v. Basuki Tjahaja Purnama aka «Ahok»". https://globalfreedomofexpression.columbia.edu/cases/public-prosecutor-v-basuki-tjahaja-purnama-aka-ahok/. Accessed September 1, 2024.

> [U]ser-generated expressive activity on the Internet provides an unprecedented platform for the exercise of freedom of expression. That is undisputed and has been recognised by the Court on previous occasions [...]. However, alongside these benefits, certain dangers may also arise. Defamatory and other types of clearly unlawful speech, including hate speech and speech inciting violence, can be disseminated like never before, worldwide, in a matter of seconds, and sometimes remain persistently available online.[16]

Although a state's action to protect religious groups from violent intimidation may in principle be legitimate – since otherwise our increasingly culturally and religiously mixed societies could be confronted with riots and acts of violence – it may also lead to state-sponsored SLAPPing against minority groups or simply unpopular views on religious dogmas. The purpose of this chapter is to examine how national and international courts deciding cases allegedly constituting SLAPPs (or legal harassment) use concepts such as hate speech/fighting words, blasphemy/defamation of religion or religious sensitivity, and the "right not to be offended", and how they balance the right to free speech against the right to be protected against gratuitous and serious harm motivated by religious considerations. The chapter will also recommend some (already developed) standards that can be used to minimise the impact of SLAPPs on the freedom of debate on religious matters.

4.1 How the Term "SLAPP" Is Construed in this Chapter

The concept of a SLAPP was identified by Penelope Canan and George W. Pring. In their 1988 paper they wrote,

> Nevertheless, every year in the United States, hundreds, perhaps thousands, of civil lawsuits are filed that are aimed at preventing citizens from exercising their political rights or punishing those who have done so. [...] We call these cases "strategic lawsuits against public participation" or SLAPPs: attempts to use civil tort action to stifle political expression. It is this political retaliation, through the law, that distinguishes SLAPPs from the commonly observed intimidation and retaliation in litigation between commercial competitors, business partners, labor and management, and regulatory agencies and licensees. Strategic lawsuits against public participation claim injury from citizen efforts to influence a government body or the electorate on an issue of public significance.[17]

16 *Delfi AS v. Estonia*, No. 64569/09 [2015] § 110, ECLI:CE:ECHR:2015:0616JUD006456909.

17 P. Canan, G.W. Pring, "Strategic Lawsuits Against Public Participation" *Social Problems*, vol. 35, no. 5 (1998): 506, 506–507 (emphasis added).

After this paper, they published a number of works focussed on SLAPPs[18] and ignited a nationwide debate on using civil lawsuits to silence public discourse. As noted by Roy L. Moore et al., "the SLAPP plaintiff does not feel defamed but rather seeks to silence critics and control public opinion about a particular issue".[19] Byron Sheldrick wrote in his book on SLAPPs in Canada that

> [w]hat all of the cases have in common, regardless of their form, is that they take place within a context of political contestation. The lawsuit, while alleging a civil claim based in common law, is a strategy within a broader political dispute. The purpose is often to put activists on the defensive, redirect their energies and resources to a costly legal battle.[20]

Thus, in the original American perception, SLAPPs are civil litigations aimed at silencing activist (essentially political) criticism and discourse. However, outside the USA the concept of SLAPPs tends to be understood more inclusively, as it were, i.e. as also extending to non-civil proceedings intended to intimidate and exhaust one's opponent, including criminal and even administrative actions, as well as to dimensions other than political activism.[21] Religious harassment, as interestingly noted by Eugene Volokh, may be both offending someone from religious positions and offending someone because of his religion.[22]

18 See, e.g., P. Canan, G.W. Pring, "Strategic Lawsuits Against Public Participation: An Introduction for Bench, Bar and Bystanders" *Bridgeport Law Review Quinnipiac College*, vol. 12, no. 4 (1992): 937; P. Canan, G.W. Pring, "Studying Strategic Lawsuits against Public Participation: Mixing Quantitative and Qualitative Approaches" *Law & Society Review*, vol. 22, no. 2 (1988): 385; G.W. Pring, "SLAPPs: Strategic Lawsuits Against Public Participation" *Pace Environmental Law Review*, vol. 7, no. 1 (1989) 3. https://digitalcommons.pace.edu/cgi/viewcontent.cgi?article=1535&context=pelr. Accessed September 1, 2024.

19 R.L. Moore, M.D. Murray, K.-H. Youm, *Media Law and Ethics* (New York: Routledge, 2021): 152.

20 B. Sheldrick, *Blocking Public Participation: The Use of Strategic Litigation to Silence Political Expression*, (Waterloo: Wilfrid Laurier University Press, 2014): 2.

21 See, e.g., Z. Emmamally, "Slapping Down SLAPP Suits in South Africa: The Need for Legislative Protection and Civil Society Action" *South African Law Journal*, vol. 139, no. 1 (2022): 1. https://hdl.handle.net/10520/ejc-jlc_salj_v139_n1_a1. Accessed September 1, 2024; or J. Bayer, P. Bárd, L. Vosyliute, N. Chun Luk, *Strategic Lawsuits Against Public Participation (SLAPP) in the European Union: A Comparative Study, v. 3*, June 30, 2021 (Brussels: Academic Network on European Citizenship Rights, 2021). https://commission.europa.eu/system/files/2022-04/slapp_comparative_study_0.pdf. Accessed November 29, 2023; or *Environmental rule of law and human rights in Asia Pacific: Strategic litigation against public participation (SLAPPs): Summary for Decision Makers* (Nairobi: UN Environment Programme, 2023). https://wedocs.unep.org/bitstream/handle/20.500.11822/43137/litigation_public_participation_SLAPPS.pdf. Accessed November 29, 2023.

22 E. Volokh, "Freedom of Speech, Religious Harassment Law, and Religious Accommodation Law" *Loyola University Chicago Law Journal*, vol. 33 (2002): 58–59.

In this chapter, we shall assume this broader definition of SLAPPs as any type of judicial proceedings, be it civil or criminal, that are intended to intimidate criticism directed against religious dogmas, figures, policies, and institutions. In this sense, the concept of SLAPPs reaches beyond the original context of civil lawsuits, extending likewise to other types of legal harassment.[23] However, we shall concentrate on the use of legal tools by public authorities to legally harass minority voices concerning religious matters.

4.2 Anti-blasphemy Laws and Their Contemporary Mutations

Anti-blasphemy laws, although still present in many jurisdictions, have changed over time. As noted by Nicholas Hatzis,

> Historically, the customary response to profane speech has been to silence the speaker through the application of blasphemy laws. Contemporary practice in Western democracies has changed in many respects and the most severe of those laws have been repealed; however, versions of blasphemy prohibitions remain common. Although this new generation of modernized blasphemy laws display some of the characteristics of their predecessors, a notable difference is that they no longer aim to protect only the established religion (where it exists) or the religion of the majority of the population; they are drafted in general terms and apply irrespective of the religious belief which is targeted by the criticism. An offshoot of blasphemy is the more recent concept of "defamation of religion", particularly present in international law. Because blasphemy has developed a bad name for itself as an instrument for the persecution of dissidents, its proponents describe the revamped blasphemy offences in different words, perhaps in an attempt to make them look more anodyne. Defamation of religion is such an attempt to rename blasphemy.[24]

23 See the discussions on legal harassment understood this way (i.e. SLAPP-like judicial proceedings extending beyond the civil lawsuit context) e.g. in OSCE, *Special Report on the Fifth Roundtable of the Safety of Journalists Project: Legal Harassment*, FOM.GAL/14/23, August 4, 2023. https://www.osce.org/files/f/documents/e/8/550009.pdf. Accessed December 2, 2023, or in a religious context in P. Côté, "Rule of Law and Religious Minorities: A Case Study of Jehovah's Witnesses" *Review of Faith & International Affairs, vol. 5, no. 3 (2007)*: 11–16. https://doi.org/10.1080/15570274.2007.9523297.

24 N. Hatzis, *Offensive Speech, Religion and the Limits of Law*, (Oxford: OUP, 2021): 115. https://doi.org/10.1093/oso/9780198758440.001.0001.

Anti-defamation-of-religion laws (originally known as anti-blasphemy) are still in force in about half of the European states,[25] though they can be grouped into those whose predominant goal is the protection of public order,[26] those whose predominant goal is the protection of a denomination and its symbols as such,[27] those whose predominant goal is the protection of "religious feelings",[28] and, finally, those whose aim is simply to penalise blasphemy.[29] In another classification (by Cristiana Cianitto), they can be divided into those which protect the religion per se (its dogmas or symbols) and those which protect people (either more individually or more collectively) who profess a religion. Surprisingly enough, she classified many more or less democratic

25 End Blasphemy Law, *Europe*. https://end-blasphemy-laws.org/countries/europe/. Accessed December 4, 2023.

26 Such as in Germany, where Article 166(1) of the Penal Code (Strafgesetzbuch, BGBl. I S. 3322 with amendments, https://www.gesetze-im-internet.de/englisch_stgb/englisch_stgb.html. Accessed December 4, 2023) provides that "[w]hoever publicly or by disseminating content (section 11 (3)) reviles the religion or ideology of others in a manner suited to causing a disturbance of the public peace incurs a penalty of imprisonment for a term not exceeding three years or a fine" (emphasis added). A similar provision is included in Article 216(3) of the Turkish Penal Code (Türk Ceza Kanunu, Resmî Gazete Sayısı No. 25611): "A person who publicly degrades the religious values of a section of the public shall be sentenced to a penalty of imprisonment for a term of six months to one year, where the act is capable of disturbing public peace". However, the latter provision has been criticised by the Venice Commission as overbroad, vague and likely to be extensively applied (see European Commission on Democracy Through Law – Venice Commission, *Opinion on Articles 216, 299, 301 and 314 of the Penal Code of Turkey* adopted by the Venice Commission at its 106th Plenary Session, Venice, March 11–12, 2016, 9–13. https://www.venice.coe.int/webforms/documents/default.aspx?pdffile=CDL-AD(2016)002-e. Accessed December 4, 2023.

27 For instance, the Italian Penal Code (Codice Penale, Testo del Regio Decreto No. 1398, October 19, 1930, with amendments) penalises public offences to religious confessions in Article 403, which reads that "[w]hoever publicly offends a religious confession, through contempt of those who professes it, is punished with a fine", as well as public vilification of items of religious worship in Article 404: "Anyone, in a place intended for worship, or in a public place or open to the public, offending a religious confession, vilifies with abusive expressions items that form objects of worship, or are consecrated to worship, or are necessarily intended for exercise of worship […] is punished with a fine".

28 For example, Article 196 of the Polish Penal Code (Kodeks karny, Dziennik Ustaw 1997 No 8, item 553 with amendments) provides that "[w]hoever offends the religious feelings of others by publicly insulting an object of religious worship or a place intended for public performance of religious rituals shall be subject to a fine, restriction of liberty or deprivation of liberty up to two years".

29 E.g., the Greek Penal Code (Ποινικός κώδικας. https://www.ministryofjustice.gr/wp-content/uploads/2019/10/%CE%A0%CE%BF%CE%B9%CE%BD%CE%B9%CE%BA%CF%8C%CF%82-%CE%9A%CF%8E%CE%B4%CE%B9%CE%BA%CE%B1%CF%82.pdf. Accessed December 4, 2023), which provides in Article 198 that "[w]hoever publicly and maliciously and by any means blasphemes God shall be punished by imprisonment for not more than two years".

states (namely Austria, Denmark, Finland, Greece, Italy, Ireland, Netherlands, San Marino, Lichtenstein, Israel, and Turkey) as having anti-blasphemy laws.[30]

Even though anti-blasphemy laws are believed by some to be compatible in the United States with the free speech clause of the First Amendment[31] and the world is still full of different anti-blasphemy (a.k.a. anti-defamation-of-religion) laws,[32] the fact remains that since the New York Supreme Court's approval for anti-blasphemy prosecutions in *People v. Ruggles*,[33] the attitude to anti-blasphemy laws has generally changed not only in the USA but also in the Western hemisphere in general. The prevailing view is that prosecuting blasphemy is not permissible from a free speech perspective, whereas different forms of sustaining religious peace can be acceptable.

4.3 US Perspective – Tolerating Blasphemy as Free Speech and Outlawing "Fighting Words"

Anti-blasphemy laws originally also existed in the USA, as a part of the English common law heritage, which was "transplanted to America"[34] (and Americans' own choices), as Sarah Barringer Gordon remarked[35]). The last person in the USA convicted of blasphemy was Abner Kneeland, whose conviction was upheld by the Massachusetts Supreme Judicial Court in 1838.[36] At the beginning of the 19th century, a court sentenced a certain Mr Chandler for holding that "the virgin Mary was a whore, and Jesus Christ was a bastard".[37]

However, in 1952, the Supreme Court ruled in *Burstyn v. Wilson* (the "Miracle" decision), a case concerning the prior licensing of a "sacrilegious" motion picture, that "from the standpoint of freedom of speech and the press, it is enough to point out that the state has no legitimate interest in protecting any or all religions from views distasteful to them which is sufficient to justify

30 C. Cianitto, "Freedom of expression and freedom of religion: Drawing the lines between hate speech, blasphemy and free speech". In: M.C. Green, T.J. Gunn, M. Hill (eds.), *Religion, Law and Security in Africa* (Stellenbosch: African Sun Media, 2018): 80, 84–88.

31 T. Dobbs, "Blasphemy and the Original Meaning of the First Amendment" *Harvard Law Review*, vol. 135, no. 2 (2021): 689, 690, where the author suggests that "none of the constitutional clauses currently thought to make anti-blasphemy laws unconstitutional – Free Exercise, Free Speech, Establishment – originally prohibited blasphemy prosecutions".

32 See J. Fiss, J. Getgen Kestenbaum, *Respecting Rights? Measuring the World's Blasphemy Laws* (Washington, D.C.: U.S. Commission on International Religious Freedom, 2017) https://www.uscirf.gov/sites/default/files/Blasphemy%20Laws%20Report.pdf. Accessed December 2, 2023.

33 *People v. Ruggles* [1811], 8 Johns. R. 290 (N.Y.).

34 For a historical overview, see J.K. Houser, "Is Hate Speech Becoming the New Blasphemy? Lessons from an American Constitutional Dialectic" *Dickinson Law Review*, vol. 144, no. 2 (2009): 571, 575–592. https://ideas.dickinsonlaw.psu.edu/dlra/vol114/iss2/6/pr. Accessed September 1, 2024.

35 S. Barringer Gordon, "Blasphemy and the Law of Religious Liberty in Nineteenth-Century America" *American Quarterly*, vol. 52, no. 4 (2000): 682–719.

36 *Commonwealth v. Kneeland* [1838] 37 Mass. 206.

37 *State v. Chandler* [1837], 2 Del. Gen. Sess. 553.

prior restraints upon the expression of those views. It is not the business of government in our nation to suppress real or imagined attacks upon a particular religious doctrine".[38] Since the *Burstyn* decision, prosecuting allegedly blasphemous speech has become incompatible with the First Amendment (and the Fourteenth, extending the First Amendment's liberties to states).

The "hate-speech exception" to the First Amendment's free speech clause has been quite consistently struck down by the US Supreme Court on several occasions, whilst the Supreme Court has also held that legislation targeting "fighting words" (i.e. speech that incites imminent lawless action) is compatible with the First Amendment. In *Chaplinsky v. New Hampshire* the Court stated,

> Allowing the broadest scope to the language and purpose of the Fourteenth Amendment, it is well understood that the right of free speech is not absolute at all times and under all circumstances. There are certain well defined and narrowly limited classes of speech, the prevention and punishment of which have never been thought to raise any Constitutional problem. These include the [...] "fighting" words – those which, by their very utterance, inflict injury or tend to incite an immediate breach of the peace.[39]

In *Brandenburg v. Ohio*, the Supreme Court deduced from its previous rulings that

> the principle that the constitutional guarantees of free speech and free press do not permit a State to forbid or proscribe advocacy of the use of force or of law violation except where such advocacy is directed to inciting or producing imminent lawless action and is likely to incite or produce such action.[40]

Finally, in *R.A.V. v. City of St. Paul*, Justice Scalia, who wrote the majority opinion, interestingly found that

> the exclusion of "fighting words" from the scope of the First Amendment simply means that, for purposes of that Amendment, the unprotected features of the words are, despite their verbal character, essentially a "nonspeech" element of communication. Fighting words are thus analogous to a noisy sound truck.[41]

This position was criticised by Justice White in concurrence, where he pointed out that "a prohibition on fighting words is not a time, place, or manner

38 *Joseph Burstyn, Inc. v. Wilson* [1952], 343 U.S. 495.
39 *Chaplinsky v. New Hampshire* [1942] §§ 571–57, 315 U.S. 568.
40 *Brandenburg v. Ohio* [1969] § 447, 395 U.S. 444 (emphasis added).
41 *R.A.V. v. City of St. Paul* [1992] § 386, 505 U.S. 377.

restriction; it is a ban on a class of speech that conveys an overriding message of personal injury and imminent violence" and that, "indeed, such a law is content based in and of itself".[42] Interestingly, the case concerned burning a cross (a clearly racist manifestation) to threaten people of colour, and the judicial appraisal of that act was overturned later in *Virginia v. Black*.[43]

Thus, the contemporary interpretation of the First Amendment assumes that very hateful content of speech is in itself insufficient to place it outside of the Free Speech clause's protection – even very crude verbal and symbolic utterances are protected so long as they do not amount to fighting words.[44] As the Supreme Court explained in *Matal v. Tam* (a case regarding the refusal of trademark registration of the music group's name "The Slants") in reaction to the propositions of both the government and some *amici curiae* advocating the protection of minority groups from degrading speech,

> no matter how the point is phrased, its unmistakable thrust is this: The Government has an interest in preventing speech expressing ideas that offend. And, as we have explained, that idea strikes at the heart of the First Amendment. Speech that demeans on the basis of race, ethnicity, gender, religion, age, disability, or any other similar ground is hateful; but the proudest boast of our free speech jurisprudence is that we protect the freedom to express "the thought that we hate".[45]

Hateful speech that, as such, does not incite imminent lawless actions ("fighting words") is under the protection of the First Amendment.

4.4 The ECHR Perspective – Balancing Interests, Combating Hate Speech and Protecting Delicate Stability

The already well-settled case law of the ECtHR holds that the 46 States Parties to the Convention must observe the duty of neutrality and impartiality in religious matters stemming from Article 9 European Convention on Human Rights (ECHR).[46] Therefore, any interference with the freedom of (and from) religion must not pursue a dominance of any particular religion, but rather be

42 *R.A.V. v. City of St. Paul* [1992] § 386, 505 U.S. 377, concurring opinion of Justice White, at § 408.

43 *Virginia v. Black* [2003] 538 U.S. 343.

44 See, e.g., *Mahanoy Area School District v. B.L., a minor, by and through her father, Levy, et al.* [2021] § 8, 594 U.S.

45 *Matal, Interim Director, United States Patent and Trademark Office v. Tam* [2017] § 25, 582 U.S.

46 See, e.g., *Metropolitan Church of Bessarabia and others v. Moldova*, No. 45701/99 [2001] § 123, ECLI:CE:ECHR:2001:1213JUD004570199; *Leyla Şahin v. Turkey*, No. 44774/98 [2005] § 107, ECLI:CE:ECHR:2005:1110JUD004477498 (and the authorities referred to therein); *Lautsi and others v. Italy*, No. 30814/06 [2011] § 60, ECLI:CE:ECHR:2011:0318JUD003081406; *Perovy v. Russia*, No. 47429/09 [2020] § 55, ECLI:CE:ECHR:2020:1020JUD004742909.

religious sensitivity protected in the framework of one of the legitimate interests. On the other hand, since the ECtHR either has to interpret the Convention in accordance with the so-called European consensus – that is, a prevailing tendency of interpretation of particular rights and freedoms (protected by the Convention as a "living instrument") – or, when no such clear tendency is sufficiently identifiable, to respect the so-called "margin of appreciation" exercised by the States Parties. The question of interfering with freedom of expression due to reasons attributable to religious beliefs, which is an area that enjoys a relatively broad margin of appreciation, is essentially decided at the national level (and supervised in respect of the necessity of the choices made there, by the Strasbourg Court).

Thus, the ECtHR has a long record of case law pertaining to the balancing of "religious sensitivity" and free speech (or rather, as it is more commonly called in Europe, freedom of expression). Whilst deciding whether the said freedom was violated, the Court verifies – pursuant to Article 10(2) ECHR[47] – whether the interference was lawful (prescribed by law), whether it pursued one of the legitimate aims described in that provision and whether it was necessary in a democratic society. In most cases (not always, though[48]) the interference is lawful and pursues some legitimate aims under the Convention, but the disputed element is the necessity of those aims, which implies that the Court must appraise whether national authorities (courts) managed to strike a fair balance between competing interests.

And in the case of SLAPPs, it is not normally the absence of a legal basis for supressing free speech or a lack of legitimate interests being pursued that occurs but precisely a failure to strike a proper balance between the protected values (undoubtedly deserving protection as such) and the freedom of imparting and receiving information and opinions.

However, when the States Parties define the interests requiring, in their view, interference with freedom of expression, they may either simply invoke Article 10(2) ECHR (the "limitation clause", which provides for a legitimate aim of protecting "rights and freedoms of others") or employ Article 9 ECHR

47 Article 10(2) Convention for the Protection of Human Rights and Fundamental Freedoms (ETS No. 005) frames the scope of interference with the freedom of expression, which is permissible under the Convention and holds that since this freedom "carries with it duties and responsibilities, may be subject to such formalities, conditions, restrictions or penalties as are prescribed by law and are necessary in a democratic society, in the interests of national security, territorial integrity or public safety, for the prevention of disorder or crime, for the protection of health or morals, for the protection of the reputation or rights of others, for preventing the disclosure of information received in confidence, or for maintaining the authority and impartiality of the judiciary".

48 See, e.g., *Unifaun Theatre Productions Limited and others v. Malta*, No. 37326/13 [2018] § 77–89, ECLI:CE:ECHR:2018:0515JUD003732613, where the Court found that since national provisions applied by domestic authorities in banning the production of a theatre play that allegedly challenged religious sensitivity were insufficiently precise, the interference was not "prescribed by law".

(protecting freedom of thought, conscience and religion[49]). Either of these approaches is applied by the Court in different cases.

For instance, in *Otto-Preminger-Institut v. Austria*, the Court admitted that "a State may legitimately consider it necessary to take measures aimed at repressing certain forms of conduct, including the imparting of information and ideas, judged incompatible with the respect for the freedom of thought, conscience and religion of others" and added, in the context of a dispute over a public display of a movie that was allegedly harmful to the religious feelings of devout Catholics, that "the respect for the religious feelings of believers as guaranteed in Article 9 can legitimately be thought to have been violated by provocative portrayals of objects of religious veneration".[50] This approach, i.e. balancing Article 10(1) against Article 9(1) freedoms in order to protect "religious feelings" against gratuitous and overly aggressive challenges, was actually criticised in the dissenting opinion, whose authors held that

> [t]he Convention does not, in terms, guarantee a right to protection of religious feelings. More particularly, such a right cannot be derived from the right to freedom of religion, which in effect includes a right to express views critical of the religious opinions of others. Nevertheless, it must be accepted that it may be 'legitimate' for the purpose of Article 10 [...] to protect the religious feelings of certain members of society".[51]

The same approach was applied in *Aydın Tatlav v. Turkey*, for example (this time concerning Islam): a state may "legitimately consider it necessary to take measures aimed at repressing certain forms of behaviour, including the communication of information and ideas deemed incompatible with respect for freedom of thought, conscience and religion of others",[52] as well as in a number of other cases.[53] However, it is indeed disputable whether the Convention actually provides for the "right to protection of religious feelings". As rightly noted by Erica Howard, the Court's repeatedly proclaimed interpretative position that freedom of speech also protects ideas which "offend, shock, or

49 Article 9(1) ECHR states that "[e]veryone has the right to freedom of thought, conscience and religion; this right includes freedom to change his religion or belief and freedom, either alone or in community with others and in public or private, to manifest his religion or belief, in worship, teaching, practice and observance".

50 *Otto-Preminger-Institut v. Austria*, No. 13470/87 [1994] § 47, ECLI:CE:ECHR:1994:0920JUD001347087.

51 *Otto-Preminger-Institut v. Austria*, No. 13470/87 [1994] § 47, joint dissenting opinion of Judges Palm, Pekkanen and Makarczyk, § 6.

52 *Aydın Tatlav v. Turkey*, No. 50692/99 [2006] § 25, ECLI:CE:ECHR:2006:0502JUD005069299.

53 E.g. *Tagiyev and Huseynov v. Azerbaijan*, No. 13274/08 [2019] or *Sekmadienis Ltd. v. Lithuania*, No. 69317/14 [2018] § 74.

disturb"[54] and that religious believers "must tolerate and accept the denial by others of their religious beliefs and even the propagation by others of doctrines hostile to their faith"[55] would consequently "suggest that a right not to be offended in one's religious feelings does not exist under Article 9 ECHR".[56]

On the other hand, in *Giniewski v. France* the ECtHR referred to the "limitation clause" of Article 10(2) ECHR (legitimate aim of protecting the "rights and freedoms of others"), and only incidentally held that this aim was "also fully consonant with the aim of the protections afforded by Article 9 to religious freedom".[57] The same was held in *Mariya Alekhina and Others v. Russia*, among others.[58]

Whether the Court views the disputed interference as pursuing the legitimate aim of protecting the rights and freedoms of others (Article 10(2) ECHR) or as serving the need to protect religious freedom (Article 9(1) ECHR) seems to be neither determined by the respondent government's argumentation (e.g. they may invoke Article 9 but nevertheless be "qualified" under the limitation clause of Article 10 – as with the Russian government in *Mariya Alekhina and Others v. Russia*[59]) nor to have a noticeable impact on the ultimate outcome of the case pending before the Court (as the examples already produced show).

For the sake of complete accuracy, one must note that, apart from the aforementioned conventional grounds of interference motivated by the

54 The phrase was used for the first time in the famous ruling in *Handyside v. the United Kingdom*, No. 5493/72 [1976] § 49, ECLI:CE:ECHR:1976:1207JUD000549372: "freedom of expression constitutes one of the essential foundations of such a society, one of the basic conditions for its progress and for the development of every man. Subject to paragraph 2 of Article 10, it is applicable not only to 'information' or 'ideas' that are favourably received or regarded as inoffensive or as a matter of indifference, but also to those that offend, shock or disturb the State or any sector of the population. Such are the demands of that pluralism, tolerance and broadmindedness without which there is no 'democratic society'".

55 This idea was first expressed in *Otto-Preminger-Institut v. Austria*, No. 13470/87 [1994] § 47: "Those who choose to exercise the freedom to manifest their religion, irrespective of whether they do so as members of a religious majority or a minority, cannot reasonably expect to be exempt from all criticism. They must tolerate and accept the denial by others of their religious beliefs and even the propagation by others of doctrines hostile to their faith. However, the manner in which religious beliefs and doctrines are opposed or denied is a matter which may engage the responsibility of the State, notably its responsibility to ensure the peaceful enjoyment of the right guaranteed under Article 9 to the holders of those beliefs and doctrines. Indeed, in extreme cases the effect of particular methods of opposing or denying religious beliefs can be such as to inhibit those who hold such beliefs from exercising their freedom to hold and express them".

56 E. Howard, *Freedom of Expression and Religious Hate Speech in Europe* (New York: Routledge, 2017): 24, 93.

57 *Giniewski v. France*, No. 64016/00 [2006] § 40, ECLI:CE:ECHR:2006:0131 JUD006401600.

58 *Mariya Alekhina and others v. Russia*, No. 38004/12 [2018] § 210.

59 *Mariya Alekhina and others v. Russia*, No. 38004/12 [2018] §§ 177–180 and 210.

protection of "religious sensitivity",[60] the latter can also be justified by the protection of morals or preventing disorder. For instance, in *İ.A. v. Turkey*, a case concerning criminal sanctions imposed on a writer of what the Court described as a book which "conveyed the author's views on philosophical and theological issues in a novelistic style" (and which, in the eyes of domestic courts, was blasphemous), the Court held that the disputed interference "pursued the legitimate aims of preventing disorder and protecting morals and the rights of others".[61] Similarly, in *E.S. v. Austria*, a case concerning the conviction of an extreme-right politician who publicly accused Muhammad of paedophilia, the Court remarked that "the impugned interference pursued the aim of preventing disorder by safeguarding religious peace, as well as protecting religious feelings, which corresponds to protecting the rights of others within the meaning of Article 10 § 2 of the Convention".[62]

It is precisely the latter grounds of interference (preventing social disorder) that seems the most convincing. Essentially, all states have no business (to quote the famous phrase of the US Supreme Court in *Burstyn*) in protecting, as such, one's religious sensitivities (let alone "feelings"), or so-called morals (being nothing more than the contemporary prudishness dominating society and a certain proportion of the highest-instance judges, who normally serve their long-prayed-for positions in the evenings of their lives and thus tend to be a bit more conservative, if not bigoted and hypocritical, than the average member of a given society), but it should have the prevention of social turmoil as an important element of the government's

60 Although, to be precise, the ECtHR has never actually invoked "religious sensitivity" as a stand-alone concept. On the other hand, judges seem to accept – invoking it on many occasions – that this is exactly what stands behind the so-called "religious feelings". Judge Sajó explained in his separate opinion in *Murat Vural v. Austria* that "[t]he Court accepted in *Otto-Preminger-Institut v. Austria* [...] that protection against indignation caused by "offensive" speech was a legitimate aim within the concept of the rights of others, at least where the right was freedom of religion. *A, B and C v. Ireland* [...] goes beyond a Convention-right-related concern. Here it was not popular religious sensitivity that was to be protected and considered by the Court in a balancing exercise. The Court said that where the case raised sensitive moral or ethical issues, the margin of appreciation would be wider (but compared to what?), so the Court was technically not even compelled to go into genuine balancing (which it did anyway, in the context of Article 8). The Court concluded that "profound moral values" of the majority entered into the realm of legitimate aims of limiting rights, namely "protection of morals"; hence, the matter was to be treated under the necessity test. Both judgments resulted in strong dissents and criticism. Under this logic, if applied to freedom of expression, the argument might go like this: the "deep sense of respect and adoration" amounts to a profound moral value; therefore – as is common in the context of disparagement of national symbols – national unity or respect for the nation as such are foundational for public morals. History shows the speech-restrictive consequences of such authority-respecting (if not outright authoritarian) approaches" (*Murat Vural v. Turkey*, No. 9540/07 [2014], ECLI:CE:ECHR:2014:1021JUD000954007, fn. 8 to the partly dissenting and partly concurring opinion of Judge Sajó).

61 *İ.A. v. Turkey*, No. 42571/98 [2005] §§ 21–22, ECLI:CE:ECHR:2005:0913JUD004257198.

62 *E.S. v. Austria*, No. 38450/12 [2018] § 41, ECLI:CE:ECHR:2018:1025JUD003845012.

agenda. This approach seems to have prevailed, for instance, in the case law of the ECtHR of the last two decades.

It is noteworthy that the defendant government's allegations concerning the legitimate aim pursued, although they are normally accepted by the Court and treated somewhat leniently, are nevertheless not binding upon the Court, who may "requalify" the goal intended by national authorities. And despite the role of the so-called master of legal characterisation normally performed by the Court through its legal assessment of the facts presented by the applicant and the choice of the Convention's provision under which they are subsumed,[63] the Court may choose another legitimate aim pursued by the interference than the one proposed by the government. It did just that in *Atamanchuk v. Russia*, where it qualified the aim pursued by the national government in penalising hate speech targeted against ethnic minorities as a protection of the rights of others rather than preventing disorder (which was proposed by the Russian government).[64]

The ECtHR case law has evolved throughout decades from more conservative stances dominating as late as some 30 years ago (as exemplified in, e.g., *Wingrove v. the United Kingdom*[65]) to a more liberal approach which entails assuming that believers must tolerate criticism towards their religion and its symbols, so long as such criticism does not constitute instigation to hatred or violence. For instance, in *E.S. v. Austria*, the ECtHR emphasised, in accordance with its already well-established line of jurisprudence, that "a religious group must tolerate the denial by others of their religious beliefs and even the propagation by others of doctrines hostile to their faith, as long as the statements at issue do not incite to hatred or religious intolerance". The simple fact that national legislation "incriminate[s] all behaviour that is likely to hurt religious feelings or amount to blasphemy" was not sufficient to endorse the findings of domestic courts in the case at hand, yet what turned out to be decisive was that domestic courts "considered that the applicant's statements had been capable of arousing justified indignation".[66] What matters is whether the expression in question is likely to lead to harmful consequences and whether the legislation is applied to protect the public order, not religious feelings as

63 See, e.g., *Soares de Melo v. Portugal*, No. 72850/14 [2016] § 65, ECLI:CE:ECHR:2016:0216JUD007285014 (where the ECtHR described itself as "Maîtresse de la qualification juridique des faits de la cause").

64 *Atamanchuk v. Russia*, No. 4493/11 [2020] §§ 39–45, ECLI:CE:ECHR:2020:0211JUD000449311.

65 *Wingrove v. the United Kingdom*, No. 17419/90 [1996] § 57, ECLI:CE:ECHR:1996:1125JUD001741990 where the Court held that "the fact remains that there is as yet not sufficient common ground in the legal and social orders of the member States of the Council of Europe to conclude that a system whereby a State can impose restrictions on the propagation of material on the basis that it is blasphemous is, in itself, unnecessary in a democratic society and thus incompatible with the Convention".

66 *E.S. v. Austria*, No. 38450/12 [2018] § 52. See also R.G. Ingram, J. Pacey, A.W. Barber, *Freedom of Speech, 1500–1850* (Manchester: Manchester University Press, 2020): 3–4.

such.[67] In other words, for the anti-blasphemy law to be legitimately applied, it is required under Article 10 ECHR that the expression in question "contained elements of violence, [... or] stirred up or justified violence, hatred or intolerance of believers".[68] Even the spread of hatred as such is insufficient because "a clear and imminent danger" must occur to justify interference motivated by the protection of public order against the consequences of hate speech. In *Gül and others v. Turkey* the Court analysed the applicants' behaviour (which consisted of publicly shouting slogans of a communist nature) and concluded that

> neither in the domestic court decisions nor in the observations of the Government is there any indication that there was a clear and imminent danger which required an interference such as the lengthy criminal prosecution faced by the applicants.[69]

The "clear and imminent danger test" has been applied since then on several occasions in cases relating to interference allegedly triggered by the need to protect social order or the rights and freedoms of others against violent speech, most recently in *Savva Terentyev v. Russia*,[70] and it has been elaborated on as an essential standard of the Article 10 ECHR jurisprudence in the dissenting opinion of Judge Pinto de Albuquerque in the *Mouvement raëlien suisse v. Switzerland* Grand Chamber ruling.[71]

One can see the similarity between the "fighting words" (expressions inciting to imminent lawless action) doctrine of the US Supreme Court and the "clear and imminent danger" test applied by the ECtHR. The Strasbourg judges themselves are well aware of that similarity, as exemplified by the joint partly dissenting opinion annexed to the Chamber judgement by judges Vučinić and Pinto de Albuquerque in the famous *Perinçek v. Switzerland* case, where they held (whilst explicitly quoting the US Supreme Court's precedents) that

> the criminalisation of genocide denial corresponds to a State policy which is necessary to fully implement the spirit and the letter of Article I of the Genocide Convention, which places an obligation on States to prevent genocide, and the United Nations General Assembly Resolution of 26 January 2007, which calls on all UN Member States "unreservedly to reject any denial of the Holocaust as a historical event, either in full or

67 *Rabczewska v. Poland*, No. 8257/13 [2022] § 62.

68 *Mariya Alekhina and others v. Russia*, No. 38004/12 [2018] § 227.

69 *Gül and others v. Turkey*, No. 4870/02 [2010] § 42, ECLI:CE:ECHR:2010:0608JUD000487002 (emphasis added).

70 *Savva Terentyev v. Russia*, No. 10692/09 [2018] § 84, ECLI:CE:ECHR:2018:0828JUD001069209.

71 *Mouvement raëlien suisse v. Switzerland*, No. 16354/06 [2012], ECLI:CE:ECHR:2012:0713JUD001635406.

> in part, or any activities to this end". At least in Europe, the soil upon which so much blood was shed during the twentieth century in order to execute terrible plans involving the extermination of entire peoples, genocide denial is to be viewed as a seriously threatening and offensive form of speech, and thus the type of "fighting words" undeserving of protection.[72]

What differentiates the interpretative standards of Article 10 ECHR from the First Amendment's free speech clause is the approach to interference motivated by the hate-speech nature of the disputed expression, though these are not justified by considerations of public order but by other legitimate aims enshrined in Article 10(2) ECHR.

4.5 Specificity of SLAPPs Relating to "Religious Sensitivity" (in Particular of Islam and Judaism)

Invoking religious sensitivity looks like a perfect engine for SLAPPs: it is sufficiently vague to cause a chilling effect, and this is exactly what SLAPPers fish for.[73] Many such cases are known from various jurisdictions.

> As Judith Miller noted in her column in the conservative *City Journal*, in the USA [n]othing gets a journalist's attention like a subpoena. While authoritarian regimes silence critics by murdering or jailing them, journalists (and other critics) in the United States face gentler, but still effective, intimidation: libel lawsuits. Over the last few years, Islamists have tried silencing reporters, scholars, and citizens by suing them for defamation, often successfully.[74]

Let us remember that "defamation of religion" (as if it could sense any dignity and have any reputation as such) is just a brand-new name invented recently for the long-standing phenomenon of blasphemy. The policy of silencing critics of religion has been successfully implemented in some states. For example, in the last few years in Poland, in line with the expectations of the conservative

72 *Perinçek v. Switzerland*, No. 27510/08 [2013] § 21, ECLI:CE:ECHR:2013:1217JUD002751008 of the partly dissenting opinion. This case was subsequently referred to the Grand Chamber and replaced with its judgement.

73 Simultaneously themselves claiming the right to the enhanced protection – either under the Free Speech or Freedom of Religious Worship clauses – afforded to verbalising their own, religiously motivated, views which sometimes may amount to incitement to hatred – see, e.g., the study on balancing religious freedom and protection of the LGBT+ minority against being targeted by hate speech in: J. Temperman, *Religious Speech, Hatred and LGBT Rights: An International Human Rights Analysis* (Leiden: Brill Nijhoff, 2021): 54–88, where the author proposes a theoretical framework (including the so-called "context theory") for balancing competing interests.

74 J. Miller, "A SLAPP Against Freedom: Attorneys Have an Effective Way to Defeat Islamic Groups' Libel Suits' City Journal", Autumn 2007. https://www.city-journal.org/article/a-slapp-against-freedom. Accessed December 8, 2023.

government in control of the law enforcement apparatus and the prosecutor's office, the public prosecution charged "blasphemers" with rapidly increasing frequency for offences stipulated in Article 196 of the Penal Code ("offending religious feelings").[75] Similar tendencies are traceable in other European states experiencing certain authoritarian or quasi-authoritarian episodes, e.g. bullying religious minorities in Russia,[76] as well as silencing critics of the Russian Orthodox Church by accusing them of alleged hatred and extremist activities.[77]

If a state is founded on the principle of secularism, it would – as an indispensable consequence – opt for penalising the disturbance of public order and would rather not penalise blasphemy or vilification of religious symbolic, and religiously motivated SLAPPs would be unlikely. However, when a state is not constitutionally separated from religion, it may be inclined to penalise blasphemy or offences of "religious feelings", and in such circumstances, the risk of religious legal harassment grows. Even lawyers may actually encounter problems dealing with the limits of public interference with the freedom of expression triggered by religiously orientated considerations. For example, Roberto Buonamano discussed human rights as a tool for protecting religious freedom and went on to claim that

> human rights law, as a product of liberal-democratic society and at the same time a vehicle for the critique of liberal values, has potential to mediate between different democratic principles (including the civic values of free expression, association and equality, as well as freedom of religion) and to determine the negotiable and necessarily tentative balance of secular politics and religious sensitivity in modern multicultural societies.[78]

The essential problem is that when a state starts actually "mediating" to "balance" secular politics and religious sensitivity, it ceases to be a "modern multicultural society". It is not a state's role to protect somebody's sensitivity ("a right not to be shocked"), and when it starts seeking a balance between any secular politics and religious sensitivity, it can no longer claim to be a

75 See Dziennik Gazeta Prawna, "Przestępstwo obrazy uczuć religijnych coraz częstsze. W 2020 r. 29 aktów oskarżenia", December 26, 2020. https://prawo.gazetaprawna.pl/artykuly/8053551,przestepstwo-obrazy-uczuc-religijnych-coraz-czestsze-w-2020-r-29-aktow-oskarzenia.html. Accessed December 5, 2023.

76 See D. Wassell, "Relentless Religious Persecution in Russia", September 1, 2021. https://religiousfreedominstitute.org/relentless-religious-persecution-in-russia/. Accessed December 5, 2023.

77 *Yefimov and Youth Human Rights Group v. Russia*, Nos 12385/15 and 51619/15 [2021], ECLI:CE:ECHR:2021:1207JUD001238515.

78 R. Buonamano, "Religious Freedom in a Secular Human Rights Order" *Politics, Religion & Ideology*, vol. 21, no. 1 (2020): 68, 90–91. https://doi.org/10.1080/21567689.2020.1732935 (emphasis added).

liberal democracy since it turns into a "tyranny" of subjective religious sensitivities dictating what public policies should or should not be.

Nonetheless, on both shores of the Atlantic, there is some acceptance for outlawing what Americans call "fighting words", or what is called in Europe "hate speech". Obviously, lessons from history were learnt in a much more dramatic way (to say the least) in Europe, and the Shoah remembrance is a sufficient reason to ban words that incite hatred motivated by religion, ethnic origin, or sexual identity. Therefore, esteemed European democracies which experienced totalitarianism in the past penalise speech that impairs religious sensitivity, though not because of that impairment, but rather due to the risk of igniting hatred and violence. Quite visibly, the "imminence" of that risk is understood much more broadly in Europe than it is in the USA, and that is for historical reasons.

However, even in the European perspective, whenever a state gets engaged in judicially protecting religious symbols, views, feelings or imaginarium it inevitably leads to SLAPPing. It is not a "government's business" to protect the religious human and ideological machinery. The government's business, though, is (only) to protect social order, the stability of which may be threatened by coexisting and very often confrontational religious views. Eugene Volokh (again) rightly noted that

> [m]uch religious discourse, and much ideological discourse more generally, involves condemnation of others' views as well as expression of one's own. One way of proving the merits of your ideas is by showing the error of rival ideas. If the government may use the force of law to suppress such condemnatory speech, then we have lost a great deal of our First Amendment protection.[79]

Indeed, if religious speech (just like artistic expression, by the way) is an expression of touching upon the transcendent – which by definition is located beyond rationality – it is hard to expect religious speakers to be overly tempered. Religions (and thus also religious expression) are by all means more emotional than rational, and emotionality may be untampered and unrestrained. It is therefore the duty of public authorities, including courts, to weigh competing interests prudently and carefully in order to preserve and protect some social stability against possible turmoil disturbing the public order.

Things get even more complicated when it comes to litigation to protect the "sensitivity" of Islamic and Judaist believers in Europe or the USA. That is because almost none of the European states (except for Turkey and some other exceptions of states with Muslim majorities) nor the USA have societies with prevailing Islamic or Judaic minorities. Therefore, for obvious reasons,

79 E. Volokh, "Freedom of Speech" 69.

the risk of state authorities getting engaged in a purely ideological (and at the same time pretending to be juridical) "crusade" is very unlikely or non-existent. On the other hand, outside the conventional Western hemisphere, the problem of SLAPPing motivated by Islam occurs sometimes in its most dramatic and brutal form – as in the case of a Nigerian atheist allegedly "blaspheming" against Islam, Mr Muhammad Mubarak Bala, who was sentenced to 24 years' imprisonment.[80] Some states with Islam as their dominant religion are in fact classic theocracies, officially combating any criticism concerning the ruling religion (as exemplified by Iran, Afghanistan, Saudi Arabia, and Mauritania). In these extreme examples, using the SLAPP label is an understatement since what happens there are actually regular, official repressions against minority views disguised in the form of some more or less ridiculous judicial proceedings.

No such religiously motivated SLAPPs are known in the case of Judaism. Even though some lawsuits were criticised as allegedly SLAPP-like,[81] they were not religiously motivated (they were not a manifestation of a tendency of Judaism to silence critics). Perhaps one of the reasons is that contemporary Judaism is actually "genetically" founded upon discussion (or rooted in a culture of discussion), and essential parts of the Talmud are actually a transcript of a discussion on various aspects of Judaism. Besides, the only state axiologically founded on Judaism is Israel, and fortunately, it is a generally democratic state (in spite of well-founded criticism against the policies of Benjamin Netanyahu's government in respect of the judiciary, for instance). And even though there is still no anti-SLAPP law in Israel, and *Khilul Hashem* (profanation of the name of God) is not unfamiliar to Judaism,[82] Israeli courts have been reported to dismiss SLAPP-like lawsuits.[83]

4.6 Conclusions

Issues related to religion, be it protecting a denomination against defamation, protecting religious symbols against vilification, or simply the good mood of believers (the so-called "right to not be offended"), are a natural field for SLAPPs to blossom in. This is because religious belief is a unique emotional

80 See the records of the criminal proceedings: Kano State High Court of Justice (Nigeria), *State v. Muhhammad Mubarak Bala*, No. K/89C/2021 [2022].

81 See the example of the District of Columbia Court of Appeals, *American Studies Association (ASA), et al., v. Simmon Bronner, et al.*, No. 19-CV-1222 [2021]. https://law.justia.com/cases/district-of-columbia/court-of-appeals/2021/19-cv-1222.html. Accessed November 30, 2023. The litigation concerned the resolution of ASA concerning the boycott of Israeli academic associations because of the Israeli policy towards Palestine. The defendants claimed that the lawsuit was a SLAPP. Ultimately, the plaintiffs lost their case in 2023.

82 G. Aran, "Khilul Hashem: Blasphemy in Past and Present Israel" *Israel Studies*, vol. 21, no. 2 (2016): 155–181.

83 See, e.g., New Israel Fund, "Precedent-Setting Decision Against SLAPP Case", February 9, 2017. https://www.nif.org/stories/social-and-economic-justice/precedent-setting-decision-against-slapp-cases/. Accessed November 28, 2023.

experience which exists beyond the sphere of rationality. When a state is founded upon the principle of religious neutrality, the risk of religiously motivated SLAPPs instituted by the state itself, or of successful legally harassing litigation with religious motivation, is low. In the case of states manifesting authoritarian or simply theocratic tendencies, the risk of religious SLAPPs increases.

In the United States, although no federal anti-SLAPP law has been adopted to date, there is a strong body of legislation at the state level aimed at preventing SLAPPs – although it is not immune to criticism based on the free speech doctrine. At the same time the US Supreme Court declared anti-blasphemy laws incompatible with the free speech clause of the First Amendment as late as 1952 (the "Miracle" decision in *Burstyn v. Wilson*), and the only type of speech criticising religion which belongs to the "certain well defined and narrowly limited classes of speech, the prevention and punishment of which have never been thought to raise any Constitutional problem", is the category of "fighting words" – expressions "which, by their very utterance, inflict injury or tend to incite an immediate breach of the peace" (*Chaplinsky v. New Hampshire*) or, as later on clarified by the Supreme Court in *Brandenburg v. Ohio*, expressions "directed to inciting or producing *imminent lawless action*". Therefore, even though religiously fiery narratives are vividly present in the US public discourse (with the prominent example of Governor Ron DeSantis, a GOP candidate in the 2024 presidential election, declaring the intention to restore religious freedom in America[84]), there seems to be no significant threat of religiously motivated SLAPPs threatening free speech in America.

On the opposite side of the Atlantic, the ECtHR clearly expects the 46 States Parties to the Convention to observe the duty of neutrality and impartiality in religious matters, in accordance with Article 9 ECHR. Nonetheless, the diversity of possible models of relations between state and religious unions in Europe makes the so-called margin of appreciation applicable to balancing freedom of expression and religious sentiments relatively broad. The Strasbourg Court has accepted interference with the freedom of expression, which was motivated by the need to balance that freedom with the freedom of religious beliefs (Article 9 ECHR) or by the need to pursue different legitimate aims enumerated in Article 10(2) ECHR (the "limitation clause"), such as protecting the public order, morals or simply the rights and freedoms of others. For decades, the case law has revealed a noticeable tendency to construe the legitimate aims (justifying interferences) more and more strictly, to apply the necessity test stringently, and to accept those justifications which invoke the need to sustain social stability. One must also note that for a long time there was no anti-SLAPP legislation at the EU level (the Directive was

84 See M. Dixon, "How religion plays into Ron DeSantis' public image — from 'armor of God' to a Bible ordered on Amazon", December 3, 2023. https://www.nbcnews.com/politics/2024-election/religion-ron-desantis-catholic-amazon-bible-rcna126855. Accessed December 1, 2023.

adopted in 2024), yet the ECtHR has demonstrated its awareness of how significant (if not devastating) a threat such litigation poses to the free flow of information and ideas.

In both the USA and Europe, the "constitutional courts" (the US Supreme Court and the European Court of Human Rights) carefully balance the interests of free speech and religious peace. The more diverse and multicultural (as well as multireligious) our societies become, the more essential is striking that fair balance for the preservation of public order. Both "constitutional courts" seem to be perfectly aware of it, at least so far.

5 Employers' Duties to Respect the Religious Freedom of Employees at the Workplace: Recent Developments

Ioanna Tourkochoriti

Abstract

This chapter argues that the legal regime that exists in Europe formed by the case law of the Court of Justice of the European Union (CJEU) does not protect employees' rights adequately compared to what is the case in other jurisdictions like the United States. It engages with case law within the European Union on wearing signs of religious affiliation in the workplace, and it focuses on jurisdictions where controversial cases have emerged, i.e. France, Belgium, and Germany. It analyses the case law of the European Court of Justice and of the European Court of Human Rights in this area, and it compares with the state of the law in the United States. Although the US Supreme Court has held that employers have an "affirmative duty" to provide a reasonable accommodation to their employees if they wish to wear signs of religious affiliation in the workplace, European courts are reluctant to recognise a similar duty. On the contrary, based on the case law of the CJEU, employers are allowed to require their employees to remove signs of religious affiliation if they need to present a "neutral" image towards customers. Further, this chapter discusses the criterion of neutrality that the CJEU articulated in its decisions and shows the differences in the understanding of neutrality across Europe and the United States. The criterion of neutrality as accepted by the CJEU has a disparate impact upon religious groups.

Keywords

freedom of religion; discrimination; access to the workplace; European Union; European Court of Human Rights; US Supreme Court

DOI: 10.4324/9781003423294-8

5.1 Introduction

This chapter argues that the legal regime that exists in Europe formed by the case law of the Court of Justice of the European Union (CJEU) does not protect employees' rights adequately compared to what is the case in other jurisdictions, like the United States. It engages with case law within the European Union (EU) on wearing signs of religious affiliation in the workplace, and it focuses on jurisdictions where controversial cases have emerged, i.e. France, Belgium, and Germany. It analyses the case law of the European Court of Justice and of the European Court of Human Rights in this area, and it compares the state of the law in the United States. Although the US Supreme Court has held that employers have an "affirmative duty" to provide a reasonable accommodation to their employees if they wish to wear signs of religious affiliation in the workplace, European courts are reluctant to recognise a similar duty. On the contrary, based on the case law of the CJEU, employers are allowed to require their employees to remove signs of religious affiliation if they need to present a "neutral" image towards customers.

Further, this chapter discusses the criterion of neutrality that the CJEU articulated in its decisions and shows the differences in the understanding of neutrality across Europe and the United States. The legal regime that exists in Europe is more restrictive towards the manifestation of religion in the public sphere. It focuses more on employers' wishes over the rights of employees. This means that the decisions of the CJEU are significantly weakening the antidiscrimination legislation that the EU has enacted with the aim to integrate religious minorities into the workplace. The criterion of neutrality as accepted by the CJEU has a disparate impact upon religious groups. This means that it constitutes indirect discrimination, which is also forbidden by the relevant EU directives against discrimination in the workplace. Intersectionality is also relevant here to the extent that the relevant legislation affects in particular women members of minority religious groups. Analysing the shortcomings of the criteria that apply in Europe, the chapter further argues that exceptions to the rule against discrimination in the workplace must be interpreted narrowly. Only a narrow interpretation is consistent with anti-discrimination law as reflected in the EU directives against discrimination in the workplace.

Employers' duties to respect the religious freedom of employees in the workplace vary around the world. This variation is due to differences in the understanding of the relation which is appropriate between religion and the state.[1] Most western democracies are based on the idea of a separation between religion and the state. The relationship between religion and the state depends

1 See I. Tourkochoriti, "The Constitutional Politics of Religion". In: M. Tushnet, D. Kochenov (eds.), *Research Handbook on the Politics of Constitutional Law* (Cheltenham: Edward Elgar, 2023): 467–482.

on several historical factors. Employers play an important role in the distributive mechanics of societies, and they are thus grounding state policies dictated by various understandings of secularism that are dominant in various states. In states where the relationship between the church and the state is based on an understanding that favours the visibility of religion in the public sphere, employers have positive obligations to accommodate the manifestation of religious belief. In states where the relationship between religion and the state is based on eliminating religion from the public sphere, employers may implement policies that limit the manifestation of belief in the workplace. The CJEU has recently issued several decisions which have defined the obligations employers have in the workplace based on a conception of neutrality that does not allow the manifestation of belief in the public sphere.

Most cases that have emerged before courts relate to the permissibility of wearing signs of religious affiliation in the workplace and to providing reasonable accommodations for religious rituals, which include prayer and religious holidays. This chapter engages with the obligations employers have within the legal system of the United States, which is protective of employees' needs for religious expression. It also engages with the standards of protection within the EU, which has since 2000 implemented antidiscrimination legislation modelled after American federal antidiscrimination law. The relevant legislation is Directive 2000/78/EC establishing a general framework for equal treatment in employment and occupation.[2] The case law of the European Court of Human Rights is also relevant in this area since the Court has long been co-defining the relevant standards in the protection of rights within Europe.

5.2 United States

The United States maintains a robust framework against discrimination in the workplace on the grounds of religion. This protection covers the manifestation of religious beliefs but does not actively discuss religion in the workplace. The legislation against discrimination in the access to the workplace in the United States foresees the possibility for a reasonable accommodation. Title VII of the Civil Rights Act of 1964 makes it unlawful for employers "to fail or refuse to hire or to discharge any individual, or otherwise to discriminate against any individual with respect to his compensation, terms, conditions, or privileges [of] employment, because of such individual's… religion".[3] Employers have a positive obligation to provide accommodation to the manifestation of belief in the workplace. Employers have an *affirmative duty* to

2 Directive 2000/78/EC establishing a general framework for equal treatment in employment and occupation, OJ L 303, December 2, 2000, 16.

3 § 2000e–2(a)(1) Civil Rights Act of 1964. https://perma.cc/24VN-QS9Y. Accessed December 28, 2024.

accommodate which requires them to do more than simply not discriminate.[4] This affirmative duty means that employers and employees need to collaborate to find a solution to reconcile the interests of both sides. On the one side, the employers' interest to define their business must respect to the extent that it is possible the employee's interest in participating in religious prayers or to wear religious dress. The Equal Employment Opportunity Commission has issued guidance according to which employers are obliged to make reasonable accommodations to the religious needs of employees whenever doing so would not create "undue hardship" on the conduct of the employers' business.[5]

The idea of "reasonable accommodation" encourages an imaginative exchange between employers and employees. Case law has defined that the accommodation requirement is "plainly intended to relieve individuals of the burden of choosing between their jobs and their religious convictions, where such relief will not unduly burden others".[6] It means adapting the work environment in a way that allows the employee to abide by her religious beliefs. As the Equal Employment Opportunity Commission (EEOC) has noted following US Supreme Court case law,[7] "employer-employee cooperation and flexibility are key to the search for a reasonable accommodation.[8] Willingness to collaborate is necessary on both sides, for them to discover an acceptable reconciliation of their interests.[9] Employers are obliged to accept limitations on their freedom to define their business image to meet the needs of their employees. Employees are also required to limit some of their freedom to meet the requirements of the employer. Employers do not have a duty to accept the proposal of the employee,[10] and the employee must cooperate with the employer if the latter does not grant the employee's preferred accommodation but

4 See G.A. Rutherglen, J.J. Donohue III, *Employment Discrimination Law and Theory* (St. Paul: Foundation Press, 2012): 508.

5 29 CFR § 1605.1 [1968]. https://www.law.cornell.edu/cfr/text/29/1605.1. Accessed December 28, 2024.

6 *Protos v. Volkswagen of Am., Inc.* [1986] 797 F.2d 129, 136. "[t]his is...part of our 'happy tradition' of avoiding unnecessary clashes with the dictates of conscience" (citation omitted).

7 *Ansonia Board of Education v. Philbrook* [1986] 479 US 60, 69.

8 Equal Employment Opportunity Commission Compliance Manual. https://www.eeoc.gov/policy/docs/religion.html.Accessed December 28, 2024.

9 *Brener v. Diagnostic Ctr. Hosp.* [1982] 671 F.2d 141, 145–146. "[E]mployee has a correlative duty to make a good faith attempt to satisfy his needs through means offered by the employer".

10 *Ansonia Bd. of Education v. Philbrook* [1986] at 69 (employer could satisfy its obligation by offering an alternative reasonable accommodation to the particular one proposed by the employee).

provides an alternative.[11] The reasonableness of the accommodation depends on the facts of each specific case. For instance, reaching a reasonable accommodation around a dress code might imply that the employer accepts that some employees might need to wear headscarves and clothing that covers more than what other employees would accept.

The US Supreme Court has issued a number of cases which affirmed this obligation, and it has defined the meaning of the positive obligations that employers have.[12] The Supreme Court held that a refusal to hire a person because the headscarf she wore pursuant to her religious obligations conflicted with the employer's neutral dress policy violates Title VII disparate treatment (direct discrimination) provision. Under US Title VII, employers are obliged to reasonably accommodate to "a religious observance or practice" unless they can prove that there would be undue hardship on the conduct of the employer's business.[13] The Supreme Court interpreted the law to mean that there is an *obligation* for the employer to accommodate, as mere neutrality is not enough.[14] Rather, the law affirmatively obliges employers not "to fail or refuse to hire or discharge any individual...because of such individual's religious observance and practice".[15] For the same Court, when an applicant requires an accommodation as an aspect of religious practice, then "it is no response that the subsequent 'failure to hire' was due to an otherwise neutral policy".[16] In other words, according to the court, even "otherwise-neutral policies" must give way to the need for an accommodation.[17] This means that employers are obliged to accommodate religious dress in the workplace unless there is serious obstruction with the accomplishment of the duties of the employee. For instance, the New York City Police Department was obliged to accommodate a traffic enforcement agent by allowing him to wear a turban on the job.[18]

11 *EEOC v. AutoNation USA Corp.* [2002] WL 31650749 (employer satisfied its initial burden by showing that it suggested possible accommodations, but the employee resigned without giving the proposed accommodations the opportunity to be implemented or tested, thus not showing good faith). *Chrysler Corp. v. Mann* [1977] 561 F.2d 1282, 1286 (where employee "refuses to attempt to accommodate his own beliefs or to cooperate with his employer's attempt to reach a reasonable accommodation, he may render an accommodation impossible. In such a case the employee himself is responsible for any failure of accommodation..."); *cert. denied* [1978] 434 US 1039.

12 *E.E.O.C. v. Abercrombie & Fitch Stores Inc.* [2015] 575 US 768.

13 42 USC. 9§ 2000e(j). https://www.law.cornell.edu/uscode/text/42/2000e. Accessed December 28, 2024.

14 *E.E.O.C. v. Abercrombie & Fitch Stores Inc.* [2015] 6. http://becketpdf.s3.amazonaws.com/Amicus-Brief-FINAL.pdf. Accessed December 28, 2024.

15 *E.E.O.C. v. Abercrombie & Fitch Stores Inc.* [2015] 6, 7.

16 *E.E.O.C. v. Abercrombie & Fitch Stores Inc.* [2015] 7.

17 *E.E.O.C. v. Abercrombie & Fitch Stores Inc.* [2015].

18 See NY Commission on Human Rights, *Jaggi v. NYPD CHR Compl.* [2004]. https://archive.citylaw.org/chr/employment/Jaggi_V_NYPD_DO.pdf. Accessed December 28, 2024.

The limits to the employers' obligation to provide a reasonable accommodation are defined in reference to the concept of "undue hardship". The EEOC has defined that the concept covers accommodations that are costly, compromise workplace safety, decrease workplace efficiency, infringe on the rights of other employees, or require other employees to do more than their share of potentially hazardous or burdensome work.[19] "Undue hardship" covers monetary costs as well as other burdens in conducting the employer's business such as diminishing efficiency in other jobs or infringing in other employee's rights or benefits.[20] Impairing workplace safety or causing coworkers to carry the employee's share of potentially hazardous or burdensome work are important elements evaluated to define whether "undue hardship" exists.[21] The EEOC has issued best practice instructions, according to which managers should be trained that the law requires making exceptions to uniformly applied dress or grooming rules, practices, or preferences. [22]

In *Groff v. DeJoy, Postmaster General*[23] decided by the Supreme Court in 2023, the Court had the opportunity to define better the scope of the obligations an employer has in this area. The court had the opportunity to define what kind of costs define the "undue hardship" requirement which may serve as a defence to an employer's refusal to provide a reasonable accommodation. The Court ruled that courts should evaluate whether a hardship would be substantial in the context of an employer's business. This means that it should be something very different from a *de minimis* burden. Courts should apply the test in a manner that considers all relevant factors in the case at hand, including the accommodations at issue and their practical impact in light of the nature, "size and operating cost of [an] employer".[24] The case concerned an employee of the US Postal Service who had a conscientious objection to working on Sundays. His employer refused to exempt him from Sunday work because this imposed on his coworkers, disrupted the workplace and workflow, and diminished employee morale. For the Court, a hardship that is attributable to employee animosity to a particular religion, to religion in general, or to the very notion of accommodating religious practice cannot be

19 See 'Religious Discrimination'. https://www.eeoc.gov/laws/types/religion.cfm. Accessed December 28, 2024.

20 *Protos v. Volkswagen of America Inc.* [1986] 797 F.2d 129, 134–135; *Brown v. Polk County* [1995] 61 F.3d 650, 655.

21 *Bhatia v. Chevron U.S.A. Inc.*, [1984] 734 F.2d 1382, 1384.

22 USDC Columbia, *United States v. Washington Metro. Area Transit Auth.*, No. 1:08-CV-01661 (RMC) [2009]. https://www.justice.gov/sites/default/files/crt/legacy/2010/12/15/wmatasettle.pdf. Accessed December 28, 2024; *EEOC v. Brink's Inc.*, No. 1:02-CV-0111 (C.D. Ill.) [2002]; see also *EEOC v. Scottish Food Systems, Inc.*, 1:13-CV00796 [2013]; *EEOC v Fries Restaurant Management d/b/a Burger King*, No. 3:12-CV-3169-M [2013].

23 *Groff v. DeJoy, Postmaster General* [2023] 600 US 447.

24 *Groff v. DeJoy, Postmaster General* [2023] 470–471.

considered "undue".[25] Impacts on coworkers are relevant only to the extent that they affect the conduct of the business. An employer must do more than conclude that forcing other employees to work overtime would constitute an undue hardship. Consideration of other options, such as voluntary shift swapping, would also be necessary. Bias or hostility to a religious practice cannot supply a defence to an employer who refuses an accommodation.

Government employees are protected in the United States as much as private employees. In fact, they are protected under federal antidiscrimination legislation, as well as under the First Amendment to the federal Constitution. A public library may not impose a dress code requiring employees not to wear clothing or ornaments symbolising religious or political affiliation.[26] Courts emphasise that wearing signs of religious affiliation is an expression of religious convictions and viewpoint, which is a matter of public concern "entitled to… [the] full protection of the First Amendment".[27]

The obligation that employers have does not extend to allowing employees to discuss freely their religion in the workplace.[28] Discussing religion in the workplace with customers is not acceptable because it may be associated by mistake with the employer's message.[29] This is the case for the private and the public sector. Government employees are not allowed to discuss their religiosity while fulfilling their duties. The key question is whether public employees' speech is occurring as part of their official duties.[30] This legal regime succeeds in allowing employees to manifest their religiosity in the workplace while protecting the employers' rights, whether it is the government or private parties, from being identified with the content of the religious beliefs of their employees. It strikes a fair balance between the employee's expressive freedoms and the employers' rights to define their businesses.

5.3 Europe

5.3.1 The Law of the European Union

The EU has recently enacted antidiscrimination legislation in the access to employment which was influenced to a great extent by American federal antidiscrimination law. Implemented in a different social and political context, antidiscrimination law operates differently in the EU. Although US legislation foresees the possibility for a reasonable accommodation for religious

25 *Groff v. DeJoy, Postmaster General* [2023] 472.
26 *Draper v. Logan County Pub. Library* [2005] 403 F. Supp. 2d 608.
27 *Draper v. Logan County Pub. Library* [2005] 617.
28 See generally, C. Mala Corbin, "Government Employee Religion" *Arizona State Law Journal* vol. 49 (2017): 1193. https://arizonastatelawjournal.org/wp-content/uploads/2018/02/Corbin_Pub.pdf. Accessed December 28, 2024.
29 *Baz v. Walters* [1986] 782 F.2d 701; *Rivera v. Choice Courier Sys. Inc., 01 Civ.2096(CBM)* [2004] WL 1444852.
30 *Garcetti v. Ceballos* [2006] 547 US 410. See C. Mala Corbin, "Government Employee Religion" 1198.

practices,[31] the EU directives do not refer to the possibility for a reasonable accommodation in the clauses protecting against discrimination on the basis of religion. The concept of reasonable accommodation appears in the EU directives only in the area of disability.[32] The absence of a clause about reasonable accommodation in the text of the EU directive in reference to freedom of religion indicates less sensibility in Europe in favour of protecting freedom of religion than in the United States.

The EU enacted Council Directive 2000/78/EC of November 27, 2000, establishing a general framework for equal treatment in employment and occupation to eliminate discrimination in the access to employment. The forbidden grounds of discrimination in the directive are religion or belief, disability, age, or sexual orientation. The Directive outlaws direct and indirect discrimination.[33] One of the aims of the Directive was to protect women members of religious minorities throughout Europe. Kimberly Krenshaw crafted the term "intersectionality" to denote all these cases where people experience discrimination on the basis of several characteristics that they have.[34] Although the term "intersectionality" is not present in the official documents on the elaboration of Directive 2000/78/EC, the idea that women may be affected differently by discrimination on the grounds of belief is present.[35] Upon proposing the Directive, the European Commission noted that discrimination on the grounds of belief affects women differently.[36] The concern to protect women as victims of multiple discrimination is present in the Preamble of the

31 42 USC § 2000e (j). https://www.law.cornell.edu/uscode/text/42/2000e. Accessed December 28, 2024.

32 Art. 5 of Directive 2000/78/EC; 42 USC § 12112. https://www.law.cornell.edu/uscode/text/42/12112. Accessed December 28, 2024.

33 The definitions provided in the text of the Directive in Article 2.2 are the following: (a) direct discrimination shall be taken to occur where one person is treated less favourably than another is, has been or would be treated in a comparable situation, on any of the grounds referred to in Article 1; (b) indirect discrimination shall be taken to occur where an apparently neutral provision, criterion or practice would put persons having a particular religion or belief, a particular disability, a particular age, or a particular sexual orientation at a particular disadvantage compared with other persons unless:

(i) that provision, criterion or practice is objectively justified by a legitimate aim and the means of achieving that aim are appropriate and necessary, or.

(ii) as regards persons with a particular disability, the employer or any person or organisation to whom this Directive applies, is obliged, under national legislation, to take appropriate measures in line with the principles contained in Article 5 in order to eliminate disadvantages entailed by such provision, criterion or practice.

34 K. Crenshaw, 'Mapping the Margins: Intersectionality, Identity Politics, and Violence against Women of Color", *Stanford Law Review* vol. 43, no. 6 (1991): 1241. https://blogs.law.columbia.edu/critique1313/files/2020/02/1229039.pdf. Accessed December 28, 2024.

35 See for instance, European Commission, Explanatory Memorandum to the Proposal for a Council Directive Establishing a General Framework for Equal Treatment in Employment and Occupation. https://eur-lex.europa.eu/legal-content/EN/TXT/?uri=COM:1999:0565:FIN. Accessed December 28, 2024.

36 European Commission, Explanatory Memorandum to the Proposal for a Council Directive Establishing a General Framework for Equal Treatment in Employment and Occupation. https://eur-lex.europa.eu/legal-content/EN/TXT/?uri=COM:1999:0565:FIN.

Directive.[37] A report by the Committee on Legal Affairs and the Internal Market of the European Parliament noted that too many women members of ethnic and religious minorities have not been integrated into the labour market within the EU.[38] The CJEU however has issued several decisions recently which weaken the protection the Directive was designed to provide to women members of minority religious groups. The Court follows in its decision a conception of neutrality which is close to the one dominant in France, which is associated with the removal of religious affiliation from the public sphere.

Asma Boungnaoui[39] involved the interpretation of Article 4(1) of Council Directive 2000/78/EC. Ms Boungnaoui was a design engineer working for a private company in France. As part of her work duties, she had to provide her services in the customers' premises. The customer complained that her headscarf had upset some of its employees. Article 4(1) of the directive allows Member States to provide that a difference in treatment based on one of the forbidden criteria of discrimination is not discriminatory if it constitutes a "genuine and determining occupational requirement, provided that the objective is legitimate and the requirement is proportionate". Although the CJEU notes the need to interpret exceptions to the principle against discrimination narrowly, it indicates that even a broad exception would be acceptable if presented as an occupational requirement objectively dictated by the "nature" of the duties of the employee. Nevertheless, the Court must be praised for not accepting that the wishes of the customer could constitute such an objective criterion.[40]

In *Achbita*,[41] a receptionist was dismissed by her employer for violating an unwritten rule that workers should not wear visible signs of their political, philosophical, or religious beliefs in the workplace. In this decision, the CJEU noted that even a neutral policy can constitute indirect discrimination. It is not inconceivable, the CJEU notes, that the referring court may conclude that an apparently neutral policy may constitute indirect discrimination on the grounds of religion when it "results, in fact, in persons adhering to a particular religion or belief being put at a particular disadvantage".[42] Indirect discrimination exists if there is no legitimate justification for the neutral policy. The Court accepts as a possibility for the employer to offer to the

37 Preamble § 4, Council Directive 2000/78/EC.

38 Report by the Committee on Legal Affairs and the Internal Market, in Report of the European Parliament on the proposal for a Council directive establishing a general framework for equal treatment in employment and occupation, (a5-0264/2000), p. 74. https://www.europarl.europa.eu/sides/getDoc.do?pubRef=-//EP//TEXT+REPORT+A5-2000-0264+0+NOT+XML+V0//EN. Accessed December 28, 2024.

39 *Bougnaoui ADDH v. Micropole SA*, C-188/15 [2017], ECLI:EU:C:2017:204.

40 *Bougnaoui ADDH v. Micropole SA*, C-188/15 [2017].

41 *Achbita v. G4S Secure Solutions NV*, C-157/15 [2017] ECLI:EU:C:2017:203; *Achbita, Centrom voor galijkheid van kansen en voor racismebestrijding v G4S Secure Solutions NV*, 13-19.855 [2017].

42 *Achbita v. G4S Secure Solutions NV*, C-157/15 [2017].

employee a post which does not involve any visual contact with customers, instead of dismissing her. This criterion is not acceptable within US antidiscrimination law because it would be considered segregating on the grounds of religion, which is contrary to Title VII.[43] Furthermore, the court held that "the desire to display in relations with both public and private sector customers a policy of political, philosophical or religious neutrality must be considered legitimate", provided that the policy "is genuinely pursued in a consistent and systematic manner", and the prohibition must be "strictly necessary" to achieve the aim pursued. The court seems to be accepting a very broad definition of what constitutes "objective justification". This definition is much broader compared to what would justify a similar policy in the United States. As analysed later, the problem with the reference to the idea of neutrality in this context is that it conceals that there is always a conception related to the visibility of religion that is at stake, which may constitute indirect discrimination against minority religious groups.[44]

In two more recent decisions the CJEU expressed the same opinion. *IX v. Wabe*[45] concerned the employee of a private childcare facility in Germany who decided to wear a headscarf while already appointed. *MH Müller Handels GmbH v. MJ*[46] concerned a sales assistant and cashier in a store who also decided to wear a headscarf while she had already been appointed. Initially, she was transferred to another post allowing her to wear the headscarf and then asked to remove it. When she refused, she was terminated. Both employers were arguing that they had implemented policies aiming to maintain neutrality in the workplace. The Court repeated that rules reflecting "a policy of political, philosophical and religious neutrality" on the part of the employer do not establish a difference of treatment between workers.[47] This is so in the first of the two cases because the employer had already required another employee wearing a religious cross to remove it. The CJEU also reflected on whether the policy might constitute indirect discrimination on the grounds of gender, religion or belief. It held that the policy may be upheld because it constitutes a legitimate aim an employer may pursue, which is to display neutrality in relations with public- and private-sector customers. For the court, in order to establish the existence of objective justification and of a genuine need on the part of the employer, account may be taken of the rights and legitimate wishes of customers or users. The policy must meet a "genuine need" on the part of

43 EEOC Compliance Manual, 73. https://www.eeoc.gov/policy/docs/threshold.html#2-II-B-3-a. Accessed September 19, 2019. See generally *EEOC v American Airlines*, 02-C-6172 (N.D. Ill.) [2002].

44 See part C and also I. Tourkochoriti, 'Is Neutrality Possible? A Critique of the CJEU on Headscarves in the Workplace from a Comparative Perspective', *The American Journal of Comparative Law* vol. 71, no. 2 (2023): 444. https://doi.org/10.1093/ajcl/avad031.

45 *IX v. Wabe*, C-804/18 [2021] ECLI:EU:C:2021:594.

46 *MH Müller Handels GmbH v. MJ*, C-341/19 [2021], ECLI:EU:C:2021:594.

47 *MH Müller Handels GmbH v. MJ*, C-341/19 [2021] § 53.

the employer. They should prove that taking into consideration inter alia the legitimate wishes of their customers or users and the adverse consequences the employer would suffer in the absence of the policy given the nature of their activities and the context in which they are carried out. The policy must also be pursued in a consistent and systematic manner. Taking into consideration customer's preference is not acceptable in the United States according to EEOC guidance.[48]

Similarly, in the second case, the court held that a similar policy may serve the aim of avoiding social conflicts within the undertaking in relation to political, philosophical, or religious beliefs. A policy that may constitute indirect discrimination may be justified by the employer's desire to pursue a policy of political, philosophical, and religious neutrality with regard to its customers or users, provided that that policy meets a genuine need on the part of the employer, which it is for that employer to demonstrate, taking into consideration the legitimate wishes of the customers or users and the adverse consequences that the employer would suffer in the absence of that policy, given the nature of its activities and the context in which they are carried out.[49] Furthermore, according to the CJEU, the difference in treatment is justified if it is appropriate for the purpose of ensuring that the employer's policy of neutrality is pursued in a consistent and systematic manner.[50] The policy may be justified if it covers all visible forms of expression of political, philosophical, or religious beliefs.

The CJEU has not issued decisions in the area of providing a religious accommodation for employees who need to arrange their work time in a way that allows them to participate in religious rituals and holidays. *Cresco v. Achatzi*[51] is a case that raised some issues related to work time and religious celebrations. An employee complained that Austrian law violated EU antidiscrimination legislation by recognising Good Friday as a paid public holiday entailing a 24-hour rest period for members of some religious groups only. The employee, who was not a member of any of these religious groups, claimed that he was discriminated against by being denied public holiday pay for work he did on a Good Friday. The CJEU found that this legal regime on Good Friday constituted direct discrimination to the extent that the public holiday pay was afforded only to employees who celebrated Good Friday and not to other employees who were part of other religious groups.[52] The ruling held that Article 21 of the Charter of Fundamental Rights of the European

48 EEOC Compliance Manual, 73. See generally *EEOC v American Airlines*, 02-C-6172 (N.D. Ill.) [2002].

49 *EEOC v American Airlines*, 02-C-6172 (N.D. Ill.) [2002] § 70.

50 *EEOC v American Airlines*, 02-C-6172 (N.D. Ill.) [2002].

51 *Cresco v. Achatzi*, C-193/17 22 [2019], ECLI:EU:C:2019:43.

52 *Cresco v. Achatzi*, C-193/17 22 [2019] § 69.

Union[53] must be interpreted as meaning that private employers must grant a right to a public holiday on Good Friday to all their employees. In this case, the CJEU must be applauded for finding direct discrimination against employees who are not members of the majority religious groups which have dictated the Good Friday rule. Another possible interpretation of the EU antidiscrimination directive could have been that EU member states should establish a legal regime which creates a duty to employers to recognise to members of other religious groups their own religious holidays as well and to provide public holiday pay for work employees decide to perform on that day. This solution would be consistent with a requirement for providing a reasonable accommodation to employers which is part of the spirit of antidiscrimination law. As analysed earlier, *Groff v. DeJoy, Postmaster General*,[54] decided by the American Supreme Court, provides some interesting insights on how this may be done.

5.3.2 The European Convention of Human Rights as Interpreted by the European Court of Human Rights

The case law of the European Court of Human Rights (ECtHR) tends to accept limits on the manifestation of religious beliefs while posing some interesting criteria that are relevant to these cases. The conception of state secularism which is dominant in the state members to the European Convention of Human Rights defines whether public employees are allowed to express their religiosity in the workplace. The ECtHR usually defers to the margin of appreciation of the states on these issues refusing to find a violation of the right to religious freedom when the government and private employers impose limits upon the wearing of signs of religious affiliation in the workplace. The relevant clauses are Articles 9[55] and 14[56] of the European Convention of Human

53 According to which: "Non-discrimination.

1. Any discrimination based on any ground such as sex, race, colour, ethnic or social origin, genetic features, language, religion or belief, political or any other opinion, membership of a national minority, property, birth, disability, age or sexual orientation shall be prohibited.
2. Within the scope of application of the Treaties and without prejudice to any of their specific provisions, any discrimination on grounds of nationality shall be prohibited".

54 *Groff v. DeJoy, Postmaster General* [2023] 600 US 447.

55 Freedom of thought, conscience, and religion. (1) Everyone has the right to freedom of thought, conscience and religion; this right includes freedom to change his religion or belief and freedom, either alone or in community with others and in public or private, to manifest his religion or belief, in worship, teaching, practice, and observance. (2) Freedom to manifest one's religion or beliefs shall be subject only to such limitations as are prescribed by law and are necessary in a democratic society in the interests of public safety, for the protection of public order, health, or morals, or for the protection of the rights and freedoms of others.

56 Prohibition of discrimination. The enjoyment of the rights and freedoms set forth in this Convention shall be secured without discrimination on any ground such as sex, race, colour, language, religion, political, or other opinion, national or social origin, association with a national minority, property, birth, or other status.

Rights protecting freedom of religion and the right not to experience discrimination, respectively.

For employees in the private sector, the ECtHR has frequently deferred to the margin of appreciation of the local authorities to decide whether their expressive interests should be limited. They have also indicated what the limits to the margin of appreciation are. Thus, the ECtHR has held that when a sign of religious affiliation is "discreet" and does not distract from the employee's professional appearance, imposing limits on the visible wearing of religious symbolic jewellery is a disproportionate limitation of the right to freedom of religion.[57] The Court evaluates whether there has been "real encroachment on the interests of others".[58] The Court has also set some important criteria which may define if limits to manifesting freedom of religion are appropriate. Restrictions on signs of religious affiliation are permissible when they are dictated by health and safety considerations.[59] Asking a nurse on a geriatric ward to remove a necklace with a cross on the basis of a uniform policy based on guidance from the Department of Health is a necessary interference with the right to freedom of religion.[60] The interference serves the need to prevent injury to the bearer herself and the patients she interacts with. In the area of health and safety, employers and domestic authorities are allowed a wider margin of appreciation.[61]

In the area of public employees, if states have decided to limit their wearing of signs of religious affiliation in the workplace, the ECtHR will most likely defer to the margin of appreciation of the state in defining neutrality and will not find a violation of the employees' freedom of religion. National legislation varies within EU member states. In Belgium, Denmark, France, Germany, and the Netherlands, courts have accepted the rights of employers to impose limits upon the wearing of signs of religious affiliation by employees. Not all of these states have legislation or regulation on the wearing of signs of religious affiliation in the workplace. France and Germany maintain bans on the wearing of signs of religious affiliation by employees in the public sector. The Bundesverfassungsgericht has held that a general prohibition on the wearing of signs of religious affiliation in public schools was incompatible

57 *Eweida and Others v. The United Kingdom*, Nos. 48420/10, 59842/10, 51671/10 and 36516/10 [2013] § 94, ECLI:CE:ECHR:2013:0115JUD004842010.

58 *Eweida and Others v. The United Kingdom*, Nos. 48420/10, 59842/10, 51671/10 and 36516/10 [2013] § 95.

59 *Eweida and Others v. The United Kingdom*, Nos. 48420/10, 59842/10, 51671/10 and 36516/10 [2013] § 98.

60 *Eweida and Others v. The United Kingdom*, Nos. 48420/10, 59842/10, 51671/10 and 36516/10 [2013].

61 *Eweida and Others v. The United Kingdom*, Nos. 48420/10, 59842/10, 51671/10 and 36516/10 [2013] § 99.

with the federal Constitution unless it is a risk to the state's neutrality or a peaceful environment in schools.[62]

Employees of the public healthcare system's rights to manifest their religion are not protected either. In *Ebrahimian v. France*,[63] the ECtHR held that an employee of the public healthcare system is also the kind of government employee who may not be offered a contract renewal if she refuses to remove her veil. The case concerned a social assistant employed in the psychiatric unit of a public health establishment in the City of Paris. For the court, the requirement of religious neutrality serves the need of protecting the rights and freedoms of others because the users of the public service were in a vulnerable situation.[64] The limits on the employee's freedom of religion pursued a legitimate aim, which was to ensure respect for all the religious beliefs held by the patients who were using the public service by guaranteeing them strict equality. It also aimed to ensure that all users enjoyed equal treatment without distinction on the basis of religion. The European Convention on Human Rights (ECHR) justified the ban on the headscarf in reference to the need to affirm the neutrality of the public hospital service, which is linked to the attitude of its staff and the requirement that patients do not have any doubts as to the impartiality of those treating them. It recognised the wide margin of appreciation states have in this area and held that public hospitals have the same margin of appreciation, as they are better placed to make decisions in their establishments than an international court. Thus, the disciplinary consequences of the applicant's refusal to remove her veil during working hours were justified in reference to the idea of neutrality.

The ECtHR has held that providers of services in the private sector may not refer to their conscientious objections to refuse to provide services to same-sex couples. An employee of a private company providing relationship counselling with a policy of requiring employers to provide services to all couples may not refer to their freedom of religion to refuse to provide services to same-sex couples.[65] The ECtHR has upheld the neutrality requirement in relation to state employees whose mission is to register official acts even if they claim that they have a conscientious objection to fulfilling their duties. The registrars who refuse to register civil partnerships considering that it is wrong for them to participate in the creation of an institution equivalent to marriage between a same-sex couple are not protected.[66] Disciplinary proceedings against them are dictated by the legitimate aim governments have to promote equal

62 Germany/Federal Constitutional Court Karlsruhe, 1 BvR 471/10, 1 BvR 1181/10 [2015] *International Labor Rights Case Law* no. 2 (2016): 91–100. https://www.doi.org/10.1163/24056901-00201016.

63 *Ebrahimian v. France*, No. 64846/11 [2015] ECLI:CE:ECHR:2015:1126JUD006484611.

64 *Ebrahimian v. France*, No. 64846/11 [2015] § 53.

65 *Ebrahimian v. France*, No. 64846/11 [2015] § 109.

66 *Eweida and Others v. The United Kingdom*, Nos. 48420/10, 59842/10, 51671/10 and 36516/10 [2013] § 106.

opportunities and to act in ways that are not discriminatory.[67] Although these rulings can be justified in reference to the need to provide goods and services to all citizens without discrimination, it is hard to see why the neutrality requirement should also cover signs of religious affiliation if there is no harm to others. Refusal to provide goods and services causes serious harm to those who are refused these goods and services.[68] Providing a good or a service while wearing signs of religious affiliation hardly causes harm to anyone, which makes limitations to wearing signs of religious affiliation in the workplace difficult to justify.

Unlike what is the case in the United States, the ECtHR has not been favourable to requests of members of minority religious groups to accommodate work time so that they are able to participate in religious rituals and celebrate religious holidays. The ECtHR has refused to recognise that Article 9 of the European Convention of Human Rights, which protects freedom of religion, includes a right to have leave from work for particular religious holidays.[69] Older decisions issued by the European Commission of Human Rights express the same attitude.[70] This is a right which is taken for granted in the United States where employers are obliged to provide a religious accommodation to employees if they wish to participate in religious rituals and other celebrations. The ECtHR's refusal to see some value on recognising rights to practice one's religion for minority religious groups was disappointing. Given that the relevant cases are rather old, there may be some hope in accepting changes to the interpretation of the freedom of religion and protection against discrimination of the European Convention of Human Rights towards recognising a right to a reasonable accommodation for minority religious groups to celebrate their holidays. If the CJEU opts to accept an interpretation of EU antidiscrimination law towards recognising reasonable accommodation for religious holidays to employees of minority religious groups as well, this could have a significant influence upon the ECtHR as well.

5.4 Is Neutrality a Good Policy to Justify Exceptions in the Application of Antidiscrimination Law?

Employers refer in Europe to the idea of neutrality to succeed in having policies which have a disparate impact upon minority religious groups. As I have analysed elsewhere,[71] the use of the concept of neutrality in this case is not very successful. Neutrality is an appealing concept which is very difficult to realise.

67 *Eweida and Others v. The United Kingdom*, Nos. 48420/10, 59842/10, 51671/10 and 36516/10 [2013] § 105.

68 See I. Tourkochoriti, 'LGBTQ Wedding Party: Conscientious Objections to the Enforcement of Antidiscrimination Law', *Tulsa Law Review* (forthcoming, 2025).

69 *Kosteski v. The Former Yugoslav Republic of Macedonia*, No. 55170/00 [2006]. https://hudoc.echr.coe.int/rus-press?i=003-1639374-1726807. Accessed December 28, 2024.

70 See *Konttinen v. Finland*, No. 24949/94 [1996] ECLI:CE:ECHR:1996:1203DEC002494994.

71 I. Tourkochoriti, 'Is Neutrality Possible?' 444.

It has a disparate impact upon minority religious groups. This is the case because it is impossible to leave aside our value commitments in any effort to make sense of the world and to devise a government policy. Neutrality is associated with keeping equal distance towards perfectionistic conceptions of the good, secular or not. The difficulty in implementing neutrality becomes obvious if we realise that governments always express value commitments in any attempt to devise a policy. Neutrality can be understood in many ways and depends on social context. In the area of employers' obligations to accommodate employees in the workplace, the employers are also grounding government policies in this area. Employers are the government's long hand due to the role that they are playing in the distributive mechanics of our societies.

As Raz has emphasised, any action that the state undertakes has an impact upon a vision of the good among those that exist within civil societies.[72] Even omissions by the government express some value because failing to help one conception of the good means hindering it.[73] If the government refuses to intervene when a conflict emerges between two social actors with unequal social power, the stronger social actor wins over. This means that the government takes a position in favour of the stronger social actor. In the area of signs of religious affiliation, if the government does not intervene to protect minority groups against discrimination, neutral policies will have a disparate impact upon minority groups which is discriminatory.

As Gadamer has emphasised in *Truth and Method*, the way we see the world is always conditioned by our perspective.[74] This perspective is conditioned by several ideas, preliminary judgements, which we make. Some of these preliminary judgements are conscious, and some are not. Our standards of social interaction are formed under the influence of several cultural factors. We convert some of those standards into legal standards of interaction. We are conscious of some of the cultural influences at play in the formation of these social standards of interaction, while we are unconscious of some others. In states that are mostly culturally homogenous, religion has been an important factor in defining the standards of social interaction. When the French Parliament was debating the ban of the burka in public places, the report prepared ahead of the relevant legislation indicated that since Christianity, the face has become the "quintessence of the person," the "noble part of the body."[75] This slip of tongue indicates that Christianity as a religious influence in the formation of the standards of social interaction in France is omnipresent. The limits on religious headscarves in the workplace, when they are not justified by health and safety considerations, can be understood from this perspective. Majority

72 J. Raz, *The Morality of Freedom*, (Oxford: Clarendon Press, 1986): 124.

73 J. Raz, *The Morality of Freedom*.

74 H.-G. Gadamer, *Truth and Method*, (New York–London: Continuum, 2004).

75 Rapport D'information Fait En Application De L'article 145 Du Réglement, No. 2262 ([Paris]: Assemblée Nationale, 2010) 32. https://www.assemblee-nationale.fr/13/pdf/rap-info/i2262.pdf. Accessed December 28, 2024.

religious groups define the standards of social interaction, which are converted into legal rules, which enable employers to ask employees to remove "conspicuous signs" of religious affiliation in reference to policies of neutrality in the workplace.

This understanding of neutrality in reference to the dominant religious influences is also obvious in the law of public holidays in France and other European states. Despite the reference to the doctrine of *laicité*, which is understood to mean a "strict" separation of church and state in France, public holidays are still associated with the dominant religious heritage of Catholicism. The lack of sensibility on behalf of the ECtHR and the CJEU to accommodate work time for employees-members of minority religious groups so that they are able to celebrate their religious holidays and to participate in rituals related to their religion can also be understood from this perspective. The social and legal rules related to public holidays have been defined by the cultural standards of the majority religious groups. In culturally homogenous states, this religious influence has now faded from public consciousness. This does not mean that it is no longer present though.

Other social and political factors also play an important role in giving content to the vague idea of "neutrality". Various states around the world have adopted different legal regimes in reference to the idea of neutrality. This situation indicates that neutrality is a concept difficult to realise. An interesting contrast exists between France and the United States. In France, state neutrality towards religion is associated with eliminating the manifestation of religion from the public sphere, whereas in the United States, it is associated with allowing the manifestation of religious belief.[76] Americans have had longer experience with trying to ensure peaceful coexistence among various religious communities. This has made courts and political actors more sensitive to the need to manifest religiosity in the public sphere and to look for accommodations in the manifestation of religious beliefs in the workplace.

By the moment of the elaboration of the federal Constitution, the dominant understanding in the United States was that peaceful coexistence among various religious groups could only be assured if equal negative liberty were to be recognised to everyone to manifest their religiosity.[77] The most important political thinkers who contributed to the conception of government in the United States emphasised the need to protect equal negative liberty for all religious groups, which would prevent the emergence of strong majority religious groups which would oppress others.[78] The multiplicity of sects and other

76 See I. Tourkochoriti, "The Constitutional Politics of Religion" 467–382.

77 See generally I. Tourkochoriti, *Freedom of Expression: The Revolutionary Roots of American and French Legal Thought* (Cambridge: Cambridge University Press, 2022).

78 J. Madison, Debates on the Adoption of the Federal Constitution, vol. 3 (Salem: Ayer Co. 1987): 330. For an analysis of freedom of religion in relation to the minority – majority dynamic and its importance for the American conception of the role of the government, see N. Feldman, *Divided by God: America's Church-State Problem and What we Should do about it* (New York: Farrar, Straus and Giroux, 2005).

interests within civil society would prevent the emergence of factions that would oppress other social groups. This variety would be reflected in a federal government which would represent all these interests existing within civil society and which would operate based on various checks and balances.[79]

In France and other European states which maintain limits to the manifestation of religion in the workplace, a different understanding of the role of the government in defining liberty is predominant. In several European states where religious institutions were mixed with state institutions, secularism was associated with the need to remove signs of affiliation with religion in the public sphere. In addition, in France and other European states, an attitude prevailed according to which it is legitimate for the government to define how the citizens express their religiosity in public. This is part of a broader attitude which legitimises government intervention in defining the content of liberty. The French Enlightenment showed distrust towards religion because it allows a greater role to the emotional aspect of humanity suppressing the rational faculties.[80] The law of 1905 separating the church and the state in France can be seen as part of a greater attitude towards the government which legitimises to dictate to the citizens how they will exercise their religious liberty. French liberalism is associated with a conception of the state as having the mission to dictate to the citizens what constitutes the "proper" exercise of one's liberty.[81] This is associated also with an understanding of the mission of the state as defining "living together" for all citizens.[82] This is an idea which exists in various official documents related to the burka ban in France in 2010 and which was the argument the ECtHR accepted in the decision related to the burka ban in public places, *S.A.S. v. France*.[83] In this decision, the ECtHR found that France's burka ban did not constitute a violation of article 9 of the ECHR protecting freedom of religion.

The CJEU in its decisions related to headscarves in the workplace by accepting the criterion of neutrality accepts the bias that is inherent in defining what neutrality means. This means that policies justified as neutral may have a disparate impact upon religious groups. The policy on the basis of which employers are allowed to implement policies of neutrality in the workplace which involve not allowing their employees to wear visible signs of religious affiliation has a

79 M.W. McConnell, "The Origins and Historical Understanding of Free Exercise of Religion", *Harvard Law Review* vol. 103, no. 7 (1990): 1479. https://doi.org/10.2307/1341281.

80 See Voltaire, *Toleration and Other Essays* (New York–London: G.P. Putnam's Sons, 1912). https://oll.libertyfund.org/titles/mccabe-toleration-and-other-essays. Accessed December 28, 2024.

81 See L. Jaume, *L'Individu Effacé ou le Paradoxe du Libéralisme Français* (Paris: Fayard, 1997).

82 R. Michaels, 'Banning Burquas: The Perspective of Postsecular Comparative Law', *Duke Journal of Comparative & International Law* vol. 28, no. 2 (2018): 213. https://djcil.law.duke.edu/article/banning-burqas-michaels-vol28-iss2/. Accessed December 28, 2024; R. Michaels, "The Böckenförde Theorem and Burqa Ban", *German Law Journal* vol. 19 (2018): 321. https://doi.org/10.1017/S2071832200022719.

83 *S.A.S. v. France*, No. 43835/11 [2014] ECLI:CE:ECHR:2014:0701JUD004383511.

disparate impact upon religious groups that consider it necessary to wear conspicuous signs of religious affiliation. They constitute indirect discrimination which is also outlawed by the EU Directive 2000/78/EC. The decisions by the CJEU on headscarves in the workplace indicate that the Court does not make the most of the legal tools against discrimination that have been enacted by the EU. The directives were enacted in order to promote social integration in the workplace for numerous minority religious groups.

Considerations of intersectionality are also at stake. As analysed earlier, although the concern to protect in particular women members of religious minorities was present upon the elaboration of the directive, the CJEU does not make the most of the legal tools it has available to protect these women. The decisions by the CJEU on headscarves in the workplace indicate that there is no willingness to implement an effective protection against discrimination for women members of religious minorities. Although American federal antidiscrimination legislation inspired the EU antidiscrimination directive, courts have not been able to interpret the directive in a way that leads to social inclusion. European courts need to familiarise themselves with the criteria courts have elaborated in this respect in the United States.

5.5 Conclusion

This chapter analysed the law related to the obligations employers have to respect freedom of religion in the workplace. It engaged with the law in the United States which provides interesting criteria that can help mediate between the interests of employers and employees. This mediation is possible thanks to the concept of "reasonable accommodation". Employers have a positive obligation to accommodate the needs of their employees in the workplace by allowing them to bear signs of religious accommodation. They are also obliged to accommodate work time in a way that allows employees to participate in religious rituals and holidays. American federal antidiscrimination law has been very influential in other parts of the world, like the EU. The EU enacted in 2000 a directive against discrimination in the workplace. Courts within the EU, however, have not been able to make the most of the legal tools that exist in the EU in this respect. Despite the American influence, antidiscrimination law is interpreted in Europe in a way that defeats its purpose. The CJEU has accepted that employers may implement policies of neutrality that have a disparate impact upon minority religious groups. This is very concerning because those affected are women members of minority religious groups. These are social members that the EU in particular aimed to protect by enacting legislation against discrimination in access to the workplace. Furthermore, European courts have not interpreted the legal tools they have available to combat discrimination in the workplace in a way that allows for accommodating work time to employees so that they are able to celebrate their religious holidays. This problem is due to the fact that the concept of neutrality, appealing as it is, is elusive. Its understanding depends on several cultural factors. It is understood differently in various parts of the world. In France, it is associated with eliminating religion from the public sphere. In the United States, it is associated with manifesting religion in the public sphere. Europeans need to think seriously about ways of integrating marginalised populations in the workplace. Although the difference in the legal regimes can be understood in reference to deep social and political factors, it is worth reflecting critically on them in reference to the results that they bring about. It is always possible to modify institutions in ways that serve social justice for minority religious groups.

Part III

Shechita and Traditional Circumcision Bans

6 *Shechita* Legal Bans in the Comparative Perspective (Historically and Today)

Iddo Porat

Abstract

In the current study, a detailed analysis of legal restrictions on ritualistic animal slaughter, or *shechita*, in various comparative settings is undertaken. The chapter deals with the historical and present debate on this phenomenon, very controversial both in Europe and beyond Europe since the 1990s. Analyses establish that civil society campaigns for the ban on *shechita*, supported by medical and veterinary authorities and activists on social media, have been effective in some, but not all, countries. The chapter will have two main aims. First, to document the historical bias against ritual animal slaughter, starting inmedieval times and culminating in 19th and 20th century European anti-Semitism, and to show the reemergence of this bias in recent decades. This reemergence, it will be shown, combines classic anti-Semitism with more recent Islamophobia (from the Right), and animal rights and anti-religious progressivism (from the Left). Second, to suggest that constitutional doctrines grounded in anti-discrimination principles are more effective than the doctrine of proportionality in protecting the religious and cultural rights of the Jewish minority in the context of *shechita*. This is because they are better equipped to expose hidden biases and prejudices against Jews than their proportionality-based counterparts.

Keywords

Shechita; animal slaughter; legal restrictions; religious freedom; historical bias

6.1 Introduction

The question of ritual animal slaughter is among the most hotly debated questions currently discussed in Europe. Campaigns addressing banning this practice have been taking place since the 1990s in Germany, Switzerland, the Netherlands, Belgium, Denmark, Luxemburg, Slovenia, Sweden, Norway, Finland, Poland, and England, and involve civil society organizations, medical or veterinary organizations, internet websites, social media and traditional

DOI: 10.4324/9781003423294-10

media, and legal challenges. They are also present outside of Europe in Australia, New Zealand, and the United States.[1]

Several such campaigns have been successful. Thus, ritual animal slaughter has been recently banned in Slovenia (2012),[2] Belgium (2017),[3] Denmark (2014),[4] and Poland (2002, overruled by the constitutional tribunal in 2014).[5] It was banned in Germany for Muslims until overruled by the constitutional court in 2002[6] and has been continuously banned since the 1930s in Sweden (1938) and Norway (1930), and since the late 19th century in Switzerland (1893).[7] A legislative attempt in Switzerland, in 2002, to relax prohibitions on ritual animal slaughter met with staunch opposition and was aborted.[8] Ritual animal slaughter was also banned recently outside of Europe, in New Zealand (2010).[9]

1 See discussions in the Introduction and in Sections 2.1, 2.3, and 2.4.

2 N. Siegal, *Butchering Laws Pit Religion Against Animal Rights*, "New York Times" January 1, 2018, A4; see G. van der Schyff, "Ritual Slaughter and Religious Freedom in a Multilevel Europe: The Wider Importance of the Dutch Case", *Oxford Journal Law Religion*, vol. 3, no. 1 (2014): 76–102. https://doi.org/10.1093/ojlr/rwt046 (discussing the bill which later became into law).

3 In June 2017, the Flemish Parliament accepted a regional decree revoking religious exemptions for the requirement of pre-stunning in all animal slaughter, to take effect from January 1, 2019. In that, it joined the Walloon region whose parliament accepted a similar decree earlier in the year, to take effect in September 2019. *See* Gerhard van der Schyff, "Reviewing the recent Ban on Ritual Slaughter in Flanders". https://verfassungsblog.de/reviewing-the-recent-ban-on-ritual-slaughter-in-flanders/. Accessed October 29, 2024.

4 See R.G. Delahunty, "Does Animal Welfare Trump Religious Liberty? The Danish Ban on Kosher and Halal Butchering", *San Diego International Law Journal*, vol. 16 (2015): 341–342; A. Withnall, "Denmark Bans Kosher and Halal Slaughter as Minister Says 'Animal Rights Come Before Religion". http://www.independent.co.uk/news/world/europe/denmark-bans-halal-and-kosher-slaughter-as-minister-says-animal-rights-come-before-religion-9135580.html. Accessed October 29, 2024.

5 Case of Constitutional Tribunal of Poland, K 52/13 [2014]. https://trybunal.gov.pl/postepowanie-i-orzeczenia/wyroki/art/7276-uboj-rytualny. Accessed October 29, 2024 (striking down a law banning slaughter without pre-stunning without religious exceptions, henceforth, the Polish ritual animal slaughter decision). See also A. Śledzińska-Simon, "A "Stunning" Decision of the Polish Constitutional Tribunal: The Ritual Slaughter Case". http://www.iconnectblog.com/2015/01/a-stunning-decision-of-the-polish-constitutional-tribunal-the-ritual-slaughter-case/. Accessed October 29, 2024.

6 German Federal Constitutional Court, *Schachten*, BVerfGE 104 [2002] – interpreting the Animal Protection Act in light of the constitutional right to freedom of religion and finding in it an exception for Muslim ritual animal slaughter).

7 F. Bergeaud-Blackler, "New Challenges for Islamic Ritual Slaughter: A European Perspective", *Journal of Ethnic and Migration Studies*, vol. 33, no. 6 (2007): 965–980. https://doi.org/10.1080/13691830701432871.

8 F. Bergeaud-Blackler, "New Challenges for Islamic Ritual Slaughter: A European Perspective," 967.

9 See J. Silver, "Understating Freedom of Religion in a Religious Industry: Kosher Slaughter (Shechita) and Animal Welfare", *Victoria University of Wellington Law Review*, vol. 42 (2011): 671–672. https://doi.org/10.26686/vuwlr.v42i4.5113.

When such campaigns receive legal treatment through challenges in European courts,[10] the main method used to decide them is balancing and proportionality.[11] Such challenges are usually couched in the following terms: religious freedom is not absolute. It is subject to those limitations that could be reasonably justified in a democratic society because of conflicting considerations – in particular because of the harms religious practices might inflict on the rights and interests of others (in the case of ritual slaughter, these would be the rights of animals or the societal interests in the prevention of unnecessary cruelty to animals). One must, therefore, assess those harms and balance them with the harms that would be inflicted on the religious community in case of a ban. The assumption behind this exercise is that it is possible to objectively assess the relative harms of ritual animal slaughter and balance them with the harms to religion caused by a ban of the practice.

US constitutional law, however, treats religious freedom claims quite differently. Under the doctrine in *Division of Employment v. Smith*,[12] (henceforth the *Smith* doctrine) there is a clear distinction between two types of religious freedom claims. When laws are "specifically directed"[13] at religious practices, and there is evidence of animus or bias against religion, those laws would be subjected to the austere "strict scrutiny review". On the other hand, "neutral law[s] of general applicability",[14] which only incidentally burden religious practices, will receive the lowest level of judicial review and would usually be left to the forces of the democratic process.

The chapter will have two aims. First, to document the long historical bias against ritual animal slaughter in Europe and the Christian world more generally, and to show the resurfacing of this bias in the last few decades, and the new shapes modern bias in Europe has taken. And secondly, to suggest that

10 See judgment of the German Federal Administrative Court, *Bundesverwaltungsgericht*, BVerwGE 99 [1995] p. 1) (maintaining that ritual animal slaughter is not mandatory under Islam and that the ban on it is therefore constitutional)*; The Cha'are Shalom Ve Tsedek v. France*, 27417/95 [2000] § 84, ECHR 2000-VII) (maintaining that ritual animal slaughter is not a mandatory practice in Judaism and therefore allowing a ban on non-mainstream-Jewish-Orthodox abattoirs to perform Jewish ritual animal slaughter in France) (henceforth the HCtHR *Cha'are Shalom* decision); The Polish ritual animal slaughter decision: Constitutional Tribunal of Poland, K 52/13 [2014] (striking down the complete ban on ritual animal slaughter in Poland); German Federal Constitutional Court, *Schachten*, BVerfGE 104 [2002] (striking down the ban on Muslim ritual slaughter in Germany).

11 See generally, V. Jackson, "Constitutional Law in the Age of Proportionality", *Yale Law Journal*, vol. 124 (2105): 3094; A. Barak, *Proportionality: Constitutional Rights and Their Limitations* (Cambridge: Cambridge University Press, 2012); M. Cohen-Eliya, I. Porat, *Proportionality and Constitutional Culture* (Cambridge: Cambridge University Press, 2013). https://doi.org/10.1017/CBO9781139134996.

12 *Employment Division v. Smith*,494 U.S. 872 [1990].

13 *Employment Division v. Smith*,494 U.S. 872 [1990] 877–878.

14 *Employment Division v. Smith*,494 U.S. 872 [1990] 879 ("The right of free exercise does not relieve an individual of the obligation to comply with a 'valid and neutral law of general applicability on the ground that the law proscribes (or prescribes) conduct that his religion prescribes (or proscribes)'") (quoting *U.S. v. Lee*, 455 U.S. 252 [1982] 263 n. 3.

the US *Smith* Doctrine, because of its emphasis on smoking out bias and prejudice, does a better job than proportionality of protecting religious and cultural minorities from bias and discrimination, and therefore is more appropriate in cases such as those pertaining to ritual animal slaughter.

The chapter will progress as follows. In Section 6.2, I outlay the historical background for ritual animal slaughter. Here I provide information as to the origins, details, and meanings of this practice in Judaism and in Islam, as well as the history of the debate and of the cultural animosity around it, starting in medieval times and culminating in 19th and 20th century European anti-Semitism. Section 6.3 will then analyze the resurrection of this debate in Europe today. This phenomenon starts roughly in the 1980s and steadily intensifies since then and combines old biases against Jews with new ones against the rising Muslim population. In this section, I provide a typology of the different aspects of the cultural animosity towards this practice, as well as the different political and ideological strands that join forces against it. In section 6.4, I engage in legal and constitutional analysis. Here I review three European cases on ritual animal slaughter and describe their analysis and the doctrine of proportionality that is at their center. I then compare the proportionality review with the US doctrine that has evolved in *Smith* and its progeny, the *Lukumi* case, as well as some of the cases that followed them, and show how this doctrine provides a better doctrinal framework than proportionality if applied to ritual animal slaughter.

6.2 Historical Background

6.2.1 Origins and Meanings

As part of the dietary restrictions imposed on their believers, both Judaism and Islam have rules regarding the way animals consumed for food should be slaughtered. These apply mainly to cattle, sheep, and poultry. In Judaism, the basis for the rules can be found in the Torah,[15] and they were originally part of the rules for the proper sacrifice of animals during the time of the two Temples, which were also, usually, consumed after the sacrifice. After the destruction of the second Temple, animal sacrifice was banned, but the rules regarding the choice of animals and other rules accompanying sacrifice remained and have been further elaborated and complicated over the years.[16]

15 The Torah does not command a particular way of slaughter but does have rules as to the prohibition on consuming blood (Leviticus 7:26; Deuteronomy 12:15, 12:23), as well as detailed rules regarding the permitted species (Deuteronomy 12:3) and parts for consumption (Genesis 32:33; Leviticus 7:24), and the separation of milk and meat (Deuteronomy 12:21), from which the rules regarding slaughter were deduced.

16 The rules in the Torah were further elaborated, first in the *Mishna* and *Gemara* (*Talmud*) in the 1st to 5th century, and then later on in Jewish law sources until they was canonized in *Shulchan Aruch* in the 16th century, which remains the central source for the current rules of Jewish slaughter.

Anthropological explanations for ritual slaughter and for animal sacrifice vary. The practice of animal sacrifice probably began with the move of man to hunting and was widespread in the ancient world. It was commonly used in ancient Greece and in the Roman world, and detailed documentation of it can be traced back to the Mesopotamian culture in the third millennium BC.[17] Anthropologists speculate that it was a way of justifying and sanctifying meat eating, which was relegated originally only to the priesthood and upper classes, and to commoners only on special festivities.[18] Others argue that it was originally a symbolic way of repenting for the killing of animals for food.[19] Other explanations have to do with the symbolic nature of blood in all cultures – either as a curing or magical element or as a purifying mechanism.[20] As to the particular form of slaughter used in Judaism and Islam – a cut to the throat and a complete drainage of blood – it is reasonable to assume that this method facilitates the preservation of meat, as it helps to prevent the meat from rotting.

Religious justifications for the practice also vary. From a religious perspective, one must note, the mere question of justification or rationale is usually secondary or irrelevant. In Judaism, the main, and usually the only, explanation to all dietary rules including the rules of slaughter, is that it is so commanded by God in the Torah. However, over the years, Judaism has provided some additional rationales which are often superimposed on the practice, or give it a rationalization, although they do not affect its binding force. First, the rules of the choice of animal and the way it is slaughtered are supposed to ensure the purity of the animal that is then transmitted to the purity, or impurity, of the person consuming it.[21] Secondly, it is claimed that ritual slaughter ensures minimal suffering for animals, in keeping with Jewish commandments

17 W.W. Hallo, "The Origin of Israelite Sacrifice", *Biblical Archaeology Review*, vol. 37 no. 6 (2011): 6.

18 W.W. Hallo, "The Origin of Israelite Sacrifice," 7. See also D. Biale, *Blood and Belief: The Circulation of a Symbol between Jews and Christians* (Oxford: Oxford University Press, 2007): 8. https://doi.org/10.1525/california/9780520253049.001.0001 – "The biblical rules that the priests fashioned for the proper disposition of animal blood enacted their ritual monopoly".

19 D. Biale, discussion Jacob Milgrom's work on blood in the bible writes that "for Milgrom since blood is equated with life, the killing of an animal for nourishment…involves a capital crime that can be expiated only by the blood of the animal itself" D. Biale, *Blood and Belief: The Circulation of a Symbol between Jews and Christians* 8. This seems to have been also one of the rationales for sacrifice in the Hellenic and Roman world.

20 D. Biale, *Blood and Belief: The Circulation of a Symbol between Jews and Christians* 26 "as with Israel blood was used by the Greeks as a purifying agent". See also "Purification rite". In: *Encyclopedia Britannica*. http://www.britannica.com/topic/purification-rite/Types-of-purification-rites. Accessed October 28, 2024.

21 See J. Silver, "Understating Freedom of Religion in a Religious Industry" 675.

that forbid cruelty to animals, some of which are written in the Torah.[22] Finally, Judaism, as well as Islam, strictly forbid eating blood, which is another rationale for the drainage of blood during ritual slaughter.

The practice in Judaism and in Islam is quite similar, but there are also important differences. In Judaism, ritual animal slaughter (*shechita*) is considered a commandment (*Mitzva*) that confers virtue on the person committing it. The particle is governed by the following essential requirements: First, performing shechita requires a professional slaughterer – a *Shochet*. The *Shochet* is in charge of both the actual slaughter and of the inspection of the animal before and after it. He (as only males can hold this office) has to be a Jew in good standing and has to go through a long and rigorous training – both practical and liturgical – including exams and a lengthy apprenticeship.[23] Second, the practice requires a special knife – a very sharp knife that must be completely smooth and without any nicks. Third, prior to being slaughtered, the animal itself has to be completely intact, externally and internally, and alive. Fourth, the killing itself has to be done by one clear strong and fast cut at the throat of the animal, dissecting, preferably entirely, the trachea, esophagus, carotid arteries, jugular veins, and vagus nerve, and allowing the blood to drain fully from the carcass. Fifth, there must be an inspection of internal parts of the carcass to see that the animal is not flawed, including inspections of the lungs in cattle. And sixth, so as to ensure a complete drainage of the blood from the carcass, there is usually a process of salting the meat – as salt absorbs fluids.[24]

This is a crude simplification, as the rules themselves are very detailed, and a flaw in any step along the way brings about the disqualification of the meat for eating (Treifa). There is also some variance between two degrees of strictness of the practice (e.g., regular *Kosher* and Glatt *Kosher*).

Islamic ritual animal slaughter is called *dhabihah* and similarly requires a clear and fast cut in the throat by a sharp knife, and the drainage of blood. But the rules in Islam are less detailed and more relaxed than in Judaism. Dhabihah requires only that the person performing the slaughter pronounce the name of Allah three times before the act, and, like in Judaism, the blood should be properly drained from the body of the animal. Unlike in Judaism not only professionals can engage in dhabihah but any Muslim. As with Judaism, there are restrictions on the animal whose meat is allowed for consumption, although there is more variance among different sects of Islam as to the extent of the prohibitions. Meats of pigs, boars, and swine are strictly prohibited in Islam, and so are meats of carnivorous animals, such as lions, tigers, cheetahs, dogs,

22 This rationale is given by Maimodes, for example, in *Guide of the Perplexed*, 3:17. It is still used as a rationale by Orthodox Jews today; see, e.g., in a recent Jewish publication in the UK: *A Guide to Shechita*, (London: Shechita UK, 2009). https://www.shechitauk.org/wp-content/uploads/2016/02/A_Guide_to_Shechita_2009__01.pdf. Accessed October 28, 2024. "The time-hallowed practice of shechita, marked as it is by compassion and consideration for the welfare of the animal, has been a central pillar in the sustaining of Jewish life for millennia".

23 See J. Silver, "Understating Freedom of Religion in a Religious Industry" 677–678.

24 J. Silver, "Understating Freedom of Religion in a Religious Industry" 676.

and cats. Meat that is not worthy of consumption is called *Haram* meat, and meat that is worthy of consumption is called *Hallal*.[25] The command to eat only *Halal* meat has its source in the Quran.[26]

6.2.2 The Controversy Around Ritual Animal Slaughter in the Modern Era

Banning ritual animal slaughter and the controversy around it are relatively recent (unlike the banning of other practices in Judaism, such as circumcision, for example, which dates back to antiquity). This is so, partly, since slaughter – the cutting of the throat of the animal and the draining of its blood – was the traditional and universal way of killing animals for centuries and so in itself did not provoke any special concern.[27] However, blood libels – folklore myths and concocted stories about Jews using the blood of non-Jews for ritual purposes[28] – which were present already in medieval times, included elements that relate to the Jewish ritual around animal slaughter. Many of the medieval blood libels depicted the victims as slaughtered at the throat or as hung from their legs like animals that are slaughtered during *shechita*.[29] Blood libels were revived in 19th- and 20th-century Europe, at which time the association with animal slaughter became more explicit, as will be described next.[30]

The direct controversy around the practice begins only when it appears to conflict with animal rights, and when new methods for killing the animal prior to slaughter are devised. This happened first in Germany in the middle

25 D. Waines, *An Introduction to Islam* (Cambridge: Cambridge University Press, 2003): 78–79. https://doi.org/10.1017/CBO9780511801037.

26 *The Holy Qur'an* (transl. N.J. Davidson, London: Penguin, 1975) 6:121: "Do not eat of any flesh that has not been consecrated in the name of Allah for that is sinful".

27 In the recent controversy over the ritual animal slaughter ban in Poland, traditional Christian butchers also objected to the ban since they used a similar method of slaughter. See A. Gliszczyńska-Grabias, W. Sadurski, "Freedom of Religion versus Humane Treatment of Animals: Polish Constitutional Tribunal's Judgment on Permissibility of Religious Slaughter Judgment of the Constitutional Tribunal of Poland of 10 December 2014, K 52/13", *European Constitutional Law Review*, vol. 11, no. 3, (2015): 599. https://doi.org/10.1017/S1574019615000280.

28 See generally A. Dundes (ed.), *The Blood Libel Legend: A Casebook in Anti-Semitic Folklore* (University of Wisconsin Press, Madison, 1991): 304, 318.

29 E. Rappaport describes how in the Blood Libel of Wessenburg, Bavaria, in 1270 "the victim is put into a head-down position like a slaughtered animal in a butcher shop…and the alleged murderers with great eagerness collect the blood, even after Passover when matzah are no longer made". E. Rappaport, *The Ritual Murder Accusation: The Persistence of Doubt and the Repetition Compulsion*. In Dundes, *The Blood Libel Legend*, 304, 318. Note the inversion, often present in anti-Semitic myths – Jews, who are strictly forbidden by their religion from eating blood, are depicted as eagerly collecting blood to be consumed as part of Jewish ritual. Some anti-Semites tried to explain this contradiction by stating that only animal blood is forbidden in Judaism, and Jews therefore compensate for this restriction by eating human blood. Dundes, *The Blood Libel Legend*, 319.

30 J. Silver, "Understating Freedom of Religion in a Religious Industry" and accompanying text.

of the 19th century, with the rise in awareness of animal rights and with the industrialization of slaughtering.

Slaughter is required, till this day, for the drainage of blood from animals consumed for food and the prevention of bacteria, regardless of whether it has a religious reason or not. During earlier times, slaughter was also considered to be the fastest and least painful way of killing the animal since the quick drainage of blood after the slaughter results in losing of consciousness of the animal within a short period of time. Today, scientists agree that the average time for loss of consciousness is 30 seconds after the slaughter and the maximum time is 2 minutes.[31] However, modern techniques that began being developed allowed for quicker ways of killing the animal before it is slaughtered, or for ways of rendering it unconscious before it is slaughtered. Such methods (whether bringing about death immediately, or only unconsciousness) are referred to as "stunning". Stunning, in the 19th century, with regards to cattle, included a blow with a big hammer to the head of the animal or a bolt that was hammered into the head. Today, an air pressure bolt-gun is used to drive the bolt through the head of the animal, and sometimes electrocution is used instead. The conflict around the practice until this day therefore stems from the fact that both Judaism and some interpretations of Islam[32] do not permit the stunning of animals prior to their slaughter. In Islam since this inhibits the flow of blood, and in Judaism both for this reason but mainly because the animal must be completely intact and alive prior to the slaughter.[33] Judaism and Islam therefore seem to require a method of killing animals for food in which the animal feels the pain of the slaughter, even if for a short period of time, whereas with stunning, this feeling of pain is reduced or eliminated.

6.2.3 Banning Campaigns and Anti-Semitism

According to Shai Lavi, banning campaigns in Germany in the 19th century originated from three movements – Progressivism which wished to make Germany more progressive, among others by providing for more humane treatment of animals; Romanticism associated also with German nationalism and anti-Semitism; and scientific health reasons having to do with hygiene in abattoirs and the inspection of healthy meat.[34]

31 The Humane Slaughter Act defines ritual slaughter as a humane method of slaughter. 7 U.S.C.A. § 1902.

32 A. Bruce, "Do Sacred Cows Make the Best Hamburgers? The Legal Regulation of Religious Slaughter of Animals", *University of New South Wales Law Journal*, vol. 34, no. 1 (2011) – "There appears to be no consistent agreement on the issue with the result that some Islamic scholars insist on the practice whereas others do not").

33 J. Silver, "Understating Freedom of Religion in a Religious Industry" 676–677.

34 S. Lavi, "Animal Laws and the Politics of Life: Slaughterhouse Regulation in Germany, 1870–1917", *Theoretical Inquiries in Law*, vol. 8, no. 1 (2007): 221–222. https://doi.org/10.2202/1565-3404.1149. See also S. Lavi, "Enchanting a Disenchanted Law: On Jewish Ritual and Secular History in Nineteenth-Century Germany", *UC Irvine Law Review*, vol. 1, no. 3 (2011): 813. https://escholarship.org/content/qt8f08j7dn/qt8f08j7dn.pdf?t=qx22aj. Accessed October 29, 2024.

Progressives, according to Shai Lavi, were concerned with the respectability of Germany and its status among civilized nations. Animal Humane Societies that were first established in Germany in the mid-19th century followed their counterparts in other European countries (England being the first in 1820) and gained popularity in the second half of that century. Progressivism also introduced a scientific element to the debate. Scientific research opposing ritual slaughter tried to show that in traditional ways of slaughter the pain extended for a long period of time (arguments were made that it took between 10 to 30 minutes for the animal to die[35]). However, even at that time, the scientific conclusions were not unanimous, and some argued that these times are vastly exaggerated. There were also debates at the time as to whether the then available methods of stunning were reliable or whether they ended up creating more pain for animals than the traditional methods.[36]

Health regulations issues included concerns that the meat produced by ritual slaughter would be unhealthy because of poor sanitary conditions or because of the drainage of blood. Most of these concerns, in retrospect, were unfounded.[37]

Finally, Romanticism and anti-Semitism, while not being at the center of the early campaigns against ritual animal slaughter, soon became the focal point of these campaigns. These ideologies coupled ideas on a romantic affinity with nature – the idea of the return to nature, to rural life and simplicity, and a wholeness of an organic connection between man and nature – with ideas on nationalism – a nostalgic return to the German Teutonic tribes, an organic conception of the German nation, and a concern for not contaminating the German nation with external elements. Jews were targets on both these accounts: first, they were a foreign element to the ethnic and national Germanic tradition, and secondly, they represented a culture which was dissociated from nature and from rural life, and, through animal slaughter, was also cruel to animals. In addition, Jews were associated with the liberal and modern strands of German society, and for that reason also, were anathema to the right-wing nationalists and conservatives.

The campaign against ritual animal slaughter therefore fit well with the rising anti-Semitism of late 19th and early 20th century, and as mentioned before, the revival of blood libels at that time created a direct association between Jewish cruelty to animals and Jewish cruelty to human beings. Studies show that there were more than 100 blood libels in Europe between 1880 and 1911. Many of them, as the one that occurred in the Prussian town of Konitz

35 R. Judd, "The Politics of Beef: Animal Advocacy and the Kosher Butchering Debates in Germany", *Jewish Social Studies. New Series*, vol. 10, no. 1 (2003): 117, 121.

36 S. Lavi, "Animal Laws and the Politics of Life" 231–232.

37 S. Lavi, "Animal Laws and the Politics of Life" 233. The only valid concern was, quite amusingly, the claim that meat produced by ritual slaughter was not as rich and tasty as meat produced by pre-stunning methods because of the drainage of blood from the meat.

in 1900, included accusations against Jewish slaughterers.[38] In these blood libels, as D. Biale writes, "Jewish ritual slaughter became conflated with ritual murder", reflecting the accusation that "Jewish ritual slaughter was a barbarous practice that bespoke the Jews' bloodthirstiness: just as they butchered their animals inhumanly so the Jews would no doubt be wont to do to their neighbors".[39] The phenomenon did not completely pass over America, as in a 1919 blood libel in the town of Pittsfield Massachusetts, in which a Jewish slaughterer and Mohel was accused of dragging a Polish boy to the synagogue and extracting two bottles of blood from him.[40]

Lavi shows how the campaign for regulating animal slaughter that was first led by Progressives and humanitarian societies in the 1870s and at that stage either allowed for exceptions for Jewish ritual slaughter or was uninterested in it, was taken over by the conservative and anti-Semitic movement, and then started targeting specifically the Jewish ritual and focusing attention on not allowing any exceptions to Judaism. The heated debate at the German Reichstag in the 1890s over a law banning Jewish *shechita* was an overt show of anti-Semitism, recognized as such by both proponents and opponents of the law.[41] A similar and more successful campaign that also involved explicit anti-Semitism was held in Switzerland, which banned *shechita* in 1893 – a ban that still holds today.[42] In Switzerland, the campaign met divisions not only on political but also on religious grounds, as the Catholic Church opposed the ban, and the polls of the plebiscite showed that the ban was supported by a majority of German Protestant Swiss but rejected by a majority of the French Catholic Swiss.[43]

The German campaign was unsuccessful eventually, but this changed during the Nazi regime. One of the first laws promulgated by Hitler, in 1933, was a ban on Jewish *shechita*, which was accompanied by similar laws in other

38 In that incident, a young man was murdered and his body carved into pieces. The blame lay on a Jewish butcher, A. Levi, because of a testament given by his neighbor Christian butcher who had most likely committed the crime. S. Lavi, "Animal Laws and the Politics of Life" 126.

39 D. Biale, *Blood and Belief* 127; See also Judd, note 32 at 120.

40 A.G. Duker, *Twentieth-Century Blood Libels in the United-States.* In: A. Dundes (ed.), *The Blood Libel Legend* 233, 249. A.G. Duker reports at least 20 cases of blood libels in the early 20th century in America. Many of them were instigated by European immigrants to the USA, especially Poles.

41 A.G. Duker, *Twentieth-Century Blood Libels in the United-States.* See also T. Kushner, "Stunning Intolerance: A Century of Opposition to Religious Slaughter", *The Jewish Quarterly*, vol. 36 (1989): 216.

42 J.M. Efron, "The Most Cruel Cut of All? The Campaign Against Jewish Ritual Slaughter in Fin-deSiècle Switzerland and Germany", *Leo Baeck Institute Yearbook*, vol. 52 (2007): 167.

43 "[T]hose in favor of the ban numbered 180,000, most of them in predominantly Protestant cantons, versus 120,000 who were opposed, who included many of the country's Catholics". read more: http://www.haaretz.com/jewish/features/.premium-1.671934. The article also notes that at the time the constitutional amendment was adopted there were only 8,000 Jews in Switzerland.

European countries and in all the countries occupied by Nazi Germany.[44] The Nazi regime, like its precursors in the 19th century, also combined anti-Semitic ideology with ideology regarding the natural world.[45] Hitler and Himmler were both vegetarians, which enhanced their opposition to *shechita*. The *Der Sturmer* magazine – the mouthpiece of Nazi propaganda – has made ample use of caricatures depicting ritual animal slaughter and referencing the way Jewish barbaric slaughter practices extended from animals to human beings. The notorious 1940 Nazi propaganda film *The Eternal Jew* by Fritz Hippler opens with a long and gruesome scene of a Jewish slaughter of a cow, extending for a whole 10 minutes out of the film's 60 minutes.[46]

6.3 The Modern Resurrection of the Debate

6.3.1 Resurrection of the Debate

In the decades following WWII, ritual animal slaughter was generally tolerated in European societies (with the exception of the few countries that did not repeal their laws banning ritual animal slaughter)[47] and did not raise controversy or debate. This may have been a result of the recent memory of the persecution of Jews by the Nazis, and possibly also of the radical diminishment of the Jewish population after the war, which reduced the extent of the phenomena.[48] In Germany, some of the laws banning ritual animal slaughter were repealed and those that were not, were not enforced.[49] It is not until the 1980s that one notices a rekindling of the debate around the practice. However, once the debate resumes, it seems to be in full force and constantly on the rise, to the point that banning the practice has become very popular in several European countries. In addition, the debate has acquired

44 Following Germany in outlawing *shechita* were Poland (1938) Italy (1938) and Sweden (1938). Norway had banned *shechita* even earlier at (1930). See F. Bergeaud-Blackler, "New Challenges for Islamic Ritual Slaughter" 965, 967.

45 For fascinating recent research as to the Nazi relationship with blood and with the natural world, see J. Chapoutot, *La Loi du Sang* (Paris: Éditions Gallimard, 2014): 34–44, which has a special section on Nazi attitudes towards Jewish ritual slaughter. The author brings evidence from H. Himmler's correspondence where he argues that the cruel attitude of Jews towards animals were a trait of the Jewish race that differed it from the Nordic race that was close to Nature. H. Himmler believed that the Buddhist monks, who spared even the life of insects, were decedents of Nordic people who emigrated from Europe to Asia during prehistoric times and attest to the Nordic affinity with nature. *Id.* at 37. Except for the law against Jewish ritual slaughter one of the first laws of the Nazi regime was a law restricting cruelty towards animals in hunting – Reichtierschutzgesetz [1933]. The author notes, however, that it was very rarely applied in practice and hunting was in effect not restricted during Nazi times, as Herman Goring, for example, was a devout hunter.

46 See D. Biale, *Blood and Belief* 128.

47 See list of countries banning ritual animal slaughter.

48 See S. Lavi, "Animal Laws and the Politics of Life" 250.

49 S. Lavi, "Animal Laws and the Politics of Life" 225.

all the attributes of a passionate and positional debate in which there is little attempt at compromise, as we will see.[50]

Surveys of the past two decades show strong popular support in several European countries for banning ritual animal slaughter. A 2013 internet survey commissioned by the *Jewish Chronicle* in Britain to YouGov (an internet-based market research company)[51] has shown that 45% of respondents supported a ban on ritual animal slaughter (27% were against and 28% were undecided). Interestingly, support for the ban was evenly distributed among Left and Right voters (Conservative, Labor, and Liberal Democrats) with the exception of the radical right-wing party UKIP, members of which have shown a considerably higher support for banning the practice (71%). A more recent internet poll, on the same website, commissioned by the RSPCA (Royal Society for the Prevention of Cruelty to Animals) found even greater popular support for a ban of ritual animal slaughter, with 77% of the people surveyed supporting the ban.[52]

To date, there are several countries that completely ban ritual animal slaughter. These include, in Europe, Switzerland (1893), Norway (1930), Sweden (1938),[53] and Denmark (2014), and outside of Europe, New Zealand (2010).[54] The Federation of Veterinarians of Europe has issued a statement that it is of the opinion that "the practice of slaughtering animals without prior stunning is unacceptable under any circumstances".[55]

50 O. Liviatan compares the debate over Muslim practices, including ritual animal slaughter in Western Europe, to the debate over abortion. Both issues, she argues, are "passionately and acrimoniously debated as positional (rather than valence) issues, with little inclination for compromise". O. Liviatan, "From Abortion to Islam: The Changing Function of Law in Europe's Cultural Debates", *Fordham International Law Journal*, vol. 36 (2013): 93–94. https://www.corteidh.or.cr/tablas/r30420.pdf. Accessed October 29, 2024.

51 F. Cranmer, "Ritual slaughter, religious male circumcision and public opinion: a YouGov poll", http://www.lawandreligionuk.com/2013/04/07/ritual-slaughter-religious-male-circumcision-and-public-opinion-a-yougov-poll/. Accessed October 29, 2024.

52 "Almost 80 percent of UK wants an end ton on stun slaughter". http://www.politics.co.uk/opinion-formers/rspca-royal-society-for-the-prevention-of-cruelty-to-animals/article/almost-80-per-cent-of-uk-wants-an-end-to-non-stun-slaughter. Accessed October 29, 2024.

53 F. Bergeaud-Blackler, "New Challenges for Islamic Ritual Slaughter" 965, 967.

54 The ban was administered through a ministerial code adopted by the Minister of Agriculture. The Animal Welfare (Commercial Slaughter). Code of Welfare 2010. https://www.mpi.govt.nz/dmsdocument/46018-Code-of-Welfare-Commercial-slaughter. Accessed October 29, 2024. The minister refused to introduce a religious exemption to the code, despite an earlier recommendation of the National Animal Welfare Advisory Committee ('NAWAC') that argued, "This is necessary to allow Jewish people to manifest their religion and belief (as provided for in the New Zealand Bill of Rights Act 1990, Public Act 1990 No 109) and because NAWAC considers that Shechita does not meet the minimum standard for commercial slaughter".

55 Slaughter of Animals Without Prior Stunning, FVE Position Paper, FVE/02/104 Final. https://fve.org/cms/wp-content/uploads/fve_02_104_slaughter_prior_stunning.pdf. Accessed October 29, 2024.

6.3.2 Sociological Analysis – Five Types of Arguments

The following is a summary of five types of arguments currently being made in banning campaigns against ritual animal slaughter in order to show how current biases and anti-Semitic tropes join old ones in today's banning campaigns. The five arguments are as follows: (1) Not Modern/Barbaric. (2) Oppressive. (3) Not Us. (4) Not Natural/Against Nature. (5) Supported by Powerful Forces.

6.3.2.1 Not Modern/Barbaric

Ritual animal slaughter is portrayed by opponents as being pre-modern, pre-liberal, irrational, archaic, barbaric, bloody, and sacrificial. In many of those campaigns, the target is both the practice of religious minorities and religion *per se*.[56] Secular societies are vocal in these campaigns and lament the surrender of logic, liberal ideas, and of vital interests and rights to religious pressure[57] – but, at the same time, and not always consciously, the target is minority religion and not Christianity.

The ancient nature of the practice and its involvement with blood and pain exacerbate the feelings of alienation that modernity has with religion in general and with Judaism and Islam in particular.[58] So is the ritualistic nature of the practice, including the use of "professionals" such as a Shochet, prayers, and ceremony, and the use of ritual instruments – the knife in animal slaughter.

56 It is so viewed by religious members. See the following on the campaign against ritual animal slaughter: "This assault on Judaism is, of course, part of a broader assault on religion, all religions, including Christianity, and the biblical understanding of life. The basic idea is that religion is primitive and ignorant and must be repressed. This is a militant form of secularism and while Muslims and Jews are today's victims, there will be many more tomorrow". M.A. Kellner, "Danish Ban on Ritual Slaughter Unites Jews and Muslims". http://www.deseretnews.com/article/865597101/Danish-ban-on-ritual-animal-slaughter-unites-Jews-and-Muslims.html?pg=all#ygx0PgTZDevChxbA.99. Accessed October 29, 2024.

57 The British Secular Society for example engages in a campaign against animal ritual slaughter as one of its ten major campaigns posted on its website: "Our campaign areas". http://www.secularism.org.uk/campaigns.html. Accessed October 29, 2024. It argues in its website that "Whilst we support the right to religious freedom, this is not an absolute right, and we do not think that exemptions should be made on religious grounds to animal welfare regulations which apply without exception to everyone else". An example of rhetoric lamenting the over-protection of religion can be seen here by the excessive hyperbole: "whatever the result may be, the claim that ritual slaughter is part of the freedom of religion, and is thus untouchable, is an incorrect one". C.M. Zoethout, "Ritual Slaughter and the Freedom of Religion: Some Reflections on a Stunning Matter", *Human Rights Quarterly*, vol. 35, no. 3 (2013) 651–672.

58 See, e.g., an interview on BBC with the Swiss animal activist E. Kessler, May 2003: "And we are today in a modern world and cannot accept many things that have been prescribed by religion in earlier times. Like stoning women that has been abandoned ritual slaughter is a very brutal thing and should be given up too". "Interview von Radio BBC mit Erwin Kessler zum Schächten in Europa". http://vgt.ch/news2003/030515.htm. Accessed October 29, 2024.

The association with sacrifice, and in particular the sacrifice of blood, is another element in the perception of this practice as barbaric or archaic and irrational. As noted earlier, ritual animal slaughter has its origins in animal sacrifice, and although the current use of the practice is designed for the purpose of food consumption, it is still associated with the symbolic sacrifice of the animal's well-being to the idolatry of religion.

As a speculation, I would like to suggest that one may see less of an objection to the ritual and irrational nature of this practice in Catholic communities than in Protestant communities (Poland being an exception for which I have no explanation).[59] There is an interesting geographical correlation between active objection to ritual animal slaughter and countries with a Protestant majority. The debates seem to be stronger in the Anglo-Saxon countries, the Nordic countries, Germany, Austria, and the German part of Switzerland (recall the objection of French Catholics to the ban on ritual animal slaughter in the plebiscite of the late 19th century). On the other hand, Spain, Italy, and France do not seem to object too strongly to this practice. This may come from the individualized nature of Protestant belief – the idea that faith is a personal and individual practice rather than a communal and familial one – and its rejection of ritual and ceremony as idolatry. On the other hand, Catholicism has retained more of its ritualistic nature as a religion, and Catholic societies tend to be more family and community oriented so that such community-based practices may be less alien to them.

6.3.2.2 Oppressive

Aligning objections to ritual animal slaughter with objections to oppression makes for the association of the Left with campaigns against this practice. The term "oppression" is often used in the context of animal rights and is used in particular in the context of opposition to animal ritual slaughter. Animals are helpless and innocent, and the graphic descriptions, photographs, and videos of religious slaughter arouse outrage against the oppression of helpless creatures. The argument of oppression also allows the coupling of those who engage in ritual animal slaughter with other categories of oppressors – white oppressors of blacks,[60] male oppressors of women, rich oppressors of the poor, and colonial oppressors of the colonized.

The argument of oppression is also associated with the use of human rights conceptualism and rhetoric, which is another aspect coupling objections to ritual animal slaughter with the progressive Left. Animal rights are often seen as the logical extension of human rights to other, non-human, groups so that cruelty towards animals is on par with human rights violations.[61] The turn to

59 I thank L. Zucca for this observation.

60 See, e.g., Facebook group called "People of Color Against Forced Genital Cutting".

61 W. Kymlicka, S. Donaldson, "Animal Rights, Multiculturalism and the Left", *Journal of Social Philosophy*, vol. 45, no. 1 (2014): 126–127. https://doi.org/10.1111/josp.12047.

rights rhetoric intensifies the debate and furthers it away from compromise, as rights, generally, serve as a trump, and as arguments of principle, and eschew compromise.[62]

6.3.2.3 "Not Us"

While the argument of oppression is usually associated with the Left, the argument of "Not Us" is usually associated with the Right. It is an argument most associated with the persecution of Jews over the ages, and anti-Semitism was often coupled by nationalism, not the least during the Nazi regime. But the current nationalistic angel of these debates has an important modern "twist" by adding Islam as a target – at times the main target – of the campaigns. Lavi has argued that Islam and Judaism are both representations of the foreign for the German society of the 1980s, but in different ways: the Jews are "strangers from within" and the Muslims "strangers from without".[63] Used by nationalists such as the racist English Defense League,[64] and by others more covertly, these types of arguments allude to the fact that those using this practice are different, alien to the culture, to the history and habits of the country, and thus threaten to fracture its integrity and organic wholeness. They also allude, either overtly or covertly, to the oriental origins of these religious communities and practices, which are ethnically and culturally different from the European ethnic and cultural origins. In this respect, the campaign against ritual animal slaughter joins the Islamophobic campaigns against the burqa and the building of Minarets, all of which are designed to stop the advent of Islam into Europe.

6.3.2.4 "Not Natural/Against Nature"

The objection to ritual animal slaughter on the account of it being averse to the protection of nature is direct, and , as described earlier, was also used in past anti-Semitic campaigns against the practice, by portraying Judaism as averse to the natural and the rural. Today too, similar associations are being made in relation to the current debate on ritual animal slaughter. Animal

62 Compared to the way, according to Liviatan, the abortion debate in Western Europe was framed by the Court, Liviatan argues, "Courts and legislatures framed debates beyond the clash of rights or worldviews, generating legal arrangements that incorporated additional social and public policy concerns for the purpose of generating compromises". However, this did not happen, according to her, with regard to conflicts over Muslim cultural practices, towards which the legal attitude was one of forced "integration and assimilation".

63 S. Lavi, "Unequal Rites – Jews, Muslims and the History of Ritual Slaughter in Germany", *Tel Aviv Yearbook for German History*, vol. 37 (2009): 164, 167. http://www.tau.ac.il/GermanHistory/Lavi.pdf. Accessed October 29, 2024.

64 See, e.g., "EDL targets Blackburn KFC in protest over Halal chicken". http://www.lancashiretelegraph.co.uk/news/8429843.EDL_targets_Blackburn_KFC_in_protest_over_Halal_chicken/?ref=rl. Accessed October 29, 2024.

societies all too often portray Judaism and Islam as inherently averse to animals and to nature, ignoring central elements in both religions that show compassion to animals and concern for nature.

It may therefore be no surprise that one finds among the vocal opponents to ritual animal slaughter many who are also engaged in ecological campaigns or are members of the Green Party. In Finland, the Green Party was vocal against ritual animal slaughter.

6.3.2.5 Supported by Powerful Forces

This last attribute is associated with the sinister and omnipotent perception of religion generally, but in particular with perception of the omnipotence of Judaism that draw also on anti-Semitic imagery and include the belief in an all-powerful Jewish lobby and a Jewish takeover of the Media. Islam, while more recently joining this club, is also at times associated with the powerful forces by using the corrupt power of oil money.

The main manifestation of this argument is in conspiracy theories that argue that powerful forces protect this practice from criticism and manipulate scientific findings.

This feature, coupled with some of the other features portrayed earlier, may also account for the very extreme, high toned, and, at times, violent nature of some of the instances of the debate, especially when taking into account the fact that, in some of the societies where the debate is held, only a few instances of the practice have occurred (in Denmark, for example, where ritual animal slaughter was banned, there was no instance of the practice for decades). Comparisons of ritual animal slaughter with murder are common in these heated debates, as are comparisons of this practice with the atrocities of the Nazis during the Holocaust. [65]

What the review in this and the previous section shows is that the debate over ritual animal slaughter is ripe with opportunities for cultural bias, prejudice, and “othering”, which must be taken into account as a background for any normative assessment of them.

This realization indicates that we must be very cautious about arguments being made in this context, and therefore must check ourselves well, using the entire arsenal of safeguards against selective bias and prejudice, before we reach normative conclusions. The next section will make the argument that constitutional law has developed tools to do just that, but that these tools are more developed in American constitutional law than in European constitutional law.

65 In the UK, for example, during one of the peaks of the debate on ritual animal slaughter, the following cartoon was circulated: cattle are seen standing outside a facility with a sign that says, *kosher meats* and one cow remarks, “I understand we’re just here to take a shower”. See Modiya Project: “Topic: Anti-Shechita”. http://modiya.nyu.edu/handle/1964/489. Accessed October 29, 2024.

6.4 Comparative Constitutional Law and Ritual Animal Slaughter

This section reviews and assesses constitutional judicial responses to challenges regarding ritual animal slaughter in Europe and compares them with actual or hypothetical similar challenges in the United States. Following the previous parts, my argument would be that constitutional law should be attuned to the dangers of cultural and religious bias. My comparative claim would be that the American *Smith* Doctrine is better equipped to do just that than the European-based proportionality analysis.

6.4.1 The Two Regimes of Religious Freedom

Comparative constitutional law provides us with two quite different regimes with regards to religious freedom – the American regime and the European regime, for which the jurisprudence of the European Court of Human Rights (ECtHR) and of the German Federal Constitutional Court (GFCC) will be the main examples.[66] The current American regime, as will be further elaborated, follows the *Smith* Doctrine according to which accommodation claims are not protected, only claims against animus-based religious discrimination that specifically target religion. In the words of a US freedom of religion scholar, the American Constitution "does not grant a right to religious exemptions from general legal obligations, but it does provide a shield against religious discrimination".[67]

The jurisprudence of the ECtHR, GFCC and specific European constitutional courts that follow their model is very different. Under the jurisprudence of the ECtHR and its analogues, there is no distinction between accommodation claims and claims against animus-based laws. There is, similarly, no distinction between neutral and generally applicable laws, and laws targeting religion. Rather, first, the court must determine whether freedom of religion is implicated, many times centering the review on the nature of the practice involved – whether, for example, it is mandatory according to a recognized religious sect, whether it is central to the religion, and so on. Secondly, if a religious activity which falls under the scope of this definition is burdened by a law, the law can stand only if it meets the requirement of the applicable limitation clause.

In the case of freedom of religion, the limitation clause in the European Convention on Human Rights (henceforth the Convention) allows for the

66 For the general division between the American and the European constitutional models, see G. Nolte (ed.), *European and US Constitutionalism* (Strasbourg: Council of Europe, 2005); M. Ignatieff (ed.), *American Exceptionalism and Human Rights* (Princeton: Princeton University Press, 2005); K. Möller, *The Global Model of Constitutional Rights* (Oxford: Oxford University Press, 2013); M. Cohen-Eliya, I. Porat, *Proportionality and Constitutional Culture*.

67 J.M. Oleske, "Lukumi at Twenty: A Legacy of Uncertainty for Religious Liberty and Animal Welafere", *Animal Law Review*, vol. 19 (2013): 295, 297.

limitation of the right to freedom of religion only for a limited set of purposes – for "the interests of public safety, for the protection of public order, health or morals, or for the protection of the rights and freedoms of others".[68] The first test of the limitation clause would therefore be to determine whether the law indeed furthers one of these purposes. The second test would be to determine whether the infringement, even if done for the proper purpose, is "necessary" or "necessary in a democratic society" for the furtherance of that legitimate purpose. Although the term "necessary" can be interpreted narrowly as excluding only such laws that impose completely gratuitous burdens, and including any law that furthers, even to a small extent, the appropriate purpose, the term was in fact interpreted as imposing a proportionality test.[69] That is, "necessary" means a law that does not impose on religion a disproportionate burden in relation to the gain achieved by the legitimate purpose.

ECtHR law therefore often boils down to a balancing test of proportionality, whereby religious freedom will be pitted against the countervailing rights and interests in order to show that the law is indeed necessary for the protection of the governmental purpose.

While it is often argued that religious freedom is substantially less protected in the United States than in Europe,[70] the cases of ritual animal slaughter show how the European seemingly protective proportionality doctrine can be a double edged sword. Proportionality, while allowing for the protection of accommodation claims, which are generally unprotected in America, can also more easily facilitate a balance in which even laws which, according to American law, might be struck down because of animus towards religion or because they single out religion can be saved if balanced with important countervailing interests.

The next sections will review the three main European constitutional cases regarding ritual animal slaughter and compare them with the analogous analysis under US law to exemplify this point.

6.4.2 Three European Cases and Proportionality

6.4.2.1 The Polish Case of Ritual Animal Slaughter

Perhaps the sole example of a constitutional analysis by a Supreme constitutional court that hinges directly on the constitutionality of ritual animal slaughter is the decision of the Polish Constitution Court in the Ritual Slaughter case[71]

68 See A. Gliszczyńska-Grabias, W. Sadurski, "Freedom of Religion versus Humane Treatment of Animals" 580.
69 See M. Cohen-Eliya, I. Porat, "The Hidden Foreign Law Debate in Heller: Proportionality Approach in American Constitutional Law", *San Diego Law Review*, vol. 46 (2009): 367, 373.
70 See note 10 and accompanying text.
71 Constitutional Tribunal of Poland, K 52/13 [2014].

In Poland, ritual animal slaughter was banned in the time of the Nazi occupation but was reinstated after the war. A law from 1997 – the Animals Protection Act (henceforth the Law) – that followed a 1993 European Union directive decision, banned animal slaughter without pre-stunning, but initially exempted ritual slaughter from the ban. The exemption was, however, removed from the law in 2002 and put back only by executive ordinances in 2004. This executive ordinance was annulled following a petition to the Constitutional Tribunal of Poland, which found that it was promulgated without due authorization from the legislature. Therefore following this court decision, the ban on animal ritual slaughter became absolute, and it was this ban that was subsequently challenged as unconstitutional in the case on animal slaughter that is the center of our review. The ban was also backed by criminal sanction of up to two years imprisonment. [72]

Note, therefore, that the type of challenge in this case is a challenge against the absence of an exemption on religious grounds from a law of general applicability. This fact has been noted by A. Gliszczyńska-Grabias and W. Sadurski, who criticize the case.[73] But the challenge comes on the background of there being such an exemption initially in the law – an exemption that was subsequently removed, reinstated by the executive, and removed again after a court petition. It also comes on the background of the EU directive which explicitly absolves ritual slaughter from the ban on slaughter without pre-stunning, and, while allowing member states to adopt a more animal protective regime, requires them to make a special notification to that effect, which Poland did. Therefore it could be argued that the exemption is the rule rather than the exception in this case.

The petitioners were representatives of the Jewish community in Poland as well as representatives of slaughterhouses that were not Jewish – since meat produced from ritual slaughter had become a business for export in Poland, especially since Turkey began importing meat from Poland – who claimed that the law without the exception conflicted with the right to religious freedom.[74]

The Court accepted the claim that freedom of religion was infringed, and then the legal analysis of the court began with the conflict between the total ban in the Law and Article 53 of the Polish constitution and Article 9 of the European Convention of Human Rights, (henceforth the Convection), both protecting freedom of religion in very similar words. Both Articles had a

72 Anna Śledzińska-Simon, *A "Stunning" Decision of the Polish Constitutional Tribunal: The Ritual Slaughter Case*, Int'l J. Const. L. Blog, January 19, 2015. http://www.iconnectblog.com/2015/01/a-stunning-decision-of-the-polish-constitutional-tribunal-the-ritual-slaughter-case/. Accessed October 29, 2024.

73 A. Gliszczyńska-Grabias, W. Sadurski, "Freedom of Religion versus Humane Treatment of Animals" 600: "This way of framing the issue [asking whether an absolute ban is constitutional] is not uncontroversial, because the law on the protection of animals does not establish a prohibition targeted at religious communities, but simply states an unconditional, general rule".

74 A. Gliszczyńska-Grabias, W. Sadurski, "Freedom of Religion versus Humane Treatment of Animals" 603.

similar limitation clause, allowing the infringement of freedom of religion only by a law which is necessary for the protection of a closed set of purposes – public safety (or State security), public order, health, morals, or the freedoms and rights of others.[75]

The purposes of security, public order and health, and the rights of others were summarily done with – the Court did not view animals as included within the "others" in the sense of the "rights of others" that were being protected[76] – leaving for discussion only the purpose of "morals". The majority opinion argued that while public morals did include a concern for the protection of animals and the alleviation of unnecessary suffering for animals, and this interest has even entered into constitutional axiology as a constitutionally protected value, the total ban on ritual slaughter was not "necessary" for the protection of public morals. Since it was evident that slaughter itself for the purpose of food is not contrary to public morals of the vast majority of the Polish people, the Court concluded that

> a total ban on one of the methods (a ritual method) – protected by the freedom of religion, and as to which scientific studies had not unambiguously determined that in every case it was more painful than other methods – was not necessary for the protection of morals.[77]

The Court further argued that it fitted with public morals because of the special importance given in Polish society to the protection of religious freedom and noted that "various methods of slaughter after stunning animals that had been permitted by law caused suffering, pain and distress to animals" and referred to hunting and other practices that allow the killing of animals without pre-stunning.

The Court also applied the test of proportionality to the case, although stating that this was not strictly required, and maintained that "the challenged provisions did not maintain proper proportion between a constitutionally safeguarded value in the form of the protection of animals and concern for their welfare on the one hand and the freedom of religion on the other".

75 Art. 53(5) of the Constitution of the Republic of Poland [1997] (https://www.sejm.gov.pl/prawo/konst/angielski/kon1.htm. Accessed October 29, 2024) reads, "The freedom to publicly express religion may be limited only by means of statute and only where this is necessary for the defense of State security, public order, health, morals or the freedoms and rights of others". Art. 9 of the Convention reads: "Freedom to manifest one's religion or beliefs shall be subject only to such limitations as are prescribed by law and are necessary in a democratic society in the interests of public safety, for the protection of public order, health or morals, or for the protection of the rights and freedoms of others". Animal Welfare (Commercial Slaughter) Code of Welfare Report.

76 Although a minority opinion by Judge T. Liszcz concluded that the right of others were also implicated, referring to people who would be offended or distressed by learning of the cruelty to animals. A. Gliszczyńska-Grabias, W. Sadurski, "Freedom of Religion versus Humane Treatment of Animals", 604.

77 Constitutional Tribunal of Poland, K 52/13 [2014].

The decision manifests an analytical blunder between the purpose test and the proportionality test that characterizes many proportionality decisions.[78] The Court claimed that no balancing was needed, as the purpose test was not met – i.e., it was not proven that the total ban fit into one of the allowed purposes for the restriction of freedom of religion. But the Court nevertheless did balance when it assessed whether the law was "necessary" to the furtherance of the purpose of public morals.

The main point about the case, however, is that the proportionality analysis did not at all relate to the reasons why the exemption from the Law was removed, or to legislative proceedings and protocols, or to the public campaign that brought about the repeal of the exemption, or to the possibility of bias motivating the Law. All of these are generally irrelevant to the proportionality test. Where present, such consideration can come into play within the "legitimate purpose test". But, as noted by many scholars, this test is seldom used as the determinative test in European-style constitutional analysis, and it is the proportionality test that takes center stage.[79] Proportionality itself does have an indirect mechanism that can help uncover illicit purposes and motivations behind a law – these are the tools of over-inclusiveness and under-inclusiveness built into the proportionality sub-tests – and indeed a certain reading of the case focusing on the parts that show such over- and under- inclusiveness can portray it as focusing on illicit motive.[80] But, unlike in American doctrine, there is no direct engagement with the issue of illicit motive, or animus, so the discussion of these issues is only indirect and less developed.

6.4.2.2 The German Schachten *Cases and the ECtHR* Cha'are Shalom *Case*

The two other European court decisions that revolved around ritual animal slaughter were also high-profile cases, and predated the Polish decision, but were not centered on a direct assessment of the constitutionality of ritual animal slaughter.

The German *Schachten* case from 2002[81] revolved mainly on the question whether the Muslim animal ritual slaughter – *dhabihah* – was a universally mandatory practice under Islam, in order to determine whether it deserved the protection under current legislation and under the German Basic Law. The German Animal's Protection Act exempted from the requirement of pre-stunning only religious rites that were mandatory in a recognized religious community. A previous case interpreting that law in the Supreme Administrative

78 See M. Cohen-Eliya and Iddo Porat, "American Balancing and German Proportionality: The Historical Origins", *International Journal of Constitutional Law*, vol. 8, no. 2 (2010): 263, 270. https://doi.org/10.1093/icon/moq004.

79 M. Cohen-Eliya and Iddo Porat, "American Balancing and German Proportionality: The Historical Origins" 268.

80 M. Cohen-Eliya and Iddo Porat, "American Balancing and German Proportionality: The Historical Origins".

81 German Federal Constitutional Court, *Schachten*, BVerfGE 104 [2002].

Court rejected a claim of a German Muslim butcher for an exemption since, the Court argued, the practice was not mandatory in Islam and furthermore since freedom of religion was not infringed as the law did not force Muslims to eat meat against their religion, and they could eat vegetarian food or import *Halal* meat. This also created inequality between Muslims and Jews, as Jewish *shechita* was considered to be mandatory and protected under the law.[82] The decision of the Federal Constitutional Court, however, accepted the Muslim butcher's claim, on the grounds of both freedom of occupation and freedom of religion, rejecting the claim that the practice was not mandatory and does not infringe freedom of religion.

The Court maintained, first, that protecting animals was a worthy cause and a proper purpose of the law, but that it can be limited by an exemption for the purpose of protecting religious freedom. The Court ruled that the interpretation of the exemption given in the law had to be one that properly balances the religious freedom of the Muslim butcher and his clients and the interest in protecting animals. The court determined that depriving Muslim butchers of their practice did not reflect such proper balance.[83]

The second high-profile case is *Cha'are Shalom Ve Tsedek v. France*.[84] This is a decision of the ECtHR concerning a petition by members of an Ultra-Orthodox community in France against the French law. The decision seems less protective to religious rights than the two decisions reviewed earlier, as it allows the State to *de facto* ban certain forms of animal ritual slaughter – namely, those of the Ultra-Orthodox Jewish sect – and as it reverts back to arguments that the German Constitutional Court rejected, that religious practitioners could obtain their meat from import and that their religious rights were therefore not infringed.[85] But this is only according to a superficial reading of the case. The case allowed for a restriction on ritual animal slaughter only since it revolved around the question of whether the State could choose which religious representative it views as authoritative for the religious community. France is traditionally tolerant to *shechita* and did not witness the same type of high-profile debates as in Germany and Scandinavia, but it has a special relationship between the State and religion. It therefore allowed for an exemption for the rule against pre-stunning but conferred the authority to the official representatives of the majority of the Jewish population to regulate the matter – the Orthodox, rather than Ultra-Orthodox, community – and gave them, in effect, a monopoly over *kosher* slaughter.

82 S. Lavi, "Unequal Rites" 84.

83 See C. Haupt, "The Nature and Effects of Constitutional State Objectives: Assessing The German Basic Law's Animal Protection Clause", *Animal Law Review*, vol. 16, no 2 (2010): 237–241 (reviewing the German *Schachten* decision and its determination regarding the mandatory nature of ritual animal slaughter).

84 *The Cha'are Shalom Ve Tsedek v. France*, 27417/95 [2000] § 84.

85 See P. Lerner, A.M. Rabello, "The Prohibition of Ritual Slaughtering (Kosher Shechita and Halal) and Freedom of Religion of Minorities", *Journal of Law and Religion*, vol. 22, no. 1 (2007): 14–15.

However, both decisions noted in passim that the permission of ritual animal slaughter was indeed proportionate and fit within the regime of the protection of religious freedom. Indeed both decisions were also later quoted to that effect in the Polish decision.

6.4.3 The American Constitutional Smith Doctrine

6.4.3.1 Smith and Lukumi

American jurisprudence is governed by Scalia's opinion in the *Smith* case of 1990. This section will review the main elements of this doctrine as applied in *Smith* and in the subsequent case of *Church of Lukumi Babalu Aye, Inc. v. City of Hialeah* (1993).[86]

The *Smith* case has laid down two main doctrinal tests: neutrality and general applicability. According to *Smith*, laws that are neutral and generally applicable would not be subject to strict scrutiny review, and only laws that specifically target religion or are based on bias and animus towards religion would be subject to such review.[87]

The *Smith* case itself, however, did not involve a law that was based on animus against religion but rather a law that was quite clearly neutral and generally applicable law – a criminal law prohibiting the use of illegal drugs, including the use of a drug called peyote. There were no indications that the law in question was designed in order to limit religious practices, and it did not single out in any way religious practices. Rather, as Justice Scalia wrote in the case, the State of Oregon had maintained an "across-the-board" prohibition of peyote in its drug laws,[88] and therefore Smith's claim for accommodation and exemption was rejected (Smith asked that he not be denied unemployment benefits on account of him being fired from his job because of violating the law by smoking peyote in a religious Indian ceremony).

The *Smith* case is usually read together with the next major free exercise Supreme Court case – *Lukumi*– which did involve animus against religion. *Lukumi* involved a municipal set of ordinances that were quite obviously designed to prevent the practices of a religious sect and were clearly singling out this practice and devaluating them in comparison to other similar non-religious practices. The practice in question was animal sacrifice, which is practiced by the Santeria religion, and the event the ordinances responded to was the intention of the head of the Santeria Church in America to build a center of that religion in the city of Hialeah, Florida. *Lukumi* further elaborated on the two main tests set by Justice Scalia in *Smith* – neutrality and general applicability – in a context which resembles in many respects that of claims against

86 *Church of the Lukumi Babalu Aye, Inc. v. City of Hialeah*, 508 U.S. 520 [1993].
87 See notes 2–4 and accompanying text.
88 *Employment Division v. Smith*, 494 U.S. 872 [1990] 884.

ritual animal slaughter in Europe. I will therefore turn to a more detailed review of this case and the way it applied the *Smith* Doctrine.

6.4.3.2 *Six Principles*

While the *Smith* Doctrine consists of only two principles or tests – neutrality and general applicability – there is considerable overlap between the two,[89] and even greater confusion as to what exactly each of them stands for.[90] It therefore makes sense to address directly some of the main principles invoked by both these tests in order to later compare them with the proportionality test used in Europe. I will analyze the *Smith* Doctrine as applied and elaborated in *Lukumi* according to six such principles.

6.4.3.2.1 ANIMUS AND DISCRIMINATORY INTENT

It is not clear from *Smith* and *Lukumi* whether the showing of animus or discriminatory intent is necessary for the purposes of subjecting a law to strict scrutiny or whether the other principles that I will discuss, such as under-inclusiveness and over-inclusiveness, are only evidentiary tools for the determination of intent, or whether they stand by themselves. However, it is certain that the showing of animus, discriminatory intent, or an object of targeting religion (I will use these terms interchangeably) would suffice to prove that a law is not neutral and therefore subject to strict scrutiny.[91] The Court has used several doctrinal tools to deduce discriminatory intent, drawing, among others, on similar tools developed in equal protection and free speech jurisprudence.

"In determining if the object of a law is a neutral one under the Free Exercise Clause" maintained the Court in *Lukumi*

> [r]elevant evidence includes, among other things, the historical background of the decision under challenge, the specific series of events leading to the enactment or official policy in question, as well as the legislative or administrative history, including contemporaneous statements made by members of the decision making body.[92]

89 In *Lukumi*, the Court wrote, "Neutrality and general applicability are interrelated, and, as becomes apparent in this case, failure to satisfy one requirement is a likely indication that the other has not been satisfied". *Employment Division v. Smith*, 494 U.S. 872 [1990] 884.

90 See, e.g., Brief for the National Association of Evangelicals and others as Amicus Curiae, pp. 1–2, On Petition for a Writ of Certiorari to the United States Court of Appeals for the Ninth Circuit, Stroman's v. Weisman: "[The jurisprudence of religious liberty] is mired in doubt because, a quarter century after this Court decided *Employment Division v. Smith*, 494 U.S. 872 (1990), followed by *Church of Lukumi Babalu Aye, Inc. v. City of Hialeah*, 508 U.S. 520 (1993), federal circuits and other lower courts cannot agree what makes a law neutral and generally applicable". https://www.scotusblog.com/wp-content/uploads/2016/03/Stromans-Brief-of-Religious-Organizations.pdf.

91 See J.M. Oleske, "Lukumi at Twenty 295, 339.

92 *Church of the Lukumi Babalu Aye, Inc. v. City of Hialeah*, 508 U.S. 520 [1993] 540.

Following these criteria, the Court in *Lukumi* quoted at length from the hearings of the city council during the legislative proceedings regarding the ordinances. A Councilman was quoted saying at the hearing that Santeria devotees "are in violation of everything this country stands for", and the city attorney as saying, "This community will not tolerate religious practices which are abhorrent to its citizens".[93] The Court also noted the fact that these resolutions took place in direct relation and in temporal proximity to the news about the intention to build the Church. It was relevant therefore that they were enacted" "because of", not merely "in spite of", "their suppression of Santeria religious practice".[94]

Other, indicia for the existence of a legislative object of targeting religion in the case were the language itself used by the ordinances, that included words such as "sacrifice" and "ritual" to describe the prohibited conduct,[95] as well as the actual effects of the ordinances, which was that only religion was detrimentally affected by the ordinances.[96] The next principles to be discussed – under-inclusiveness and over-inclusiveness – were also used as indirect evidence for illicit motive.

6.4.3.2.2 UNDER-INCLUSIVENESS: FACIALLY AND IN APPLICATION

The Court in *Lukumi* noted that the "ordinances were gerrymandered with care to proscribe religious killings of animals but to exclude almost all secular killings".[97] In other words, the ordinances were under-inclusive in not including within their scope similar activities with no religious motive. Under-inclusiveness could be facial, i.e., apparent from the terms of the legislation itself. This was the case with some of the ordinances which, as noted earlier, specifically targeted religious activities such as "ritual" or "sacrifice", thus leaving out of their scope non-religious types of animal killings.

However, even when an ordinance was neutral facially, or "on its face", the Court noted that it could look into its application. Rejecting *Hialeah*'s claims that at least one of the ordinances was neutral and broad since it had no mention of religion in its text – the ordinance punished "whoever [...] unnecessarily [...] kills any animal", – the Court wrote,

> The problem [...] is the interpretation given to the ordinance by [Hialeah] and the Florida attorney general. Killings for religious reasons are deemed unnecessary, whereas most other killings fall outside the prohibition. The city, on what seems to be a per se basis, deems hunting,

93 *Church of the Lukumi Babalu Aye, Inc. v. City of Hialeah*, 508 U.S. 520 [1993] 541–542.
94 *Church of the Lukumi Babalu Aye, Inc. v. City of Hialeah*, 508 U.S. 520 [1993] 540.
95 *Church of the Lukumi Babalu Aye, Inc. v. City of Hialeah*, 508 U.S. 520 [1993] 534–535.
96 *Church of the Lukumi Babalu Aye, Inc. v. City of Hialeah*, 508 U.S. 520 [1993] 535 (courts should look into the "effect of a law in its real operation").
97 *Church of the Lukumi Babalu Aye, Inc. v. City of Hialeah*, 508 U.S. 520 [1993] 542.

> slaughter of animals for food, eradication of insects and pests, and euthanasia as necessary. There is no indication in the record that respondent has concluded that hunting or fishing for sport is unnecessary. Indeed, one of the few reported cases [...] concludes that the use of live rabbits to train greyhounds is not unnecessary.[98]

6.4.3.2.3 OVER-INCLUSIVENESS

Another aspect of neutrality, or its absence, and possible indication for illegitimate motive is the over-inclusiveness of the law. The Court noted that "the legitimate governmental interests in protecting the public health and preventing cruelty to animals could be addressed by restrictions stopping far short of a flat prohibition of all Santeria sacrificial practice". For example, "regulation of conditions and treatment, regardless of why an animal is kept, is the logical response to the city's concern, not a prohibition on possession for the purpose of sacrifice", [99] and public health concerns can be addressed by regulations as the proper disposal of carcasses rather than the prohibition of slaughter.

6.4.3.2.4 SELECTIVE EXEMPTIONS AND "DEVALUATION" OR RELIGION

A particular aspect of under-inclusiveness that was accorded special notice in *Lukumi* as well as in following cases is the occurrence of "selective exemptions" – that is, exemptions from a general rule that exist only for secular reasons but not for religious reasons. Such exemptions, the Court maintained, professed a "devaluation" of religion, as they expressed the view that religion reasons are of lower value than other reasons. The Court wrote,

> As we noted in *Smith*, in circumstances in which individualized exemptions from a general requirement are available, the government 'may not refuse to extend that system to cases of "religious hardship" without compelling reason.' Respondent's application of the ordinance's test of necessity devalues religious reasons for killing by judging them to be of lesser import than nonreligious reasons. Thus, religious practice is being singled out for discriminatory treatment.[100]

6.4.3.2.5 A LEGITIMATE INTEREST IS NOT ENOUGH

The Supreme Court in *Lukumi* addressed the District Court's ruling that affirmed the ordinances. It noted that the lower court's view was that

> [a]lthough [...] the city's concern about animal sacrifice was 'prompted' by the establishment of the Church in the city... the purpose of the

98 *Church of the Lukumi Babalu Aye, Inc. v. City of Hialeah*, 508 U.S. 520 [1993] 537.
99 *Church of the Lukumi Babalu Aye, Inc. v. City of Hialeah*, 508 U.S. 520 [1993] 538.
100 *Church of the Lukumi Babalu Aye, Inc. v. City of Hialeah*, 508 U.S. 520 [1993] 537.

> ordinances was not to exclude the Church from the city but to end the practice of animal sacrifice, for whatever reason practiced.

The lower court also argued that "specifically regulating [religious] conduct" does not violate the First Amendment "when [the conduct] is deemed inconsistent with public health and welfare" and that the "ordinances' effect on petitioners' religious conduct was "incidental to [their] secular purpose and effect".[101]

The Court expressly rejected this analysis. A critical point of the *Smith* Doctrine is that the availability of a legitimate governmental interest behind the legislation – the prevention of animal cruelty – does not cure a selective treatment of religion and its singling out versus other types of activities: "The principle that government, in pursuit of legitimate interests, cannot in a selective manner impose burdens only on conduct motivated by religious belief is essential to the protection of the rights guaranteed by the Free Exercise Clause".[102]

6.4.3.2.6 NO BALANCING AND NO EVALUATION OF RELIGIOUS BELIEF

The District Court's ruling in the *Lukumi* case was handed down before *Smith* and therefore applied to the case a pre-*Smith* strict scrutiny balancing test despite viewing it as involving accommodation. The Court in *Lukumi* notes that the District Court "proceeded to determine whether the governmental interests underlying the ordinances were compelling and, if so, to balance the governmental and religious interests". The Court quoted from the District Court that wrote that this "balance depends upon the cost to the government of altering its activity to allow the religious practice to continue unimpeded versus the cost to the religious interest imposed by the government activity".[103]

This passage of the District Court was also expressly rejected in *Lukumi*. It was rejected since it no longer fit with current doctrine post-*Smith*. But more than that, it was rejected since it contradicted one of the main tenets of the *Smith* Doctrine – the avoidance of balancing and of the need to assess the strength of the religious claim or of the authenticity of religious belief.

In a famous passage in *Smith* Justice Scalia wrote that

> [i]t may fairly be said that leaving accommodation to the political process will place at a relative disadvantage those religious practices that are not widely engaged in; but that unavoidable consequence of democratic government must be preferred to a system in which each conscience is a law unto itself or in which judges weigh the social importance of all laws against the centrality of all religious beliefs.[104]

101 *Church of the Lukumi Babalu Aye, Inc. v. City of Hialeah*, 508 U.S. 520 [1993] 529.
102 *Church of the Lukumi Babalu Aye, Inc. v. City of Hialeah*, 508 U.S. 520 [1993] 543.
103 *Church of the Lukumi Babalu Aye, Inc. v. City of Hialeah*, 508 U.S. 520 [1993] 529.
104 *Employment Division v. Smith*, 494 U.S. 872 [1990] 890 (emphasis added).

Scalia therefore thought that it would be worse to allow judges to balance between the social importance of laws and religion, than to suffer a disadvantage to minority religion. One of the reasons was that such balancing necessarily required the Court to evaluate the centrality or importance of religious claims, so that it could balance them with social importance. "Repeatedly" wrote Scalia, "and in many different contexts, we have warned that courts must not presume to determine the place of a particular belief in a religion or the plausibility of a religious claim".[105]

6.5 Applying *Smith/Lukumi* to the Animal Slaughter

How would the claims against animal ritual slaughter brought in the European cases fare under the US *Smith* Doctrine? Following the review of the European cases and the way they are set in their cultural and historical context, as well as the main principles of the American *Smith* Doctrine, I would argue in this section that the *Smith* Doctrine provides a better framework for the assessment of these cases.

Note that my point here will not be to compare the actual outcomes of the European cases with the hypothetical outcomes of similar cases under American law, nor would such a project be a fruitful one. The reason is that doctrine is always filtered by judicial discretion, and thus never fully determined. Therefore, as we have seen, some of the proportionality cases in the European cases arrived at outcomes that were favorable to minority religion (e.g. the Polish ritual animal slaughter case and the German *Shachten* case) while others did not (e.g. the first German *Shachten* case, as well as, to an extent, the ECtHR *Cha'are Shalom* case). And similarly, the *Smith* Doctrine, while arguably more determinate than proportionality, leaves many questions open and is often lamented for the doctrinal confusion it creates, especially in the "hard" cases that lie in between the "easy" cases of *Smith* and *Lukumi*. My point, rather, would be to show that the kind of considerations that each of these doctrines puts to the fore, and the focus of the analysis in each, makes a better case for minority religion claims under the American regime, at least to the extent that ritual animal slaughter is a representative example. I will focus on the Polish case.

Recall that the review in the Polish animal ritual case focused on determining whether the total ban on ritual slaughter was "necessary for the furtherance of public morals", which, as mentioned earlier, meant, determining where the balance between public morals (the protection of animals) and freedom of religion lies. The five principles of the *Smith/Lukumi* doctrine, however, would focus attention on quite different questions and factors.

Animus and Discriminatory Intent: The *Smith*/Lukumi doctrine would attempt to determine whether animus and bias were in any way involved in the motivations behind the Polish Animal Protection Law and in particular behind

105 *Employment Division v. Smith*, 494 U.S. 872 [1990] 885–887.

the absence (or extraction) of the religious exemption from the Law. As with the *Lukumi* case, the legislative hearings behind the Law would be a pertinent piece of evidence, as well as the public debate that accompanied legislation and that might have affected it. The *Smith* Doctrine would therefore allow for evidence regarding the nationalistic and, at times, anti-Semitic and Islamophobic overtones of the Polish public debate over animal ritual slaughter.[106] It would also have required a close look at the legislative hearings and pronouncements of members of parliament, which could have found problematic pronouncements such as those that were documented earlier in the legislative hearings in the *Lukumi* case. General background evidence relating to animus would also be relevant for the constitutional analysis – the general Islamophobic atmosphere and the rise in anti-Semitism in current Europe, as well as the long history of anti-Semitism in Poland, including anti-Semitism revolving around the particular practice of ritual animal slaughter (recall that Poland adopted anti-*shechita* laws even before it was occupied by the Nazis, based on overt anti-Semitism, in 1938). Such evidence would serve as a background raising suspicion that animus was involved in the Law, the way the general unpopularity of Santeria in America was relevant for raising a similar suspicion in the *Lukumi* case. Note that all the factors reviewed earlier – legislative hearings and pronouncements, public debate, general background of animus – are completely absent from the proportionality-based review in the Polish case.

Another factor that is completely absent from the Polish review and would be pertinent under the *Smith/Lukumi* animus review is the history of the law itself – the fact that it included a religious exemption that was subsequently removed from the law, the fact that even when the exemption was reinstated by the government this brought about a petition that resulted in its repeal, and the fact that the total ban persisted despite an express EU endorsement of religious exemptions.[107] All these facts in the history of the law can be used as indications that the law was not "neutral" with regard to religion, and may have resulted from bias and animus. At the very least, this history would show that the Law differs from laws, such as in *Smith*, that do not even contemplate a conflict with religion, and in which the conflict is completely incidental to

106 See L. Janion, "Wspólnoty mięsa. Konstruowanie tożsamości grupowej wokół sporu o ubój rytualny", *Kultura Popularna* no 4 (2014): 49 (English abstract): "Tatars cement their collective identity of meritorious Poles while add an element of being the victims of political quarrels and religious discrimination. Animal rights activists deny being anti-Semitic or Islamophobic, but they present themselves as more civilized and humane than the minority. Thus, the view on the superiority of the majority's culinary practices is strengthened. Both groups refer to the nationalist discourse and the category of being Polish".

107 This is indeed the usual case with bans on ritual animal slaughter. See, e.g., the ban in New Zealand promulgated by the Minister of Agriculture. The Minister did not include an exception for religious slaughter despite an early recommendation to do so by the National Animal Welfare Advisory Committee.

the law. [108] The legislative history shows that the conflict with religion was very much at the background of the entire process of legislation and that the law can even be said to be more restrictive than an existing standard – to the extent that EU law provides a European standard.

As noted earlier, the discriminatory effect of the law was also considered in *Lukumi* as a possible indication for the lack of neutrality and existence of animus. In the Polish case, as in *Lukumi*, the law adversely affects only minority religions – Islam and Judaism – which would be pertinent to the review, and does not enter in any direct way into the proportionality review in the Polish case.[109]

Under-Inclusion and Selective Exemptions – this aspect of the Polish law would be immediately at the center of a *Smith/Lukumi* review, and indeed the *Lukumi* case itself provides for good arguments that directly apply to the ritual slaughter case. Petitioners against a ritual animal slaughter law, such as in Poland, would no doubt argue that the law is under-inclusive or singling out religion, or has selective exemptions, or devaluates religious reasons, either expressly or in application, in not banning similar activities that result in pain and suffering for animals. These other activities include hunting, rodent extermination, unsupervised small-scale slaughter that is done in farms, cruel transport and living conditions of farm animals, and so on. Note that the Polish Court did indeed point to some of these factors, but not in any doctrinally orderly manner. They were used as an indication that general morality did not object to a religious exemption from animal cruelty norms, and they could have been used under the first proportionality test also, to show that there is no rational connection (or at least not a good one) between the law and its objective. However, the *Smith/Lukumi* review makes this type of analysis much more central to the constitutional review. Indeed it can be seen as one of the primary indications to bias, as it shows a double standard – one that applies to the majority and one to the minority religion.

Over-Inclusion – this factor too would be immediately picked up in the animal slaughter case if reviewed under the *Smith/Lukumi* doctrine. One could argue that careful inspection of religious slaughter, making sure that the handling of cattle is done properly, and that the slaughter itself is done as quickly and efficiently as possible, would reduce much of the concerns around

108 See, for example, the difference between the laws in *Lukumi* that were enacted directly in relation to the coming of the Santeria church to town, and the laws in Merced that predated the conflict by a long time and did not anticipate it. See also in Newark Police Department "the medical exemption raises concern because it indicates that the Department has made a value judgment that secular (i.e., medical) motivations for wearing a beard are important enough to overcome its general interest in uniformity but that religious motivations are not".

109 Effects obviously do matter in a proportionality review, but not as indications for animus. The review would need to show that the harmful effects on minorities outweighs the benefit to the entire society, maybe adding into the calculus the fact that there might be extra harm when someone is the sole bearer of the social cost.

religious slaughter without banning it completely. Examples from other countries (South Africa, Australia) of compromises between concerns for animals and religion that resulted in less than a total ban would also be indications for the over-inclusiveness of the regulation. Again, proportionality has tools to review over-inclusion – especially the second test of proportionality, the least restrictive means test – but these would not be as directly related to animus, and therefore, they would be more malleable than in the American case.

Legitimate Interest Is Not Enough: proponents of the absolute ban on ritual animal slaughter often argue that it is not motivated by anti-Semitism or Islamophobia, but rather by a secular legitimate interest – preventing cruelty for animals. As the *Lukumi* case shows, such claims may have better answers in the *Smith/Lukumi* type reviews than in the proportionality review that takes governmental interests at face value and balances them with religious hardship.

No Balancing and No Evaluation of Religious Belief: Recall that one of the express motivations of the *Smith* reasoning is to avoid judicial balancing between the public interest and religion, and leave it to the political and democratic process. The European proportionality analysis, on the other hand, cannot avoid such balancing. The Polish decision attempts to be an exemption, as the court almost expressly wished to avoid assessing the validity and strength of the religious claim and the balancing of it versus the animal rights/ public morals interest. But, as A. Gliszczyńska-Grabias and W. Sadusrki rightly write, it could not really achieve this. In order to assess whether a total ban was "necessary" for the furtherance of public morals, the court had to, and in effect did, assess the gravity of the infringement of religious freedom versus the gravity of the public moral concern. In other cases, such as in the German *Shachten* case and in the HCtHR *Cha'are Shalom* case, this was done even more expressly and included an evaluation of the obligatory nature or centrality of a religious practice according to its own terms - as in evaluating whether ritual slaughter was mandatory under Islam (*Shachten*) or whether having *Kosher* meat imported as a replacement for local slaughter is religiously neutral under Jewish law (*Cha'are Shalom*).

Balancing and evaluation of religious reasons do not inherently point to less protection of minority of religion, but they may. This is apparent if one takes into consideration the fact that balancing has to be done according to a certain standard. The yard stick for the balance in a European-type proportionality analysis is a community-based set of values, enshrined in the constitutional order. This is especially formalized in German jurisprudence, and the Polish decision shows the clear influence of German constitutional jurisprudence. While the Polish decision identified consensual public morals with toleration to minority religion, the potential of such a test to reflect bias towards minority religion is more than evident. The shared mores and habits of society may very well be the opposite of what minority religion and culture stands for.

6.6 Conclusion

The chapter attempted to show the extensive background of bias and prejudice in disputes around ritual animal slaughter in Europe, and to argue that in such cases doctrines that are attuned to fleshing out bias – such as the American *Smith* Doctrine – are preferable to proportionality.

The discussion in this chapter does not mean to say that the Polish ritual slaughter case, for example, or its counterparts in Germany and in the ECtHR would necessarily be easy cases under American post-*Smith* review. A. Gliszczyńska-Grabias and W. Sadurski, e.g., argue that the case should not be reviewed as one of singling out religion but as one of generally applicable law. In addition, the mere fact that a religious exemption was contemplated but not included is not enough in and of itself to show bias and non-neutrality. The reasons for not exempting religion are also of crucial importance, and may turn out to indicate neutrality, or be viewed as compelling. But it does seem that a history of anti-religious sentiment around a law, coupled with under- and over-inclusiveness, and awareness to a general standard favoring exemption, carry considerable weight in terms of the legal analysis in America, and they are almost completely absent in the European formal analysis.

The history and jurisprudence of the practice of two minority religions in Europe provide a rich example of the shortcomings of the European alternative to *Smith* – the proportionality doctrine – and of some of the advantages of *Smith* in the area of minority protection.

7 Animal Welfare and the Right to Freedom of Religion before the CJEU

The Case of Stunning and Ritual Slaughter

Gerhard van der Schyff

Abstract

This chapter discusses the issue of abolishing religious exemptions from the obligation to stun animals before slaughter in the interest of animal welfare. The chapter focuses on the ruling of the Court of Justice of the European Union in the matter of *Centraal Israëlitisch Consistorie van België and Others v. Vlaamse Regering*. It concludes that Member States are in principle allowed to require stunning in the context of ritual slaughter but that the margin of appreciation in this case was probably too wide. For this reason, the possible effects of a narrower margin are investigated. The chapter also argues that the cumulative effect of abolishing religious exemptions across the European Union should be considered when deciding whether the right to freedom of religion was limited in a proportionate manner.

Keywords

animal welfare; ritual slaughter; religious slaughter; stunning of animals; fundamental rights; freedom of religion; limitation of rights; Belgium; Flanders Court of Justice of the European Union; European Court of Human Rights; Constitutional Court of Belgium; Charter of Fundamental Rights of the European Union; European Convention on Human Rights; Treaty on European Union; Treaty on the Functioning of the European Union; EU law; ECHR law

7.1 Setting the Scene

A question that continues to vex policymakers, lawyers, and judges across Europe today is that of the legal regulation of ritual or religious slaughter, as required by many adherents of Judaism and Islam. According to this practice, animals may not be stunned when they are slaughtered, as this would

DOI: 10.4324/9781003423294-11

contradict religious tenets and render such meat unfit for human consumption. While many jurisdictions across Europe allow religious exemptions from stunning animals, such exemptions have become controversial in some states in the cause of animal welfare. In the past few years, Denmark amended its legislation to require blanket stunning, while the Netherlands nearly scrapped its religious exemptions.[1] Other states, such as Sweden, have required blanket stunning for decades.[2]

In light of recent developments in that country, Belgium provides fertile ground for examining the legal regulation of ritual slaughter. This is especially true given the European Union (EU) law dimension of the case and its significance for other jurisdictions facing similar issues. Belgium has always recognised religious exemptions to the stunning of animals.[3] However, in 2017, Flanders and Wallonia, two of Belgium's three federal regions, each adopted decrees which scrapped such religious exemptions.[4] The Flemish and Walloon decrees were challenged before the country's Constitutional Court. In 2019, the Constitutional Court submitted three references for preliminary rulings to the Court of Justice of the European Union (CJEU) regarding the Flemish decree, which was essentially the same as the Walloon decree.[5] In his opinion in 2020, Advocate General Hogan proposed that scrapping the exemptions did not accord with EU law.[6] The CJEU did not follow the Advocate General's opinion and ruled in *Centraal Israëlitisch Consistorie van België and Others v. Vlaamse Regering* in 2020 that scrapping the religious exemptions was not precluded by EU law.[7] This ruling was duly copied by the Constitutional Court in 2021 in two judgements concerning the Flemish and Walloon decrees, respectively.[8] To

1 See J. Janssen, "Dierenwelzijnargumenten tegen en godsdienstige argumenten voor deze slachtmethode" *Tijdschrift voor Religie, Recht en Beleid*, no. 5 (2015): 34.

2 See G. van der Schyff, "Ritual Slaughter and Religious Freedom in a Multilevel Europe: The Wider Importance of the Dutch Case" *Oxford Journal on Law and Religion* 3 (2014): 76, 78.

3 See S. Wattier, "Ritual Slaughter Case: The Court of Justice and the Belgian Constitutional Court Put Animal Welfare First" *European Constitutional Law Review*, vol. 18 (2022): 264, 267.

4 S. Wattier, "Ritual Slaughter Case" 267–268.

5 Belgian Constitutional Court's case No. 53/2019 [2019], §§ A63.3, B.28. https://www.const-court.be/public/e/2019/2019-053e.pdf. Accessed June 25, 2024.

6 Opinion of AG Hogan in case C-336/19 *Centraal Israëlitisch Consistorie van België and Others v. Vlaamse Regering* [2020] § 88, ECLI:EU:C:2020:695.

7 *Centraal Israëlitisch Consistorie van België and Others v. Vlaamse Regering*, C-336/19 [2020] § 96, ECLI:EU:C:2020:1031.

8 Belgian Constitutional Court's case No. 117/2021 [2021]. https://www.const-court.be/public/e/2021/2021-117e.pdf. Accessed June 25, 2024, and Belgian Constitutional Court's case No. 118/2021 [2021]. https://www.const-court.be/public/e/2021/2021-118e.pdf. Accessed June 25, 2024.

date, the Brussels Capital Region is the only Belgian region to still allow religious exemptions to the stunning of animals.[9]

The CJEU's judgement in *Centraal Israëlitisch Consistorie van België and Others* is of particular importance, as it is the first on the European plane to consider whether religious exemptions to stunning can be removed without violating the right to freedom of religion. Although the topic of ritual slaughter featured in its case law in the past, this basic question was never before addressed by the CJEU. For instance, in *Liga van Moskeeën en Islamitische Organisaties Provincie Antwerpen, VZW and Others v. Vlaams Gewest* the CJEU in 2018 confirmed the validity of an EU rule that ritual slaughter without stunning the animal first must always take place in approved slaughterhouses.[10] The place of slaughter was thus the main issue before the Court and not ritual slaughter as such. As for the European Court of Human Rights (ECtHR), in 2000 the question before the bench in *Cha'are Shalom Ve Tsedek v. France* was not whether the ritual slaughter of animals without stunning them could be banned but whether the organisation in question could be denied permission for such slaughter while another organisation was allowed to do so.[11] The ECtHR only ruled on the question in 2024, when in *Executief van de Moslims van België v. Belgium* it decided that the Flemish and Walloon decrees did not violate the ECHR's guarantees on freedom of religion or the prohibition of discrimination, thereby reaching a similar conclusion to that of the CJEU four year years earlier.[12]

Given the significance of the legal issue, the purpose of this contribution is to critically analyse the CJEU's judgement in *Centraal Israëlitisch Consistorie van België and Others* as the first of its kind. The importance of this judgement is reinforced by the fact that it is relevant not only to the Belgian situation, but also to EU law and to each of the 27 Member States when they comply with such law. Where relevant, reference will be made to the ECHR and ECtHR case law regarding ritual slaughter. Although this contribution was largely completed before the ruling in *Executief van de Moslims van België*, some preliminary observations will be included in the light of the judgement.

9 S. Wattier, "Ritual Slaughter Case" 269. See also G. van der Schyff, S. Sottiaux, "Debating Ritual Slaughter in Belgium: A Multilevel Fundamental Rights Perspective". In: K. Lemmens, S. Parmentier, L. Reyntjens (eds.), *Human Rights with a Human Touch: Liber Amicorum Paul Lemmens* (Cambridge: Intersentia, 2019): 715, 720.

10 *Liga van Moskeeën en Islamitische Organisaties Provincie Antwerpen, VZW and Others v. Vlaams Gewest*, C-426/16 [2018], ECLI:EU:C:2018:335; see also *Oeuvre d'assistance aux bêtes d'abattoirs v. Ministre de l'Agriculture et de l'Alimentation and Others*, C-497/17 [2019], ECLI:EU:C:2019:137 on labelling products resulting from ritual slaughter without stunning animals as organic.

11 *Cha'are Shalom Ve Tsedek v. France*, No. 27417/95 [2000], ECLI:CE:ECHR:2000:0627JUD002741795.

12 *Executief van de Moslims van België v. Belgium*, Nos. 16760/22 and 10 others [2024], ECLI:CE:ECHR:2024:0213JUD001676022.

In studying the CJEU's ruling in *Centraal Israëlitisch Consistorie van België and Others*, the attention turns first to explaining what is meant by ritual slaughter and stunning in the context of animal welfare (Section 7.2). After this the case of ritual slaughter in Belgium is outlined with particular reference to the Flemish decree (Section 7.3)[13], followed by the applicable EU law framework in Council Regulation (EC) no. 1099/2099 on the Protection of Animals at the Time of Killing of September 24, 2009[14] (Section 7.4). This is followed by a brief summary of the preliminary references made by the Belgian Constitutional Court to the CJEU (Section 7.5) and an explanation of the CJEU judgement and opinion by the Advocate General (Section 7.6). The judgement and the opinion are then analysed, paying particular attention to whether the abolition of the religious exemptions from the stunning of animals violated the right to freedom of religion under Article 10(1) of the Charter of Fundamental Rights of the European Union[15] (CFREU) (Section 7.7), before concluding the discussion (Section 8).

7.2 Ritual Slaughter, Stunning, and Animal Welfare

As various religions do, authorities in Judaism and Islam prescribe dietary laws for their adherents. These laws cover issues ranging from the types of food that may be eaten by their followers to the methods used for its preparation.[16] When dietary laws are met, food is considered *kosher* in Judaism and *halal* in Islam.[17] With regard to the preparation and consumption of meat, various religious laws can be distinguished in these religions.[18] Importantly, both these religions prohibit their followers from consuming certain types of animals, as well as blood.[19] And when an animal fit for human consumption is slaughtered, particular rites are prescribed by each religion. In Judaism, the practice of such slaughter is known as *shechita* and in Islam *dhabihah*. The act of slaughtering an animal in accordance with religious rites or precepts is generally described as ritual slaughter or religious slaughter. The terms 'ritual slaughter'

13 Flemish Decree of 7 July 2017 amending the Law of August 14, 1986, on the protection and welfare of animals, regarding permitted methods of slaughtering animals [Decreet houdende wijziging van de wet van 14 augustus 1986 betreffende de bescherming en het welzijn der dieren, wat de toegelaten methodes voor het slachten van dieren betreft] [2017], https://www.ejustice.just.fgov.be/eli/decreet/2017/07/07/2017030639/staatsblad. Accessed October 25, 2024.

14 Council Regulation (EC) No 1099/2009 of September 24, 2009, on the protection of animals at the time of killing (Text with EEA relevance) [2009] OJ L 303.

15 Charter of Fundamental Rights of the European Union [2007] OJ C 303.

16 *Cha'are Shalom Ve Tsedek*. No. 27417/95 [2000] § 13.

17 S. Wattier, "Ritual Slaughter Case" 266.

18 See further P. Lerner, A.M. Rabello, "The Prohibition of Ritual Slaughtering (Kosher Shechita and Halal) and Freedom of Religion of Minorities", *Journal of Law and Religion*, vol. 22, no. 1 (2007): 9–12.

19 See C.M. Zoethout, "Ritual Slaughter and the Freedom of Religion: Some Reflections on a Stunning Matter", *Human Rights Quarterly*, vol. 35 (2013): 651, 653–655.

and 'religious slaughter' can be considered synonyms.[20] This contribution uses the term 'ritual slaughter' because it is prevalent in the academic debate on the subject and is commonly used both in the Belgian context and in the judgements of the CJEU and the ECtHR.

Where the religious conventions or rules governing ritual slaughter in Judaism and Islam are not observed, the meat may be rejected and considered unfit for human consumption. The regulations regarding ritual slaughter in these two religions know various facets. These regulations may pertain among others issues to the knife and method used for cutting, the person permitted to slaughter the animal, the saying of a prayer over the animal, or the inspection of the animal's meat once it has been slaughtered.[21] It suffices to note that while there are commonalities between the two religions, there are also differences between them in this respect.[22] Differences may also exist within each religion, as evidenced in the *Cha'are Shalom Ve Tsedek* case decided by the ECtHR. The case concerned a Jewish association in France which did not recognise the meat as slaughtered by another such association, as they preferred a stricter adherence to the rules about the inspection of the slaughtered animal in determining whether its meat was "perfectly pure, or *glatt*".[23] Moreover, it goes without saying that not all followers of these religions may agree with or subscribe to the practice of ritual slaughter either.

Various interfaces can be distinguished when it comes to the present-day legal regulation of ritual slaughter, as alluded to in the introduction. These can relate to the state restricting such slaughter to slaughterhouses, such as in *Liga van Moskeeën en Islamitische Organisaties Provincie Antwerpen, VZW and Others* to who is permitted to carry it out, such as in *Cha'are Shalom Ve Tsedek*. The most debated interface across Europe today probably concerns the relationship between ritual slaughter and the legal requirement of stunning animals. The purpose of stunning is to render an animal immediately unconscious during the process of slaughter through a variety of techniques.[24]

20 See G. van der Schyff, S. Sottiaux, "Debating Ritual Slaughter in Belgium" 717; C.M. Zoethout, "Ritual Slaughter and the Freedom of Religion" 652; P. Lerner, A.M. Rabello, "The Prohibition of Ritual Slaughtering" 9.

21 See C.M. Zoethout, "Ritual Slaughter and the Freedom of Religion" 656. See also A.Z. Zivotofsky, *Religious Rules and Requirements – Judaism* (Cardiff: Dialrel, 2010). https://www.dialrel.net/dialrel/images/dialrel-wp1-final.pdf. Accessed December 18, 2023; H. Anil, M. Miele, K. von Holleben, F. Bergeaud-Blackler, A. Velarde, *Religious Rules and Requirements – Halal Slaughter* (Cardiff: Dialrel, 2010). https://www.dialrel.net/dialrel/images/dialrel_report_halal.pdf. Accessed December 18, 2023.

22 P. Lerner, A.M. Rabello, "The Prohibition of Ritual Slaughtering" 11.

23 *Cha'are Shalom Ve Tsedek*. No. 27417/95 [2000] §§ 31–33, 60.

24 See G. van der Schyff, "Ritual Slaughter and Religious Freedom in a Multilevel Europe" 79; K. von Holleben, M. von Wenzlawowicz, N. Gregory, H. Anil, A. Velarde, P. Rodriguez, B. Cenci Goga, B. Catanese, B. Lambooij, *Report on Good and Adverse Practices – Animal Welfare Concerns in Relation to Slaughter Practices from the Viewpoint of Veterinary Sciences* (Cardiff: Dialrel, 2010) 79–80. https://www.dialrel.net/dialrel/images/veterinary-concerns.pdf. Accessed December 18, 2023.

This can involve gassing, mechanical, or electrical methods.[25] A distinction is also made between so-called pre-cut and post-cut methods.[26] This refers to whether the animal is stunned before its throat is cut or immediately thereafter. An additional distinction is drawn between reversible and non-reversible methods.[27] Reversible methods mean that the animal can be revived and regain conscious after stunning, such as some electrical methods allow, whereas non-reversible methods exclude this by resulting in the animal's death. Stunning today is usually advanced in the cause of animal welfare as a way to prevent animals from suffering unnecessary pain when slaughtered. This is especially so regarding pre-cut stunning. In this regard, the EU-funded DIALREL report on the comparative ranking of risks from a veterinary sciences perspective concluded that "pain and suffering during the cut" was "high" during "neck cutting without stunning" and "stunning post neck cutting", but "low" when "stunning prior to neck cutting" was practised.[28] Also, for "pain and suffering during the post-cut period", the rating was "low" for pre-cut stunning, "intermediate" for post-cut stunning and "high" when there was no stunning.[29]

Many legal jurisdictions today require that animals be stunned in some manner to reduce their distress, pain and suffering when slaughtered.[30] Whether stunning is compatible with ritual slaughter rites in Judaism and Islam is controversial though. While some religious authorities, such as the position taken by the Islamic rector of Al-Azhar University in Cairo in 1982, accept the practice provided it does not result in the death of the animal, others argue that it violates the regulations on ritual slaughter under all circumstances.[31] When stunning is rejected, meat that has not been properly slaughtered may not be consumed for fear of violating religious law. Against this background, the opposition between those in favour of blanket stunning for the benefit of animal welfare and those who would make or maintain an exemption for Jewish and Islamic ritual slaughter on religious grounds is evident. It is this tension that underlies the CJEU's judgement in *Centraal Israëlitisch Consistorie van België and Others* and which will be investigated in the following sections. The purpose in this regard is not to engage in or settle a religious or theological debate, but to focus on the legal questions involved, especially from the perspective of freedom of religion.

25 G. van der Schyff, "Ritual Slaughter and Religious Freedom in a Multilevel Europe" 79.
26 G. van der Schyff, "Ritual Slaughter and Religious Freedom in a Multilevel Europe" 79.
27 G. van der Schyff, "Ritual Slaughter and Religious Freedom in a Multilevel Europe" 79.
28 K. Von Holleben et al, *Report on Good and Adverse Practices* 70.
29 K. Von Holleben et al, *Report on Good and Adverse Practices* 70.
30 See S. Ferrari, R. Botton, *Legislation Regarding Religious Slaughter in the EU Member, Candidate and Associated Countries* (Cardiff: Dialrel, 2010). https://www.dialrel.net/dialrel/images/report-legislation.pdf. Accessed December 18, 2023.
31 See G. van der Schyff, "Ritual Slaughter and Religious Freedom in a Multilevel Europe" 79; P. Lerner, A.M. Rabello, "The Prohibition of Ritual Slaughtering" 11–12.

7.3 The Case of Ritual Slaughter in Belgium

Before the sixth state reform in Belgium, animal welfare was a federal competence. Since July 1, 2014, the subject has become a regional competence. This means that each region can decide to amend the Law of August 14, 1986, on the Protection and Welfare of Animals for itself. The default position under the 1986 Law, as expressed in Articles 15 and 16, was that vertebrate animals could only be killed after stunning. Mindful of the right to freedom of religion, it was decided to exempt ritual slaughter from this requirement in Article 16(1).[32] Each of the three regions saw attempts to scrap the exemption after the topic became a regional competence. With exemption of the Brussels Capital Region, where a bill to that effect was rejected on June 17, 2022, Flanders and Wallonia each adopted decrees which scrapped the exemption from stunning for ritual slaughter.[33] In this regard, Article 15(2) of the Flemish decree, adopted on July 7, 2017, departs from the Law of 1986 by providing that

> [i]f the animals are slaughtered according to special methods required for religious rites, the stunning must be reversible and the animal's death must not be caused by stunning.[34]

Electronarcosis was deemed the most effective stunning method as it is non-lethal and allows an animal to regain consciousness without any negative effect.[35] Wallonia adopted two decrees, both of which were similar to that in Flanders by requiring that reversible stunning be practised in the case of ritual slaughter.[36]

32 Belgian Law of 14 August 1986 on the protection and welfare of animals [Wet van 14 augustus 1986 betreffende de bescherming en het welzijn der dieren] [1986]); *Centraal Israëlitisch Consistorie van België and Others v. Vlaamse Regering*, C-336/19 [2020] § 11; G. van der Schyff, S. Sottiaux, "Debating Ritual Slaughter in Belgium" 719.

33 See S. Wattier, "Ritual Slaughter Case" 269; G. van der Schyff, S. Sottiaux, "Debating Ritual Slaughter in Belgium" 718–720.

34 Flemish Decree of 7 July 2017 amending the Law of August 14, 1986, on the protection and welfare of animals, regarding permitted methods of slaughtering animals (Decreet houdende wijziging van de wet van 14 augustus 1986 betreffende de bescherming en het welzijn der dieren, wat de toegelaten methodes voor het slachten van dieren betreft [2017]). The translated quote is taken from *Centraal Israëlitisch Consistorie van België and Others v. Vlaamse Regering*, C-336/19 [2020] § 12.

35 Flemish Decree of 7 July 2017 amending the Law of August 14, 1986, on the protection and welfare of animals, regarding permitted methods of slaughtering animals (Decreet houdende wijziging van de wet van 14 augustus 1986 betreffende de bescherming en het welzijn der dieren, wat de toegelaten methodes voor het slachten van dieren betreft [2017]). The translated quote is taken from *Centraal Israëlitisch Consistorie van België and Others v. Vlaamse Regering*, C-336/19 [2020], § 13. Initially, an exemption was made for bovine animals to be stunned using post-cut stunning, as the practice of electronarcosis was not yet as advanced in their case.

36 See in particular Art. D.57(1) of the Walloon Decree of 4 October 2018 on the Walloon animal welfare code [Décret relatif au Code wallon du Bien-être des animaux] [2018]. The first was the Walloon Decree of 18 May 2017 amending Articles 3, 15 and 16 and inserting an Article 45ter into the law of 14 August 1986 on the protection and welfare of animals [Décret modifiant les articles 3, 15 et 16 et insérant un article 45ter dans la loi du 14 août 1986 relative à la protection et au bien-être des animaux] [2017].

The provision in the Flemish decree is based on the report commissioned by the Flemish minister responsible for animal welfare in which an independent party entered into a dialogue with various stakeholders on ritual slaughter and stunning.[37] The report concluded that reversible stunning took maximum account of animal welfare while also respecting the spirit of ritual slaughter by not causing an animal's death but allowing it to die by bleeding out as required in ritual Jewish and Islamic slaughter.[38] According to the report, the balance struck was proportionate within the framework of religious freedom, whilst noting that this was acceptable to at least part of the Muslim community and only to a limited or no extent for the Jewish community.[39] The report met with agreement in the decree's preparatory documents, which stressed the importance of stunning "to eliminate all avoidable animal suffering in Flanders".[40]

Following the adoption of the Flemish and Walloon decrees, the official representations of the Jewish and Muslim communities in Belgium, as well as a number of non-governmental organisations and individuals, approached the country's Constitutional Court in 2019 to annul them.[41] It is important to note that the Constitutional Court rules on constitutional norms, however this remit is interpreted widely allowing the Court in many cases to take note of international law and EU law.[42] Consequently, a range of legal arguments based on various instruments were put to the Court, the essence of which alleged that the decrees violated EU secondary law, freedom of religion, the separation of church and state, freedom of occupation and the principle of equality and non-discrimination.[43] As the two decrees are similar in wording and the Court's ultimate decision in both cases confirmed the constitutionality of the decrees, this discussion will only focus on the Flemish case. This is primarily because the Flemish decree formed the basis for the preliminary references the Court made to the CJEU. As questions of EU law were raised, the

37 P. Vanthemsche, Rapport over de dialoog met de geloofsgemeenschappen met het oog op een significante verbetering van het dierenwelzijn bij de praktijk van ritueel slachten en de overgang naar een algemeen verbod op onbedwelmd slachten of 2017. https://www.friscris.be/nl/publications/rapport-over-de-dialoog-met-de-geloofsgemeenschappen-met-het-oog-op-een-significante-verbetering-van-het-dierenwelzijn-bij-de-praktijk-van-ritueel-slachten-en-de-overgang-naar-een-algemeen-verbod-op-onbedwelmd-slachten(6d92edab-4998-4e76-a25d-e4a8e2034229).html.Accessed December 18, 2023.

38 P. Vanthemsche, Rapport, 57.

39 P. Vanthemsche, Rapport.

40 *Centraal Israëlitisch Consistorie van België and Others v. Vlaamse Regering*, C-336/19 [2020] § 13.

41 Belgian Constitutional Court's case No. 52/2019 [2019]. https://www.const-court.be/public/e/2019/2019-052e.pdf. Accessed December 18, 2023; regarding the Flemish decree; and case No 53/2019 [2019] regarding the Walloon decree.

42 See S. Wattier, "Ritual Slaughter Case" 278; Stefan Sottiaux, *Grondwettelijk recht* (Cambridge: Intersentia, 2016): 454–455.

43 Belgian Constitutional Court's case No 52/2019 § B.15.

Constitutional Court decided to make three references to the CJEU. The applicable EU law framework will be outlined first and then the references.

7.4 The EU Law Framework on Ritual Slaughter and Animal Welfare

On the topic of ritual slaughter, Regulation no. 1099/2009 on the Protection of Animals at the Time of Killing is now the standard piece of EU legislation and has replaced Directive 93/119/EC on the Protection of Animals at the Time of Slaughter or Killing of December 22, 1993.[44] The Regulation reflects the duty in Protocol no. 33 on Protection and Welfare of Animals attached to the Treaty of Amsterdam of 1997 to pay full regard to the welfare of animals in a number of policy areas.[45] This duty of the EU and the Member States was recast in Article 13 of the Treaty on the Functioning of the European Union (TFEU)[46] by the Treaty of Lisbon in 2009. Today, the provision recognises animals as 'sentient beings' and retains the earlier qualification that Member States' legal provisions and practices relating to religious rites, cultural traditions, and regional heritage must be respected when taking full regard of animal welfare.[47]

As its predecessor, Regulation no. 1099/2009 provides a number of minimum animal welfare requirements that Member States need to follow in the process of slaughtering animals for a variety of purposes, including the 'production of food' according to Article 1(1).[48] In this regard, the Regulation stipulates that animals must be spared "any avoidable pain, distress or suffering during their killing".[49] The Regulation does not apply to a number of situations, such as the animals killed in the process of "scientific experiments", "during hunting or recreational fishing activities" and "during cultural or sporting events".[50] Although the term 'slaughter' is sometimes used, the Regulation speaks more generally of the 'killing' of 'animals'. Where 'killing' is

44 Council Directive 93/119/EC on the Protection of Animals at the Time of Slaughter or Killing of December 22, 1993 [1993] OJ L 340/21; Council Regulation no. 1099/2009 (EC) on the Protection of Animals at the Time of Killing of September 24, 2009 [2009] OJ L 303/1.

45 See recitals 4 and 15 of Regulation no. 1099/2009. Protocol no. 33 was derived from Declaration no. 24 on the Protection of Animals attached to the Treaty of Maastricht of 1992.

46 Treaty on the Functioning of the European Union (consolidated version) [2016] OJ C 202.

47 See generally S. Mangiameli, "Article 13 [Animal Protection]". In H.-J. Blanke, S. Mangiameli (eds.), *Treaty on the Functioning of the European Union: A Commentary* (Cham: Springer, 2021): 331–346; M. Klamert, "Article 13 TFEU". In: M. Kellerbauer, M. Klamert, J. Tomkin (eds.), *The EU Treaties and the Charter of Fundamental Rights: A Commentary* (Oxford: Oxford University Press, 2019): 389–390.

48 See recitals 34, 35, 57 on minimum welfare requirements.

49 Art. 3(1) of Regulation no. 1099/2009.

50 To which is added the slaughter of "poultry, rabbits and hares" for their owners' private domestic consumption. See Art. 1(3)(a)(i)-(iii) of Regulation no. 1099/2009.

defined as "any intentionally induced process which causes the death of an animal", the latter being defined as "any vertebrate animal, excluding reptiles and amphibians".[51]

In Article 4(1) of the Regulation, one of its central rules is explained, namely that animals may only be killed after stunning, thereby providing for pre-cut stunning.[52] The effects of stunning – namely, the loss of consciousness and sensibility – must last until the death of the animal.[53] In Annex I, the Regulation also contains a list of stunning methods, including their specifications.[54] However, the requirement in Article 4(1) of the Regulation that animals be stunned before they are slaughtered is not a blanket requirement. This is because Article 4(4) of the Regulation provides for an exemption from pre-cut stunning and states the following:

> In the case of animals subject to particular methods of slaughter prescribed by religious rites, the requirements of paragraph 1 shall not apply provided that the slaughter takes place in a slaughterhouse.[55]

The practice of ritual slaughter is thereby exempted from stunning, provided it takes place in a slaughterhouse as regulated in Article 2(k) of the Regulation. By 'religious rite', the Regulation refers to "a series of acts related to the slaughter of animals and prescribed by a religion", according to Article 2(g). Although the Regulation does not mention any religion by name, it should be clear that both ritual Jewish and Islamic slaughter, as described earlier, fall under the exemption. In order to have a clear picture of the exemption for ritual slaughter, it is important to mention Article 26 of the Regulation on stricter national rules. Apart from allowing existing stricter national rules, Article 26(2) allows Member States to adopt stricter rules in a number of areas laid down by the Regulation.[56] In this context, Article 26(2)(c) states that stricter national rules may be adopted for the "slaughtering and related operations of animals in accordance with Article 4(4)". While ritual slaughter is exempted from the requirement in Article 4(1) that animals always be stunned, the exemption itself may be subject to stricter national rules. In

51 To which is added the slaughter of "poultry, rabbits and hares" for their owners' private domestic consumption. See Art. 2(a), (c) of Regulation no. 1099/2009.

52 Stunning is defined as "any intentionally induced process which causes loss of consciousness and sensibility without pain, including any process resulting in instantaneous death".

53 Art. 4(1) of Regulation no. 1099/2009.

54 These are stunning by mechanical, electrical and gassing methods, as well as by lethal injection.

55 In this regard, the position in Regulation no1099/2009 is the same as in Directive 93/119/EC, which provided for an exemption in Art. 5(2).

56 Apart from stricter national rules, Art. 26(1) of Regulation no. 1099/2009 does not prevent Member States from maintaining existing national rules aimed at ensuring a more extensive protection of animals when they are killed. In this way, Member States are not required to scale back their protection of animal welfare in meeting the requirements set by the Regulation.

setting stricter rules, a Member State may not "prohibit or impede the putting into circulation within its territory of products of animal origin" from other Member States on account that those products do not meet its own stricter rules.[57]

7.5 Three References for Preliminary Rulings

The interplay between the adoption of stricter national rules by a Member State, under Article 26(2)(c) of Regulation no. 1099/2009, versus the exemption for ritual slaughter in Article 4(4) from the requirement that animals must always be stunned played a central role in the CJEU's ruling in *Centraal Israëlitisch Consistorie van België and Others*. In this regard, the Belgian Constitutional Court raised three questions.[58] The CJEU only sought the opinion of Advocate General Hogan on the first two questions, and in its judgement, the Court also examined these questions together.[59]

The CJEU reformulated the first *two questions* as essentially referring to whether Article 26(2)(c) of the Regulation, "read in light of Article 13 TFEU and Article 10(1) of the Charter, must be interpreted as precluding the legislation of a Member State which requires, in the context of ritual slaughter, a reversible stunning procedure which cannot result in the animal's death".[60] The *third* question asked whether the Regulation would violate Articles 20, 21, and 22 CFREU, on equality and respect for religious diversity, if it allowed Member States to require stunning in all cases of slaughter, while the killing of animals in the context of cultural, sporting, hunting, and recreational events does not require stunning.[61] On the first two questions, the CJEU ruled that the Regulation did not preclude national legislation which required reversible stunning in the context of ritual slaughter, which was at odds with the Advocate General's opinion that the religious exemption from stunning in Article 4(4) had to be respected. As to the third question, the CJEU ruled

57 Art. 26(4) of Regulation no. 1099/2009.

58 *Centraal Israëlitisch Consistorie van België and Others v. Vlaamse Regering*, C-336/19 [2020] § 32.

59 *Centraal Israëlitisch Consistorie van België and Others v. Vlaamse Regering*, C-336/19 [2020] § 32. Read separately, the *first* question concerned whether the Flemish decree could, under Art. 26(2)(c) of Regulation no. 1099/2009, derogate from the religious exemption from stunning under Art. 4(4) by requiring stunning in all cases, including ritual slaughter. And if this was possible, the *second* question was whether the possibility of derogating from the religious exemption violated the right to freedom of religion under Art. 10(1) CFREU.

60 *Centraal Israëlitisch Consistorie van België and Others v. Vlaamse Regering*, C-336/19 [2020] § 39.

61 *Centraal Israëlitisch Consistorie van België and Others v. Vlaamse Regering*, C-336/19 [2020] § 32.

that there was no violation of the mentioned CFREU articles.[62] The rest of this contribution will focus on the first two questions, as they formed the basis of the ruling, especially from the perspective of religious freedom. The third question relates primarily to the issue of equality rights and requires a study of its own.[63] In what follows, the judgement and the opinion will be outlined and then analysed.

7.6 Explaining the CJEU Judgement and the Advocate General's Opinion

The main difference between the Court and the Advocate General related to the nature of the legislative framework created by Regulation no. 1099/2009 in the context of the religious exemption from stunning in Article 4(4).[64] The Court's interpretation was arrived at based on a reading of recitals 15 and 18 of the Regulation. The exemption, the Court explained by referring to recital 15, reflected the wording of Article 13 TFEU, which refers to the need to protect animal welfare, but in a way, that takes into account the different approaches in the Member States, particularly with regard to religious rites.[65] The Court also referred to recital 18 that under the exemption "a certain level of subsidiarity" must be left to each Member State.[66] On this basis, the Court held that while the Regulation provides a framework for reconciling the right to freedom of religion and animal welfare, this balance is not established by the

62 See too S. Wattier, "Ritual Slaughter Case" 273. This was, briefly, because cultural and sporting events could not be understood as food production activities in the sense of Art. 1(1) of Regulation no. 1099/2009, while 'hunting' and 'recreational fishing' would be rendered meaningless if animals had to be stunned first (*Centraal Israëlitisch Consistorie van België and Others v. Vlaamse Regering*, C-336/19 [2020] §§ 88–91). Taken together, the CJEU ruled that the Regulation "did not disregard the cultural, religious and linguistic diversity guaranteed" under Art. 22 CFREU (§ 93).

63 See G. Harpaz, A. Reich, "Kosher and Halal Slaughtering Before the Court of Justice: A Case of Religious Intolerance?", *European Public Law*, vol. 28, no. 1 (2022): 35, 49–50. Consider also E. Howard, "Ritual Slaughter and Religious Freedom: Liga van Moskeeën" *Common Market Law Review*, vol. 56, no. 3 (2019): 803, 805, 816–624; A. Peters, "Religious Slaughter and Animal Welfare Revisited: CJEU, Liga van Moskeeen en Islamitische Organisaties Provincie Antwerpen", *Canadian Journal of Comparative and Contemporary Law*, no. 5 (2019): 269, 281–295 on addressing the regulation of ritual slaughter on non-discrimination grounds. See also S. Wattier, "Ritual Slaughter Case" 281–282 and regarding the ECHR the ruling in *Executief van de Moslims van België v. Belgium*, Nos. 16760/22 and 10 others [2024], §§ 125–151.

64 Y. Nakanishi, "Case C-336/19 Centraal Israëlitisch Consistorie van België: Animal Welfare and Freedom of Religion", *Maastricht Journal of European and Comparative Law*, vol. 28, no. 2 (2021): 687, 691–694. https://doi.org/10.1177/1023263X211027497 lists the differences between the judgement and opinion.

65 *Centraal Israëlitisch Consistorie van België and Others v. Vlaamse Regering*, C-336/19 [2020] § 44.

66 *Centraal Israëlitisch Consistorie van België and Others v. Vlaamse Regering*, C-336/19 [2020] § 45.

Regulation itself, but must be found by the Member States.[67] This meant that Member States could in principle derogate from the exemption, under Article 26(2)(c) of the Regulation, even to the extent of requiring stunning in the case of ritual slaughter.[68] When adopting stricter rules, Member States though had to respect the right to freedom of religion in Article 10(1) CFREU.[69]

Advocate General Hogan came to a different conclusion about the taking of stricter national rules under Article 26(2)(c). The adoption of such rules could only "take place within the context of and with full regard to the nature of the derogation provided for by Article 4(4)" of the Regulation.[70] This did not include the "elimination or quasi-elimination" of the religious exemption from stunning, but did allow for the adoption of additional "technical conditions or specifications" aimed at minimising the suffering of the slaughtered animals.[71] This reading was also based on recital 18 but stressed the need to maintain the religious exemption in combination with Member States only having "a certain level of subsidiarity" when derogating.[72] Any other interpretation of the Regulation, he opined, would interfere with the right to freedom of religion in Article 10(1) CFREU and had to be justified under the Charter's limitation provision under Article 52(1).[73]

However, as explained, the Court disagreed and held that when derogating from Article 4(4) of the Regulation, a Member State may in principle require stunning in the case of ritual slaughter. The Court noted that the word 'religion' had to be understood in a broad sense and that ritual slaughter fell within the scope of the right to manifest religion in Article 10(1) CFREU, as previously decided in *Liga van Moskeeën en Islamitische Organisaties Provincie Antwerpen, VZW and Others*.[74] In this regard, it recognised that the Flemish decree interfered with the right by requiring stunning, which resulted in an examination of the decree under Article 52(1) CFREU.[75]

In this regard, the Flemish decree clearly met the requirement that the interference had to be provided by law.[76] The judgement then found that the

67 *Centraal Israëlitisch Consistorie van België and Others v. Vlaamse Regering*, C-336/19 [2020] § 47.

68 *Centraal Israëlitisch Consistorie van België and Others v. Vlaamse Regering*, C-336/19 [2020] § 48.

69 *Centraal Israëlitisch Consistorie van België and Others v. Vlaamse Regering*, C-336/19 [2020] §§ 48–49.

70 Opinion of AG Hogan in case C-336/19, § 70.

71 Opinion of AG Hogan in case C-336/19, §§ 69, 75.

72 Opinion of AG Hogan in case C-336/19, § 71. See also § 72.

73 Opinion of AG Hogan in case C-336/19, § 73. Such justification was deemed difficult, if not impossible, to achieve (§ 73).

74 *Centraal Israëlitisch Consistorie van België and Others v. Vlaamse Regering*, C-336/19 [2020] § 52.

75 *Centraal Israëlitisch Consistorie van België and Others v. Vlaamse Regering*, C-336/19 [2020] §§ 53–55.

76 *Centraal Israëlitisch Consistorie van België and Others v. Vlaamse Regering*, C-336/19 [2020] § 60.

'essence' of the right to freedom of religion was respected. This was because the decree only addressed one aspect of ritual slaughter by requiring reversible stunning, without prohibiting such slaughter in its entirety.[77] This opened the door to reviewing the legitimate aim and proportionality of the interference. It was also clear that by pursuing stricter national rules in the interest of animal welfare, as required under Article 13 TFEU, the decree met a "general interest objective" recognised by the EU.[78] The judgement then focused in some detail on the proportionality of the interference. The limitation analysis was conducted with special reference to the ECtHR case law on the right to freedom of religion in Article 9(1) ECHR. This is because Article 10(1) CFREU 'corresponds' to that right according to Article 52(3) CFREU, which provides that

> [i]n so far as this Charter contains rights which correspond to rights guaranteed by the [ECHR], the meaning and scope of those rights shall be the same as those laid down by the [ECHR]. This provision shall not prevent [EU] law providing more extensive protection.

In this regard, the Court copied the notion of a "wide margin of appreciation" for the state from the case law of the ECtHR.[79] This margin was caused by the "absence of consensus at EU level", which the Court derived from Regulation no. 1099/2009, as it allowed religious exemptions from stunning on the one hand but also allowed stricter national rules on the subject on the other.[80] As a consequence of the margin, 'special weight' had to be given to the role of the 'domestic policymaker' when reviewing the necessity of the interference with the right to freedom of religion, which in this case meant the Flemish legislature.[81] It was pointed out that the decree was in line with the scientific consensus emerging from the opinions of the European Food Safety Authority that pre-cut stunning reduces animal suffering at slaughter.[82] In view of this, the Court found that the Flemish legislature did not exceed its margin of appreciation when it adopted this position in the decree.[83] Moreover, in accordance

77 *Centraal Israëlitisch Consistorie van België and Others v. Vlaamse Regering*, C-336/19 [2020] § 61.

78 *Centraal Israëlitisch Consistorie van België and Others v. Vlaamse Regering*, C-336/19 [2020] §§ 62–63.

79 *Centraal Israëlitisch Consistorie van België and Others v. Vlaamse Regering*, C-336/19 [2020] § 67.

80 *Centraal Israëlitisch Consistorie van België and Others v. Vlaamse Regering*, C-336/19 [2020] § 69. This was also deduced from recitals 18 and 57 of Regulation no. 1099/2009.

81 *Centraal Israëlitisch Consistorie van België and Others v. Vlaamse Regering*, C-336/19 [2020] § 67.

82 *Centraal Israëlitisch Consistorie van België and Others v. Vlaamse Regering*, C-336/19 [2020] § 72. Reference was also made to recital 6 of Regulation no. 1099/2009.

83 *Centraal Israëlitisch Consistorie van België and Others v. Vlaamse Regering*, C-336/19 [2020] §§ 73–74.

with Article 26(4) of the Regulation, the decree did not prohibit or impede the putting into circulation of animal products from Member States which still observe the religious exemption in Article 4(4).[84] These facts and arguments led the CJEU to answer the Belgian Constitutional Court that the Flemish decree did not violate the right to freedom of religion in Article 10(1) CFREU when it required that reversible pre-cut stunning also be practised in the context of ritual slaughter.[85] Based on these answers and after considering the other arguments advanced by the parties, the Constitutional Court upheld both the Flemish and Walloon decrees.[86]

7.7 Analysing the CJEU Judgement and the Advocate General's Opinion

In evaluating the CJEU's ruling, the attention will turn to (i) the CJEU's interpretation of Regulation no. 1099/2009 in the light of Article 13 TFEU, (ii) the interference with the right to freedom of religion in Article 10(1) CFREU, and (iii) the justification of the interference according to the limitation provision in Article 52(1) CFREU.

7.7.1 Article 13 TFEU and Regulation no 1099/2009

The Court and the Advocate General, as explained, differed fundamentally as to whether Article 26(2)(c) of Regulation no. 1099/2009 precludes, by definition, a derogation from the religious exemption in Article 4(4) which requires pre-cut stunning in the case of ritual slaughter. The Court's view that stunning is not excluded is preferable to that of the Advocate General because it is more in line with the logic of Article 13 TFEU.

Article 13 TFEU is a horizontal provision on animal welfare which sets relevant standards for the interpretation of EU primary and secondary law, such as the Regulation.[87] This provision, it may be recalled, demands 'full regard' for animal welfare regarding a number of EU policy fields, while also requiring respect for the different approaches in the Member States, particularly with regard to religious rites. The effect is that the duty in Article 13 TFEU to protect animal welfare is counterbalanced and even restrained by

84 *Centraal Israëlitisch Consistorie van België and Others v. Vlaamse Regering*, C-336/19 [2020] § 78. This included such products from non-EU Member States.

85 *Centraal Israëlitisch Consistorie van België and Others v. Vlaamse Regering*, C-336/19 [2020] §§ 81, 96.

86 Belgian Constitutional Court's case Nos. 117/2021 and 118/2021 [2021]. See S. Wattier, "Ritual Slaughter Case" 277–282.

87 See M. Klamert, "Title II Provisions Having General Application". In: M. Kellerbauer, M. Klamert J. Tomkin (eds.), *The EU Treaties and the Charter of Fundamental Rights: A Commentary* (Oxford: Oxford University Press, 2019): 377, 378. This must be distinguished from the question whether the provision is justiciable.

the approaches in the Member States.[88] The Advocate General's reading of the religious exemption to ritual slaughter in Article 4(4) of the Regulation strikes this balance for the Member States in the spirit of maximising harmonisation. The opinion effectively interprets Article 4(4) as a standstill provision of sorts. Member States *with* existing religious exemptions from stunning *must* maintain them in line with Article 4(4). On the other hand, only Member States *without* such exemptions, such as Sweden, *may* continue to require stunning in the case of ritual slaughter. This is because Article 26(1) of the Regulation allows such Member States to maintain their more extensive protection of animal welfare at the time of the Regulation's coming into force.

The standstill approach is arguably at odds with the idea underlying Article 13 TFEU, namely that of respecting national diversity among the Member States and allowing each state to express and develop its own legal provisions and customs in this regard.[89] Article 13 TFEU could also be viewed in light of a provision such as Article 4(2) of the Treaty on European Union (TEU),[90] which requires that the EU respect the national identities of the Member States to the extent such identity inheres in their "fundamental structures, political and constitutional, inclusive of regional and local self-government".[91] This provision calls on the EU to respect the 'core' of the Member States' constitutional orders, which according to the German Constitutional Court means that "sufficient space is left to the Member States for the political formation of the economic, cultural and social living conditions".[92] It would, therefore, be all the more remarkable if the Regulation were to strike a balance as definitive between the values of religious freedom and animal welfare for the Member States as that contemplated by the Advocate General. Instead, it makes more sense, as the Court also ruled, to understand the Regulation as establishing a framework on the basis of which Member States themselves can reconcile freedom of religion and animal welfare.[93]

88 See S. Mangiameli, "Article 13 [Animal Protection]" 339.

89 S. Mangiameli, "Article 13 [Animal Protection]" 342 critically on the provision leaving "ample room to discretion as to its enforcement" in Member States.

90 Treaty on European Union (consolidated version) [2016] OJ C 202.

91 See generally G. van der Schyff, "The Constitutional Relationship between the European Union and its Member States: The Role of National Identity in Article 4(2)", *European Law Review*, vol. 37 (2012): 563.

92 German Federal Constitutional Court, 2 BvE 2/08 (*Lissabon*) [2009] § 249, ECLI:DE:BVerfG:2009:es20090630.2bve000208. The Court highlighted that in its opinion "[t]hese important areas [...] include cultural issues such as the disposition of language, the shaping of circumstances concerning the family and education, the ordering of the freedom of opinion, press and of association and the dealing with the profession of faith or ideology".

93 *Centraal Israëlitisch Consistorie van België and Others v. Vlaamse Regering*, C-336/19 [2020] § 47.

7.7.2 Interfering with the Scope of Freedom of Religion

On the basis of the foregoing and in the context of Article 51(1) CFREU, according to which the Charter is to be observed by the EU and its Member States when they implement EU law, the main question is not whether the EU legislature respected the right to freedom of religion when it adopted the Regulation but whether the Flemish legislature did so when it exercised the power to derogate under Article 26(2)(c) of the Regulation.[94] This is because the Regulation itself does not interfere with the right to freedom of religion under Article 10(1) CFREU, obviating the need for a limitation analysis under Article 52(1) CFREU, but protects this right by exempting ritual slaughter from stunning under Article 4(4).[95] Only when a Member State, such as the Flemish decree in the case of Belgium, derogates on the basis of Article 26(2)(c) of the Regulation from the exemption in Article 4(4), does a limitation analysis become possible.

Although the CJEU did not elaborate on this point, the judgement was noteworthy in how it established that the right to freedom of religion had been interfered with.[96] As required under Article 52(3) CFREU, the ruling used the "meaning and scope" of the right to freedom of religion in Article 9(1) ECHR as a benchmark for interpreting and applying the corresponding right in Article 10(1) CFREU. A close reading and comparison of the judgement with the legal situation under the ECHR, as it applied then, shows that the CJEU protected freedom of religion more comprehensively than did the ECtHR in the case of ritual slaughter. While the CJEU followed the ECtHR in giving a broad meaning to 'religion' and finding that ritual slaughter fell within the scope of the right to freedom of religion, it arguably set the threshold *lower* than the ECtHR in finding an interference with the right.[97]

In *Cha'are Shalom Ve Tsedek*, the ECtHR held that there would be an interference with "the freedom to manifest one's religion only if the illegality of performing ritual slaughter made it impossible" for religious adherents "to eat meat from animals slaughtered in accordance with the religious prescriptions they considered applicable".[98] In that case, the applicant organisation in France could 'easily obtain' meat that fit its requirements from Belgium, meaning there was no interference.[99] The same could be said in *Centraal Israëlitisch Consistorie van België and Others* of religious adherents in Flanders, as they

94 *Centraal Israëlitisch Consistorie van België and Others v. Vlaamse Regering*, C-336/19 [2020] § 49.

95 The CJEU (*Centraal Israëlitisch Consistorie van België and Others v. Vlaamse Regering*, C-336/19 [2020] § 44) referred to Art. 4(4) of Regulation no. 1099/2009 as a "positive commitment of the EU legislature" to protecting Art. 10(1) CFREU.

96 *Centraal Israëlitisch Consistorie van België and Others v. Vlaamse Regering*, C-336/19 [2020] § 55.

97 *Centraal Israëlitisch Consistorie van België and Others v. Vlaamse Regering*, C-336/19 [2020] § 52.

98 *Cha'are Shalom Ve Tsedek*. No. 27417/95 [2000] § 80.

99 *Cha'are Shalom Ve Tsedek*. No. 27417/95 [2000] § 81.

could still obtain qualifying meat from the Brussels Capital Region, as well as from other Member States and beyond. Also, in accordance with Article 26(4) of the Regulation, Flanders did not refuse animal products from other Member States because they do not comply with its own stricter national rules.[100]

According to the ECHR threshold, as set in *Cha'are Shalom Ve Tsedek*, there would have been no interference with the right to freedom of religion in Article 10(1) CFREU.[101] Yet the CJEU departed from this high threshold, as a simple *de facto* interference with ritual slaughter through the requirement of reversible pre-stunning was sufficient to invoke the limitation provision in Article 52(1) CFREU. Although the CJEU did not reference this, the judgement could be considered an example of EU law providing "more extensive protection" to a corresponding Charter right under Article 52(3) CFREU. The level of protection set under the ECHR, it should be recalled, is only a floor, which EU law may exceed but not derogate from.[102] By setting the threshold lower in finding an interference with the right, the CJEU made it easier for the applicants to claim its protection, while placing the onus on the state to prove that the interference was indeed justified. This, it has been argued, is the proper way for a right with a limitation clause to operate.[103] The effect is that the bearers of a right are also free to exercise that right, instead of imposing a high burden of proof on them before they can rely on that right's protection before the state.

Interestingly, in *Executief van de Moslims van België*, decided four years after *Centraal Israëlitisch Consistorie van België and Others*, the ECtHR applied a lower threshold similar to the one used by the CJEU in finding that removing religious exemptions to stunning was sufficient to interfere with the right to freedom of religion.[104] To reach this conclusion, the ECtHR distinguished the facts from those in *Cha'are Shalom Ve Tsedek* where the question was whether one organisation could be denied permission to conduct ritual slaughter, while another organisation had been granted permission.[105] Why this factual difference should lead to a different finding as to interference

100 *Centraal Israëlitisch Consistorie van België and Others v. Vlaamse Regering*, C-336/19 [2020] § 78.

101 The opinion of AG Hogan in case C-336/19, §§ 85–86 noticed the same but argued that Arts. 4(4) and 26 of Regulation no. 1099/2009 provided a more 'specific protection' to freedom of religion than was required under Art. 9 ECHR. The CJEU (*Centraal Israëlitisch Consistorie van België and Others v. Vlaamse Regering*, C-336/19 [2020] § 18) did not address the matter explicitly and only referenced the ECHR threshold in relation to the applicant's arguments.

102 See S. Peers, S. Prechal, "Article 52". In: S. Peers, T. Hervey, J. Kenner, A. Ward (eds.), *The EU Charter of Fundamental Rights: A Commentary* (Oxford: Hart Publishing, 2021) 1611, 1651–52.

103 See G. van der Schyff, "Ritual Slaughter and Religious Freedom in a Multilevel Europe" 90–92.

104 *Executief van de Moslims van België v. Belgium*, Nos. 16760/22 and 10 others [2024] § 88.

105 *Executief van de Moslims van België v. Belgium*, Nos. 16760/22 and 10 others [2024] §§ 82–83.

remains unclear. It seems that the ECtHR has developed its case law on this point, perhaps given the difficulties caused by its stance in *Cha'are Shalom Ve Tsedek* and also to align itself more closely with the CJEU on this topic.

7.7.3 Justifying the Interference with Freedom of Religion

When evaluating the limitation under Article 52(1) CFREU, attention will also be paid to the effect of Article 9(2) ECHR, the limitation provision applicable to the right to freedom of religion in Article 9(1) ECHR. This is because the CJEU referred to this provision and the applicable ECtHR case law in its analysis.[106] This seems to be in recognition of the Explanations to the Charter with regard to Article 52(3) CFREU, which indicate that where corresponding rights such as Article 10(1) CFREU on freedom of religion are involved, the 'authorised limitations' under the ECHR also apply.[107] In what follows, particular attention will be paid to the 'essence' rule in Article 52(1) CFREU, the margin of appreciation doctrine, and the proportionality of the interference with religious freedom.[108] The question of whether the interference was provided for by law and pursued a legitimate aim or general EU interest was not open to real doubt and will therefore not be treated as such.[109]

7.7.3.1 Essence Rule

The CJEU, it may be recalled, found no violation of the essence of Article 10(1) CFREU, as the Flemish decree did not prohibit ritual slaughter as such but only restricted an aspect of it by requiring reversible and pre-cut stunning.[110] This finding is in line with earlier CJEU case law that the essence of a right is only violated upon that right being extinguished.[111] This does not entail a proportionality exercise but an objective test of whether all aspects of a right have been restricted. The question remains how the application of this

106 *Centraal Israëlitisch Consistorie van België and Others v. Vlaamse Regering*, C-336/19 [2020] §§ 57–58.

107 Explanations Relating to the Charter of Fundamental Rights [2007] OJ C 303/17, 33.

108 Art. 52(1) CFREU mentions both proportionality and necessity, these limitations grounds are closely related and are treated together. See also S. Peers, S. Prechal, "Article 52" 1633–1634.

109 Although a legitimate aim, it is important to recall the words of Peters (n 59) 296 that "we must pay attention that concern for animal welfare is not played out against respect for human dignity and against religious and cultural pluralism".

110 *Centraal Israëlitisch Consistorie van België and Others v. Vlaamse Regering*, C-336/19 [2020] § 61.

111 See S. Peers, S. Prechal, "Article 52" 1632; K. Lenaerts, "Limits on Limitations: The Essence of Fundamental Rights in the EU" *German Law Journal*, vol. 20 (2019): 779, 792–793 on this approach. See also the criticism of G. Harpaz, A. Reich, "Kosher and Halal Slaughtering Before the Court of Justice" 45; M. de Blois, "Centraal Israëlitisch Consistorie van België vs Vlaamse Regering: Is het Hof van Justitie van de EU "koosjer" als het om de vrijheid van godsdienst gaat?", *Tijdschrift voor Recht, Religie en Beleid*, vol. 12 (2021): 99, 105.

limitation requirement is to be understood in the context of Article 52(3) CFREU. A textual comparison of the two limitation provisions shows that whereas Article 52(1) CFREU requires that a limitation of a right respects its 'essence', a similar requirement is not found in Article 9(2) ECHR. Both provisions though require that a limitation (i) must be provided by law, (ii) serve a legitimate aim, and (iii) be proportional.[112] Although Article 9(2) ECHR does not contain a similar requirement on essence, this difference with Article 52(1) CFREU is not likely to lead to any difficulties in applying Article 52(3) CFREU on corresponding rights. This is because a finding under Article 52(1) CFREU that a right was *extinguished* would most likely also correspond to its violation under a limitation provision such as Article 9(2) ECHR. In other words, it is difficult to imagine the extinction of an ECHR right not resulting in its violation and hence its 'essence', as understood in accordance with Article 52(1) CFREU.

7.7.3.2 Margin of Appreciation

This brings the discussion to the margin of appreciation given its important role in finding that Article 10(1) CFREU had not been violated by the Flemish decree. The effect of a margin in EU law is to allow the Member State, in this case the Flemish legislature, partial or full latitude in deciding an issue such as the proportionality of an interference.[113] Whereas under the former the CJEU leaves the decision to the Member State but stipulates how it is to be made, under the latter, it exercises "only superficial control of the relevant national measure, leaving substantive leeway for the Member State legislature".[114] When the distinction is applied to *Centraal Israëlitisch Consistorie van België and Others*, it can be put that the legislature was given a full margin. The CJEU observed, for instance, that Member States had a 'broad discretion' to each preserve their "specific social context" in terms of the Regulation.[115] This raises the question of whether the margin of appreciation was justified.

It is submitted that Regulation no. 1099/2009 implies a margin of appreciation for Member States. This is because, in light of Article 13 TFEU as explained, the Regulation only creates a framework for Member States with

112 Compare J. Kühling, "Fundamental Rights". In A. von Bogdandy, J. Bast (eds.), *Principles of European Constitutional Law* (Oxford: Hart Publishing, CH Beck, 2009): 479, 503; W.A. Schabas, *The European Convention on Human Rights: A Commentary* (Oxford: Oxford University Press, 2015): 420.

113 J. Zglinski, "The Rise of Deference: The Margin of Appreciation and Decentralised Judicial Review in EU Free Movement Law" *Common Market Law Review*, vol. 55, no. 5 (2018): 1341, 1344–1347.

114 J. Zglinski, "The Rise of Deference: The Margin of Appreciation and Decentralised Judicial Review in EU Free Movement Law" *Common Market Law Review*, vol. 55, no. 5 (2018), 1347.

115 *Centraal Israëlitisch Consistorie van België and Others v. Vlaamse Regering*, C-336/19 [2020] § 71.

which to reconcile freedom of religion and animal welfare.[116] However, the applicable margin is arguably narrower than that adopted by the CJEU in this case.[117] The CJEU, it may be recalled, noted that ECtHR case law grants Member States a "wide margin of appreciation" in respect of Article 9 ECHR and referred to the "absence of consensus at EU level" to support a similar margin in EU law.[118] However, in the context of ritual slaughter in *Cha'are Shalom Ve Tsedek*, there was no reference to a 'wide margin' but only to a 'margin'.[119] Also, that case concerned a particular association which was denied the right to carry out such slaughter.[120] *Centraal Israëlitisch Consistorie van België and Others*, on the other hand, constitutes a more far-reaching interference with the right to freedom of religion by removing the religious exemption as such, which pleads for a narrower margin given the range of the interference.[121] While the Regulation may show a lack of consensus at EU level, as the CJEU noted, the nature of the interference arguably limits the discretion of states in the absence of a common position on ritual slaughter. On this basis, there could also be grounds to question the width of the margin granted Belgium by the ECtHR in *Executief van de Moslims van België*, where a narrower margin was not accepted.[122]

7.7.3.3 Proportionality

As a consequence of the margin of appreciation implied in Regulation no. 1099/2009, it can be argued that the Flemish legislature was entitled to decide whether to allow the religious exemption under Article 4(4) or to require stunning under Article 26(2)(c). To interpret the margin otherwise would be to undo the margin. In this regard, the CJEU's approach was consistent with a wide or full margin of appreciation, as it essentially limited its role to examining whether the Flemish decision-making process was proper.[123] However, based on

116 *Centraal Israëlitisch Consistorie van België and Others v. Vlaamse Regering*, C-336/19 [2020] § 47.

117 See also A. Reich, G. Harpaz, "Kosher and Halal Slaughtering Before the European Court of Justice: Voting with Your Trolley Instead of an Outright Ban?", *Texas International Law Journal*, vol. 57 (2021): 39, 55.

118 *Centraal Israëlitisch Consistorie van België and Others v. Vlaamse Regering*, C-336/19 [2020] § 67.

119 *Cha'are Shalom Ve Tsedek*. No. 27417/95 [2000] § 84.

120 *Cha'are Shalom Ve Tsedek*. No. 27417/95 [2000] § 2.

121 Compare A. Reich, G. Harpaz, "Kosher and Halal Slaughtering Before the European Court of Justice" 55; G. van der Schyff, "Ritual Slaughter and Religious Freedom in a Multilevel Europe" 96.

122 *Executief van de Moslims van België v. Belgium*, Nos. 16760/22 and 10 others [2024], §§ 105–106.

123 For instance, the CJEU referred to the decree's preparatory documents (*Centraal Israëlitisch Consistorie van België and Others v. Vlaamse Regering*, C-336/19 [2020] § 73) and noted that the legislature relied on the scientific consensus that pre-cut stunning is "the optimal means of reducing the animal's suffering at the time of killing" (§§ 72, 75).

the argument for a narrower margin, more care may have been warranted to ensure that the aim of the interference was achieved by less restrictive measures, thereby better protecting the right to freedom of religion in Article 10(1) CFREU.[124] For instance, the CJEU could have required that the decision to derogate from the religious exemption in Article 4(4) be revisited after a period of time.[125] In this way, the legislature would have to weigh the competing values of animal welfare and freedom of religion afresh in deciding whether the limitation of ritual slaughter was still proportional given current societal views and scientific evidence. The far-reaching limitation of the right to freedom of religion would thus still be allowed, but on a conditional basis. However, while acknowledging that the Flemish legislature had considered less restrictive measures in its decision-making process, the CJEU stopped short of investigating such measures more closely.[126] A comparable position was followed four years later by the ECtHR in *Executief van de Moslims van België*.[127]

A narrower margin of appreciation may also require a closer inspection into *how* the decree established that ritual slaughter was no longer exempted from the stunning of animals required by Article 4(1) of the Regulation. The relevant Flemish provision, which was quoted in full earlier, reads that in the event of ritual slaughter, stunning *must* be reversible and *must* not cause the death of the animal. The idea was that such a procedure would be compatible with religious requirements.[128] Although this was undoubtedly not the intention of the legislature, the impression or effect may be that the wording of the decree defines or codifies a religious practice and thus goes beyond the simple

124 See G. van der Schyff, "Ritual Slaughter and Religious Freedom in a Multilevel Europe" 97; A. Reich, G. Harpaz, "Kosher and Halal Slaughtering Before the European Court of Justice" 52 and compare J. Zglinski, "The Rise of Deference" 1346 in general.

125 Cf. G. van der Schyff, 'Considering the Relationship Between Law and Religion in the Netherlands: The Case of Ritual Slaughter". In J.W. Sap, C. M. Zoethout, G. van der Schyff, *Ritual Slaughter, Animal Welfare and the Freedom of Religion* (Amsterdam, VU University Press: 2017) 75, 87; G. van der Schyff, "Ritual Slaughter and Religious Freedom in a Multilevel Europe" 102. A. Reich, G. Harpaz, "Kosher and Halal Slaughtering Before the European Court of Justice" 53–55 propose the labelling of meat instead of abolishing the religious exemption in the context of a narrow margin and refer to the *Cassis de Dijon* judgment (*Rewe-Zentral AG v. Bundesmonopolverwaltung für Branntwein*, 120/78 [1979], ECLI:EU:C:1979:42. According to J. Zglinski, "The Rise of Deference" 1344, there was no margin in the latter case, leading to doubts whether their proposal factors in the margin sufficiently. Arguably, the absence of a margin precludes stunning being required, as opposed to a margin which would allow stunning in principle.

126 *Centraal Israëlitisch Consistorie van België and Others v. Vlaamse Regering*, C-336/19 [2020] §§ 62, 72–73.

127 *Executief van de Moslims van België v. Belgium*, Nos. 16760/22 and 10 others [2024], § 117. As to the role of the less restrictive test as such, see the concurring opinions of judges Koskelo and Kūris and that of judge Yüksel.

128 P. Vanthemsche, Rapport 57.

abolition of the exemption.[129] The ECHR system, like the EU, does not dictate to Member States how they should structure their relationship with religion, but Article 9(1) ECHR requires that such a relationship must respect freedom of religion.[130] In this context, doubts are warranted as to whether the Flemish decree was indeed proportionate to achieve its aim and whether the margin of appreciation covers a situation under Article 10(1) CFREU where a legislature in effect prescribes the form of religious rites. The CJEU did not address this question. However, it probably fell within the remit of the reference made by the Belgian Constitutional Court, as it asked not only whether the decree could derogate from Article 4(4) of the Regulation but also whether its "alternative stunning procedure" for ritual slaughter was permissible.[131] In these circumstances, it might have been prudent for the CJEU to have ruled that while derogation under the decree could extend stunning to all animals in line with the Flemish legislature's wish, it precluded the specific "alternative stunning procedure" for religious rites.[132]

Apart from these remarks on the Flemish decree as such, it is appropriate to briefly address another dimension of the proportionality analysis in order to provide a complete picture. In its ruling, the CJEU noted that the CFREU, like the ECHR, is a 'living instrument' that needs to be interpreted in the light of 'present-day conditions'.[133] This meant that the increased importance of animal welfare in many democratic societies may 'be taken into account to a greater extent in the context of ritual slaughter and thus help to justify the proportionality of legislation'.[134] This position implies that any of the 27 EU Member States or their regions may decide to derogate from the religious exemption in Article 4(4) of the Regulation. This seems to be far from reality at present, as most states still adhere to the exemption.[135]

129 G. van der Schyff, "Recent Legislation on Ritual Slaughter in Flanders Evaluated: Perspectives from the Separation of State and Religion and Freedom of Religion", *Religie en Samenleving*, no. 1 (2017): 5, 13, 15.

130 Consider the implications of European Commission of Human Rights, *Darby v. Sweden*, No 11581/85 [1989] § 45, for the case at hand. The Commission explained that a state church system as in Sweden at the time in itself did not violate Art. 9 ECHR but that it had to be operated in a manner that protected the right to freedom of religion.

131 *Centraal Israëlitisch Consistorie van België and Others v. Vlaamse Regering*, C-336/19 [2020] § 32.

132 A similar question was raised before the Belgian Constitutional Court's case Nos 117/2021 and 118/2021 [2021] §§ B.31.4, B.34. The Court issued an interpretative guidance, holding that the provision could not be read as defining a religious practice, as that would violate state neutrality in religious affairs. Instead, it had to be read as offering the possibility of reversible stunning in the context of ritual slaughter. The question is whether this is sufficient. Preferable would have been a reformulation of the decree to align with state neutrality.

133 *Centraal Israëlitisch Consistorie van België and Others v. Vlaamse Regering*, C-336/19 [2020] § 77.

134 *Centraal Israëlitisch Consistorie van België and Others v. Vlaamse Regering*, C-336/19 [2020] § 77.

135 *Centraal Israëlitisch Consistorie van België and Others v. Vlaamse Regering*, C-336/19 [2020] § 78.

Suppose though that all Member States or even the majority were to follow the Flemish example. While each individual derogation might be proportionate, it is questionable whether the cumulative effect of all of them would also constitute a proportionate interference with the right to freedom of religion under Article 10(1) CFREU. In other words, the effect of an EU-wide derogation could mean that each individual derogation would represent a much greater interference with the right than if it were the only derogation in the EU. This is because an EU-wide derogation would lead to the *de facto* impossibility of ritual slaughter without the stunning of animals throughout the EU.[136] A related consequence could very well be that it becomes prohibitively expensive or almost impossible in practice for religious adherents in the EU to access meat that suits their requirements, including from third countries.[137] The equation changes when this happens, as the limitation of a religious *practice* turns into a *de facto* limitation of what may be *consumed* based on religious conviction. In this regard, the CJEU could take inspiration from *Cha'are Shalom Ve Tsedek* in which the ECtHR opined that Article 9(1) ECHR would be interfered with if that happens.[138] Instead of finding an interference this way, an approach which was rejected earlier, the CJEU could use this test to determine whether the right to freedom of religion in Article 10(1) CFREU was violated, in which event, the relevant Member State might have to consider means less restrictive of the right when protecting animal welfare.[139] The ECtHR, in *Executief van de Moslims van België*, considered such an approach, as the question whether religious adherents had access to meat satisfying their requirements was examined as part of the necessity test.[140] In this case, however, the ECtHR found that the applicants had not established that the contested decrees made it more difficult for them to have access to such meat.[141]

7.8 To Conclude

The CJEU judgement in *Centraal Israëlitisch Consistorie van België and Others* illustrates the complexity of balancing the right to freedom of religion and animal welfare in a multi-level context that includes EU law and Member

136 This would be irrespective of whether such meat would still be available according to Art. 26(4) of Regulation no. 1099/2009.

137 See also L. Hehemann, "Religious Slaughtering, a Stunning Matter: Centraal Israëlitisch Consistorie van België and Others", *European Papers*, no. 6 (2021): 111, 117; G. Harpaz, A. Reich, "Kosher and Halal Slaughtering Before the Court of Justice" 47; G. van der Schyff, "Ritual Slaughter and Religious Freedom in a Multilevel Europe" 101 speaks of 'reasonable access' to such meat. Consider also A. Reich, G. Harpaz, "Kosher and Halal Slaughtering Before the European Court of Justice" 48–51 on the functioning of the internal market in this respect.

138 *Cha'are Shalom Ve Tsedek*. No. 27417/95 [2000] §§ 80–81.

139 See again §§ 69 and 75 of the opinion of AG Hogan in case C-336/19 which arguably mention such measures.

140 *Executief van de Moslims van België v. Belgium*, Nos. 16760/22 and 10 others [2024] § 122.

141 *Executief van de Moslims van België v. Belgium*, Nos. 16760/22 and 10 others [2024] § 122.

State law and in which not only the CFREU plays a role but also the ECHR. In many respects, the Court's judgement can serve an example on how this sometimes-difficult balance can be achieved. As outlined, however, while recognising that Member States may in principle require stunning in the context of ritual slaughter, it would have been prudent to allow the Flemish legislature a narrower margin of appreciation than was the case. On a general note, it would be incorrect to view the judgement as the last word on the topic of ritual slaughter and stunning. The very nature of the EU legal framework in this regard means that the topic is to be debated in the Member States while respecting the right to freedom of religion in Article 10(1) CFREU. The margin of appreciation entails that Member States are to take primary responsibility for their decision-making on whether to derogate from the religious exemption in Article 4(4) of Regulation no. 1099/2009.[142] This leaves them room for manoeuvre, taking into account the requirements of their own separation of powers and constitutional sources, while respecting the possibilities and limits of EU law, in particular regarding the CFREU.

142 See also J. Kühling, "Fundamental Rights" 507, who recommends an EU margin of appreciation doctrine to make the case law on fundamental rights more dynamic so that rights do "not lose their framework character for the entire legal order".

8 Ritual Male Circumcision and Children's Rights

Rhona Schuz

Abstract

In recent years, anti-circumcision activists have started to use children's rights discourse in order to promote their agenda. For example, in 2013, the Parliamentary Assembly of the Council of Europe (PACE) adopted a resolution and recommendation on the Child's Right to Physical Integrity, which inter alia expressed concern that ritual male circumcision violated children's rights protected by the UN Convention on the Rights of the Child; it urged Member States to consider forbidding the practice on children who were not old enough to consent and recommended inclusion of the child's right to physical integrity into relevant Council of Europe standards. Concerns about the impact of this resolution on Jewish and Muslim communities in Europe led to the passing of a further PACE resolution on the Right to Freedom of Religion in 2015. The latter urges States to come to "reasonable accommodations" in relation to controversial religious practices, so as to ensure effective equality in exercise of the right to freedom of religion. The resolution specifically states that States should "provide for ritual circumcision of children not to be allowed unless practiced by a person with the requisite training and skill, in appropriate medical and health conditions" in order to ensure compliance with the rights of the child. These two resolutions reflect not only a divergence of approach as to the scope of the right to freedom of religion but also in relation to the question of whether ritual circumcision is per se a human rights violation.

Against the background of the 2013 PACE resolution and other recent attempts to ban or limit the practice of ritual male circumcision, this chapter will analyze critically the various bases of the claim that ritual male circumcision violates children's rights and show that the claims made by the anti-circumcision advocates are based on fundamental misconceptions in relation to children's rights. On the contrary, it will be argued that a child born into a religion which practices ritual male circumcision has a right to be circumcised. For reasons of convenience, the chapter will refer to Jewish and Muslim boys since these are the main religions which practice ritual male circumcision, but the arguments apply equally to other religions in which circumcision is considered to be a religious precept.

DOI: 10.4324/9781003423294-12

Keywords

anti-circumcision; autonomy; benefits; best interests; bodily integrity; Convention on the Rights of the Child; rights discourse; freedom of religion; interference; Jewish; medical; Muslim; right to identity; right to highest standard of health; ritual circumcision; parental rights; Prophylactic; risks

8.1 Introduction

In October 2013, the Parliamentary Assembly of the Council of Europe (PACE) adopted a resolution and recommendation on the Child's Right to Physical Integrity (the PACE Resolution),[1] which *inter alia* expressed concern that ritual male circumcision violated children's rights protected by the UN Convention on the Rights of the Child (CRC);[2] it urged Member States to consider forbidding the practice on children who were not old enough to consent and recommended inclusion of the child's right to physical integrity into relevant Council of Europe standards. In an earlier article,[3] I argued that this resolution illustrates some of the pitfalls of children's rights discourse and highlights the risks of self-proclaimed children's rights advocates taking a monolithic, oversimplistic approach to rights analysis. I also exposed the defects in the process of the passing of the PACE Resolution and questioned which institutions should have the authority to make value judgments concerning children's rights.

In September 2015, the PACE adopted a new resolution on the Right to Freedom of Religion,[4] which urges States to come to "reasonable accommodations" in relation to controversial religious practices so as to ensure effective equality in exercise of the right to freedom of religion. The resolution specifically states that States should "provide for ritual circumcision of children not to be allowed unless practiced by a person with the requisite training and skill, in appropriate medical and health conditions" in order to ensure compliance with the rights of the child. The clear implication of this statement is that ritual circumcision is not a human rights violation, provided that it is carried out by a qualified person in proper conditions.

1 Resolution 1952: Children's Right to Physical Integrity, Parliamentary Assembly Council of Europe [2013] UN Doc. 13297.

2 Convention on the Rights of the Child [1989] 1577 UNTS 3 (hereinaft CRC), ratified by all States apart from the United States.

3 R. Schuz, "The Dangers of Children's Rights' Discourse in the Political Arena: the Issue of Religious Male Circumcision as a Test Case", *Cardozo Journal of Law and Gender*, vol. 21 (2015): 347.

4 Resolution 2076 of Parliamentary Assembly Council of Europe: Freedom of Religion and Living Together [2015]. https://www.assembly.coe.int/nw/xml/XRef/Xref-XML2HTML-en.asp?fileid=22199&lang=en. Accessed November 2, 2024.

While the latest resolution of the PACE appears to have put an end to the efforts of anti-circumcision activists to use the Council of Europe[5] as a vehicle to promote their agenda, it has not prevented intense campaigns against circumcision in some quarters[6] and attempts to pass legislation banning or restricting ritual male circumcision in a number of European States, including Iceland[7] and Denmark.[8] While to date, none of these attempts has been successful,[9] the view that the practice violates the human rights of the child seems to be relatively widespread. Accordingly, it is appropriate to rehearse the arguments on which this view is based and to explain why they are flawed, and why a ban on ritual male circumcision would in fact violate a child's human rights. Section 8.2 of this chapter will outline the religious and medical background to the practice of ritual male circumcision. Section 8.3 will then discuss critically in turn each of the human rights claims made in relation to the practice, and Section 8.4 will summarize the conclusions.

8.2 The Religious and Medical Background[10]

8.2.1 The Religious Background

Ritual male circumcision is a widespread practice among Jews and Muslims and is also practiced by other tribes and some Christian communities.[11] The percentage of boys who are circumcised is as high as 99% in many Muslim

5 The Committee of Ministers had previously expressed reservations about the resolution on the Right to Physical Integrity and decided that no further action should be taken in relation thereto, Comm. of Ministers, Children's Right to Physical Integrity, Parliamentary Assembly Recommendation 2023 (2013), CM/AS(2014)Rec2023 final [2014]. https://www.wcd.coe.int/ViewDoc.jsp?id=2173161&Site=CM&BackColorInternet=C3C3C3&BackColorIntranet=EDB021&BackColorLogged=F5D383. Accessed March 21, 2024.

6 A.J. Jacobs, K.S. Arora, "Ritual Male Infant Circumcision and Human Rights", *The American Journal of Bioethics*, vol. 15, no. 2 (2015): 30, 37. https://doi.org/10.1080/15265161.2014.990162.

7 "Iceland law to outlaw male circumcision sparks row over religious freedom". https://www.theguardian.com/society/2018/feb/18/iceland-ban-male-circumcision-first-european-country. Accessed October 21, 2024.

8 M. Clante Bendixen, "Denmark: Renewed debate on circumcision of boy". https://ec.europa.eu/migrant-integration/news/denmark-renewed-debate-circumcision-boys_en. Accessed October 21, 2024.

9 See e.g. "Danish Parliament Rejects Ban on Boys Circumcision". https://www.news/article/29-danish-parliament-rejects-ban-on-boys-circumcision. Accessed October 21, 2024; "Iceland Dumps Proposed Ban on Male Circumcision". https://bioedge.org/uncategorized/iceland-dumps-proposed-ban-on-male-circumcision/. Accessed October 21, 2024; C. Liphshiz, "Proposal to ban male circumcision scrapped from Finland bill". https://www.timesofisrael.com/proposal-to-ban-male-circumcision-scrapped-from-finland-bill/. Accessed October 21, 2024.

10 This part is a revised version of R. Schuz, "The Dangers of Children's Rights' Discourse in the Political Arena".

11 R. Cohen-Almagor, "Should liberal government regulate male circumcision performed in the name of Jewish tradition?", *SN Social Science*, vol. 1, no. 8 (2021): 7. https://doi.org/10.1007/s43545-020-00011-7.

States and 97% of Jewish boys in Israel.[12] The origin of the practice of neonatal circumcision in Judaism[13] is in the Divine command to Abraham in the following passage:

> [You shall] keep My covenant, [you] and [your] seed after [you] throughout their generations. This is My covenant which [you] shall keep between Me and you and [your] seed after [you]; every male among you shall be circumcised. And [you] shall be circumcised in the flesh of your foreskin; and it shall be a token of the covenant [between] Me and you. And he that is eight days old shall be circumcised among you, every male throughout your generations, he that is born in the house or bought with money of any foreigner, that is not of [your] seed. He that is born in [your] house, and he that is bought with [your] money, must needs be circumcised: and My covenant shall be in your flesh for an everlasting covenant. And the uncircumcised male who is not circumcised in the flesh of his foreskin that soul shall be cut off from his people; he [has] broken My covenant.[14]

The duplication within these verses and in other places in the Old Testament[15] together with the severe implications of not being circumcised[16] perhaps explain the cardinal importance which has been attached to this commandment by Jews ever since biblical times,[17] in Israel and in the Diaspora. Indeed, it is one of the few commandments that is widely observed by Jews who regard themselves as entirely secular.[18] Another indication of the fundamental nature and importance of this commandment is that it overrides the laws of the Sabbath

12 R. Cohen-Almagor, "Should liberal government regulate male circumcision performed in the name of Jewish tradition?", *SN Social Science*, vol. 1, no. 8 (2021): 7. https://doi.org/10.1007/s43545-020-00011-7.

13 For evidence that male circumcision was also performed by other early civilizations, see M. Yavuz, T. Demir, B. Dogangen, "The Effect of Circumcision on the Mental Health of Children: A Review", *Turkish Journal of Psychiatry*, vol. 23 (2012): 1.

14 Gen. 17,9:14 (trans. Soncino (ed.), London: Soncino Press, 1964).

15 Lev. 12,3 (repeating the commandment of circumcision of male newborns on the eighth day).

16 While lack of circumcision does not prejudice the Jewish status of a male born to a Jewish mother, it remains an essential element of conversion to the Jewish faith.

17 Exod. 4, 24. Moses himself was nearly punished with death for not circumcising his second son, Eliezer, even though he was at the time travelling to Egypt to free the Children of Israel from slavery, in accordance with the Divine command. He was saved when his wife performed the circumcision. See also Yoreh Deah, Laws of Circumcision 260:1 (the leading Rabbinical codex of Jewish law, the Shulhan Aurch, written by Rabbi Yosef Karo in the 16th century, stating that the commandment to circumcise one's son is greater than the other positive commandments) (in Hebrew).

18 In the HCJ case *Plonit v. Ploni*, 8533/13 [2014] § 17 (Justice Neor), § 4 (Justice Rubenstein) referring to Jewish tradition that the Jewish people will be redeemed in the merit of their having kept the commandment of circumcision). It is estimated that 98% of Jewish males worldwide are circumcised. R. Cohen-Almagor, "Should liberal government regulate male circumcision performed in the name of Jewish tradition?" 8.

and thus where the eighth day after birth falls on the Sabbath, the circumcision is performed even though cutting the skin is normally prohibited on the Sabbath.[19]

As seen in the quote, the Bible does not give any reason for the commandment other than that it is a sign of the covenant between the Creator of the world and the Jewish people. Rabbinical sources, developing this idea further, state that the purpose of the circumcision is to distinguish between Jews and other nations[20] and that the reproductive organ was chosen as the location of the sign of the covenant since this is the source of the existence of the human race.[21] Another explanation offered is that the Creator made man with a redundant foreskin so that he could complete the creation of his own body, and this would teach him that he must also strive to perfect his soul, the prime purpose of life, according to Jewish philosophy.[22]

The approach to male circumcision in Islam is somewhat different. Circumcision is not mentioned in the Koran and is based on prophetic tradition. While for Muslims circumcision is not an absolute command, it is strongly recommended and is of great symbolic significance, being seen as passage into manhood.[23] There is no prescribed age for circumcision in Islam, but it is usually carried out when a boy reaches the age of 7.[24] An expert opinion in one case claimed that lack of circumcision would render null and void prayer by a Muslim male, which is obligatory after the age of 10.[25] Due to the religious and social importance of the practice,[26] nearly all Muslim boys are circumcised,[27] even where their parents are not practicing Muslims.[28] Interestingly, in the prophetic traditions, male circumcision is mentioned under the heading of

19 By way of contrast, other positive commandments, such as blowing the ram's horn on the New Year or taking the Four Species on the Festival of Tabernacles, do not override the Sabbath and so are not performed when the festival falls on the Sabbath. E. Ki Tov, *The Book of our Heritage. Nisan: The Jewish Year and Its Days of Significance* (Jerusalem: Feldheim Publishers, 1978): 41, 163.
20 *Sefer Hachinuch* (Book of Education), commandment 2.
21 *Sefer Hachinuch* (Book of Education), commandment 2.
22 *Sefer Hachinuch* (Book of Education), commandment 2.
23 M. Yavuz, T. Demir, B. Dogangen, "The Effect of Circumcision on the Mental Health of Children" 2.
24 M. Yavuz, T. Demir, B. Dogangen, "The Effect of Circumcision on the Mental Health of Children" 2.
25 *In Re* S (specific issue order: religion: circumcision) [2004] EWHC 1282, [24] (Fam).
26 *In Re* S (specific issue order: religion: circumcision) [2004] EWHC 1282, [24] (Fam), 1, 4. The expert claimed that lack of circumcision would cause the boy embarrassment; M. Yavuz, T. Demir, B. Dogangen, "The Effect of Circumcision on the Mental Health of Children".
27 *In Re* S [2004] [24] 1, 4 (the expert claimed that lack of circumcision would cause the boy embarrassment); M. Yavuz, T. Demir, B. Dogangen, "The Effect of Circumcision on the Mental Health of Children".
28 *In Re* J [1992] 2 FCR 34 (an application by the nonpracticing Muslim father for permission to circumcise his son against the wishes of the nonpracticing Christian mother).

cleanliness, together with the clipping of nails,[29] the use of toothpicks, and the cutting of mustaches.[30]

8.2.2 Medical Aspects of Male Circumcision

In the 19th century, some doctors started circumcising newborn boys for preventative-hygienic reasons,[31] and the practice spread in some Western, largely Anglo-American countries.[32] However, the prevalence of nonritual circumcision decreased in the second half of the 20th century.[33] Nonetheless, in the United States, over one half of newborns were circumcised between 1999 and 2010.[34] Globally, it has been estimated that 13.3 million boys are circumcised each year.[35] Over the last few decades, there has emerged a divergence of medical opinion as to the desirability of performing circumcision, other than in cases where it is medically indicated.[36] One of the most up-to-date and authoritative reports on the subject is that published in 2012 by the American Academy of Pediatrics (AAP) following a thorough investigation of the subject by a taskforce set up for this purpose.[37] They summarize their conclusions as follows:

> Evaluation of current evidence indicates that the health benefits of newborn male circumcision outweigh the risks; furthermore, the benefits of newborn male circumcision justify access to this procedure for families

29 M. Yavuz, T. Demir, B. Dogangen, "The Effect of Circumcision on the Mental Health of Children" 3.

30 W. Dekkers, C. Hoffer, J.-P. Wils, "Bodily Integrity and Male and Female Circumcision", *Medicine, Health Care and Philospohy*, vol. 8 (2005): 179, 181. https://doi.org/10.1007/s11019-004-3530-z.

31 M. Fox, M. Thompson, "Short Changed? The Law and Ethics of Male Circumcision", *The International Journal of Children's Rights*, vol. 13 (2005): 161, 162, 170–173 (providing a historical medical narrative); R. Cohen-Almagor, "Should liberal government regulate male circumcision performed in the name of Jewish tradition?" 7.

32 M. Fox, M. Thompson, "Short Changed?" 162 (in continental Europe and Scandinavia, the rate of non-therapeutic male circumcision is very low); H. Askola, "Cut-Off Point? Regulating Male Circumcision in Finland", *International Journal of Law, Policy and the Family*, vol. 25, no. 1 (2011): 100. https://doi.org/10.1093/lawfam/ebq018.

33 W.D. Dunsmuir, E.M. Gordon, "The History of Circumcision", *BJU International*, vol. 83, no. spec. 1. (1999): 1–12. https://www.doi.org/10.1046/j.1464-410x.1999.0830s1001.x.

34 S. Blank, M. Brady, E. Buerk, W. Carlo, D. Diekema, A. Freedman, L. Maxwell, S. Wegner, "Male Circumcision", *Pediatrics*, vol. 130, no. 3 (2012): 756. http://pediatrics.aappublications.org/content/130/3/e756.full.html. Accessed November, 1 2024. Hereinafter: AAP Report.

35 W. Dekkers, C. Hoffer, J.-P. Wils, "Bodily Integrity and Male and Female Circumcision" 180. For percentage of circumcised males per country, see R. Cohen-Almagor, "Should liberal government regulate male circumcision performed in the name of Jewish tradition?" 14.

36 M. Benatar, D. Benatar, "Between Prophylaxis and Child Abuse: The Ethics of Neonatal Male Circumcision", *The American Journal of Bioethics*, vol. 3, no. 2 (2003): 35, 48 (discussing the medical evidence available two decades ago).

37 AAP Report 756.

> who choose it. Specific benefits from male circumcision were identified for the prevention of urinary tract infections,[38] acquisition of HIV,[39] transmission of some sexually transmitted infections, and penile cancer. Male circumcision does not appear to adversely affect penile sexual function/sensitivity or sexual satisfaction [...] Significant acute complications are rare.

Similarly, an article published in the prestigious US medical journal *Mayo Clinical Proceedings*, strongly supports neonatal circumcision.[40] In particular, this paper draws attention to the fact that while there has been a decrease in neonatal circumcision, there has been an increase in the incidence of circumcision in the male population as a whole.[41] In light of the considerable medical advantages of performing the procedure at a young age, the paper calls for newborn circumcisions to be funded by healthcare schemes and argues that this is cost-effective in the long term.[42]

Opponents of circumcision dispute the scientific validity of the findings on which these and earlier pro-circumcision medical papers are based[43] and point

38 A meta-analysis showed that the incidence of urinary tract infection in circumcised infants was ten times less than in their uncircumcised counterparts, B.J. Morris, S. Moreton, J.N. Krieger, "Critical Evaluation of Arguments Opposing Male Circumcision: A Systematic Review", *Journal of Evidence-Based Medicine*, vol. 12, no. 4 (2019): 263, 265. https://doi.org/10.1111/jebm.12361.

39 See also J. Morris, S. Moreton, J.N. Krieger, "Critical Evaluation of Arguments Opposing Male Circumcision: A Systematic Review", *Journal of Evidence-Based Medicine*, vol. 12, no. 4 (2019): 263, 265. https://doi.org/10.1111/jebm.12361; R.V. Short, „Male Circumcision: A Scientific Perspective", *Journal of Medical Ethics*, vol. 30, no. 3 (2004): 241. https://www.doi.org/10.1136/jme.2002.002576 (pointing out that the rates of HIV are much lower in third world countries, where Islam is the majority religion, than in non-Islamic neighbouring States); C. De Lange, "AIDS Prevention: Africa's Circumcision Challenge", *Nature* no 503 (2013): 182. https://doi.org/10.1038/503182a (in Africa, around three million males have been circumcised as part of a program to combat HIV, and there are plans to circumcise many more); and A. Marcell, "Greater benefits of infant circumcision", https://www.hopkinsmedicine.org/news/articles/2012/10/greater-benefits-of-infant-circumcision. Accessed November 2, 2024.

40 B.J. Morris, S.A. Bailis, T.E. Wiswell, "Circumcision Rates in the United States: Rising or Falling? What Effect Might the New Affirmative Pediatric Policy Statement Have?", *Mayo Clinical Proceeding*, vol. 89, no. 5 (2004): 677–686. https://www.doi.org/10.1016/j.mayocp.2014.01.001 ("neonatal circumcision should logically be strongly supported and encouraged as an important evidence based intervention akin to childhood vaccination.".

41 B.J. Morris, S.A. Bailis, T.E. Wiswell, "Circumcision Rates in the United States: Rising or Falling? 678.

42 B.J. Morris, S.A. Bailis, T.E. Wiswell, "Circumcision Rates in the United States: Rising or Falling? What Effect Might the New Affirmative Pediatric Policy Statement Have?", *Mayo Clinical Proceeding*, vol. 89, no. 5 (2004), 684.

43 R.S. Van Howe, "Peer-Review Bias Regarding Circumcision in American Medical Publishing". In: G.C. Denniston, F.M. Hodges, M.F. Milos (eds.), *Male and Female Circumcision: Medical, Legal, and Ethical Considerations in Pediatric Practice* (New York: Kluwer, 1999): 357.

to a number of adverse effects of circumcision.[44] However, these claims are convincingly refuted by a recent systematic literature review, that brings a large body of high quality evidence showing the medical benefits of circumcision together with the low risk of complications and explains the flaws in the allegedly contrary evidence.[45]

8.3 Children's Rights

8.3.1 Use of Children's Rights Discourse in the Circumcision Debate

Historically, bans on religious male circumcision were part of spiritual and/or physical attacks on Jews. In the 2nd century BCE, the Greek leader Antiochus IV, in his attempt to suppress Judaism and Hellenize Jews, prohibited circumcision on pain of death.[46] Two centuries later, the Roman emperor Hadrian also forbade circumcision.[47] In contrast, the modern anti-circumcision lobby, which emerged toward the end of the 20th century, is not expressly directed against Jews and indeed seems to be largely a response to the practice of routine medical neonatal circumcision in the United States.[48] Indeed, one of the main motivations for this development seems to be the dissatisfaction of men who had been circumcised for nonreligious reasons.[49] Over the years, opponents of circumcision have started using arguments based on children's rights, a concept which has been rapidly gaining acceptance, largely as a result of the 1989 UN CRC. It has been suggested that anti-circumcision activists turned to human rights arguments since neither the medical evidence nor moral arguments could justify removing the decision about infant circumcision from parents.[50] Indeed, the children's rights argument has become a powerful vehicle in the campaign against ritual circumcision, as can be seen

44 R. Cohen-Almagor, "Should liberal government regulate male circumcision performed in the name of Jewish tradition?" 8.

45 B.J. Morris, S. Moreton, J.N. Krieger, "Critical Evaluation of Arguments Opposing Male Circumcision".

46 1 Macc 1:63–64.

47 A.M. Rabello, "The Ban on Circumcision as a Cause of Bar Kochba's Rebellion", *Israel Law Review*, vol. 29, no. 1–2 (1995): 176.

48 D. Schultheiss, "The History of Foreskin Restoration". In: G.C. Denniston, F.M. Hodges, M.F. Milos (eds.), *Male and Female Circumcision* 285–294. https://doi.org/10.1007/978-0-585-39937-9_23.

49 Thus, a survey among men who belonged to an organization providing support for those interested in foreskin restoration revealed that 91% of them were Christians and that only 9% had been circumcised for religious reasons, R.W. Griffiths, "Current Practices in Foreskin Restoration. The State of Affairs in the United States, and Results of a Survey of Restoring Men". In: G.C. Denniston, F.M. Hodges, M.F. Milos (eds.), *Male and Female Circumcision* 295. https://doi.org/10.1007/978-0-585-39937-9_24.

50 A. Viens, "Value Judgment, Harm and Religious Liberty", *Journal of Medical Ethics*, vol. 31 (2004): 241, 245.

from the 2013 PACE Resolution and from the press coverage of the attempts to impose a ban.

The opponents of ritual male circumcision claim that the practice violates the child's right to physical integrity and the child's autonomy, and is inconsistent with their best interests. Conversely, I and others have argued that permitting circumcision actually promotes some of the child's rights – including the right to identity, the right to freedom of religion, the right to the best attainable standard of health, and the right to autonomy – as well as their best interests.[51] The following analysis will consider the various claims in relation to each of these rights and the best interests of the child.

8.3.2 The Right to Bodily Integrity

The child's right to physical integrity is derived *inter alia* from the obligation imposed on State Parties by Article 19 of the CRC to take all appropriate measures to

> [p]rotect the child from all forms of physical or mental violence, injury or abuse, neglect or negligent treatment, maltreatment or exploitation, including sexual abuse, while in the care of parent(s), legal guardian(s) or any other person who has the care of the child.[52]

There is no official definition of physical integrity, which like its synonym bodily integrity, is an inherently ambiguous notion.[53] However, it is clear that many physically invasive procedures which are not medically required are routinely performed on children, such as ear piercing, immunization and cosmetic orthodontic surgery, correction of a simple harelip, and administration of human growth hormone to short children. Yet, there does not seem to be any condemnation of these procedures,[54] which are considered acceptable because of the limited degree of interference involved and/or because of the benefits

51 R. Schuz, "The Dangers of Children's Rights' Discourse in the Political Arena"; A.J. Jacobs, K.S. Arora, "Ritual Male Infant Circumcision and Human Rights"; B.E. Rivin, D.S. Diekema, A.C. Mastroianni, J.N. Krieger, J.D. Klausner, B.J. Morris, "Critical Evaluation of Adler's Challenge to the CDC's Male Circumcision Recommendations", *International Journal of Children's Rights*, vol. 24, no. 2 (2016): 265.

52 Comment No. 13: The Right of the Child to Freedom From All Forms of Violence, 3(b)(c), (e)(f), UN Doc. CRC/C/GC/13 [2011]. www2.ohchr.org/english/bodies/crc/docs/CRC.C.GC.13_en.pdf. Accessed November 2, 2024.

53 W. Dekkers, C. Hoffer, J.-P. Wils, "Bodily Integrity and Male and Female Circumcision" 189; for discussion of the various approaches to physical integrity, see R. Schuz, "The Dangers of Children's Rights' Discourse in the Political Arena" 364–366.

54 B.J. Morris, S. Moreton, J.N. Krieger, "Critical Evaluation of Arguments Opposing Male Circumcision: A Systematic Review" 276. A.J. Jacobs, K.S. Arora, "Ritual Male Infant Circumcision and Human Rights" 32 claim that rights rhetoric is used selectively in relation to circumcision, ignoring the various other elective procedures which are no less invasive or permanent.

of the interference for the child involved. Accordingly, it is appropriate to use these two criteria when assessing whether circumcision is an impermissible violation of bodily integrity.

Possible parameters for evaluating the degree of interference with bodily integrity include duration of the effect, degree of actual bodily invasion, functional impact, experiential impact, and risks involved.[55] Viewed under the first two parameters, duration of the effect and degree of actual bodily invasion, circumcision would indeed seem to be a violation of bodily integrity. The effect of circumcision is permanent, and the degree of bodily invasion in the removal of the foreskin seems high. However, the other three parameters (functional impact, experiential impact, and risks) do not provide support for this conclusion. While there is no consensus as to whether the foreskin has any valuable use,[56] there is no clear evidence that circumcision has any negative impact on bodily function.[57] In addition, the weight of the evidence shows that there is no negative experiential impact on circumcised males[58] and that the risks involved in properly performed infant circumcision are minimal.[59] By way of comparison, the degree of interference involved in immunization does not seem to be significantly less. While, on the one hand the injury to the skin caused by the injection appears minor and heals very quickly, the vaccine, which may contain a live, albeit weak, strain of the disease itself, permeates into the blood stream and is designed to have a long-lasting effect. Moreover, relatively minor adverse reactions to vaccinations are common, and they carry a small risk of serious disability and even death.[60]

Turning to the benefits of the interference, we saw earlier that there is strong evidence of the short- and long-term prophylactic medical benefits of circumcision. It can be argued that, in practice, these benefits are greater than those resulting from immunization for the particular child since in the light of

55 Pain has been rejected as a relevant parameter both because of the difficulty of measuring it and because of the availability of pain relief. D. Benatar, M. Benatar, "How Not to Argue About Circumcision", *American Journal of Bioethics*, vol. 3, no. 2 (2003): W4. https://humanities.uct.ac.za/sites/default/files/content_migration/humanities_uct_ac_za/225/files/selected-papers_Benatar%2520How%2520not%2520to%2520argue%2520about%2520circumcision.pdf. Accessed November 2, 2024.

56 M. Benatar, D. Benatar, "Between Prophylaxis and Child Abuse: The Ethics of Neonatal Male Circumcision", *American Journal of Bioethics*, vol. 3 (2003): 35, 42.

57 AAP Report; M. Benatar, D. Benatar, "Between Prophylaxis and Child Abuse".

58 W. Dekkers, C. Hoffer, J.-P. Wils, "Bodily Integrity and Male and Female Circumcision" 185; US Centers for Disease Control and Prevention (CDC), Draft Recommendations for Providers Counseling Male Patients and Parents Regarding Male Circumcision, for Providers Counseling Male Patients and Parents Regarding Male Circumcision. https://www.cdc.gov/nchhstp/newsroom/docs/factsheets/mc-factsheet-508.pdf. Accessed November 2, 2024. ("Circumcision is simpler, safer and less expensive for newborns and infants than for adult males") ("Adult men who undergo circumcision generally report minimal or no change in sexual satisfaction or function.") – hereinafter CDC Draft Recommendations.

59 AAP Report; B.J. Morris, S.A. Bailis, T.E. Wiswell, "Circumcision Rates in the United States".

60 M. Benatar, D. Benatar, "Between Prophylaxis and Child Abuse" 37.

the overall herd immunity, the risk of contracting the disease involved is minimal. In addition, where ritual circumcision is concerned, there are likely to be emotional and social benefits, as well as medical ones.[61] Indeed, some of the aesthetic invasive procedures mentioned earlier, which involve more risks than circumcision, are carried out on children purely on the basis of the emotional benefit.[62]

The relevance of different types of benefit in determining legitimacy of interference with bodily integrity is supported by the philosophical claims that it is only "within a particular moral narrative that one can determine whether specific uses of the body are to be praised, condemned, or regarded as morally neutral"[63] and that accordingly, "every alteration or apparent violation of the human body must be considered in its own medical, religious, and cultural context."[64]

In summary, it can be seen, that while technically, ritual circumcision is a violation of bodily integrity, it cannot be convincingly distinguished from other procedures which are allowed both in relation to the degree of interference and the benefits of that interference. Significantly, male circumcision can be clearly distinguished from female genital mutilation (FGM), which is outlawed in many Western States, on the basis that FGM does not have any medical benefits and causes real and irreparable damage to the woman.[65]

8.3.3 Autonomy and Participation Rights

It is claimed that circumcision of young children involves a breach of the child's autonomy, synonymously referred to as his right to self-determination, because he does not consent to the procedure. This claim is based on Article

61 A.J. Jacobs, K.S. Arora, "Ritual Male Infant Circumcision and Human Rights" 32. This seems to be the basis of the holding of the English court in *Re* J [1992] 4 All ER 614 that a decision by both parents to ritually circumcise their child is lawful.

62 These include cosmetic orthodontic surgery, correction of a simple harelip, and administration of human growth hormone to short children, A.J. Jacobs, "The Ethics of Circumcision of Male Infants", *Journal of Medical Ethics*, vol. 15, no. 1 (2013): 60, 63.

63 W. Dekkers, C. Hoffer, J.-P. Wils, "Bodily Integrity and Male and Female Circumcision" 179.

64 W. Dekkers, C. Hoffer, J.-P. Wils, "Bodily Integrity and Male and Female Circumcision" 179.

65 Attempts to make an analogy between ritual male circumcision and FGM are clearly flawed, B.E. Rivin, D.S. Diekema, A.C. Mastroianni, J.N. Krieger, J.D. Klausner, B.J. Morris, "Critical Evaluation of Adler's Challenge to the CDC's Male Circumcision Recommendations" 284 and were criticized by the Council of Europe Committee of Ministers: Children's Right to Physical Integrity – Parliamentary Assembly Recommendation 2023 (2013), UN Doc. CM/AS(2014) Rec2023 final [2014]. https://wcd.coe.int/ViewDoc.jsp?id=2173161&Site=CM&BackColorInterwnet=C3C3C3&BackColorIntranet=EDB021&BackColorLogged=F5D383. Accessed November 2, 2024. See also M. Freeman, "The Morality of Cultural Pluralism", *The International Journal of Children's Rights*, vol. 3 (1995): 10–12 (assessing the importance of the value of physical integrity to women in countries where FGM is practiced and concluding that the various social justifications of the practice are outweighed by the significant adverse physical and psychological effects; whereas applying the same test to ritual male circumcision, which has only the "remotest similarity to female circumcision" leads to the opposite conclusion).

12 of the CRC, which recognizes the child's right to participate in decisions concerning him and to have due weight attached to his views in accordance with his age and degree of maturity. It is argued that the child's participatory rights require delaying the making of important decisions that have irreversible consequences until the child has the capacity to participate in the decision-making, unless such delay is likely to be prejudicial. Accordingly, the PACE Resolution on Physical Integrity and other opponents of circumcision[66] take the view that *brit milah* should be delayed until the child is old enough to make the decision for himself. It has also been argued that circumcision violates a child's autonomy in the sense of his right to an open future[67] because of its irreversible nature.[68]

However, many of these arguments are based on unsubstantiated allegations about the impact of circumcision.[69] Moreover, they are all based on the assumption that the child will not be prejudiced by delaying the circumcision. This assumption reflects a number of misconceptions concerning the differences between performing circumcision in infancy and later in life and does not take into account the practical consequences of delay. Firstly, delay means that the child is deprived of the medical and other benefits of circumcision during his childhood.[70] Secondly, it cannot seriously be disputed that circumcision of an older child or adult is a much more complex and risky procedure,[71] both from a medical and psychological perspective.[72] Thirdly, there are substantial barriers to later circumcision, including having to contend with the unpleasant physical, emotional, and psychological implications of undergoing

66 See, e.g, R. Merkel, H. Putzke, "After Cologne: Male Circumcision and the Law. Parental Right, Religious Liberty or Criminal Assault?", *Journal of Medical Ethics*, vol. 39, no. 7 (2013): 444–449. https://www.doi.org/10.1136/medethics-2012-101284.

67 J. Feinberg, *Freedom and Fulfilment: Philosophical Essays* (Princeton: Princeton University Press, 1994): 76–97.

68 R.T.J. Darby, "The Child's Right to an Open Future: Is the Principle Applicable to Non-Therapeutic Circumcision?", *Journal of Medicine Ethics*, vol. 39 (2003): 463. https://doi.org/10.1136/medethics-2012-101182.

69 E.g., that it reduces sexual pleasure, R.T.J. Darby, "The Child's Right to an Open Future 465.

70 M. Benatar, D. Benatar, "Between Prophylaxis and Child Abuse" 37; B.E. Rivin, D.S. Diekema, A.C. Mastroianni, J.N. Krieger, J.D. Klausner, B.J. Morris, "Critical Evaluation of Adler's Challenge to the CDC's Male Circumcision Recommendations" 303.

71 The risks are between 10 and 20 times greater, B.J. Morris, S. Moreton, J.N. Krieger, "Critical Evaluation of Arguments Opposing Male Circumcision: A Systematic Review" 274–275; R. Cohen-Almagor, "Should liberal government regulate male circumcision performed in the name of Jewish tradition?" ("Evidence suggests that children should be circumcised in the early days or weeks of life, when the circumcision is safest, and unlikely to leave any trauma on the young infant."); CDC Draft Recommendations: "Circumcision is simpler, safer and less expensive for newborns and infants than for adult males".

72 B.J. Morris, S.A. Bailis, T.E. Wiswell, "Circumcision Rates in the United States" 683; A.J. Jacobs, "The Ethics of Circumcision of Male Infants" 63 ("Adult circumcision simply is not a reasonable substitute for infant circumcision.").

circumcision as an adolescent or adult.[73] In the case of Jews or Muslims, these barriers might well give rise to considerable anxiety and even cause an identity crisis. Thus, Mazor argues that since "we cannot provide the child with – even roughly – the same choice facing the parents once he attains majority," there can be no breach of his right to self-determination.[74]

The best way to give effect to the child's participatory rights in cases where delaying making a particular decision may be prejudicial is to assess how the child would decide if he had the capacity to do so, in accordance with Rawls' concept of "substitute judgment."[75] This approach in turn involves considering what is likely to be the child's view about the decision in the future.[76] In the current context, the question to be determined is whether when the child reaches adolescence or adulthood, he will wish that he had been circumcised as an infant or not.[77] It can surely be assumed that the vast majority of Jewish and Muslim males would, in fact, wish to have been circumcised as children[78] in the light of the benefits this provides for them.[79] This proposition is supported by the limited available evidence.[80] While there is always a chance that the child will later abandon his religion, he may still be satisfied with the medical benefits of the circumcision. In any event, the circumcision does not restrict the child's future religious freedom, as it does not in any way require him to practice his religion or preclude him from joining another religion. In particular, since many circumcisions are carried out for medical or prophylactic nonreligious reasons, the circumcision does not per se provide clear evidence of the circumcised child's birth religion and so cannot be accurately described

73 B.J. Morris, S. Moreton, J.N. Krieger, "Critical Evaluation of Arguments Opposing Male Circumcision: A Systematic Review" 274–275.

74 J. Mazor, "The Child's Interests and the Case for the Permissibility of Male Infant Circumcision", *Journal of Medicine Ethics*, vol. 39, no. 7 (2013): 421, 422–425. https://www.doi.org/10.1136/medethics-2013-101318.

75 J. Rawls, *A Theory of Justice* (Cambridge: Belknap, 1999): 208.

76 G. Dworkin, "Paternalism". In: R. Sartorius (ed.), *Paternalism* (Minnesota: University of Minnesota Press, 1984): 28 (referring to this approach as "future-oriented consent").

77 M.D.A. Freeman, "A Child's Right to Circumcision", *BJU International Suppl.* vol. 83 no. 1 (1999): 74, 76. 10.1046/j.1464-410x.1999.0830s1074.x.

78 M.D.A. Freeman, "A Child's Right to Circumcision" 74, 76. J. Mazor, "The Child's Interests and the Case for the Permissibility of Male Infant Circumcision" 426 (claiming that most Jewish males would choose to be circumcised as adults, if they had not been circumcised as infants).

79 A.J. Jacobs, K.S. Arora, "Ritual Male Infant Circumcision and Human Rights" 32, argue that autonomy issues are not independent of beneficience.

80 J. Badger, "Consent to Circumcision Survey". https://www.circlist.com/surveys/badger-03.html. Accessed October, 2 2024 (a large general survey published on the internet, in which most of the men questioned did not express regret about being circumcised and indicated that they had or would circumcise their sons. There is no breakdown of the reasons for circumcision, but clearly, many were not ritual, because in 32% of cases, the doctor had made the decision to circumcise, and in 26% of cases, the interviewee did not know who had made the decision.

as a permanent seal which can never be broken off.[81] Thus, the circumcision does not in reality violate his right to an open future.

Accordingly, if we take the view that the purpose of the child's right to self-determinism is to bring him "to the threshold of adulthood with the maximum opportunities to form and pursue life-goals that reflect as closely as possible an autonomous choice,"[82] we might conclude that not circumcising a Jewish or Muslim child is, in fact, a breach of that child's autonomy. Indeed, a ban on ritual circumcision would in fact be violating the child's right to an open future, because it would prevent his parents from providing him with the opportunity to have been circumcised at a time when the risks involved were significantly less and without the need to overcome the barriers associated with later circumcision.

8.3.4 The Child's Right to Freedom of Religion and Culture

While much of the debate about ritual circumcision has referred to the parents' right to freedom of religion, it has not always been appreciated that the child's own right to freedom of religion is also engaged. Article 14(1)–(2) of the CRC requires State Parties to "respect the right of the child to freedom of thought, conscience and religion" and to "respect the rights and duties of the parents [...] to provide direction to the child in the exercise of his or her right in a manner consistent with the evolving capacities of child." The latter provision clearly assumes that a child takes on the religion chosen for him by his parents and recognizes that a child's freedom of religion is dependent upon allowing his parents to teach and guide him in religious practice. It is important to emphasize that this provision is protecting the child's rights, and not only that of the parents.

Article 14(3) strengthens the requirement to respect the child's right to freedom of religion by providing that "[f]reedom to manifest one's religion or beliefs may be subject only to such limitations as are prescribed by law and are necessary to protect public safety, order, health or morals, or the fundamental rights and freedoms of others." Moreover, Article 30 provides specific protection for a child belonging to an ethnic or religious minority, who should "not be denied the right [...] to enjoy his or her own culture and, to profess and practice his or her own religion." It is abundantly clear that any ban on circumcision would violate the freedom of religion of a Jewish or Muslim child and would deny him the right to practice his own religion and enjoy his own culture. In particular, within Judaism, while the parent has the responsibility for circumcising his son, the circumcision has religious significance for the child as denoting the relationship between him and his Creator and a spiritual sanction

81 As alleged by R. Merkel, H. Putzke, "After Cologne".

82 J. Eekelaar, "The Interests of the Child and the Child's Wishes: The Role of Dynamic Self-Determinism", *International Journal of Law, Policy and the Family*, vol. 8, no. 1 (1994): 42, 53. https://doi.org/10.1093/lawfam/8.1.42.

is imposed on noncircumcised males.[83] Accordingly, the parent's act in arranging for the circumcision to be performed clearly comes within the meaning of providing direction to the child in the exercise of his religion in Article 14(2).[84] Similarly, it seems that within Islam, lack of circumcision has religious repercussions.[85]

8.3.5 The Child's Right to Identity

Under Article 8 of the CRC, States undertake to respect the right of the child to preserve his or her identity. Ya'ir Ronen maintains that protection of identity "necessitates exploration of culture as a context of personal meaning and is founded on empathic understanding of an individual child's experience."[86] It seems clear that identity must include religion, as well as culture, at least in so far as these have any meaning to the child. Bearing in mind that circumcision has historically and still is treated as a primordial sign of identification and of belonging to a religious group for both Jews[87] and Muslims,[88] any attempt to outlaw the practice of circumcision of children cannot be consistent with respecting the right of the child to preserve his identity.[89] Indeed, a decision of the Finnish Supreme Court that ritual male circumcision is lawful relied *inter alia* on the benefits to the child in developing his identity and his attachment to his social and religious community.[90]

8.3.6 The Child's Right to Highest Attainable Standard of Health

Article 24 of the CRC provides that States "recognize the right of the child to the enjoyment of the highest attainable standard of health", and Article 24(2)(f) mandates States to develop preventative healthcare services. The child's right to health has been defined as "the right to opportunities to survive, grow

83 Accordingly, the comment in the PACE Explanatory Memorandum (n 1) para. 21 that a naming ceremony can be an alternative to circumcision displays complete ignorance of the religious imperative of *brit milah*.

84 S. Baum, "Religious Circumcision: Free from Interference?", *UCL Jurisprudence Review*, vol. 1 (1999): 18.

85 *In Re* S [2004].

86 Y. Ronen, "Redefining the Child's Right to Identity", *International Journal of Law, Policy and the Family*, vol. 18, no. 2 (2004): 147–148.

87 *Sefer Hachinuch* stating that one of the purposes of circumcision is to distinguish between Jews and other nations.

88 M. Yavuz, T. Demir, B. Dogangen, "The Effect of Circumcision on the Mental Health of Children" 6 (describing circumcision as a sign of social belonging in Turkey).

89 M.D.A. Freeman, "A Child's Right to Circumcision" 74.

90 H. Askola, "Cut-Off Point?"; H. Aora, A.J. Jacobs, K.S. Arora, "Ritual Male Infant Circumcision and Human Rights" 32 (circumcision "initiates boys into a community that may provide emotional and spiritual advantages throughout life, and possibly beyond.").

and develop, within the context of physical, emotional and social well-being, to each child's full potential."[91]

On the basis of the medical evidence of the prophylactic effects of male circumcision, it can be argued that outlawing the practice prevents children from enjoying the highest standard of health.[92] Not only does such a ban increase the risk that children will suffer from certain illnesses, but it may also have a negative effect on emotional and social welfare of those children who belong to communities in which circumcision is a religious imperative and/or has great social significance. Accordingly, even if, in light of the lack of consensus in relation to the significance of the medical benefits of circumcision, States are not obliged to make circumcision available to all children,[93] any attempt to prevent those parents who wish to circumcise their children from doing so can be seen as a violation of children's right to health.

8.3.7 Best Interests

Article 3(1) of the CRC provides that "[in] all actions concerning children, whether undertaken by public or private social welfare institutions, courts of law, administrative authorities or legislative bodies, the best interests of the child shall be a primary consideration." In addition, the "best interests of the child" standard is to serve as a principle of interpretation in cases where the scope of the rights in the Convention is not clear or there are conflicts between different rights.[94] Thus, for example, assuming that ritual circumcision were considered a breach of the child's right to physical integrity, the conflict between that right and other rights of the child, which are promoted by the practice should be resolved by the best interests principle.

The best interests standard is notoriously indeterminate and subjective, and there are formidable difficulties in applying it to the issue of ritual male

91 Committee on the Rights of the Child, General Comment No. 15: Right of the Child to the Enjoyment of the Highest Attainable Standard of Health (art. 24), UN Doc CRC/C/GC/15 [2013].

92 B.E. Rivin, D.S. Diekema, A.C. Mastroianni, J.N. Krieger, J.D. Klausner, B.J. Morris, "Critical Evaluation of Adler's Challenge to the CDC's Male Circumcision Recommendations" 288; A.J. Jacobs, K.S. Arora, "Ritual Male Infant Circumcision and Human Rights" 63.

93 However, it has been argued that in the light of the wide ranging medical protection which circumcision provides, it is unethical to leave boys uncircumcised. B.J. Morris, S. Moreton, J.N. Krieger, "Critical Evaluation of Arguments Opposing Male Circumcision: A Systematic Review" 276.

94 Commitee on the Rights of the Child, General Comment No. 14 (2013) on the Right of the Child to Have His or Her Best Interests Taken as a Primary Consideration, UN Doc. CRC/C/GC/14 [2013] § 33; although this may lead to circular reasoning since the Children's Rights Committee enjoins us to bear in mind the child's rights when assessing his best interests, see R. Schuz, "The Dangers of Children's Rights' Discourse in the Political Arena" 377–378.

circumcision at the collective level,[95] since the circumstances of Jewish and Muslim children cannot possibly be compared to those of other children.[96] The attempt of Committee on the Rights of the Child's to define the purpose of the best interests standard, as being "to secure the holistic physical, psychological, moral and spiritual integrity of the child and promote his or her human dignity",[97] is of limited assistance,[98] both because there can be no objective test of each of these types of integrity and because they may not necessarily go hand in hand. Thus, for example, even if it is assumed that circumcision is a violation of physical integrity, it might well be necessary for the psychological and spiritual integrity of Jewish and Muslim children.[99]

Similarly, the definition of the Committee on the Rights of the Child does not shed any light on the extent to which the best interests assessment should focus on the short-term interests of the child or on his long-term interests. This is pertinent to the religious circumcision debate, because even if the circumcision does not serve the child's interests at the time of its performance, it might certainly do so in the long term since it prevents him from having to undergo the procedure later on in life when it would be more risky and more complicated.[100]

The Committee on the Rights of the Child has recognized that since children are not a homogeneous group, diversity must be taken into account when assessing their best interests.[101] Thus, it states, "[A]lthough children and young people share basic universal needs, the expression of those needs

95 As opposed to the case of a dispute between the parents, when the court can consider the impact of circumcision on the particular child, as in the two English mixed-faith cases, *In Re* J [1992]; *In Re* S [2004] [24].

96 J. Mazor, "The Child's Interests and the Case for the Permissibility of Male Infant Circumcision" 422–427.

97 *General Comment No.14* (n 99), para. 5 (this formulation is very similar to that in the first version of the draft Convention); see P. Alston, "The Best Interests Principle: Towards A Reconciliation of Culture and Human Rights", *International Journal of Law, Policy and The Family*, vol. 8 (1994): 10.

98 J. Schiratzki, "Banning God's Law in the Name of the Holy Body: The Nordic Position on Ritual Male Circumcision", *The Family in Law*, vol. 5 (2011): 35, 45. https://esh.diva-portal.org/smash/get/diva2:549517/FULLTEXT01.pdf. Accessed November 2, 2024 (noting that the lack of a closer interpretation of Art. 3 explains why it has been invoked both as an argument for and against ritual circumcision).

99 H. Askola, "Cut-Off Point?" 107–108 (this conflict was addressed by the Finnish Supreme Court, which held that in assessing best interests, the court must take into account the seriousness of the physical interference and the weight of the reasons put forward to justify the interference. Its conclusion was that in the light of the benefits accruing to the child from ritual male circumcision, it is "a defensible (and minor) interference.").

100 A. Berhns, "Note, To Cut Or Not To Cut?: Addressing Proposals To Ban Circumcision Under Both A Parental Rights Theory And Child-Centered Perspective In The Specific Context Of Jewish And Muslim Infants", *William & Mary Bill of Rights Journal*, vol. 21, no. 3 (2013): 925, 948. https://scholarship.law.wm.edu/cgi/viewcontent.cgi?referer=&httpsredir=1&article=1651&context=wmborj. Accessed November 2, 2024; J. Mazor, "The Child's Interests and the Case for the Permissibility of Male Infant Circumcision" 422.

101 General Comment No. 14 § 55.

depends on a wide range of personal, physical, social and cultural aspects, including their evolving capacities." In particular, the Committee states that the right of the child to preserve his or her identity "must be respected and taken into consideration in the assessment of the child's best interests"[102] and that "[t]he identity of the child includes characteristics such as sex, sexual orientation, national origin, religion and beliefs, cultural identity, personality."[103]

As seen earlier, the Finnish Supreme Court, adopting this approach, held that ritual male circumcision did promote the best interests of the Muslim child in question because it "can be considered to be positive for the boy child, the development of his identity, and his attachment to his religious and social community."[104] Conversely, in the English case of *Re J*,[105] the fact that the child was not being brought up as a practicing Muslim and would have little contact with Muslims was an important consideration in the court's conclusion that it was not in the best interests of the child to be circumcised against the wishes of the non-Muslim mother, as requested by the nonpracticing Muslim father. However, the court made clear that every case depends upon its own facts and indicated that there would be circumstances in which it would order circumcision against the wishes of one parent, even where the latter parent was not Jewish or Muslim.

By way of contrast, the Cologne court did not take into account the specific circumstances of the child in question when holding that the parental consent to circumcision was inconsistent with the welfare of the child.[106] Schiratzki suggests that other decision-makers, such as legislators and medical personnel, tend to interpret best interests of the child in the light of what is considered to be "normal."[107] She claims that in the Nordic States, the practice of ritual circumcision by a tiny minority is considered not normal because of the long history of religious homogeneity in this region and the prevalent understanding that religion should be limited to personal belief.[108] This approach seems inconsistent with that advocated by the Committee on the Rights of the Child, which mandates taking into account cultural factors in determining best interests.

Overall, in the light of the discussion in this chapter, the claim that circumcision is not in the best interests of Jewish and Muslim children seems untenable in light of the evidence that this is what most such children would want together with the medical, social, and emotional benefits thereof. In addition, account

102 General Comment No. 14 § 55.
103 General Comment No. 14 § 55; see also General Comment No. 13 § 12 (educational needs and social and family background are also to be taken into account).
104 H. Askola, "Cut-Off Point?" 108.
105 *In Re* J [1992].
106 LG Cologne, Judgment, Ns 169/11, [2012]. https://www.dur.ac.uk/law/news/?itemno=15002&rehref=%2Flaw%2Fnews%2Farchive%2F&resubj=%20Headlines. Accessed November 2, 2024.
107 J. Schiratzki, "Banning God's Law in the Name of the Holy Body Schiratzki", 46.
108 J. Schiratzki, "Banning God's Law in the Name of the Holy Body Schiratzki", 47.

should be taken of the general principle that it is in the best interests of children that their parents make decisions for them.[109] Finally, it should be borne in mind that Article 3 of the CRC does not mandate that the best interests of the child be the sole or even the principal consideration in decisions concerning children but rather that it should be one of the main considerations.[110] Thus, it is permissible to take into account parental interests.[111] Outlawing ritual circumcision would be a serious violation not only of the parents' freedom of religion but also of their parental autonomy,[112] an interest that also protects the child.[113]

8.4 Conclusion

In recent years, the question of whether ritual male circumcision is a human rights violation has been debated by activists, politicians, and scholars from a number of disciplines, including medicine, philosophy, bioethics, and law. Much of the debate has involved selective use of rights rhetoric[114] and/or been based on unreliable information about the risks and consequences of circumcision. The claim that the practice constitutes a breach of the child's right to bodily integrity does not give sufficient weight to the significant medical and psychological benefits of the practice. Moreover, the child has a variety of other rights which are promoted by ritual male circumcision. These include autonomy interests, the right to freedom of religion, the right to identity, and the right to the highest standard of health. Accordingly, there can be little doubt that ritual male circumcision promotes the best interests of Jewish and Muslim children and that any attempt to ban the practice would in fact result in a violation of the child's rights, as well as those of his parents.

Finally, it is appropriate to comment on the wider implications of the discussion in this article for the debate on the boundaries of religious freedom in the modern world. While it seems clear that religious freedom, like culture, should not be "accorded the status of a metanorm which trumps rights,"[115] the impact of religious practices on human rights cannot be assessed without

109 B.E. Rivin, D.S. Diekema, A.C. Mastroianni, J.N. Krieger, J.D. Klausner, B.J. Morris, "Critical Evaluation of Adler's Challenge to the CDC's Male Circumcision Recommendations" 288; Art 5 CRC requires States to respect parental rights to provide direction and guidance in the exercise of the child's rights.

110 General Comment No. 14 § 39.

111 General Comment No. 14 § 39.

112 A. Viens, "Value Judgment, Harm and Religious Liberty" 246 (concluding that parental interests must be protected because it has not been proven that male circumcision is harmful).

113 Inter alia by limiting external interference which might destabilize the family unit. See, e.g., J. Goldstein, A. Freud, A. Solnit, *Before the Best Interests of the Child* (New York: Free Press, 1979): 9.

114 R. Schuz, "The Dangers of Children's Rights' Discourse in the Political Arena"; A.J. Jacobs, K.S. Arora, "Ritual Male Infant Circumcision and Human Rights" 37.

115 P. Alston, "The Best Interests Principle" 1, 20.

taking into account the religious context of the practices.[116] Thus, for example, assessment of the benefits of a practice which might justify a technical breach of physical integrity has to take into account the emotional and social benefits from the perspective of a member of the religion involved. Moreover, care must be taken in ensuring that all relevant rights are taken into consideration. The analysis of the debate concerning ritual male circumcision in this chapter shows that there is a real risk of a selective approach to rights and of ignoring a child's own right to freedom of religion.

116 M. Freeman, "The Morality of Cultural Pluralism" 12, 16; S. Baum, Religious Circumcision: Free from Interference?", 13–14.

Part IV

The Constitutional Boundaries of Religious Accommodation of Jewish and Muslim Minorities: National Perspectives

9 The Constitutional Boundaries of Religious Accommodation

The Israeli Perspective

Aviad Hacohen

Abstract

The right to "freedom of religion" – as well as the "ancillary" rights and its various derivatives, including freedom of religious belief, freedom of conscience, freedom of religion, freedom of worship, the right to access and worship the holy places – is recognized today in the law of the State of Israel as a constitutional right of the highest order.

Although it has no explicit name anchored in the law, there are many laws and, more than that, many dozens of rulings that recognized the right indirectly and implicitly anchored it, and worked to develop and preserve it.

The lack of the right to freedom of religion anchored in an explicit law stems both from the lack of a formal "constitution" document in the State of Israel and mainly from political considerations.

In view of this state of affairs, over the years, attempts have been made to establish the status of the right and to expand it through court rulings, especially the Supreme Court and High Court of Justice. These efforts have been crowned with success on the practical level, and there is hardly any case (except in cases where the right to freedom of religion is withdrawn from other rights and values, within the framework of the balance between them, as is customary in other legal systems) that points to an unjustified and disproportionate violation of this right.

It is possible that with the completion of the constitutional process in Israel, which has been ongoing since its establishment more than 75 years ago, there will also be a remedy for anchoring the right in an orderly constitutional document and in an explicit manner. Time will tell if the end of such a process will take shape. Until then, the right to be carried on the ship of ruling, here and there, was discussed, while its sailors did everything possible to strictly guard it and prevent damage to it.

Keywords

freedom of religion; freedom from religion; freedom of worship; freedom of conscience; equality; constitution; Basic Laws; hurting religious feelings;

DOI: 10.4324/9781003423294-14

Jewish and democratic state; constitutional right; marriage and divorce; holy places; burial; bigamy; Proselytism; conversion; *kashrut* (dietary laws)

9.1 Preface

Friday, May 14, 1948, was supposed to be a day of celebration in the State of Israel. In a brief but momentous ceremony, David Ben-Gurion stood on the stage of the Tel Aviv Museum and read aloud the Declaration of Independence. "We hereby proclaim the establishment of a Jewish state in the Land of Israel, to be known as the State of Israel",[1] he declared to the cheers of those present, and continued,

> The State of Israel will devote itself to the development of the country for the benefit of all its inhabitants; it will be based on the foundations of liberty, justice, and peace as envisioned by the prophets of Israel; it will ensure complete equality of social and political rights to all its citizens, irrespective of religion, race, or gender; it will guarantee freedom of religion, conscience, language, education, and culture; it will safeguard the Holy Places of all religions; and it will be faithful to the principles of the Charter of the United Nations.[2]

These paragraphs were meant to express the great vision of the State of Israel as a "Jewish and democratic state," a phrase that later became something of a *motto* – a vision and purpose – enshrined in the Basic Laws of the State of Israel.[3] Alongside these, another, somewhat lesser-known paragraph was added, stating,

> We declare that from the moment the Mandate ends, tonight, the eve of the Sabbath, the 6th of Iyar 5708, May 15, 1948, until the establishment of the elected, regular authorities of the state in

1 The Declaration of the Establishment of the State of Israel. https://www.gov.il/en/pages/declaration-of-establishment-state-of-israel. Accessed January 5, 2025.

2 As is well-known, freedom of religion is among the principles included in the Universal Declaration of Human Rights (https://www.un.org/en/about-us/universal-declaration-of-human-rights. Accessed October 27, 2024). Art. 18 of the Declaration states, "Everyone has the right to freedom of thought, conscience, and religion; this right includes freedom to change his religion or belief, and freedom, either alone or in community with others and in public or private, to manifest his religion or belief in teaching, practice, worship, and observance [...]. Freedom to manifest one's religion or beliefs shall be subject only to such limitations as are prescribed by law and are necessary to protect public safety, order, health, or morals, or the fundamental rights and freedoms of others". [All emphases here and throughout the article are mine unless otherwise stated – A. H.].

3 Basic Laws of the State of Israel. https://m.knesset.gov.il/en/activity/pages/basiclaws.aspx&ved=2ahUKEwifj97_vq-JAxWoFBAIHSIQJ8QQFnoECBkQAQ&usg=AOvVaw0jSxkFDYWLE8MiKyAw6-vA. Accessed October 20, 2023.

> accordance with a constitution to be adopted by the elected Constituent Assembly no later than October 1, 1948, the People's Council shall act as the Provisional State Council, and its executive branch, the People's Administration, shall constitute the provisional government of the Jewish state, which shall be called Israel.

As the members of the Provisional State Council exited the building where the proclamation was read, they encountered spontaneous dancing circles welcoming the newly born state.

The joy, however, did not last long. Within a few hours, Arab armies launched a coordinated assault on the newborn entity. The State of Israel began its War of Independence, which concluded more than a year later, on July 20, 1949, leaving behind thousands of dead and wounded. A total of 4,762 soldiers fell in the campaign, and 915 civilians were killed in hostile actions connected to it, approximately 0.9% of the roughly 630,000 inhabitants of the Yishuv at the outbreak of the war. Roughly 1 in 111 inhabitants fell in the battle that left its mark on the nation's history for many years to come.

In the tumult of war, the completion of the constitution was also postponed. The Declaration of Independence explicitly stated that the governance of the new state would be "in accordance with a constitution to be adopted by the elected Constituent Assembly no later than October 1, 1948."[4]

4 Incidentally, Section 11 of the Law and Administration Ordinance No. 1 of 5708-1948: May 19, 1948 (as Amended to May 20, 1981, OCW CD 30 (IL)), established a "continuity clause" in the following terms: "The law that existed in the Land of Israel on the 5th of Iyar 5708 (May 14, 1948) shall remain in force, insofar as it is not inconsistent with this Ordinance or with other laws that may be enacted by the Provisional Council of State or pursuant to it, and subject to changes resulting from the establishment of the state and its authorities." It is possible that this clause could serve as an additional legal basis for the enshrinement of freedom of religion in Israeli law since in the Mandatory law, which was "the law in effect in the Land of Israel" prior to the establishment of the State of Israel, freedom of religion was enshrined in several legal provisions. For example, Art. 15 of the Mandate Charter provided that the Mandatory authority "shall ensure complete freedom of conscience and free exercise of all forms of worship, limited only by the necessity of maintaining public order and morality. No discrimination of any kind shall be made between the inhabitants of Palestine on the grounds of race, religion, or language. No person shall be excluded from Palestine on the sole ground of his religious belief." Similarly, Art. 17(1)(a) of the King's Order-in-Council stated that "the High Commissioner shall have full power and authority [...] to issue orders necessary for the peace, order, and good government of Palestine, provided that no order shall be issued restricting complete freedom of conscience and the free exercise of all forms of worship, except as necessary for maintaining public order and morality, and no order shall be issued that discriminates in any way between the inhabitants of Palestine on the grounds of race, religion, or language." Similar provisions were found in other laws that applied under Mandatory law. This approach is also reflected in the "Religious Communities Ordinance", through which the Mandatory authorities granted freedom of action to every "religious community" in matters of "personal status", including marriage, divorce, wills, inheritance, and religious endowments.

The first Knesset – the Israeli parliament – began its work on February 14, 1949, several months after the date mentioned in the Declaration of Independence. It was declared that in addition to serving as the legislative body, the Knesset would also act as the "Constituent Assembly" whose task would be to draft the constitution of the State of Israel. To that end, a Constitution, Law, and Justice Committee was established and began its work with great zeal.

Since then, much has changed. Governments have risen and fallen, Knessets have been elected and dissolved, but a formal constitution for Israel remains absent. Even more than 75 years after the date set in the Declaration of Independence, the drafting of the constitution remains incomplete. Over the years, dozens of proposals were introduced and failed, but for numerous and varied reasons – beyond the scope of this discussion – the constitutional process remains unfinished.

Members of the Knesset may not have anticipated that the process would take so long, but they understood that in Israel's political climate, the brief period allotted for the completion of the constitution in the Declaration of Independence – four and a half months – would not suffice. Therefore, on June 13, 1950, the Knesset adopted a resolution initiated by Member of Knesset Yizhar Harari, of the Progressive Party, which stated,

> The first Knesset entrusts the Constitution, Law, and Justice Committee with the task of preparing a draft constitution for the state. The constitution will be built chapter by chapter, such that each chapter will constitute a basic law in itself, which will eventually be combined into the constitution of the state.

Even the enactment of these Basic Laws, which were intended – according to the resolution – to "eventually be combined into the state's constitution", proceeded slowly. From 1950 until today, 13 Basic Laws have been enacted.[5] Initially, these laws established the institutions of governance: the Knesset, the government, the military, the presidency, the judiciary, and the State Comptroller. In later years, additional Basic Laws were enacted, such as Basic Law: Human Dignity and Liberty[6] and Basic Law: Freedom of Occupation[7], which enshrined various human rights and granted them constitutional status.

5 Two of them, Basic Law: The Government and Basic Law: Freedom of Occupation, were re-enacted several times for reasons that are beyond the scope of this discussion.

6 Basic Law: Human Dignity and Liberty. https://m.knesset.gov.il/EN/activity/documents/BasicLawsPDF/BasicLawLiberty.pdf&ved=2ahUKEwiLy5LXz6-JAxXvUlUIHWr_DJkQFnoECBQQAQ&usg=AOvVaw3QNxFtRI9XCi8fAeTpUhYq. Accessed October 20, 2023.

7 Basic Law: Freedom of Occupation. https://m.knesset.gov.il/EN/activity/Documents/BasicLawsPDF/BasicLawOccupation.pdf&ved=2ahUKEwia3YqA0K-JAxXQFhAIHa1YNFoQFnoECBIQAQ&usg=AOvVaw21pstW65QHvfhqibShpm0Z. Accessed October 20, 2023.

As mentioned, the completion of the formal constitutional document was never achieved. In this respect, both Israel and the United Kingdom – remains the only country in the world without a formal constitution.

Over the years, the Supreme Court sought to fill the void by creating "constitutional rights" out of "nothing" through "judicial legislation". In a long series of rulings, the Court determined that various human rights were "constitutional basic rights", granting them a special status and greater weight. This extensive jurisprudence solidified the status of these basic rights in substantive law, strengthening and developing them.

Nevertheless, the facts cannot be denied: even after 75 years, Israel still lacks a formal constitution.

Moreover, three fundamental human rights, which are the cornerstone of any worthy constitution, are missing from the Basic Laws enacted over the years: the principle of equality and the prohibition of discrimination, freedom of religion, and freedom of expression. The reasons for this omission are diverse and manifold, but we will not delve into them here. Instead, we will focus on the last of these rights, freedom of religion, which is the subject of this volume.

The explicit mention of these three rights – by their commonly accepted names – does not appear in any of Israel's laws. Although the Declaration of Independence, which lacks formal legal status, emphasizes that the State of Israel "will ensure freedom of religion," this phrase, "freedom of religion," is not found anywhere in Israeli legislation.

The avoidance of explicitly mentioning "the sacred name" did not arise in a vacuum. Similar to the omission of the principle of equality from the Basic Laws,[8] the reason for this was primarily political. Explicit recognition of this fundamental principle would have entailed a demand for equality among the different religions in the State of Israel, as well as between the different streams within Judaism: the dominant Orthodox stream, alongside the smaller Conservative and Reform streams. The same applies to the desire of those who opposed explicit recognition of the principle of "freedom from religion", which is a corollary of the principle of "freedom of religion".

For various reasons, mainly political, the State of Israel has thus far refrained from granting explicit legal recognition to the principle of equality among all religions or among the different streams, as well as to the principles of "freedom of religion" and "freedom from religion".

Practically speaking, as mentioned earlier, these rights are enshrined in Israel's constitutional law, but primarily by virtue of judicial rulings rather than explicit legislation.

8 Unlike "freedom of religion" and "freedom of expression", the principle of equality, which is absent from the Basic Laws, is at least reflected in a long series of other important laws that embody it, such as the "Equal Rights for Women Law", the "Equal Rights for People with Disabilities Law", the "Equal Opportunities in Employment Law", and others.

9.2 The Enshrinement of the Principles of Equality in Matters of Religion and Freedom of Religion in Israeli Legislation

In the absence of an explicit constitutional source, the Knesset and the courts of Israel have established these fundamental principles within the legal framework of the state. This has been done "case by case", step by step.

One of the most notable examples is the first law enacted in the State of Israel: the Law and Administration Ordinance, 1948. Alongside the establishment of various fundamental legal structures (such as the prohibition of "secret legislation" and the requirement that all laws be published in the Reshumot [the official gazette] as a condition for their validity), this law included a clause addressing "official days of rest in the State of Israel".

Section 18A of the law states that "the Sabbath and the Jewish holidays [...] shall be the established days of rest in the State of Israel". At the same time, the law emphasizes that "non-Jews are entitled to observe their days of rest on their Sabbaths and holidays. These holidays shall be determined for each community by a government decision to be published in the Reshumot".

Although the essence of this section is primarily declarative, highlighting its social character (the right of every person to rest from work, even if they are not religious) and not necessarily its religious character, the law has had practical implications – particularly in labor law – regarding the right of an employee to rest, even for religious reasons and not just for social reasons, on the "day of rest" designated by their religion.

Yet, as emphasized, despite this section reflecting the principle of equality and nondiscrimination between members of different religions and exuding the pleasant fragrance of the principle of freedom of religion, the explicit term "freedom of religion" is not mentioned.

To complete the picture, we can add that a similar section was established in 2018 in Section 10 of the Basic Law: Israel – The Nation-State of the Jewish People (known as the Nation-State Law), but this section too is primarily declarative in nature.[9]

Another law, enacted in the early days of the state, is the "*Kosher* Food for Soldiers Ordinance, 1948", which mandated that "all Jewish soldiers[10] in the Israel Defense Forces be ensured the right to eat *kosher* food".

Another legislative provision expressing the importance of maintaining the fundamental principle of equality between members of different religions

9 For a detailed interpretation of this provision, see A. Hacohen, "Interpretation of Article 10: Days of Rest and Statutory Holidays". In: Y. Shany, Y.Z. Stern (eds.), *Commentary on the Basic Law: Israel – the Nation-State of the Jewish People* (Jerusalem: The Israel Democracy Institute, 2023): 297–335.

10 The guarantee of kosher food for every "Jewish soldier in the IDF" highlights the absence of a similar provision guaranteeing similar religious freedom and *halal* food for non-Jewish soldiers. For example, for a Muslim soldier who, for religious reasons, eats only *halal* meat, which must be slaughtered according to Islamic principles. In practice, since Muslims also rely on Jewish slaughter and permit the consumption of meat slaughtered according to Jewish law, this right is *de facto* preserved for all Muslim soldiers serving in the IDF.

appears in the Law for the Protection of Holy Places and various ordinances regulating their status. This is already alluded to in the previously mentioned paragraph from the Declaration of Independence, which states that the State of Israel "will safeguard the Holy Places of all religions". Later, the Law for the Protection of Holy Places, 1967, also enshrined the obligation to protect "freedom of access" to the holy sites for members of all religions. Thus, Section 1 of this law states, "The Holy Places shall be protected from desecration and any other harm, and from anything that could impair the freedom of access of members of religions to the places sacred to them or their feelings toward these places".[11] Other sections of the law established criminal penalties for the desecration of holy sites.

Similar provisions were enacted in Israel's main criminal law: the Penal Code, 1977.[12]

After years of struggle against the monopoly held by the "Chevra Kadisha" – the Jewish burial societies in Israel, all of which are conducted according to Orthodox halakhic law – a change also occurred in this area. Following a lengthy struggle, including legal proceedings, the State of Israel recognized the right to "freedom of religion" and "freedom from religion" in matters of burial as well. This recognition was enshrined by the Knesset in the Alternative Civil Burial Law, 1996,[13] which allows a Jew to be buried in a "civil" cemetery whose regulations do not necessarily follow Jewish law.[14]

In 1994, Prof. Aharon Barak, who would later become president of the Supreme Court, wrote an article in which he argued that since 1992, there has been a significant change in the status of constitutional basic rights, including freedom of religion. This change, he claimed, followed the enactment of Basic Law: Human Dignity and Liberty. According to Barak, although the explicit term "freedom of religion" is not mentioned in this Basic Law – unlike other rights such as liberty, privacy, and more – it can be considered part of the right to human dignity, which is explicitly mentioned in the Basic Law and even in its title.[15]

This position was adopted by many of the Supreme Court justices (though not all), and they expressed it in a long series of rulings over the 30 years that

11 A similar clause can be found in Sec. 3 of Basic Law: Jerusalem as the Capital of Israel. An important law relating to the non-Jewish religious communities is The Religious Communities Ordinance (their organization), a law that, despite its enactment back in the mandate period before the establishment of the State of Israel, still stands in force.

12 Penal Law, 5737-1977. https://www.icj.org/soginationallegislat/israel-penal-law-5737-1977/&ved=2ahUKEwiHvuzq0K-JAxXHJRAIHdDjACgQFnoECBwQAQ&usg=AOvVaw1u3Afi_ZYO5iFJqeYXi5d5. Accessed October 20, 2023.

13 Alternative Civil Burial Law, 5756-1996.

14 Similarly, the courts have recognized a person's right to have their body cremated, even though this is contrary to Jewish law.

15 See A. Barak, *Interpretation in Law*. Vol. 3 *Constitutional Interpretation* (Nevo, Jerusalem, 1994): 225 in Hebrew.

have passed since. Barak succinctly summarized this view in 2014 when he wrote,

> Basic Law: Human Dignity and Liberty does not recognize freedom of religion as an independent constitutional right. Freedom of religion is recognized in Israel as a constitutional right only if it can be seen as a derivative of the right to human dignity. Only those aspects of freedom of religion that stem from a person's humanity – from their freedom of will, their autonomy, and their ability to write the narrative of their life within society – are granted constitutional status in Israel. These aspects are broad. Indeed, there is a close connection between freedom of religion and human dignity as the humanity of the person. The freedom to believe in God is one of the most important expressions of a believer's ability to express their personality and identity as a human being. God is central to the life story of the believer. Freedom of religion – and the freedom of religious worship derived from it – is the freedom of every person in Israel to believe in God and to carry out all actions that their faith requires, to refrain from all actions their faith forbids, all in order to practically realize their faith.[16]

9.3 The Enshrinement of the Principles of Equality in Matters of Religion and Freedom of Religion in Israeli Court Rulings

As mentioned earlier, in the absence of a formal constitutional document, the constitutional enshrinement of the principle of equality among all religions, as well as the fundamental principles of "freedom of religion" and "freedom from religion", and, similarly, freedom of expression (and initially, also freedom of occupation), has primarily been achieved through "judicial legislation" via the rulings of Israeli courts, particularly the Supreme Court.

The Supreme Court has approached this "case by case," anchoring freedom of religion as a recognized and obligatory right in Israeli law and working to strengthen it.

One of the earliest expressions of the enshrinement of the principle of freedom of religion in Israel occurred incidentally in a case where an individual was criminally prosecuted for the offense of bigamy. The defendant argued in his defense that his religion – Judaism – permitted him to marry more than one wife.

In rejecting this claim, the court, among other things, addressed the status of the right to freedom of religion in the State of Israel. Justice Landau wrote, "Freedom of conscience and worship is one of the personal liberties

16 A. Barak, *Human Dignity: The Constitutional Right and Its Offshoots*, Vol. II (Jerusalem: Nevo, 2014): 770 [Hebrew].

guaranteed to every individual under any enlightened democratic regime".[17] However, the court rejected the defendant's claim on the merits, ruling that even if Jewish law allowed bigamy, its values would be outweighed by other values, primarily the protection of human dignity – and the dignity of women in particular – before which the right to freedom of religion must give way. Moreover, in this case, even according to those who argued that bigamy was permissible under Jewish law, it was not mandated by it.[18]

Thus, like freedom of expression and freedom of occupation, the court created the right to freedom of religion as if out of nothing, based on the assumption that the State of Israel is a democracy, and no democracy worthy of the name lacks freedom of religion and worship as one of its foundations.[19]

Another expression of the enshrinement of the principle of freedom of religion in the State of Israel is given in a series of court rulings that dealt with the permission to sell pork and meat products that are not *kosher* according to Jewish (and Muslim[20]) religious law.

The essence of the law is found in Section 9.1, which states, "A person shall not raise, keep, or slaughter pigs."[21]

Here too, an indirect expression of "freedom from religion" and the principle of equality among different religions is found in Section 2 of the law, which exempts from its application localities listed in the law's appendix where a significant Arab-Christian population resides whose religious principles do not require abstention from consuming pork.

17 *Yosipoff v. Attorney General*, Criminal Appeal 112/50 [1951] 5 P.D. 487.

18 Regarding this matter, see the remarks of Justice Silberg in the same case: "There is no doubt that freedom of conscience also includes freedom of religion. However, for a prohibitive provision of law to be seen as infringing on freedom of religion, it is not enough to prove that the religion does not prohibit the act; it must also be proven that the offense is a commandment of the religion, that the religion commands and obligates the act. Not everything permitted by religion must be permitted by law, since the two domains do not completely overlap: one deals with matters between man and God and between man and fellow man, while the other also deals with matters between man and the state". *Yosipoff v. Attorney General*, Criminal Appeal 112/50 [1951] 496. Justice Silberg reiterated this fundamental position regarding the nature and limits of freedom of religion in another case: "Freedom of religion does not mean the freedom to do whatever religion permits, but rather to fulfill what religion commands". HCJ, *Malham v. Qadi Court*, 49/54 [1954] 8 P.D. 913.

19 In this way, the court also enshrined freedom of expression, which is not explicitly mentioned in either the Declaration of Independence or any other law. In this context, it is worth noting that the term "democracy" does not appear in the Declaration of Independence either, and it was explicitly mentioned in Israel's laws for the first time in the late 1980s, nearly 40 years(!) after the establishment of the state.

20 As emphasized in the explanatory notes to various laws on this matter, the avoidance of non-*kosher* meat, especially pork, is motivated not only by religious reasons but also – some would say primarily – by national and historical considerations. For further discussion, see D. Barak-Erez, *Outlawed Pigs Law, Religion, and Culture in Israel* (Madison: University of Wisconsin Press, 2007).

21 "Slaughtering" (nechira) refers to the killing of a pig for the purpose of eating it.

As a kind of "complement" to this law, which only prohibits pig breeding but not the sale, consumption, or eating of pork, many local authorities enacted "bylaws" that also prohibited the sale of pork within their jurisdictions. These laws, which openly conflicted with constitutional principles of equality, freedom of occupation, and freedom of religion, were challenged in several court rulings, primarily by merchants seeking to sell non-*kosher* meat.

In a long series of rulings in the 1950s and 1960s, the court ruled that prohibitions on raising, marketing, and selling pigs, when based on religious reasons, were invalid due to their violation of the fundamental principles of liberty and freedom of occupation, as well as freedom of religion.

An explicit and central expression of freedom of religion was given in a case involving a non-Orthodox Jewish community that sought to hold prayer services on Rosh Hashanah and Yom Kippur in a hall owned by Kfar Shmaryahu, a local council near Herzliya. The local council refused, with the true reason for its refusal being a desire to avoid providing a public space for a community that did not pray according to the Orthodox liturgy.

In accepting the petition, the court spoke of the public authority's obligation to treat all religious streams equally, ruling that discrimination against one of them constitutes an infringement on freedom of religion.[22]

Although freedom of religion was not, and still is not, explicitly enshrined in any Israeli law, the court viewed it as a binding principle by virtue of Israel being a democratic state. In practice, the court thereby granted this principle constitutional status, creating it "out of nothing," even in the absence of an explicit legal norm.

The court, in a ruling by Justice Haim Cohn, wrote,

> Freedom of religion and worship was guaranteed to every citizen of Israel in the Declaration of the Establishment of the State; and although this Declaration is not a law that can serve as the basis for a cause of action, this freedom is but 'one of the individual liberties guaranteed to every person in any enlightened democratic regime.' The very existence and guarantee of this freedom involves the risk of division between different religious streams and movements; but this risk does not diminish freedom of religion and worship in the least; for if you say otherwise, you abolish the entire doctrine of religious freedom.[23]

Justice Zussman added in this context,

22 In this case, the infringement is not absolute, as no one prevented the community from praying elsewhere. Nonetheless, the discrimination against them based on their religious beliefs and way of life constitutes a certain infringement on their freedom of religion.

23 HCJ, *Peretz v. Kfar Shmaryahu*, 262/62 [1962] P.D. 16(3) 2107.

> Not only has the responsibility for religious matters not been entrusted to a local council, but it is not for the council to decide that the residents of the locality shall pray in this manner and not in that manner. Uniform worship and prayer may have been common during the Thirty Years' War, when rulers upheld the principle of *cuius regio, eius religio* ["whose realm, his religion"]. But the Declaration of Independence promised freedom of religion and worship to all citizens of the state, and even if the Declaration itself does not grant a right enforceable by legal action, the way of life of the state's citizens was determined therein, and all authorities in the state must follow its principles.[24]

The court reaffirmed this position on various occasions. For instance, it rejected a petition by a woman who sought to change her last name to that of the man with whom she lived and had children, even though the two were not married. During the deliberation, Justice Haim Cohn (who was in the minority) wrote the following:

> As for religion and morality, beliefs and opinions differ among the people. What one sees as religiously obligatory, another sees as contrary to morality; and the moral commandment of one is a religious prohibition for another. In a free and democratic state, the secular legislator does not purport to resolve disagreements over beliefs and opinions. Every person is entitled to conduct their steps and life path according to their own conscience, as long as they do not violate the law.[25]

In another context, the court addressed the petition of a company seeking to import into Israel – contrary to the prevailing practice until that time[26] – meat that is not *kosher* according to Jewish religious law. In doing so, the court ruled that the principle of "freedom from religion" –which some view merely as a derivative of "freedom of religion" and not an independent right – is, in fact, a fundamental constitutional right:

> It is a supreme principle in Israel – rooted in the rule of law (in its substantive sense) and in the jurisprudence of the court – that both freedom of religion and freedom from religion are preserved for every citizen and resident [...] From the supreme principle of freedom of religion and freedom from religion follows the rule that no religious

24 HCJ, *Peretz v. Kfar Shmaryahu*, 262/62 [1962] P.D. 16(3) 2116.

25 HCJ, Schik *v. Ministry of the Interior*, 353/70 [1971] 25(1) P.D. 549.

26 Later, following the petition and the enshrinement of the principle of freedom of occupation in the Basic Laws, a law was passed mandating that all meat imported into Israel be *kosher*. See Import of Frozen Meat Law [1994] 5754-1994; Meat and Meat Products Law [1994] Dinim Vol. 5, 2898.

> commandments shall be imposed on those who are not observant and on those who do not wish to observe religious commandments.[27]

In that ruling, Justice Or wrote,

> Protecting the feelings of one part of the public may easily turn into an infringement on the feelings of another part of the public. The tension between freedom of religion and freedom of conscience, one aspect of which is freedom from religion, is inherent and unavoidable. Both principles are noted in the Declaration of Independence as foundational ideas upon which the State of Israel is based. In the delicate balance between freedom of religion and freedom from religion, it is crucial to remember that the mere fact that one segment of the public holds different opinions, beliefs, and behaves differently – even if this offends another segment of the public—does not justify preventing the first group from continuing to think, believe, and act according to their own views, beliefs, and customs.[28]

Justice Cheshin added,

> Religious commandments cannot be imposed on those who are not observant or who do not wish to observe them; such commandments cannot be imposed – neither directly nor indirectly – except by the primary legislator, the Knesset. The principle of the separation of religion and state is to be upheld according to the laws enacted by the Knesset. Only by law, at the national level, can religious commandments be enforced.[29]

The principle of freedom of religion has also been enshrined in a series of court rulings dealing with the obligation to provide equal representation to various streams within Judaism in government institutions. For instance, in a case concerning the representation of the "Masorti Movement" (associated with the Conservative stream), the court, through Justice Zamir, added the following regarding the importance of religious tolerance:

> In a democratic society, different groups, including rejected minority groups, have the right to express themselves in the realms of culture,

27 HCJ, *Mitrael Ltd. v. The Prime Minister and Minister of Religious Affairs*, 3872/93 [1993] 47(5) P.D. 506.
28 HCJ, *Mitrael Ltd. v. The Prime Minister and Minister of Religious Affairs*, 3872/93 [1993] 47(5) P.D. 500.
29 HCJ, *Mitrael Ltd. v. The Prime Minister and Minister of Religious Affairs*, 3872/93 [1993] 47(5) P.D. 498.

> religion, and tradition, each group in its own way.[30] Every individual lives according to their faith. Not only that, but it is also advantageous for society to have a diversity of perspectives, ways of life, and institutions. Diversity enriches, reflects the reality of life, contributes to the improvement of life, and gives practical meaning to freedom.[31]

The principle of freedom of religion has also come to the forefront in various cases concerning conversion to Judaism and religious conversion in general. In the absence of explicit legislation regulating the conversion process,[32] one of the contentious issues has been petitions seeking recognition of non-Orthodox conversions performed by non-Orthodox rabbis. In one of the important rulings on this matter, Chief Justice Shamgar wrote,

> Freedom of religion and conscience is one of the foundational principles of our legal system. This freedom is among the values that form the normative foundations governing our system since the establishment of the state. Freedom of religious conversion is protected under the framework of freedom of religion and conscience. Therefore, a reasonable interpretation of the current legal situation indicates that the authorities should not interfere in this domain of individual autonomy, and that the decision of a resident or citizen to convert to another religion, on the one hand, and the decision to accept a person into the fold of the religion they choose to join, on the other hand, should remain free from governmental intervention and regulation. Religious conversion is a private matter. In a free society, every person may convert to another religion as they wish. No formal governmental approval is required for this. The need for approval arises only in matters concerning personal status, and indeed this is the case in most countries with systems similar to ours. In Israel, religious affiliation carries many legal implications concerning personal status, and nothing more.[33]

Although the court has recognized the constitutional status of the rights to freedom of religion and freedom of worship, it has also ruled on several occasions that, like other human rights, these rights are not absolute. In certain circumstances, these rights yield to other values, rights, and interests.

30 This verse has been widely used in discussions about issues of religion and state and the principle of freedom of conscience. However, its original biblical wording (Hab. 2:4) is slightly different: "But the righteous shall live by his faith.".

31 SCJ, *Masorti Movement v. Minister of Religious Affairs*, 1438/98 [1999] 53(5) P.D. 376–377.

32 Regarding the absence of legislation on this issue and its background, see A. Hacohen, "Conversion According to Dat Moshe (Jewish Law) and (The State of) Israel: A Big Mess, Fuss and Chaos". In: S. Afek, O. Grosskopf, S. Lifshitz, E. Spiegelman (eds.), *Law, Defense and Literature – Essays in Honour of Menachem Finkelstein* (Jerusalem: Nevo, 2020), 713–751 [in Hebrew].

33 SCJ, *Pessaro Goldstein v. Minister of the Interior*, 1031/93 [1995] 49(4) P.D. 661.

This principle was expressed in a series of rulings concerning the freedom of access to holy sites and worship at those sites, even when the exercise of such freedoms could, with a high degree of likelihood, lead to public disorder and endanger human safety. In one case, the court rejected a petition by a group of Jewish worshippers seeking to pray on the Temple Mount. In rejecting the petition, Justice Barak wrote,

> In an organized society, the exercise of individual rights must sometimes yield to the public good. This happens only when the harm to the public interest is significant and the probability of its occurrence is high. Regarding freedom of religious worship and freedom of expression, a substantial harm, whose likelihood is close to certain, is required to justify limiting these liberties.[34]

In another ruling, the court expressed a similar view by grounding freedom of religion in the broader right to "freedom of expression". The primary issue in this case, rooted in international public law, concerned the Israel Defense Forces' right to seize real property in areas under belligerent occupation to secure access for worshippers to a holy site – in this case, the Cave of the Patriarchs in Hebron. In dismissing the petition challenging the legality of the Israel Defense Forces' actions, Justice Procaccia wrote,

> Freedom of religion is a fundamental constitutional right of the individual, one that holds a superior status even in relation to other constitutional human rights. Freedom of worship is an expression of freedom of religion and a branch of freedom of expression [...]. A person expresses themselves in the realm of religious belief through religious worship. The constitutional protection given to freedom of worship is therefore fundamentally similar to the protection afforded to freedom of expression, and the appropriate constitutional balancing formula for one is applicable to the other. It is a constitutional right of great strength, carrying significant weight in the balance against opposing societal values.[35]

Nevertheless, Justice Procaccia acknowledged that sometimes freedom of religion and worship must yield to other values and rights:

> Where the exercise of the right to worship creates a near certainty of severe and substantial harm to public safety, and no reasonable means exist to avert the danger, the value of public safety will prevail, and the constitutional right must give way. However, where reasonable means exist that can mitigate the risk, they should be utilized, particularly when

34 SCJ, *Salomon v. Chief of Jerusalem District Police*, 4044/93 [1995] 49(5) P.D. 621.
35 SCJ, *Hess v. Commander of IDF Forces in the West Bank*, 10356/02 [2004] 58(3) P.D. 465–466.

> a constitutional right of significant weight is at stake. The greater the constitutional right in the hierarchy of rights, the greater the need to exhaust reasonable and available means to minimize the danger to public safety.[36]

Another unique expression of the principle of freedom of religion occurred in a case before the Supreme Court involving a petition that sought to compel a Jewish burial society to act contrary to its usual practice, which followed Jewish religious law. In a minority opinion, Justice Yitzhak Englard argued that the attempt to force a burial society operating according to Jewish law to follow practices contrary to Jewish law infringed upon the "freedom of religion" of its members. He wrote,

> In my opinion, this court is not fundamentally authorized to compel a religious body – whether public or private – to act in contradiction to the religious law to which it adheres. Such coercion constitutes a serious violation of the principle of freedom of religion. This violation is permissible only through explicit legislative decree, such as when the actions of the religious body constitute a criminal offense under the Penal Code, or when the legislature, for important reasons, prohibits the religious body from acting according to its religious commandments. In the absence of an explicit legal provision, one cannot compel a person to violate religious commandments, whether they be light or severe. Furthermore, this court is not authorized to question the correctness of the legal ruling issued by the body competent under religious law. The court does not adjudicate religious law, and the personal views of the judge regarding the nature of the faith or the correctness of the legal ruling – whether it is consistent or in line with the spirit of the times – are irrelevant [...] If the legal ruling causes harm to the views of those who rely on the services of the religious body, it is appropriate to find a satisfactory solution. However, coercion to violate religious commandments is not the right solution in a democratic state that respects the principle of freedom of religion.[37]

9.4 Exceptions to the Principle of Freedom of Religion and Freedom from Religion

As mentioned earlier, although it is now widely accepted that the principles of freedom of religion and freedom from religion constitute fundamental constitutional rights in the State of Israel, there are still prominent "islands" where these principles are violated. Most of these infringements have been

36 SCJ, *Hess v. Commander of IDF Forces in the West Bank*, 10356/02 [2004] 58(3) P.D. 465.
37 *Shavit v. Hevra Kadisha Rishon LeZion*, Civil Appeal 6024/97 [1999] 53(3) P.D. 645.

"corrected" – to some extent – through judicial rulings, but these remain practical corrections rather than legal ones, as they have not been incorporated into legislation.

Perhaps the most notable of these violations is the absence of freedom of religion in matters of "marriage and divorce" in Israel. The principle of freedom to marry is enshrined in Article 16 of the Universal Declaration of Human Rights (1948), which states,

> Men and women of full age, without any limitation due to race, nationality, or religion, have the right to marry and to found a family. They are entitled to equal rights as to marriage, during marriage, and at its dissolution.

Nevertheless, the Knesset, already in the early days of the state, enacted the Rabbinical Courts Jurisdiction (Marriage and Divorce) Law, 1953.[38] This law imposes a dual restriction on the freedom of religion – and especially on the freedom from religion – of Jews in Israel concerning "matters of marriage and divorce".

Section 1 of the law establishes a unique and exclusive jurisdiction: "Matters of marriage and divorce of Jews in Israel, citizens or residents of the state, shall be under the exclusive jurisdiction of rabbinical courts". Section 2 further provides an exclusive rule concerning the applicable law, stating, "Marriages and divorces of Jews in Israel shall be performed according to Jewish law".

Thus, the Israeli legislature has effectively mandated that all "Jews in Israel" must marry only through Orthodox religious ceremonies ("according to Jewish law"[39]), preventing them from marrying in civil ceremonies, let alone engaging in "interfaith marriages" with people of other religions or same-sex marriages, which are prohibited under Jewish law and are not recognized as valid marriages.

Furthermore, as noted earlier, the legislature did not limit itself to determining which law would govern marriages but also assigned exclusive jurisdiction over such matters to rabbinical courts (and not civil courts), which rule according to Orthodox Jewish law.

Similar arrangements apply to members of other religions (except for those without religious affiliation), so the only "official" way to marry in Israel is through religious ceremonies, with judicial authority over marriage matters assigned to religious courts.

38 Rabbinical Courts Jurisdiction (Marriage and Divorce) Law, 5713-1953. For the background to the enactment of the law and the controversies preceding it, see A. Hacohen, "Marriage According to the Laws of Moses and (The State of) Israel". In: D. Hacohen, M. Lissak (eds.), *Crossroads of Decisions in Israel* (Beer Sheva: Ben-Gurion University of the Negev, 2010): 40–87 [Hebrew].

39 Although the legislature used the renewed term "Torah law", the courts interpreted it from the outset—and continue to do so today – as synonymous with Orthodox halakhah according to the Shulchan Aruch, the fundamental legal code of Orthodox Judaism.

This is the formal legal framework. In practice, however, over the years, various "Bypass" roads have been developed that allow those who do not wish to marry through religious ceremonies or rely on religious courts to marry in ways that are recognized by the state.

One "Bypass" is to marry outside the borders of Israel in a country that recognizes civil marriages or marriages that are not recognized – or even outright prohibited – under Orthodox Jewish law (such as interfaith marriages or same-sex marriages). These marriages, performed outside of Israel (often in neighboring Cyprus), are recognized for the purposes of Israeli law under principles of international public law. Those married in this way are granted the full "civil" rights afforded by the state to married couples. Another "Bypass" – a refinement of regular civil marriage – is "consular marriage", in which the marriage is registered in another country without the physical presence of the couple in that country.

A third way to obtain civil rights in Israel without resorting to religious marriage is through the status of "common-law partners", whereby cohabitation for a significant period grants couples, under certain circumstances, the same civil rights as those given to married couples, without being formally recognized as "married".

The creation of these dual tracks – religious and civil – often leads to conflicts between different legal systems, and courts are frequently required to address the issues that arise from this peculiar situation.

Another, though indirect, infringement on freedom of religion in Israel comes through various laws that, in practice, limit a person's religious freedom. For example, the criminal prohibition(!) against "inducing religious conversion", particularly the conversion of minors. Historically, this law was intended to combat Christian missionary activities. While the law does not prohibit "religious conversion" per se, the imposition of a criminal ban on "inducing religious conversion" limits a person's ability to freely act in this area and subtly distinguishes between "conversion to Judaism" – referred to in Hebrew as giyur, which is permitted and even supported by the state – and conversion from Judaism to another religion.[40]

Another area that seems to include certain limitations on freedom of religion (as well as freedom of occupation) is the realm of *kashrut* (Jewish dietary laws). Despite original Jewish law not requiring a product or business (such as a factory, restaurant, hotel, or hall) to have a *kashrut* certificate, let alone one issued by a specific rabbinical authority, the entire *kashrut* certification process in Israel has been handed over to the Chief Rabbinate of Israel.[41]

40 On this matter, see A. Hacohen, "Proselytism and the Right to Change Religion in Israel". In: S. Ferrari, R. Cristofori (eds.), *Law and Religion in the 21st Century* (Farnham–Surrey: Ashgate, 2010): 261–278.

41 This arrangement is primarily enshrined in the Prohibition of Fraud in *kashrut* Law, 5743-1983. Although this law appears to be a "consumer protection" law, designed to prevent the misleading of consumers who seek *kosher* food, it effectively grants the Chief Rabbinate a quasi-monopoly over all matters of *kashrut* in Israel.

As a result, a person is not allowed to present their business or product as *kosher* unless they have received a *kashrut* certificate issued by the Chief Rabbinate (or its authorized bodies, such as local religious councils). Moreover, there are restrictions on importing kosher products into Israel. Even if these products are recognized as *kosher* by a rabbinical authority abroad, their *kashrut* status must receive additional recognition from the Chief Rabbinate, without which they cannot be imported as *kosher* products.

Another import restriction is set out in the Meat and Meat Products Law (1994), which prohibits the import of meat into Israel without a *kashrut* certificate. Since the Chief Rabbinate, following Orthodox Jewish law, effectively holds a monopoly on issuing kashrut certificates, all meat imported into Israel is subject to its supervision and approval, and only *kosher* meat is allowed to be imported. Petitions to the Supreme Court seeking to overturn this practice, citing discrimination and violation of freedom of religion, have been dismissed.[42]

In addition to these arrangements enshrined in primary legislation – laws passed by the Knesset – there are also numerous regulations, bylaws, or "administrative guidelines" that in practice infringe upon freedom of religion and freedom from religion. For example, the inscription of Gregorian calendar dates on tombstones has been prohibited in most Jewish cemeteries in Israel for decades. Most Jewish cemeteries in Israel have long followed Orthodox Jewish law, sometimes even its stricter interpretations.[43]

As a result, those wishing to hold "civil burial ceremonies" were denied the possibility of being buried in these cemeteries, which are funded by the state (through the National Insurance Institute). Change came after several petitions were filed with the Supreme Court, following which the Alternative Civil Burial Law, 1996, was enacted. This law requires the state to establish "civil" cemeteries, where a person can be buried – at state expense – without religious symbols. However, despite this right being enshrined in law, its implementation has been slow, and in practice, the vast majority of Jewish burials in Israel are still conducted in cemeteries managed according to Orthodox Jewish law.

9.5 Court Rulings Attempting to "Balance" Freedom of Religion and Freedom from Religion

Over the years, as courts navigated issues of religion and state, they – particularly the Supreme Court in its capacity as the High Court of Justice – have sought to find creative solutions to balance, as much as possible, the

42 See, e.g., *Mitral v. Minister of Commerce*, 7198/93 [1994] 48(2) P.D. 844.

43 E.g., women were prevented from eulogizing their loved ones, and gender separation between men and women was enforced at the cemetery, against the wishes of the families. These arrangements were declared "illegal" by the courts. See, e.g., *Asaf Bar v. Chief Rabbinate of Petach Tikva*, 6526/05 [2006].

fundamental principle of "freedom of religion" with "freedom from religion". For example, courts have prohibited the opening of stores selling pork in city centers but allowed such commerce in industrial zones or in communities where the majority of the population desired to consume it,[44] required public hospitals to permit the entry of chametz (leavened bread) during Passover for those who wish to consume it,[45] recognized conversions performed according to Jewish religious law but outside the official state rabbinical court system,[46] and more.

It should be emphasized that in many of these rulings, the issue of "freedom of religion" is not addressed in isolation. Constitutional principles such as equality, nondiscrimination, and freedom of occupation are often intertwined in the discussion. Nonetheless, these rulings also express the application of the principles of "freedom of religion" and "freedom from religion". For instance, rulings that permitted commerce on the Sabbath under certain conditions in city centers,[47] mandated equitable allocation of public land to different streams of Judaism for building synagogues, required local authorities to allow "family swimming hours" for both men and women together at a municipal swimming pool (where the local authority had prohibited this on grounds of religious modesty),[48] required religious councils to include women as members despite opposition from the Chief Rabbinate on halakhic grounds,[49] required the inclusion of women in the electoral body that selects rabbis (despite Orthodox rabbinical opposition on religious grounds[50]), allowed the construction of a ritual bath (mikveh) in a neighborhood where the majority of residents were not religious and opposed its construction,[51] granted exemption from military service on religious grounds,[52] and allowed the use of public mikvehs for non-Orthodox conversions, among other examples.

44 HCJ, *Knesset Member Marina Solodkin v. Beit Shemesh Municipality*, 953/01 [2004] 58(5) P.D. 595.

45 HCJ, *Secular Forum v. Minister of Health*, 1550/18 [2020]. Despite the ruling, it was largely emptied of its content following an amendment to the Patient's Rights Law [1996] (https://hamoked.org/files/2013/155880_eng.pdf/. Accessed October 27, 2024), allowing the hospital director, under certain conditions, to prohibit the entry of chametz to the hospital during Passover.

46 HCJ, *Martina Regachova v. Ministry of the Interior*, 7625/06, [2016].

47 AAA, *Bremer v. The Tel Aviv-Jaffa Municipality*, 2469/12 [2013].

48 HCJ, *Shlomi Shukron v. Kiryat Arba Local Council*, 3865/20 [2020].

49 HCJ, *Shakdiel v. Minister of Religious Affairs*, 153/87 [1988] 42(2) P.D. 244.

50 HCJ, *Poraz v. Mayor of Tel Aviv*, 953/87 [1988] 42(2) P.D. 309.

51 HCJ, *Soloduch v. Rehovot Municipality*, 10907/04 [2010].

52 Regarding this matter, see also the Defense Service Law [consolidated version] [1986] Section 40. https://www.jewishvirtuallibrary.org/israel-defense-service-law-1986. Accessed October 27, 2024.

9.6 Conclusion

The right to "freedom of religion" – along with its associated and derivative rights, including freedom of religious belief, freedom of conscience, freedom from religion, freedom of worship, and the right of access to holy places and the right to worship there – is now recognized in Israeli law as a fundamental constitutional right.

Although it is not explicitly enshrined in any specific law, there are numerous legislative acts, and more than that, dozens of court rulings that have recognized, enshrined, and worked to develop and preserve this right.

The absence of explicit legislative enshrinement of the right to freedom of religion stems partly from the lack of a formal constitution in Israel but primarily from political considerations.

In light of this reality, over the years, efforts have been made to solidify and expand the status of this right through court rulings, especially in the Supreme Court. These efforts have been largely successful in practical terms, and it is rare to find cases (except where the right to freedom of religion has yielded to other rights and values in the process of balancing, as is customary in other legal systems) that demonstrate unjustified or disproportionate infringements on this right.

It is possible that with the completion of Israel's constitutional process – which has been ongoing since its founding over 75 years ago – there will eventually be a formal enshrinement of this right in a comprehensive constitutional document. Time will tell whether this process will come to fruition. Until then, the right to freedom of religion remains subject to the vicissitudes of judicial rulings, with its "sailors" doing all they can to safeguard it and prevent harm to it.

10 Jewish and Muslim Claims to Religious Freedom, Participation, and Benefits Under Article 4 (1) and (2) of the German Basic Law – and Their Constitutional Limits

Hans Michael Heinig

Abstract

This chapter examines the protection of religious minorities under German constitutional law using the example of Jews and Muslims. To this end, the current legal instruments are presented and, in particular, the mode of operation of religious freedom under the Basic Law is explained. Its individual protection dimension is presented using several examples, as well as its cooperative dimension. In addition to the separation of state and religion, German constitutional law on religion is also characterised by cooperative elements, which in themselves are subject to the principle of equality. The forms of cooperation between the state and Muslim and Jewish religious organisations are traced. The chapter also addresses deficits in implementation in legal practice.

Keywords

antidiscrimination; chaplaincy; cooperation; equality; financial funding; holidays; religious; Islamic headscarf; Kipah; minority rights; neutrality; religious freedom; religious scope; religious limits; religious dimensions; religious instruction; religious societies; taxation of members; school; Shoah; secularity; self-understanding; slaughtering; theology at state universities

10.1 Introduction: The Fundamental Rights Protection of Religious Minorities from Democratic Majorities

Liberal-democratic orders are characterised by a double concept of freedom: they oscillate between individual self-determination and collective self-government. Effective protection of fundamental rights and democratic legitimation

DOI: 10.4324/9781003423294-15

of political authority are indissolubly linked in this conception of order, but they are also in permanent tension with one another.[1]

This is also reflected in the way religious freedom and its limits are dealt with. Obligations to the law that applies to everyone and religiously justified exceptions to such general obligations compete with each other. Partly, special attention is paid to individual protection, partly to the democratic obligation of "neutral" laws for all. The problem becomes even more pressing when it comes to religious minorities. The interests of religious majorities are usually taken into account by the democratic majority in collectively binding decisions. The situation is different for religious minorities, which can be distinguished from a religious or secular majority culture. Then it depends in particular on what exactly one understands by "neutrality" (see Section 10.4.) and how minority-protective aspects of fundamental rights are reflected here.

The protection of minorities is not only achieved through special exemption clauses for certain religious minorities but also through further diversity-oriented structures of the legal system: prohibitions of discrimination, equal status in general cooperation, and support by the state but also the positive adaptation of special interests of individual religious cultures into the legal system can play a role.

The following chapter will take a closer look at how German law, guided by the constitutional guarantee of equal religious freedom, deals with two very different religious minorities, Jews and Muslims.[2] Their religious interests are partly congruent (e.g. *shechita*, different religious weekly rhythms than in Christianity, religiously accentuated clothing); in both cases, religious life in Germany is strongly influenced by migration experiences. However, their historical, political and socio-cultural starting points are completely different: Germany's political culture includes an enduring awareness of the responsibility that falls to the people who perpetrated the Shoah. Religious conflicts with a Jewish connection always stand in the long shadow of National Socialism. This factor does not apply to Muslims. In Germany, Islam cannot look back on a long cultural history (unlike in Austria, for example).

Religious conflicts with a Muslim connection therefore take on a different dimension: rather in the long shadow of Islamic fundamentalism, including its trail of violence, as well as a considerable Islamophobic attitude in parts of the German population. While anti-Semitism is widespread among the general population but absolutely taboo in the dominant political culture in Germany,

1 J. Habermas, *Faktizität und Geltung Beiträge zur Diskurstheorie des Rechts und des demokratischen Rechtsstaats* (Frankfurt am Main: Suhrkamp, 1992).

2 Some passages on Muslim rights in this article are based on H.M. Heinig, *Rechtliche Rahmenbedingungen für die Entfaltung muslimischen Lebens in der Bundesrepublik Deutschland* (Göttinger: Universität Göttingen, 2023). https://doi.org/10.47952/gro-publ-134. Accessed May 3, 2024.

the same is not true of resentments or even hostility towards Muslims.[3] Politicians are more inclined to take up anti-Muslim sentiments, including through legislation. Fundamental rights as minority rights are then of particular importance in order to set limits to such tendencies and to counteract them. The Federal Constitutional Court has repeatedly done this in recent years with reference to the fundamental right of freedom of religion and religious discrimination bans.

10.2 People of Faith, Membership, Organisational Landscape

Secular law on religion is characterised by a specific mixture of individual and corporate rights. Traditionally, the corporate dimension is very pronounced in Germany. The background to this is the experience of a bi-confessional legal space after Luther's Reformation, which (initially at the imperial level, then also in the individual territories of the empire) sought to resolve tensions and conflicts through a polity of equality between Catholicism and Protestantism. This had a lasting effect, even when the individualisation of law took hold at the end of the 18th century: The "religious parties" of the Peace of Westphalia became in the course of enlightened natural law thinking "religious societies", associations of members of a confession.[4] To this day, the legal institution of the religious society plays a decisive role in the exercise of corporative religious rights (see Sections 10.7, 10.9, and 10.10). They act in cooperation with the state as religious authorities, for example for theological institutes and faculties at state universities or for religious instruction in public schools, as well as in chaplaincy in the military and in publicly funded hospitals.

In light of the guarantee of negative religious freedom, legal membership in a religious society cannot be established by descent or family affiliation but only by individual, even implied, declaration. In Christianity, baptism is the central point of reference for establishing legal membership. In order to be able to exercise the rights of such a membership-based religious society, organised Judaism in Germany had to develop a membership law based on individual declaration, independently of the theological principle of maternity.[5]

After 1945, under the impact of the Shoah, the model of the "Einheitsgemeinde" (unified community), which encompassed liberal, conservative, and orthodox

3 For the perspective of social science see G. Pickel, *Weltanschauliche Vielfalt und Demokratie. Wie sich religiöse Pluralität auf die politische Kultur auswirkt* (Gütersloh: Bertelsmann, 2019). https://www.bertelsmann-stiftung.de/fileadmin/files/BSt/Publikationen/GrauePublikationen/Religionsmonitor_Vielfalt_und_Demokratie_7_2019.pdf. Accessed November 16, 2024; for the approach of the right wing party Alternative für Deutschland on Muslims see H.M. Heinig, *Säkularer Staat – viele Religionen: Religionspolitische Herausforderungen der Gegenwart* (Hamburg: Kreuz Verlag, 2018): 61–70.

4 H.M. Heinig, *Prekäre Ordnungen historische Prägungen des Religionsrechts in Deutschland* (Tübingen: Mohr Siebeck, 2018): 4.

5 J. Kunze, *Bürgerliche Mitgliedschaft in Religionsgemeinschaften: Studie über die Rechtsbeziehungen der Mitglieder zu den römisch-katholischen*, (Göttingen: Göttinger Universitätsverlag, 2013).

traditions, prevailed. All synagogue communities were represented in the Central Council of Jews in Germany as an umbrella organisation. In the 1990s, there took place a massive immigration of Jews from the territory of the former Soviet Union, deliberately sought by the German government. This immigration drastically changed the character of the Jewish communities but at the same time saved them from imminent disappearance. Since the 1990s, there has also been a trend towards "reconfessionalisation". New (mostly liberal but also orthodox) congregations have arisen independent of the Central Council and the "Einheitsgemeinden". In addition, the orthodox Chabad Lubavitch movement plays an important role alongside or in many communities.[6]

German religion policy initially found it difficult to keep up with the reorganisation of the Jewish organisational landscape and to adapt the instruments for promoting Jewish life in Germany to the extended pluralisation.[7]

Today, an estimated 225,000 Jews live in Germany, 91,000 of whom are members of a synagogue congregation.[8] This means, conversely, that roughly half of the Jews living in Germany are not members of a Jewish religious society. Some, but by no means all, are what are known as "secular Jews".

This phenomenon of "believing without belonging" is even more pronounced among Muslims in Germany. The mosque communities have far more users than members. Whether and under what conditions their associations are religious societies in the legal sense is one of the most controversial issues in German law on religion. Many Muslims do not bind themselves as formal members to a specific legal entity; the communities and their associations also tend to differentiate themselves along ethnic rather than theological lines. The largest Islamic association, the Türkish Islamic Union of the Institution for Religion (DITIB), is closely linked to the religious authority in Ankara, which reports to the Turkish president, and is controlled from there. This poses a challenge to the law on religion because integration and foreign policy tensions repeatedly arise in which religion acts as a kind of proxy. In addition to DITIB, there are other umbrella associations with different characteristics. The question of how sub-organisations view human rights and democracy arises from time to time. Numerous Islamic organisations are monitored by the intelligence services on federal and state level. The exact number of members in the legal sense in mosque communities cannot be reliably determined, as official statistics only record membership of religious societies organised under public law, and Muslim

6 M. Demel, "Idee und Entwicklung der jüdischen Gemeinden und Landesverbände". In: *Autonomie und Gesetz: Zum Verhältnis von Staat und Religion Die jüdische Gemeinschaft in Deutschland* (Berlin: Zentralrat der Juden in Deutschland, Hentrich & Hentrich, 2024): 146–165.

7 H.M. Heinig, *Die Verfassung der Religion* (Tübingen: Mohr Siebeck, 2014): 172.

8 "Judentum", https://mediendienst-integration.de/gruppen/judentum.html. Accessed May 3, 2024.

associations have largely not yet achieved this status. The figures provided by the largest association, DITIB, fluctuate between 200,000 (2007)[9] and 800,000 members (2017[10]; current figure: 400,000);[11] presumably this also includes family relatives who are not members in the legal sense. It is assumed that a total of around 5.3 million people with a Muslim religious affiliation lived in Germany in 2019.[12]

Muslim and Jewish life in Germany unfolds in a religiously and culturally heterogeneous and dynamic overall situation:[13] In the area of East Germany, the former German Democratic Republic, the vast majority have no firm commitment to a religious community and describe themselves as atheist or completely uninterested in religion. In West Germany, the Protestant and Catholic churches are losing popularity dramatically year after year. The former "people's churches" are literally eroding. However, the degree of religious diversity is also increasing, particularly as a result of migration. In Berlin alone, over 250 religious and worldview societies shall be active.[14] Most recently, the number of Orthodox Christians in Germany has risen sharply due to war refugees from Ukraine.

10.3 Legal Sources and Legal Forms of the State Law on Religion

The law on religion uses the general legal forms of state law: primacy is given to the federal constitution with its fundamental rights guarantees; the Basic Law also determines the distribution of competencies for legislation and law enforcement between the federal and state levels.[15] In Germany, for example, the federal government has general legislative powers for the law of associations, civil law or social and labour law – areas of law that are also indirectly relevant to the law on religion. However, the core competence for the enactment of laws relating to religion lies with the federal states.

9 "Mitgliederzahlen: Islam". https://remid.de/info_zahlen/islam. Accessed May 3, 2024.

10 "DITIB 2017: Klare Vision für Deutschland – DITIB startet mit konzentrierter Projektarbeit in das neue Jahr". https://www.ditib.de/detail1.php?id=562&lang=de. Accessed May 3, 2024.

11 "Bund der muslimischen Frauen. Starke Frau – Starke Gesellschaft". https://www.ditib.de/default1.php?id=6&sid=12&lang=de#:~:text=Diese%20sind%20an%20die%20Türkisch,der%20DITIB%2DMoscheen%20organisiert%20sind. Accessed May 3, 2024.

12 K. Pfündel, A. Stichs, K. Tanis, *Muslimisches Leben in Deutschland 2020* (Nürnberg: Bundesamt für Migration und Flüchtlinge, 2021). https://www.bamf.de/SharedDocs/Anlagen/DE/Forschung/Forschungsberichte/fb38-muslimisches-leben.pdf?__blob=publicationFile&v=16. Accessed May 3, 2024.

13 For an overview see D. Pollack, G. Rosta, *Religion in der Moderne. Ein internationaler Vergleich* (Frankfurt am Main: Campus, 2022).

14 "Religion und Weltanschauung". https://www.berlin.de/sen/kultgz/religion-und-weltanschauung. Accessed May 3, 2024.

15 W. Heun, *The Constitution of Germany: A Contextual Analysis* (Oxford: Hart, 2011).

The law on religion also has specific legal characteristics. Austria, for example, has special statutes for individual religious cultures, including Jews and Muslims;[16] in Germany, on the other hand, contractual agreements with individual religious societies play an important role.[17] In general, they are ratified by parliamentary act and then also have the status of a formal statute in the hierarchy of norms. Such agreements have also been concluded between the Central Council of Jews in Germany and the Federal Republic,[18] as well as between the federal states and the local synagogue communities and their regional associations.[19] This contracts serve in particular to take account of the specific religious interests of a certain religious culture in the legal system.

In the Islamic spectrum, however, only two small city states (Hamburg and Bremen) have concluded such a treaty, whereby the treaty in Hamburg was not ratified but merely brought to the attention of parliament by the government.[20]

10.4 Secularity of Law and Neutrality of the State as Protection of Religious Minorities from Democratic Overpowering

Majorities, not religious truths, are decisive for democratic decision-making. The basis of state action is its democratic legitimacy, not its theological legitimacy of any kind: "All state authority emanates from the people", states Article 20 § 1 of the Basic Law (GG).[21]

The liberal-democratic constitutional order of the Basic Law prohibits state religion and state ideology in the meaning of "worldview" ("Weltanschauung"). The principle of freedom is intended to protect people in their diversity. The state must be able to be a "home" for all of them. All religions and world views have equal rights. The state must not identify with any of them. In this sense, it is religiously and worldview neutral.[22]

16 W. Wieshaider, "Comme à travers un kaléidoscope: le statut des minorités religieuses en Autriche". In: M. Ventura (ed.), *The Legal Status of Old and New Religious Minorities in the European Union* (Granada: Editorial Comares, 2021): 185–201.

17 G. Robbers, *Law and Religion in Germany* (Alphen aan den Rijn: Kluwer, 2013): 146ff.

18 A. Hense, "Vergangenheit als staatliche Verpflichtung". In: *Autonomie und Gesetz* 255–268.

19 J. Lutz-Bachmann, "Gleich oder doch anders? Die Staatsverträge der jüdischen Gemeinden mit den Ländern". In: *Autonomie und Gesetz* 127–145; J. Lutz-Bachmann, *Mater rixarum?* (Tübingen: Mohr Siebeck, 2015).

20 J. Lutz-Bachmann, "Gleich oder doch anders? Die Staatsverträge der jüdischen Gemeinden mit den Ländern".

21 German Constitutional Law. https://www.gesetze-im-internet.de/englisch_gg/englisch_gg.html. Accessed November 17, 2024. H.M. Heinig, "The concept of religious neutrality under German Constitutional Law", *Quaderni di Diritto e Politica Ecclesiastica* vol. 21 (2018): 57–67.

22 German Constitutional Law. https://www.gesetze-im-internet.de/englisch_gg/englisch_gg.html. Accessed November 17, 2024. H.M. Heinig, "The concept of religious neutrality under German Constitutional Law", *Quaderni di Diritto e Politica Ecclesiastica* vol. 21 (2018): 57–67.

However, neutrality in the sense of German constitutional law means neither blindness towards German cultural history, which has also been influenced by Christian and Jewish traditions, nor exclusionary secularism. With the preamble (***nominatio dei***), the freedom of religion, the prohibition of religious and ideological discrimination, the provisions on religious instruction and chaplaincy in state institutions, the Basic Law establishes a constitutional system of law on religion that is open to the religions and worldviews of its citizens, precisely so that the state itself does not become religious, civil-religious or ideological.

The ban on the state church also means that the state cannot and must not give its own answer to the question of religious truth. There should be no state theology. If the state opens itself up to the religions and worldviews of its citizens (such as religious instruction in public schools), theological questions are left to them. This is why the Basic Law ties in with their self-organisation in religious societies: as associations of believers, these are authorised to speak for them vis-à-vis the state and to represent them in the legal sense. This need not be accompanied by a hierarchically structured theological doctrinal office (like in the catholic church) but by an authority to speak for the religious society as such.

The religious and worldview neutrality of the state does not prevent the state from pursuing to a certain extent a policy on religion as long as it serves purely secular public interests. The constitution recognises that religions are phenomena of ambivalence.[23] They can have an extremely socially productive effect (by providing meaning, comfort, and mobilising civil society involvement), but they can also have destructive consequences (religious extremism that seeks to violently limit individual self-determination). The liberal state therefore has an interest in the "domestication" of religious forces that threaten social peace (negative formulation) and (positive formulation) in religious cultures that develop "forms of life that accommodate the liberal-democratic order" (Jürgen Habermas). Public authorities may pursue this interest as long as they respect religious liberty and prohibitions on discrimination – admittedly a difficult balancing act at times, because in practice, this can be a gateway to prejudice and preferential treatment.

As we will see in a moment, both sets of norms, religious freedom and equality rights, do not per se preclude the state from protecting the rights of third parties and other constitutional principles or from pursuing other public welfare interests (as long as they are reflected in constitutional rights and obligations). The state can therefore without violating its duty of neutrality forbid a religious organisation that actively opposes the free and democratic constitutional order.[24] It can take the monstrous crimes suffered by European Jewry

23 H.M. Heinig, *Öffentlich-rechtliche Religionsgesellschaften: Studien zur Rechtsstellung der nach Art. 137 Abs. 5 WRV korporierten* (Berlin: Duncker & Humblot, 2003): 39.

24 BVerwG, *Schutzerklärungen v. Scientology*, 6 A 6/05, NVwZ [2006] 694; BVerwG, 6 A 3/13, NVwZ [2014] 1573.

under the Nazi regime as an impetus to make collective reparations to the synagogue communities and their associations without becoming religiously biased.[25] By establishing theological research institutions and degree courses at state universities that are committed to general academic standards, it can exert an indirect influence on the further development of religious cultures, provided that partners willing to cooperate can be found who are prepared to contribute their religious expertise.[26]

10.5 The Fundamental Right of Freedom of Religion under the Basic Law

10.5.1 Scope of Protection of Freedom of Religion and the Importance of Self-Understanding

The central norm of the German constitutional law on religion, the "lex regia", is Article 4 § 1 and § 2 of the Basic Law, the guarantee of religious freedom. It states, "(1) Freedom of faith, freedom of conscience and freedom of religious and worldview beliefs shall be inviolable. (2) The undisturbed practice of religion shall be guaranteed". In jurisprudence and legal practice, a distinction is made between the question of what behaviour a fundamental right generally protects and the freedom that is effectively guaranteed in concrete terms after a comparison with the rights of third parties and public welfare interests defined by the legislator.

In personal terms, it should first be noted that Article 4 § 1 and § 2 is a "human right", not a civil right. Anyone can invoke freedom of religion in Germany, not just citizens.

The general protection of religious freedom, the scope of protection, is extremely broadly defined under the Basic Law. It is the case that the constitutional text distinguishes between belief, confession, and religious practice. However, case law has combined these partial guarantees into a uniform, broadly conceived area of protection. In the words of the Federal Constitutional Court:

> Article 4 § 1 and § 2 of the Basic Law contains a unified fundamental right to be understood extensively [...]. It extends not only to the inner freedom to believe or not to believe [...] but also to the outer freedom to profess and propagate one's faith, to promote one's faith and to persuade others away from their faith [...]. This includes not only ritual acts and the practice and observance of religious customs, but also religious education and other forms of expression of religious and worldview life

25 M. Demel, *Gebrochene Normalität* (Tübingen: Mohr Siebeck, 2011).

26 C. Waldhoff, "Islamische Theologie an staatlichen Hochschulen". In: W. Rüfner, D. Pirson, S. Muckel, M. Germann, E. Friesenhahn (eds.), *Handbuch des Staatskirchenrechts der Bundesrepublik Deutschland* vol. 1 (Berlin: Duncker & Humblodt, 2020): 154–155; H.M. Heinig, *Prekäre Ordnungen historische Prägungen des Religionsrechts in Deutschland* 279.

> [...]. This includes the right of individuals to align their entire behavior with the teachings of their faith and to act in accordance with this conviction, i.e. to live in accordance with their faith; this does not only concern imperative beliefs [...].[27]

In other words, the freedom of religion in the Basic Law guarantees something like a religion-specific freedom of action, in which the religious motivation of an action that can also be interpreted in a non-religious way from the outside is sufficient to open up the scope of protection.[28] This broad understanding of religious freedom is particularly important for religious cultures in which everyday life is determined by religion – for example, through meal rules. The fundamental right to freedom of religion protects the right to align one's entire life with one's own religious beliefs – even (or especially) if these may be alien to the majority society.

The protection of fundamental rights is a significant protection of the individual. Therefore, the self-understanding of the holder of the fundamental right is central for the question of whether a behaviour falls under the freedom of religion, especially since the state itself has no religious competence.[29] The protection of minorities has always played an important role in religious freedom. The religious self-understanding is relevant, on the one hand, in relation to the majority society but, on the other hand, also in conflicts of interpretation within a religious culture.

The religious-cultural ideas of the majority society cannot be decisive in determining the scope of protection. In particular, religious orthodoxy and orthopraxy are also protected, even if a part of society that considers itself enlightened or progressive takes offence. However, holders of fundamental rights must make their self-understanding plausible. When they can fulfil this task, their perspective is decisive. Other religious doctrinal traditions within their religious culture do not reduce the protection of fundamental rights.

To give an example: As a Muslim woman, you can also refer to Islamic clothing practices if these are controversial amongst the believers. In the words of the Federal Constitutional Court:

> When assessing what is to be regarded as the practice of religion and belief in individual cases, the self-understanding of the religious and worldview communities concerned and of the individual holder of fundamental rights must not be overlooked [...]. Muslim women who wear

27 2 BvR 1333/17, *Kopftuch III* [2020] BVerfGE 153, 1 nb. 78.

28 H.M. Heinig, "Religions- und Weltanschauungsfreiheit". In: W. Rüfner, D. Pirson, S. Muckel, M. Germann, E. Friesenhahn (eds.), *Handbuch des Staatskirchenrechts der Bundesrepublik Deutschland* vol. 1 559–613; A. von Ungern-Sternberg, "Religionsverfassungsrecht". In: M. Herdegen (ed.), *Handbuch des Verfassungsrechts: Darstellung in transnationaler Perspektive* (München: Beck, 2021): 1335–1390.

29 M. Morlok, "Art. 4". In: H. Dreier (ed.), *Grundgesetz Kommentar*, vol. 1 (Tübingen: Mohr Siebeck, 2013) nb 60.

> a headscarf tied in the manner typical of their faith can [...] invoke the protection of freedom of religion and belief under Article 4 § 1 and § 2 of the Basic Law. The fact that different views on the so-called covering requirement are held in Islam [...] is irrelevant in this respect, since the religious basis of the choice of clothing is in any case sufficiently plausible in terms of spiritual significance and outward appearance.[30]

The same applies to doctrinal disputes over questions of religious lifestyle among Jews of liberal, conservative and orthodox provinces.

10.5.2 Dimensions of Religious Freedom

According to the Basic Law, all fundamental rights, including freedom of religion, are primarily defensive rights against the state. They protect a sphere of freedom against state interference. However, the Federal Constitutional Court has developed further dimensions of fundamental rights over the course of time: fundamental rights also constituted objective-law principles of the legal system ("system of values"). As such, they would have a transmission effect. For example, fundamental rights values must be taken into account in the interpretation and application of indeterminate legal terms and general clauses, including in the legal relationship between private individuals. In this way, freedom of religion has an impact on employment law when it comes to the contractual relationship between employer and employee.[31] The employer's right to issue instructions is therefore restricted by the employees' freedom of religion: A balance should be struck as far as possible between company requirements and the religious interests of the employee. If, for example, a Muslim employee in a supermarket refuses to put alcoholic drinks on the shelves for reasons of conscience, the employer must endeavour to assign him other tasks. Dismissal is only a secondary consideration.[32] However, if it is foreseeable for the employee at the time the contract is concluded that there will be conflicts of interest, he must disclose these. A Jewish sales employee in a store, for example, cannot unilaterally and without further notice refuse to work on Saturday if it was foreseeable that the store would be open on that day.

In addition, fundamental rights oblige the state to protect the legal interest guaranteed by fundamental rights and to combat interference by third parties. The criminal liability of disturbing the practice of religion (Section 167 StGB) or incitement to hatred against religious minorities that threatens public peace

30 2 BvR 1333/17, *Kopftuch III* [2020]nb. 80.

31 U. Di Fabio, "Art. 4 [Glaubens-, Gewissens- und Bekenntnisfreiheit, Kriegsdienstverweigerung]". In: G. Dürig, R. Herzog, R. Scholz (eds.), *Grundgesetz Kommentar* (München: Beck, 2024), Beck-online, nb. 224; M. Germann, "Art. 4". In: *BeckOnline Kommentar Grundgesetz*, Beck-online, nb. 77.

32 *Kündigung wegen Glaubenskonflikts*, 2 AZR 636/09 [2011] BAGE 137, 164.

(Section 130 StGB), for example, can be understood as a result of the state's duty to protect.[33] However, obligations to protect almost never convey an entitlement to specific state action. The state has a wide margin of discretion and judgement here.

10.5.3 Limits of Religious Freedom

No fundamental right is unlimited. As rights to prevent interference, fundamental rights must be able to be restricted; otherwise, no state order would be possible. In the tradition of Kant, it must be remembered that the freedom of the one finds its limit in the equally justified freedom of the other. Unlike most other fundamental rights, Article 4 § 1 and § 2 of the Basic Law does not contain a reservation of statutory rights, i.e. the parliamentary legislator cannot invoke arbitrary ideas of the common good to justify infringements of this fundamental right. A conflicting constitutional right or value is always required. Conflicting fundamental rights and other legal interests of constitutional status (such as the state objective provisions in Article 20a GG on environmental protection and animal welfare) can justify an interference with religious freedom.

The legal situation is somewhat different in the case of corporative freedom of religion.[34] For the right of self-determination of religious societies, Article 140 GG in conjunction with Article 137 § 3 WRV[35] expressly recognises the barrier of the "law applicable to all".[36] At first glance, this would appear to give the democratic legislator far-reaching scope for intervention. However, as in the case of individual religious freedom, there is another hurdle here too: in both constellations (individual and corporative), restrictions on religious freedom must be brought into an appropriately balanced relationship with freedom itself. Interventions in fundamental rights are subject to the principle of proportionality or (in the case of fundamental rights without statutory reservation) the principle of establishing practical concordance: conflicting rights should be given their relative weight in relation to each other, i.e. collisions should not simply be resolved unilaterally to the detriment of one side. Here, too, the self-image of the fundamental right bearers must be considered when determining the relative weight of their interests. Otherwise, there is a risk of religious interests being filtered, distorted, and marginalised by

33 B. Fateh-Moghadam, *Die religiös-weltanschauliche Neutralität des Strafrechts* (Tübingen: Mohr Siebeck 2019).

34 H.M. Heinig, *Öffentlich-rechtliche Religionsgesellschaften* 593; M. Germann, "Art. 4". In: *BeckOnline Kommentar Grundgeset* nb. 47.

35 Die Verfassung des Deutschen Reichs [1919] RGBl. III, 401–402.

36 *Katholischer Chefarzt*, 2 BvR 661/1 [2014] BVerfGE 137, 273; M. Morlok, "Art. 4" nb.109, 126.

requirements of rational comprehensibility in the context of the proportionality test.[37] At the same time, due to the principle of equal status of the holders of fundamental rights and constitutional rights, one side cannot be given the final decision; this must remain the responsibility of the state and, ultimately, the courts.

However, this also means that religious freedom is not a super fundamental right that supersedes all other rights but can be restricted with good reason. There is always a dispute as to when such a good reason exists – especially when it comes to protecting the interests of a minority religion. The parliamentary legislature is the first to decide whether there are good reasons for restricting religious freedom. The executive always needs a legal basis for interfering with religious freedom. The legislature, for its part, is subject to a principle of proportionality that is handled quite strictly in the practice of the Federal Constitutional Court; in the specific application of a law in individual cases, the particular circumstances must be considered; the concrete application must also be proportionate.

In this way, the principle of proportionality based on fundamental rights sets relevant limits for the democratic majority, the exact course of which then depends on the specific circumstances. The democratic generality of the law and consideration for individual interests as an expression of a kind of individual justice are mediatised by means of the principle of proportionality.

10.6 Individual Protection of Religious Liberty – Selected Legal Issues

The environments in which interference with religious freedom occurs are diverse, as are the legal interests that are used as justification in legal practice. Various cases can be used as examples to show what balancing legal interests in conflicting legal positions actually means in German constitutional law.

A functioning legal system, for example, sometimes requires the cooperation of citizens. Such obligations may then only apply to the extent that they are absolutely necessary: a photo showing the face may be required for official ID cards; a headscarf with no influence on the biometric function of the image, on the other hand, is harmless; an unconditional ban would therefore be unconstitutional.[38] The situation is similar when questioning witnesses in court. For the judicial assessment of evidence, it is necessary to be able to see the facial expressions of the witnesses. Otherwise, the religious clothing of

37 See in different (Canadian) context to this problem B.L. Berger, "Freedom of Religion". In: N. Des Rosiers, P. Macklem, P. Oliver (eds.), *Oxford Handbook of the Canadian Constitution* (Oxford: Oxford University Press, 2017): 755–776. https://doi.org/10.1093/law/9780190664817.003.0036.

38 § 7 Personalausweisverordnung (Verordnung über Personalausweise, eID-Karten für Unionsbürger und Angehörige des Europäischen Wirtschaftsraums und den elektronischen Identitätsnachweis (Personalausweisverordnung – PAuswV, BGBl. I S. 1460 No 54) provides therefore an exemption on religious grounds from the general rule that headgear is forbidden.

witnesses or the audience is of no concern to the court. If the state orders a personal appearance – for example, in a court case – it must take into account the holiday requirements of the parties to the proceedings. For example, a Jewish witness cannot be forced to appear in court on a high Jewish holiday if he can plausibly demonstrate that he wishes to observe the holiday.

The state aim of animal welfare (Article 20a GG) justifies the ban on slaughtering, but exceptions must be possible with regard to the requirements of religious communities, in particular in relation to high religious holidays, whereby animal welfare is then ensured as far as possible through qualification requirements and conditions.[39]

In the funeral sector, the obligation to either cremate a deceased person or bury them in a coffin is intended to protect the environment and the post-mortem dignity of the deceased. Some federal states expressly provide for exceptions to the coffin requirement for religious reasons.[40]

This must be distinguished from the so-called lying-in-place periods, i.e. the reburial of a grave after a certain period of rest. This is not an exemption, but an extended benefit. There is no constitutional right to this in public cemeteries; however, public authorities can extend the legally stipulated resting periods for religious reasons. In addition, religious communities can operate cemeteries. Numerous Jewish synagogue communities make use of this, as do Muslim mosque communities in some cases.

In the absence of a conflicting constitutional legal interest, a general ban on public full-face veils, as known in France (so-called burqa ban), is out of the question in Germany.[41] However, a clear field of vision may be required for the purpose of road safety when driving a motor vehicle or in comparable situations.

The school sector plays a major role in the public perception of religious conflicts. Here, the state's educational mandate in Article 7 § 1 GG competes with the religious freedom of pupils and the right of parents to raise their children religiously in Article 6 § 1 GG in conjunction with Article 4 § 1 and § 2 GG. The state's educational mandate also includes making provisions for the proper functioning of the school system. The right of school staff to follow a religious dress code can therefore be restricted if it poses a concrete threat to school peace. However, a general ban on public school teachers wearing headscarves or kippahs would be unconstitutional, according to the Federal Constitutional Court.

39 *Slaughtering*, 1 BvR 1783/99 [2002] BVerfGE 104, 337; H.M. Heinig, "Art. 4". In: A. Voßkuhle, P.M. Huber (eds.), *Grundgesetz – Kommentar* (München: CH Beck, 2024) nb. 55, 87.

40 See § 11 Bestattungsgesetz Niedersachsen (Gesetz über das Leichen-, Bestattungs- und Friedhofswesen (BestattG) vom 08. 12. 2005 (Nds. GVBl. S. 381); § 13 Bestattungsgesetz Rheinland-Pfalz, GVBl. 1983, 69; § 18 Friedhofs- und Bestattungsgesetz Hessen, GVBl. I 2007, 338.

41 H.M. Heinig, "Art. 4" 82.

An even more far-reaching protection of freedom applies to pupils. The religiously and ideologically neutral state (see Section 10.4.) must accept the religious orientation of pupils; any school conflicts (such as pressure from classmates to observe fasting rules or to dress in a certain way) cannot be dealt with in such a way that clothing with religious connotations is banned. Limits are only reached when religious clothing makes it impossible to achieve the school's goals (e.g. when the entire face is covered by a burka).[42]

Alienating or distancing pupils from their religion of origin is not a legitimate goal of school activities, although the school should create the educational foundations for a responsible and self-determined life. In this respect, the religious wishes of parents and pupils may have to take a back seat, depending on the circumstances. It is difficult to draw precise boundaries, and case law is not free from fluctuations. The general obligation to attend school is now considered to be of paramount importance and generally prevails over religious freedom.[43] This also applies to participation in coeducational sports and swimming lessons or school trips. In the background of the restrictive jurisdiction is the concern about "parallel societies", without it being legally determined what exactly this should mean in a religiously and culturally diversified society that is committed to individual freedom. Applications for exemption from sex education lessons are consistently rejected, but sensitivity to the diversity of sexual-ethical orientations is required by law. In everyday school life, the organisation of lessons does not have to take special account of individual needs such as prayer times. However, school exemptions are required for high religious holidays; these exemptions are partly guaranteed by contract (for Judaism) and partly based on statute or ministerial decrees.[44]

To "compensate" this relatively strict regime (e.g. no right of homeschooling based on religious concerns), the constitution guarantees religious instruction in public schools (which is always tricky to put into practice for minority religions due to organisational requirements such as minimum pupil numbers). But an extensive private religious school system, as in France, has therefore not developed in Germany. However, the right to establish and operate private schools with a religious profile alternative to public schools is expressly guaranteed under constitutional law. There are 16 Jewish schools on this basis in Germany.[45] The establishment of private Muslim schools is still in its infancy.

Also, pupils may not be denied the opportunity to pursue religious needs in the public school system, at least not if this does not disrupt the running of the

42 U. Di Fabio, "Art. 4 [Glaubens-, Gewissens- und Bekenntnisfreiheit, Kriegsdienstverweigerung]" nb.154.

43 A. von Ungern-Sternberg, "Religionsverfassungsrecht" 1335–1390; C. Waldhoff, *Neue Religionskonflikte und staatliche Neutralität* (München: CH Beck 2010).

44 H. Rubin, "Jüdische Religionsausübung im schulischen Alltag". In: *Autonomie und Gesetz* 206–220.

45 "Jüdische Krippen, Kindergärten und Schulen". https://www.bildungsserver.de/onlineressource.html?onlineressourcen_id=59376. Accessed May 3, 2024.

school.[46] Freedom of religion in public schools does not give rise to a right to the provision of a special infrastructure, such as a prayer room. Nevertheless, prayers during breaks are just as permissible in principle as a practice of fasting (even if the latter can be at the expense of school performance and have a correspondingly negative impact on the assessment).

The higher education sector is currently discussing whether the Jewish and Muslim holiday calendars should be taken into account when scheduling examinations.[47] The problem arises for Jews in particular with compulsory examinations on Saturdays. While entitlements to school holidays are extensively regulated by statutory, contractual agreement, or ministerial decree, there are no comparable regulations for the postsecondary education sector.

There can also be a collision between parental educational ideas and the state legal system outside of school. The Basic Law attaches great importance to the parents' right to educate their children. The state's guardianship mentioned in Article 6 § 2 GG comes only into play when the well-being of the child requires state intervention. Therefore, the religiously motivated circumcision of boys is expressly permitted by the legal system (Section 1631d BGB) if it is carried out lege artis, whereas genital mutilation of girls is prohibited by criminal law (Section 226a StGB).[48]

Religiously influenced clothing worn by civil servants cannot simply be attributed to the employer.[49] Wearing a headscarf, a kippah, or a visible cross on the neck on duty in public service is therefore not per se a violation of religious and worldview neutrality of the state.[50] Depending on the area in question, however, other constitutional interests may also be affected, such as the functioning of the judiciary, which is particularly dependent on trust in the neutrality and impartiality of the court system. These functional conditions are primarily ensured by qualification requirements and rules regarding bias. The restraint of individuality in the exercise of the judicial office is also symbolically represented in the obligatory official dress of judges and prosecutors (robes). The Federal Constitutional Court goes so far as to allow the legislator to prohibit the addition of a headscarf or kippah to the official robes.[51] It may be objected that ultimately anti-religious resentment is being rewarded here. Whether the prohibition of a kippah or headscarf for judges and public

46 Critical to the Case Law of the Federal Administrative Court (6 C 20.10 [2011] BVerwGE 141, 223) H.M. Heinig, "Religionsfreiheit im Schul- und Mitgliedschaftsrecht", *Zeitschrift für evangelisches Kirchenrecht* vol. 61, no. 2 (2016): 202.

47 *Die Religionsfreiheit von Jüdinnen und Juden respektieren!: Das nordrhein-westfälische Feiertagsrecht an der Glaubensfreiheit ausrichten!* ([Berlin]: Tikvah Institut, 2023). https://tikvahinstitut.de/wp-content/uploads/Policy-Paper-ReliFrei-NRW_online.pdf. Accessed Mai, 3 2024.

48 M. Germann, "Art. 4". In: *BeckOnline Kommentar Grundgesetz* nb. 50.3.

49 *Kopftuch*, 2 BvR 1436/02 [2003] BVerfGE 108, 282.

50 *Kopftuch*, 2 BvR 1436/02 [2003] BVerfGE 108, 282; *Kopftuchverbot Nordrhein-Westfalen (Kopftuch II)*, 1 BvR 1181/10 [2015] BVerfGE 138, 296.

51 2 BvR 1333/17, *Kopftuch III* [2020].

prosecutors in the courtroom is really necessary to ensure the acceptance of court decisions and the perception of their independence und impartiality would have to be proven in more detail. A blanket assertion, measured against the usual prognosis requirements for justifying encroachments on fundamental rights, cannot actually be sufficient.[52]

The question of religious freedom is particularly sensitive in social contexts that are largely controlled by the state: in addition to the school system just discussed, the military and prisons are worthy of mention. Here, the Basic Law seeks to compensate for the loss of freedom associated with such institutions by guaranteeing chaplaincy. However, consideration is also given to individual concerns and special circumstances, insofar as this is permitted by the purpose of the institution. For example, many Länder statutes stipulate that prisoners must be allowed to follow the food regulations of their religious community and that they may have a reasonable number of religious writings and objects of religious use.[53] If you talk to imams and rabbis who care for Muslim or Jewish prisoners, they sometimes perceive considerable deficits in the enforcement of the law. While prison laws clearly state the religious rights of prisoners, prison administrations repeatedly seem to find it difficult to adequately fulfil these rights.

10.7 Corporative Religious Freedom – Selected Legal Issues

The European Convention on Human Rights accurately states that freedom of religion includes the right to "manifest one's religion or belief … in community with others" (Article 9 § 1 ECHR[54]). Most religious cultures are characterised by processes of community building and insist on communal religious practices. This usually requires a certain degree of organisation. This corporate side of religion is also protected by the Basic Law in terms of freedom. Freedom of religion includes the right to join together with other believers (freedom of religious association).[55] The fundamental right of freedom of religion under Article 4 § 1 and § 2 of the Basic Law applies to religious associations ("religiöse Vereine") and religious societies ("Religionsgesellschaften"). Religious organisations acquire legal personality according to general civil law. Alternatively, religious societies may be granted the rights of a public corporation (Article 140 GG in conjunction with Article 137 § 2 WRV). There is a constitutional

52 H.M. Heinig, "Art. 4" nb. 86.

53 P. Weller, *The Accommodation of Religious Minority Beliefs in Prisons in Germany and the United States*, Doctor Thesis, (Fiesole: EUI, 2020). https://cadmus.eui.eu/bitstream/handle/1814/67090/Weller_2020_LAW.pdf?sequence=1&isAllowed=y. Accessed May 3, 2024.

54 European Convention on Human Rights as amended by Protocols Nos. 11, 14, and 15 supplemented by Protocols Nos. 1, 4, 6, 7, 12, 13, and 16 https://www.echr.coe.int/documents/d/echr/convention_ENG. Accessed November 15, 2024.

55 M. Morlok, "Art. 137 WRV". In: H. Dreier (ed.), *Grundgesetz Kommentar*, vol. 3 (Tübingen: Mohr Siebeck, 2018) nb. 26.

entitlement to this status if the association is law-abiding and offers a guarantee of durability. However, the German legal system does not have a special recognition or licensing procedure like in other European countries.

Insofar as the organisation serves the general cultivation of religion, it is referred to as a "religious society" in the technical legal sense. Religious organisations that only realise partial purposes form "religious associations" (see also Section 10.2.). The terminology is characterised by the rational law of the Enlightenment, i.e. it does not follow a theological doctrine of the church (ecclesiology). However, it has clearly developed against the background of the social structure of the Christian churches: the churches themselves are religious societies, their charitable institutions are religious associations.

Organised Judaism in Germany has adapted to these types of organisation. Most synagogue communities are organised as corporations under public law due to the expanded organisational possibilities offered by this legal institute. Newly founded communities, such as liberal ones, are initially constituted according to general association law.

The situation is different regarding organised Islam. It is not easy to classify the organisations found here (in the sociological sense) under the legal category of "religious society" (see also Section 10.9.).[56] The precise assessment of some Islamic associations is the subject of important court decisions.[57] These work out that the constitution does not require "ecclesiasticalisation" but rather the self-organisation of believers for the all-sided cultivation of religion. This requirement is based on legitimate secular legal concerns: the safeguarding of negative religious freedom and the religious and worldview neutrality of the state in cooperative relationships. In the case of religious societies, the state knows who belongs to it and for whom it can speak. Such self-organisation can also be based on a division of tasks, as is common in Islamic umbrella structures, as long as the top level also fulfils religious functions of sufficient importance.

One may doubt that the German case law to this topic is consistently convincing.[58] Anyone observing the political debate and administrative practice might also occasionally get the impression that the discussion about the legal status of umbrella organisations takes the place of the problems that really need to be addressed: the external control of religious organisations by foreign government authorities, the hybrid character of organisations in which

56 H.M. Heinig, "Religionsgemeinschaft/Religionsgesellschaft': Herkunft, aktuelle Bedeutung und Zukunft einer religionsverfassungsrechtlichen Zentralkategorie", *Zeitschrift für evangelisches Kirchenrecht* vol. 64, no. 1 (2019): 1. https://www.doi.org/10.1628/zevkr-2019-0001.

57 6 C 2/04 [2005] BVerwGE 123, 49; *Anspruch islamischer Dachverbände auf Einrichtung von Religionsunterricht an öffentlichen Schulen Beschlus*, 6 B 94/18 [2018] BVerwG, NVwZ 2019, 236.

58 Critical observations: D. zu Hohenlohe, "Islamische Dachverbände als Religionsgesellschaften – ein Zwischenbericht", *Zeitschrift für evangelisches Kirchenrecht* vol. 64, no. 1 (2019): 79. https://www.doi.org/10.1628/zevkr-2019-0005.

party-political and religious activities ultimately merge, the question of adherence to the law and the constitution, and sufficient social power in light of the weakly developed membership structure.

In addition to the formation of religious associations, it goes without saying that the freedom of religion also protects the internal organisation according to faith and the organisation's specific activities. In consideration of religious freedom, the state may also have to accept deviations from the requirements of general association law in the organisational structure.[59]

In addition to the regulation and management of own affairs in an administrative-technical sense by religious societies, freedom of religious activities also includes the entire area of joint religious affairs, from the holding of religious services, religious teachings and missionary activities to charitable and religiously motivated social and youth work.[60]

However, there are also limits to corporative freedom, which are generally defined by the non-religious provisions that apply to all: buildings used for religious worship must comply with public building law. Fire protection and emission control regulations must be observed for public events. Data protection law must be observed for missionary activities. The provisions of burial law apply to the operation of a cemetery (see also Section 10.6 on this topic).

10.8 Equal Treatment and Non-discrimination Rules

Traditionally, equal treatment provisions are of particular importance for minority religions. The Basic Law contains a variety of equal treatment provisions that are intended to counteract discrimination on religious and ideological grounds: The very guarantee of equal freedom of religion has a fundamentally egalitarian effect. In addition, the Basic Law consistently refers to religious communities or religious societies in the area of corporative law on religion. The terminology is deliberately designed to be inclusive. For example, all religious communities, not just the two larger Christian churches, are entitled to religious instruction in public schools (Article 7 § 3 sentence 1 GG), the legal form of a public corporation (Article 140 GG in conjunction with Article 137 § 5 sentence 2 WRV) or access to state institutions for the purpose of chaplaincy (Article 140 GG in conjunction with Article 141 WRV).

State discrimination on grounds of religion or belief is also expressly prohibited by Article 3 § 3 GG and Article 33 § 3 GG and Article 140 GG in conjunction with Article 136 § 2 WRV. Article 136 § 1 and 2 WRV (equal access to state offices; equal exercise of civil and civic rights).

These guarantees of equality, which are initially binding on the state, also have an impact on civil law in accordance with the aforementioned statements on the dimensions of fundamental rights (Section 10.5). Therefore, the

59 *Bahá'í case*, 2 BvR 263/86 [1991] BVerfGE 83, 341.
60 M. Morlok, "Art. 137 WRV" nb. 48.

constitutional prohibitions of discrimination on religious and worldview grounds are also relevant for general contract law, labour law, and tenancy law.

However, this so-called indirect third-party effect of fundamental rights is now overlaid by provisions of European law. As a result of the overlay of European law, equality issues are increasingly moving to the centre of the law on religion.[61] Economics-related prohibitions of discrimination have always played a prominent role in the law of the European Union; in the course of its development into a political union, this path has continued: the only explicit competence of the Union in terms of religion policy concerns antidiscrimination measures (Article 19 TFEU[62]). Directives were passed on this basis, which were implemented in Germany through the General Equal Treatment Act. This also explicitly covers indirect discrimination, i.e. provisions and practices that are religiously neutral but regularly have a religion-specific effect.

Union law also has an impact on the freedoms protected under constitutional law on religion, such as the question of the extent to which religious communities may make religious affiliation a prerequisite for establishing an employment relationship: The European Court of Justice has adopted a more restrictive stance here than was previously customary in Germany under the influence of the case law of the Federal Constitutional Court – with significant consequences for legal practice, considering that the two churches are among the largest employers in Germany, particularly thanks to the refinancing of charitable activities by the welfare state.[63] Although there were already a large number of Muslim employees in church social institutions before this, it has now been clarified by the courts that a specific religious affiliation can only be required in exceptional cases (such as responsibility for religious education or for the religious profile of an institution), but not in general for all doctors, nursing staff, office staff and other employees. The case law also binds Jewish and Muslim organisations.

10.9 Cooperation between Organised Islam and the State

As mentioned in Section 10.4, the German separation of organised religion and state is characterised by openness and a willingness to cooperate. In the words of the Federal Constitutional Court:

> The religious and worldview neutrality required of the state is … not to be understood as distancing in the sense of a strict separation of state and church, but as an open and overarching attitude that equally promotes freedom of belief for all denominations.[64]

61 A. Tischbirek, "Ein europäisches Staatskirchenrecht?", *Der Staat* vol. 58, no. 4 (2019): 621.
62 Treaty on the Functioning of the European Union [2012] OJ C 326, 47–390.
63 C-414/16, *Egenberger* [2018] ECLI:EU:C:2018:257.
64 *Headscarf Decision*, 6 C 20/10 [2011] BVerfGE 108, 282, 300.

This openness to cooperation of course also applies to organised Islam. In principle, the entire spectrum of cooperation is open to organised Islam: the operation of institutions that provide services financed by the welfare state (care for the elderly, hospitals, kindergartens); the establishment of Muslim religious instruction at public schools; research and teaching of Islamic theology at state universities; the operation of a private higher education institution run by a Muslim organisation; chaplaincy in prisons, in state hospitals, in the German armed forces; the operation of a cemetery with a special religious profile; participation in supervisory bodies of public broadcasting and the exercise of some rights to broadcast; and the possibility of collecting membership fees in the form of a tax from religious societies organised under public law.

However, legal cooperation requirements must also be met. In some constellations, for example, there must be a "religious society" in the technical legal sense (as in Article 7 § 3 GG, Article 140 GG in conjunction with Article 137 § 5 sentence 2 WRV and Article 141 WRV) – and then the academic dispute as to the conditions under which mosque associations and Islamic umbrella organisations constitute such a society takes on very practical significance (see Section 10.2 and 10.7).

Nevertheless, in order to achieve progress in cooperation, politicians sometimes try to help themselves with tricks and auxiliary constructions. For example, the agreement between Hamburg and Muslim associations simply refers to the Islamic contracting parties as "Islamic religious societies". On a symbolic level, this was intended to signal recognition, albeit without any constitutional relevance: the treaty was not ratified in the form of a law (unlike concordats and Protestant state-church treaties and the state treaties with the Jewish associations) and, due to the primacy of the constitution, such a treaty cannot dispose of constitutionally defined characteristics.

The "Beirat" models developed for Islamic religious education and Islamic theology at state universities are particularly noteworthy.[65] The translation with "advisory board" would be misleading, because it is precisely not about advice but rather about decisive participation rights in theological questions regarding staff decisions, curricula, study, and examination regulations, which otherwise fall to a religious society. In some cases, the religious boards have found explicit statutory protection. Their appeal lies in the fact that the participation rights of Islamic organisations are structured in such a way that their character as a religious society in the technical legal sense is not decisive. Ultimately, however, it remains an open question as to whether religious education organised in this way constitutes religious instruction within the meaning of Article 7 § 3 GG or an aliud. In other words, whether it is at the disposal of the legislator.

In addition to the question of access to religious constitutional institutions, other problems and solutions play an important role in policy on religion. In

65 C. Schmischke, *Das Beiratsmodell* (Göttingen: Göttinger Universitätsverlag, 2018).

2006, the German government founded the German Islam Conference as a forum for dialogue (involving a wide range of state and civil society actors). Similar formats can also be found at state and municipal levels. In the wind shadow created by the relationships of trust established in this way, various forms of state project funding and other ways of cooperation have been established. The federal government will foreseeably step up its efforts to contribute to the creation of an Islamic welfare association. It is also endeavouring to establish a Muslim military chaplaincy – and, indirectly, to enable imam training in Germany following a degree in Islamic theology at German universities.

Here, however, as in all constitutional law on religion, the belief-neutral state is dependent on partners who are willing and able to cooperate in order to fill the guiding principle of an integrative and open separation with life. The ability to cooperate, depending on the area and scope, includes a certain degree of professional organisation, a certain social power, a sufficient guarantee of adherence to the law and the constitution (in particular respect for human dignity; recognition of the fundamental state structure principles of Article 20 GG as a binding political order in Germany; adoption of the basic principles of constitutional law on religion, such as the separation of state and religious organisations; and respect for religious freedom, including the right of all people to change or abandon their religion), and an organisational structure that enables sufficient religious autonomy of the believers – in contrast to primarily political control by a foreign state for the purpose of diaspora politics or by a foreign political party.[66] This last aspect in particular is difficult to define precisely in legal practice. The federal and state governments set different legal priorities when dealing with the guiding legal doctrines laid down in the Basic Law, supported, by the way, by very heterogeneous expert advice from legal scholars so that the impression of a consistent administrative practice that strictly follows the constitutional obligations does not arise.

To summarise, one can say: the cooperation of state authorities at the federal level, in 16 federal states, and their municipal level with "the Islam" in its organisational diversity and multifaceted spiritual movements oscillates between goodwill; constructive help for sufficient cooperation skills, awkwardness, and uncertainty; consideration for sensitivities critical to Islam not intended or recognised by constitutional law; and very tangible security concerns with regard to Islamic threats to internal security.

66 Critical observations: V. Beck, "Religionspolitik zur Verwirklichung von Freiheit und Gleichheit der Religion". In: K. Abmeier, A. Jacobs, T. Köhler (eds.), *Rechtliche Optionen für Kooperationen zwischen deutschem Staat und muslimischen Gemeinschaften* (Münster: Aschendorff Verlag, 2019): 55–70.

10.10 Cooperation between Organised Jews and the State

In contrast, it becomes clear how different the situation is when it comes to the state's cooperation with organised Jewry in Germany. Three aspects are particularly noteworthy.

Synagogue communities and their associations (see Section 10.2) are quite obviously "religious societies" in the technical legal sense. There is no comparable debate to the one about the legal status of Muslim organisations. As in most cases, synagogue communities and their associations are corporations under public law. The state offers to collect membership fees in the form of a tax. In addition, special exemptions or considerations are granted in numerous areas of law in connection with the public law status. For example, religious societies under public law are automatically recognised as providers of child and youth welfare services, and in planning urban development, special consideration must be given to their interests.

Against the backdrop of the Shoah, the synagogue communities and their associations receive considerable financial funding from the federal and state governments based on treaties[67] (e.g. 22 Mio € per annum federal funding; 10 Mio. € per annum in Baden-Württemberg; 6,6 Mio per annum in Hessen). This is not limited to the subsidising of individual cultural, social and integration projects, as is the case with Islamic organisations, but is provided in a comprehensive form to support all tasks, including specifically religious activities. However, it is also designed to cover the considerable financial requirements for security measures for Jewish institutions in the face of anti-Semitic threats. Just how real these threats are was seen in Halle in 2019, when an armed assassin tried to break into a Jewish community celebration to indiscriminately kill as many people as possible.

As mentioned earlier, the Jewish community in Germany is small (approximately 100,000 members out of a population of 83 million). In different constellations, however, the German state is attempting to make restitution for the crimes committed during the Nazi era by placing the Jewish communities in a similar position they would have been in without the attempt to eradicate them.[68] For example, Jewish representatives are involved in broadcasting councils and other supervisory bodies in which civil society is to be represented in its diversity (although far larger religious communities are not represented).

It can also be observed in other places that the cooperative instruments of the law on religion are to be used as comprehensively as possible. For example, there is an institute for (liberal and conservative) Jewish theology at the University of Potsdam; and a Jewish university in Heidelberg, which is supported by the Central Council of Jews in Germany. There are also private Jewish schools, whose attendance satisfies state compulsory education

67 J. Lutz-Bachmann, "Gleich oder doch anders?" 127–145; J. Lutz-Bachmann, *Mater rixarum?*.
68 M. Demel, *Gebrochene Normalität*.

requirements (see Section 10.6), and day care centres in several federal states, albeit on a manageable scale (16 Jewish schools, 20 Jewish day care centres). In school practice, efforts can be observed to make Jewish religious instruction possible regardless of the low number of participants – for example, by offering it outside of the timetable and in the rooms of synagogue congregations across the year groups.

10.11 Conclusion

Under the Basic Law, German case law on religious liberty shows currently a tendency in favour of the individual-protective dimension of religious freedom. The fundamental right is not subject to a simple reservation by law. Only conflicting constitutional interests justify any interference with this fundamental right at all. In other words, interferences with religious freedom cannot be made in pursuit of arbitrary political ends but must serve a constitutional good. This tends to set higher hurdles for democratic majority decisions than for other encroachments on fundamental rights.

Any infringement of religious freedom must nevertheless have a basis in parliamentary law, and it must also be proportionate – even in individual cases. The intensity of judicial scrutiny regarding proportionality thus becomes the decisive adjusting screw for the constitutional control of religiously based exceptional claims. The Federal Constitutional Court practice – in international comparison – is an intensive proportionality test, which has repeatedly become decisive, particularly in cases relating to Islam.

However, the court also emphasises the leeway that the democratic legislator has in the accommodation of religion. The parliament has the right of first access when it comes to the concretisation of the conflict constellation between different rights and constitutional interests. In real life, legislative practice proves to be quite volatile in questions of exemption clauses for religion, dependent on political coincidences, while basic principles of jurisdiction on religious freedom (broad scope; importance of individual self-understanding; limitation of infringements by the proportionality test) prove to be relatively stable, despite all the changes in religious cultures and social practices (individualisation, secularisation, pluralisation).

Muslims tend to suffer particularly from this volatility in the political process because anti-Muslim stereotypes and resentments are being introduced into the democratic process under the impression of growing right-wing populism. This development becomes a litmus test for the value of the promises of equality and freedom that the constitution makes to Muslims and Jews, as well as to all other believers and non-believers. In too many areas, the legal reality, the law in action, is still too far away from the situation intended by the constitution, the constitutional law in the books. This also has to do with blurred boundaries to anti-constitutional political Islamism under the organised Muslims, with their lack of professionalism in the self-organisation but also with hesitancy and deficits in enforcement on the part of state authorities that are questionable in terms of the rule of law. The example of organised Judaism in Germany shows that things can be different when dealing with religious minorities, that the state can also come up with wise solutions and sustainable cooperation based on the benevolence demanded by religious freedom. However, it remains to be seen how long this role model will last. How resilient will the far-reaching consensus in Germany among the political elite be about that there should be no room for anti-Semitism in political communication and political decision-making? The traditional ("bourgeois" and far-right) and immigrant (often Israel-related) anti-Semitism might put the current arrangement of accommodating Jewish religious needs under increased pressure.

11 Recent Developments in Belgian Case Law on the Regulation of Relations between the State and Religions

Stéphanie Wattier

Abstract

After highlighting the constitutional framework governing the relations between the State and religions in Belgium, the chapter aims to analyse major recent case law in that ambit, and, more particularly, the issues of "Belgian *laïcité*", the ban on the full veil in the public space, religious and moral courses in public schools, the Covid crisis, and ritual slaughter. In a context of secularisation of Belgian society, the number of rulings on religious matters is paradoxically increasing, especially where the Islamic and Jewish religions are concerned.

Keywords

Belgium; constitutional framework; case law; courts; Constitutional Court; Council of State; recent evolutions; secularism; *laïcité*; burqa law ban; religious courses; Covid crisis; ritual slaughter

11.1 Introduction

A series of preliminary observations are necessary in order to propose an assessment and to understand the scope of the legal decisions handed down in recent years on the regulation of relations between the State and religions in Belgian case law.

The first observation can be presented in the form of a paradox: while Belgian society is becoming more secular – as is the case in most European countries – there is a growing tendency to go to court invoking the violation of religious freedom. This can also be seen in the case law of the European Court of Human Rights, which has become increasingly abundant since 1993, when the *Kokkinakis v. Greece*[1] judgement was handed down and considered to mark a major turning point in that area.

1 *Kokkinakis v. Greece*, 14307/88 [1993], ECLI:CE:ECHR:1993:0525JUD001430788.

DOI: 10.4324/9781003423294-16

The second finding – connected to the first one – is quantitative: the decisions handed down by Belgian courts on matters of religion and belief in recent years number in the hundreds. They affect all types of courts, i.e., all the judicial courts, the administrative courts (mainly the Council of State) and the Constitutional Court.

The third observation relates to the religions involved in the cases dealt with by the judges: in recent years, a very large number of court decisions concern Islam – and to a lesser extent Judaism – compared with other religions (like Catholicism, which was the largely dominant religion when Belgium became independent in 1830). In this respect, it should be noted that a recent study by researchers at UCLouvain revealed that Islam has become the second religion in Belgium, after Catholicism.[2] Moreover, according to a research of the Pew Research Center, it is estimated that by 2030, there will be more than 10% of Muslims in Belgium,[3] which means an increase of 80% compared to 2010 (638,000 Muslims in Belgium at that time, itself based on an estimation). The difficulty with these figures is that, as in a number of other European countries, censuses are prohibited in Belgium, so they are highly imprecise. Several sociologists of religion therefore urge caution when using these figures.[4]

In the light of these observations, this chapter focuses on some of the major decisions handed down in recent years concerning the regulation of relations between states and religions in Belgian case law (Section 11.3), insofar as it is impossible to analyse all the jurisprudence handed down. Before doing so and to contextualise the analysis, it briefly reviews the constitutional framework governing these relations (Section 11.2).

11.2 Constitutional Framework Governing the Relations between the State and Religions

Adopted on February 7, 1831, the Belgian Constitution[5] does not expressly specify the type of relations to be maintained between religions and the State. However, four articles of the Constitution can be used to characterise these relations: Articles 19, 20, 21, and 181.

2 It was a survey on values and the quest for meaning carried out by Olivier Servais (UCLouvain) and Justine Vleminckx (UCLouvain), conducted by Sonecom among a sample of 650 French-speaking Belgians aged 16 and over between May and July 2019. For more details, see A.-F. de Beaudrap, “Les Belges sont croyants, mais pratiquants peu réguliers”. https://www.cathobel.be/2021/02/les-belges-sont-croyants-mais-pratiquants-peu-reguliers. Accessed December 6, 2023.

3 “Event Transcript: The Future of the Global Muslim Population”. https://www.pewresearch.org/religion/2011/01/27/md2-event-transcript/. Accessed December 13, 2023.

4 C. Torrekens, “La présence musulmane en Belgique”. https://www.laicite.be/magazine-article/la-presence-musulmane-en-belgique/. Accessed December 13, 2023.

5 The Belgian Constitution, Legal Affairs and Parliamentary Documentation Department of the Belgian House of Representatives, D/2021/4686/04. https://www.dekamer.be/kvvcr/pdf_sections/publications/constitution/GrondwetUK.pdf. Accessed October 27.

More precisely, Article 19 of the Constitution guarantees freedom of religion, stating that "freedom of worship, its public practice and freedom to demonstrate one's opinions on all matters are guaranteed, but offences committed when this freedom is used may be punished". Article 20 specifies that "no one can be obliged to contribute in any way whatsoever to the acts and ceremonies of a religion or to observe its days of rest". Article 21, first paragraph stipulates that

> the State does not have the right to intervene either in the appointment or in the installation of ministers of any religion whatsoever or to forbid these ministers from corresponding with their superiors, from publishing the acts of these superiors, but, in this latter case, normal responsibilities as regards the press and publishing apply.

Those three articles have never been modified since 1831, except concerning the new numeration of the Constitution that took place in 1994. The three principles they contain apply to all religions, whether or not they are recognised by the Belgian State. In 1831, Articles 19, 20 and 21 very well reflected the position of the Parliament and the population vis-à-vis religions. In broad terms, the Constitution of 1831 was a compromise between Catholic members of the National Congress – who wanted freedom of religion and autonomy of churches (Articles 19 and 21) – and Liberals who wanted the right not to be obliged to believe in or manifest membership of any religion (Article 20) and the priority of civil over religious marriage ceremonies (Article 21(2)).[6]

As far as the funding of recognised religions is concerned, Article 181 of the Constitution mandates the State to finance their ministers. Concretely, this article specifies that "the salaries and pensions of ministers of religion are paid for by the State; the amounts required are charged annually to the budget". Six religions are currently recognised and financed by the Belgian State: Catholicism, Protestantism, Judaism, Anglicanism, Islam, and Orthodoxy.

Catholicism and Protestantism have been recognised ever since the independence of Belgium (18 Germinal year X and April 18, 1802, Act). Judaism was organised by three decrees of 17 March 1806 and Anglicanism by the royal decrees of 18 and 24 April 1835. For a century and a half, there were only four recognised religions, before the Belgian legislator decided to recognise Islam and Orthodoxy. To understand why Islam and Orthodoxy have been recognised, we need to remember that the 1960s saw a massive influx of immigrants in response to the labour shortage experienced by Belgium at the time following the two World Wars. Most immigrant workers

6 Art. 21(2) of the Belgian Constitution (https://www.dekamer.be/kvvcr/pdf_sections/publications/constitution/GrondwetUK.pdf. Accessed October 26, 2024) states that "a civil wedding should always precede the blessing of the marriage, apart from the exceptions to be established by the law if needed".

came from the Mediterranean Basin: mainly Morocco,[7] Turkey, Greece, Spain, and Italy. Unlike the Italian and Spanish workers, who were able to benefit from the services of ministers of Catholic religion (as most of them were Catholics), immigrant workers from Morocco, Turkey, and Greece did not have this option. As the majority were, respectively, Muslim and Orthodox, they practised religions that were not recognised by the Belgian legislator and therefore had no ministers or places of worship funded by the State. The legislator was then convinced that recognition of their religion would enable Muslim and Orthodox immigrants "to feel more integrated"[8] since this recognition would mean that they would have ministers and places of worship funded by the State. The legislator therefore recognised the Islamic faith in the law of July 19, 1974, and the Orthodox faith in the law of April 17, 1985.

As regards the constitutional principles, Articles 19, 20, 21, and 181 of the Constitution taken together govern "church-state relations" and are

> an early example of Belgian political tradition of consensus. Though the bright, young, liberal, and sometimes anticlerical politicians wanted to propagate modern freedoms, they also wanted to retain absolute governmental supervision of the church. Catholic politicians and the Belgian church, however, were unwilling to allow their voices to go unheard.[9]

The Belgian Constitution is unique in that it henceforth recognises and funds non-denominational philosophical organisations in addition to recognised religions. More precisely, in 1993, a second paragraph was added to Article 181 of the Constitution. The adoption of this paragraph was the result of a political evolution that had begun in 1980. Article 181 of the Constitution had been opened for revision in 1978, in 1981, and in 1987 without being effectively revised. Then, a new proposition had been introduced on the basis of Resolution 36/15 of the United Nations General Assembly of October 28, 1981, relative to the elimination of all forms of intolerance and discrimination based on religion or conviction. This proposition showed the importance of pluralism in Belgium and the necessity to finance non-confessional organisations. After being discussed for years in the Parliament, new Article 18, § 2, of the Constitution was adopted with a quasi-unanimity in 1993. Quickly after

7 See H. Bousetta, M. Martiniello, "L'immigration marocaine en Belgique: du travailleur immigré au citoyen transnational". In: K. Bichara, C. Roosens (eds.), *Belges et Arabes. Voisins distants, partenaires nécessaires* (Louvain: Presses Universitaires de Louvain, 2004): 67–81.

8 Report by the Commission of Justice on the proposition of law of 11 December 1973 recognising the Islamic faith and secular philosophy, ord. sess. 1973–1974, no. 104, p. 2.

9 R. Torfs, "Church and State in France, Belgium, and the Netherlands: Unexpected Similarities and Hidden Differences", *Brigham Young University Law Review* no. 4 (1996): 949.

this vote, the so-called organised *laïcité* asked to be recognised as a non-confessional organisation. This recognition took place through the June 21, 2002, Act. For the time being, it is the only recognised organisation. For many years now, the Belgian Buddhist Union has asked to be recognised on the basis of Article 181 § 2, of the Constitution. Although preliminary projects have been passed on several occasions by the relevant minister of justice, none of them has yet come to fruition.[10]

11.3 Major Recent Case Law on the Regulation of Relations between the State and Religions

Over the past 15 years, certain decisions handed down by Belgium's supreme courts (essentially the Council of State and the Constitutional Court) have had a greater impact on the jurisdictional landscape than others concerning the relations between the State and religions. We propose to focus on five issues in particular – namely, Belgian *laïcité* (secularism; Section 11.3.1.), the ban on the full veil in the public space (Section 11.3.2.), religious and moral courses in public schools (Section 11.3.3.), the Covid crisis (Section 11.3.4.), and ritual slaughter (Section 11.3.5.). The decisions are presented in chronological order.

11.3.1 The Belgian Laïcité

The French *laïcité* and the Belgian *laïcité* are often confused. A ruling by the Belgian Council of State on December 21, 2010, is useful in trying to better understand the difference between these two concepts. More specifically, in a case that initially concerned the wearing of the Islamic veil, the Council of State stated that "the Belgian Constitution has not established the Belgian State as a *laïc* State. The concepts of *laïcité*, a philosophical conception among others, and neutrality are distinct".[11] In other words, the French *laïcité* (secularism) can be described as political secularism insofar as it is a principle of constitutional rank. Article 1 of the French Constitution states that "France shall be an indivisible, secular (*laïque*), democratic and social Republic". In Belgium, by contrast, *laïcité* is best described as "philosophical" because *laïcité* or *organised laïcité* (those two are words synonyms) is an organisation that is defined as

> a non-denominational community [...] recognised and organised by law [...] for those who do not participate in any religion, who do not wish

10 The last preliminary project for its recognition was adopted by the Council of Ministers in March 2023, but Buddhism is still awaiting a vote by the Federal Parliament, which is competent to recognise new religions and philosophies.

11 Ruling of Belgian Council of State, 210.000 [2010], 6.7.2 (unofficial translation).

> to establish a privileged relationship with a deity in their way of life, and who therefore wish to organise certain aspects of life that are usually regulated by a religion, excluding any reference to religion.[12]

This definition can also be applied to any non-confessional philosophical organisation, such as Buddhism, which is currently awaiting recognition by the legislator.

The Belgian *laïcité* is an organisation recognised by the law – in this case that of June 21, 2002 – which receives public funding from the State in the same way as the other six recognised religions. In 1993, the Constitution was revised to include a second paragraph in Article 181, which now allows non-confessional philosophical organisations to be recognised by law and to have their "delegates" funded by the State in the same way as ministers of religions.

The ambiguity that exists between the political *laïcité* of France and the philosophical *laïcité* of Belgium regularly raises the question of inserting the principle of *laïcité* – this time political – in the Belgian Constitution.[13] However, Belgium remains legally very different from France on one important point that seems difficult to reconcile with the political version of *laïcité*, – namely, the public funding of recognised religions. While the Belgian States funds six recognised religions, the 1905 French law of separation prohibits direct public funding of any religion (with the exception of Alsace Moselle, which remains under the Concordat regime).

11.3.2 Ban on Wearing Full-Face Veils in the Public Space

Following in the footsteps of its French neighbour a few months earlier, the Belgian legislator passed a law on June 1, 2011, "prohibiting the wearing of any clothing which totally or mainly conceals the face". Even if the law does not expressly say so, a reading of the preparatory work reveals that the intention was to ban the wearing of the full Muslim veil and, more specifically, the burqa and the niqab. In the same sense, the law also states that it does not apply to

12 Project of law of December 10, 2001, on the Central Council of Non-Confessional Philosophical Communities in Belgium, delegates and institutions responsible for managing the material and financial interests of recognised non-confessional philosophical communities, Doc. parl., Ch. repr., sess. ord. 2001–2002, n°1556/001, p. 4.

13 An entire dossier was devoted to the specific nature of Belgian *laïcité*, how it differs from the French system and whether the principle of political *laïcité* should be – or not – enshrined in the Belgian Constitution. See X. Delgrange (ed.), "Les débats autour de l'inscription du principe de laïcité politique dans la Constitution belge", Cahiers du CIRC vol. 4 (2020). https://www.circ.usaintlouis.be/wp-content/uploads/2018/09/Cahier-du-CIRC-3-3.pdf. Accessed October 27, 2024.

festive events, such as carnivals. The law was quickly nicknamed "anti-burqa" or "anti-niqab" law.

More concretely, this law inserted the following new Article 563*bis* into the Belgian Criminal Code:

> Persons who, unless otherwise provided by law, appear in a place that is accessible to the public with their faces completely or partially covered or hidden, such as not to be identifiable, shall be liable to a fine of between fifteen and twenty-five euros and imprisonment of between one and seven days, or only one of those sanctions. However, paragraph 1 hereof shall not concern persons who are present in a place that is accessible to the public with their faces completely or partially covered or hidden where this is provided for by employment regulations or by an administrative ordinance in connection with festive events.[14]

Immediately after its publication in the *Official Journal* (*Moniteur belge*), the Law was challenged before the Constitutional Court. The Muslim applicants sought to have the Law annulled on the grounds that it was contrary to Article 19 of the Constitution (freedom of religion) read in conjunction with Article 9 of the European Convention on Human Rights. In its ruling no. 145/2012 of December 6, 2012, the Constitutional Court ruled against the applicants and validated the law, deeming it to comply with the Constitution. The Court validates the threefold legitimate objective of "public safety, equality between men and women and a certain conception of 'living together' in society". According to the Court, "[s]uch objectives are legitimate and fall within the category of those enumerated in Article 9 of the European Convention on Human Rights, namely the maintenance of public safety, the prevention of disorder and the protection of the rights and freedoms of others".[15] It should be noted, however, that the European Court of Human Rights, in its landmark decision *S.A.S v. France* – concerning the French law banning the wearing of the full veil, in which Belgium was an intervening party – held that only "living together" could be considered a legitimate objective relating to the protection of the rights and freedoms of others.

14 This traduction of new Art. 563*bis* of the Criminal Code comes from: *S.A.S. v France*, 43835/11, § 41, ECLI:CE:ECHR:2014:0701JUD004383511.

15 Belgian Constitutional Court, 145/2012 [2012], B.18 (unoffical translation).

Like the ruling of the European Court of Human Rights, the Belgian Constitutional Court's decision has been commented by many authors,[16] and it would be impossible to summarise the content of the doctrinal differences on this subject here. The main highlight to remember is that the wearing of the full veil in the Belgian public space is now a criminal offence, with the sole exception of places of worship, about which the law said nothing but which the Constitutional Court considered should be subject to a reservation of interpretation. It is hard to imagine that the full veil could be banned from places of worship, especially Muslim ones.

To complete the analysis of the Belgian "burqa ban Law", it is interesting to note that the concept of *vivre ensemble* was initially used by the French government to emphasise that "voluntary and systematic concealment of the face is problematic because it is quite simply incompatible with the fundamental requirements of 'living together' in French society".[17] Then, this notion was taken up by the Belgian legislator and affirmed by the Belgian Constitutional Court, which held that

> the individuality of every subject of law (*sujet de droit*) in a democratic society is inconceivable without his or her face, a fundamental element thereof, being visible. [...] [I]t was entitled to take the view that the creation of human relationships, being necessary for living together in society, was rendered impossible by the presence in the public sphere, which quintessentially concerned the community, of persons who concealed this fundamental element of their individuality.[18]

Even if the *vivre ensemble* is not a legal concept that would be listed among the legitimate aims of Paragraph 2 of Articles 8 and 9 of the European Convention on Human Rights to justify a limitation to freedom, the Court finds that the "burqa ban Law" can be regarded "as proportionate to the aim pursued, namely the preservation of the conditions of 'living together' as an element of

16 See, among many others, L.-L. Christians, S. Minette, S. Wattier, "Le visage du sujet de droit: la burqa entre religion et sécurité", *Journal des Tribunaux* (2013): 234–245; N. Renuart, "Brevet de conventionnalité pour l'interdiction du port du voile intégral dans l'espace public. Commentaire de l'arrêt de Grande Chambre rendu dans l'affaire S.A.S. contre France (1er juillet 2014)", *Chroniques de droit public* (2013): 440–450; S. Ouald-Chaib, "Grote Kamer EHRM velt arrest over boerkaverbod", *Tijdschrift voor Mensenrechten* (2014): 15–16; C. Ruet, "L'interdiction du voile intégral dans l'espace public devant la Cour européenne: la voie étroite d'un équilibre", *La Revue des droits de l'homme. Actualités Droits-Libertés* (2014). https://doi.org/10.4000/revdh.862; Y. García Ruiz, "Convivencia y símbolos religiosos en Europa tras la sentencia "SAS c. Francia" del Tribunal Europeo de Derechos Humanos", *Revista general de derecho europeo* no. 35 (2015): item 415712.

17 See *Exposé des motifs*, Assemblée nationale de France, projet de loi n° 2520 (May 10, 2010), quoted by *S.A.S. v. France*, 43835/11 [2014] § 25.

18 Belgian Constitutional Court, 145/2012 [2012] B.21 (unofficial translation).

the 'protection of the rights and freedoms of others'"[19] in the same vein as the Belgian Constitutional Court.

Incidentally, after several years of the coronavirus crisis and the imposition of the wearing of masks in many public places, we might also wonder about the consistency of the restrictions in a law such as the burqa ban on human rights.

11.3.3 Religious Courses and Moral Lessons in Public Schools

Ruling no. 34/2015 of March 12, 2015, handed down by the Constitutional Court[20] is undoubtedly an important ruling of those recent years since it is at the root of a revolution in official education in the French Community. On this subject, it should be briefly recalled that Belgium is made up of three communities (Flemish-, French-, and German-speaking) and that since 1988 they have had sole competence for education. This judgement of 2015 was handed down at the start of a preliminary question put to the Constitutional Court on the orientated nature of "lessons in morality inspired by the spirit of free examination" that pupils may follow at public school instead of religious classes. In fact, by virtue of Article 24 of the Constitution, schools run by the public authorities must offer, until the end of compulsory education (18 years), the choice between the teaching of one of the recognised religions and non-confessional organisations. For the moment, only one philosophical organisation is recognised and funded in Belgium: the so-called "*laïcité organisée*" ("organised secularism"), which is a kind of humanist non-religious organisation. In its judgement, the Constitutional Court considered that "lessons in morality inspired by the spirit of free examination" involve the dissemination of information or knowledge in an "objective, critical and pluralistic" manner, in accordance with the case law of the European Court of Human Rights. The Constitutional Court was in particular referring to the judgement *Folgerø and others v. Norway*, in which the Grand Chamber of the Strasbourg Court considered that

19 This point of view was not shared by all the 17 judges of the Grand Chamber. The Court holds by 15 votes to 2 that there has been no violation of Arts. 8 and 9 of the Convention. One dissenting opinion is formulated by two judges (Judges Nußberger and Jäderblom). According to those two judges, "the very general concept of 'living together' does not fall directly under any of the rights and freedoms guaranteed within the Convention" and that is the reason why they doubt that "Law prohibiting the concealment of one's face in public places pursues any legitimate aim under article 8 § 2 or article 9 § 2 of the Convention".

20 About this decision, see, among others, L.-L. Christians, M. El Berhoumi, "De la neutralité perdue à l'exemption du cours de morale. Commentaire de l'arrêt 34/2015 de la Cour constitutionnelle", *Journal des Tribunaux* vol. 20, no. 6606 (2015): 437–444. https://dial.uclouvain.be/downloader/downloader.php?pid=boreal%3A177470&datastream=PDF_01&disclaimer=3c365ed91f08af495a717898813c787fbb5708e6a3af3c7dc766a860c6404f19. Accessed October 27, 2024; J. Lievens, "Grondwettelijk Hof maakt komaf met verplichte keuze tussen godsdienst en zedenleer", *Die Juristenkrant* no. 306 (2015): 3.

> the second sentence of article 2 of Protocol No. 1 implies on the other hand that the State, in fulfilling the functions assumed by it in regard to education and teaching, must take care that information or knowledge included in the curriculum is conveyed in an *objective, critical and pluralistic manner*. The State is forbidden to pursue an aim of indoctrination that might be considered as not respecting parents' religious and philosophical convictions. *That is the limit that must not be exceeded* (§ 84).

Noting that the current system in the French Community only authorises parents and children to choose between "courses of religion" and "moral courses inspired by free spirit", the Constitutional Court considers that the French Community only offers "orientated" courses and, therefore, does not comply with the Strasbourg case law. According to the Constitutional Court, it must be possible for the students to be exempted from religious and moral lessons.

To meet this requirement of the Constitutional Court, the legislator of the French Community decided to create a new course called the Philosophy and Citizenship Course.[21] Since September 2016, all public school pupils have been obliged to take one hour of this new course. For the second hour, pupils[22] can choose between a course in one of the recognised religions, non-confessional organisation, or one additional hour of philosophy and citizenship. As consequence, in practice, there is no longer any obligation to take religion classes in public schools in the French Community.

11.3.4 Religious Freedom, Places of Worship and Covid-19 Crisis

Not a single country in the world escaped the Covid-19 crisis. From an infectious disease that appeared in Wuhan in China in November 2019, it quickly became a pandemic, and the UN declared a global public health emergency at the end of January 2020.[23] Every state in the world took measures to restrict freedoms in an attempt to contain the pandemic. Some of these restrictions inevitably affected religious freedom. In Belgium, numerous laws and royal and ministerial orders were adopted, and a number of them have been challenged in court on the grounds that they would contravene human rights.[24] Among this

21 About this new course, see, among others, X. Delgrange, "La Belgique francophone accouche douloureusement d'un cours de philosophie et de citoyenneté non désiré par tous", *Revue du droit des religions* no. 5 (2018): 107–132. https://www.doi.org/10.4000/rdr.397.

22 In fact, the choice in made by their parents by virtue of Art. 24 of the Belgian Constitution.

23 D. Cucinotta, M. Vanelli, "WHO Declares COVID-19 a Pandemic", *Acta Biomedica* vol. 91, no. 1 (2020): 158.

24 For a general overview of those measures, see F. Bouhon, E. Slautsky, S. Wattier (eds.), *Le droit public belge face à la crise du COVID-19. Quelles leçons pour l'avenir?* (Paris: Larcier, 2022).

case law, a ruling by the Council of State (the country's highest administrative court) is particularly noteworthy. Handed down on December 8, 2020, this decision concerns restrictions on the freedom to meet in places of worship, which the Jewish community complained about and won before the High Administrative Court.

To understand the scope of the ruling, it should first be remembered that collective exercise of religious freedom was banned during the "first wave" of the pandemic in Belgium, from March 14 to June 8, 2020. It was then reauthorised during the summer of 2020 with strict health rules and a limited number of people. As the situation once again gave cause for concern in early autumn, a new Ministerial Order of October18, 2020, restricted religious freedom to meetings of 40 people. Due to a "second wave" of the epidemic confirmed in the end of October, several other ministerial orders were adopted. More precisely and chronologically, the Ministerial Order of October 28, 2020, introduced major restrictions on freedom of religion. This decree was subsequently amended by a Ministerial Order of November 1, 2020, followed by a Ministerial Order of November 28, 2020. These measures initially applied until November 19 under the Ministerial Order of October 28, 2020, then were extended until December 13 by the Ministerial Order of November 1, 2020, and until January 15, 2021, by the Ministerial Order of November 28, 2020. These various decrees were challenged before the Council of State, as discussed in the ruling of December 8, 2020.

The applicants criticised the rules contained in the ministerial orders according to which religious ceremonies could, for health reasons, only take place with a maximum of ten people for recording purposes with a view to broadcasting via all available channels, that funerals and cremations could bring together a maximum of 15 people, and that weddings could only take place with the presence of the spouses, witnesses, the civil registrar, or the minister of religion, all in compliance with strict hygiene and distancing measures.

The applicants claimed a violation of Article 19 of the Constitution, read in conjunction with Article 9 of the European Convention on Human Rights[25] and Articles 18 and 27 of the International Covenant on Civil and Political Rights[26]. According to them, the Ministerial Order entailed a national ban on religious freedom, with only a few exceptions that were "tailor-made" for the Roman Catholic faith and prohibited collective religious freedom by the Jewish

25 European Convention on Human Rights [1950], CETS No. 213.

26 International Covenant on Civil and Political Rights [1966]. https://www.ohchr.org/en/instruments-mechanisms/instruments/international-covenant-civil-and-political-rights. Accessed October 27, 2024.

community. In its ruling of December 8, 2020,[27] the Council of State ruled that the measures in the Ministerial Order were disproportionate to the legitimate objective of protecting public health. In its reasoning, the Council of State considers that "by simply authorising the same exception for religious weddings and funerals, the opposing party has not, *prima facie*, taken sufficient account of what the religions themselves consider to be important ceremonies".[28] In view of the relaxation of certain measures – and in particular the reopening of so-called non-essential shops from December 1, 2020 – the Council of State considered that the severe restriction on freedom of religion resulting from the ban on collective worship was not proportionate to the objective pursued and that the plea was serious. The Council of State considered the measures an obstacle for two of the applicants who had planned for a long time to organise their Jewish wedding and that the measures had a particularly serious impact on the religious ceremonies that would take place at the end of the year. Therefore, the Ministerial Order was annulled.

But the reason why the ruling is remarkable is not only that the Ministerial Order was annulled but also that the Council of State enjoined the minister of justice to enter into dialogue with the recognised religious denominations in order to write and adopt his new order. More precisely, the Council of State enjoined the Belgian State to replace the Ministerial Order "with regulations that do not disproportionately restrict the collective exercise of worship" and stated that "the replacement must be carried out in consultation with representatives of religious and non-confessional communities".[29] Otherwise said,

27 About this ruling, see S. Wattier, F. Xavier, "Les restrictions à la liberté de religion durant la deuxième vague de coronavirus: analyse des arrêts du Conseil d'État", *Journal des Tribunaux* no. 6851 (2021): 241–246 ; M. Servais, "Des mesures provisoires au secours de la liberté de culte ou de la santé publique ? Note sous C.E. 8 décembre 2020", *Administration publique* (2021): 511–517; J. Bernaerts, A. Overbeeke, "Case Law on the Freedom of Religion During the COVID-19 Crisis in Belgium", *Journal of Church and State* vol. 64, no. 4 (2022): 663–682. https://doi.org/10.1093/jcs/csac073; L.-L. Christians, "La déstabilisation sanitaire de la liberté de culte en droit belge. Entre troisième vague Covid-19 et postmodernité". In: L. Danto, C. Burgun (eds.), *L'Église en état d'urgence. Droit canonique et gestion de la pandémie de la Covid-19* (Paris: Les Editions du Cerf, 2021): 151–179; L.-L. Christians, A. Overbeeke, "Le droit belge des cultes au défi de la crise sanitaire de la covid-19. Légistique de crise entre vieux réflexes et nouvelles réalités", *Revista General de Derecho Canónico y Derecho Eclesiástico del Estado* vol. 54, no. 1 (2020): 1–23; L.-L. Christians, "COVID-19, Law and Religion in Belgium", *Fides & Libertas* (2021): 67, https://www.doi.org/10.5281/zenodo.570190; F. Judo, "De Raad van State, de COVID-maatregelen en de erediensten – een consistent verhaal?", *Rechtskundig Weekblad* no. 34 (2021): 1357–1360; F. Judo, "De Geest is niet gehaast (note sur C.E., 28 mai 2020 - Covid - Cultes)", Juristenkrant (2020): 12; P. Minsier, "La religion au temps du Corona : une liberté comme les autres". In: S. Parsa, M. Uyttendaele (eds.), *La pandémie de Covid-19 face au droit.* Vol. 2 *Analyse et perspective d'une crise et de ses lendemains* (Limal: Anthemis, 2022): 389–402.

28 *Congregation Yetev Lev Dsatmar Antwerp Limited e.a.*, no. 249.177 [2020] (unofficial translation).

29 *Congregation Yetev Lev Dsatmar Antwerp Limited e.a.*, no. 249.177 [2020] (unofficial translation).

the administrative court required that the State to enter into dialogue with representatives of religious and non-confessional organisations to review the health regulations. In doing so, the Council of State asked the federal government to ensure that the content of the new order met the demands of religious and non-confessional organisations. For the time being, there is no dialogue between public authorities and religious and non-confessional communities institutionalised under Belgian law. By comparison, this is the case at European Union level, where Article 17 of the Treaty on the Functioning of the European Union (TFEU)[30] states as follows: "Recognising their identity and their specific contribution, the Union shall maintain an ***open, transparent and regular dialogue*** with these churches and organisations".[31]

In Belgian law, the beginnings of an institutionalisation of such a dialogue emerged three days after the "march against terror" held in Brussels on April 17, 2016, in tribute to the victims of the terrorist attacks of March 22, 2016, when the prime minister and the minister of justice received all the representatives of recognised religions and non-confessional organisation. The outcome of this meeting was the desire to create "a permanent body for consultation with representatives of recognised religious denominations".[32] The 2016 initiative aimed to create a dialogue with representatives of recognised religious and non-confessional organisations only. In its ruling of December 8, 2020, the Council of State called for dialogue with "representatives of religious and non-confessional communities", without specifying if these communities must be recognised or not.

The new Ministerial Order adopted on the basis of the dialogue that took place authorised a maximum of 15 people for any ceremony, not including the registrar and the minister of religion. It allowed religious ceremonies to be held at the end of the year (such as Christmas mass, Hanouka, etc.) in strict

30 Treaty on the Functioning of the European Union (consolidated version) [2012] OJ C 326/47.

31 About Art. 17 TFEU, see L.-L. Christians, "Droit et religion dans le Traité d'Amsterdam : une étape décisive ?". In: Y. Lejeune (ed.), *Le Traité d'Amsterdam. Espoirs et déceptions* (Bruxelles: Bruylant, 1998): 195–225; L.-L. Christians, "La condition juridique du religieux dans la construction d'une Europe post-nationale. Du Traité d'Amsterdam au Projet de Constitution européenne", *Annales d'études européennes* (2004): 117–133; J. Duffar, "Les relations entre l'Union européenne et les Églises". In: R. Puza, N. Doe (eds.), ***Religion et droit en dialogue: collaboration conventionnelle et non-conventionnelle entre État et religion en Europe*** (Leuven: Peeters, 2006): 278 ff ; S. Wattier, "Juridical Challenges of the Dialogue Between the European Union and Religious and Non-Confessional Organisations", *Quaderni di diritto e politica ecclesiastica* vol. 20, no. 2 (2017): 475–496; S. Wattier, "Quel dialogue entre l'Union européenne et les organisations religieuses et non confessionnelles? Réflexions au départ de la décision du Médiateur européen du 25 janvier 2013", *Cahiers de droit européen* (2015): 535–556. https://pure.unamur.be/ws/portalfiles/portal/54166030/D1107.pdf. Accessed October 27, 2024.

32 About this initiative of dialogue in the press, see A. Belga, "Attentats: Charles Michel veut une concertation permanente avec les représentants des cultes", https://www.rtbf.be/article/attentats-de-bruxelles-charles-michel-veut-une-concertation-permanente-avec-les-representants-des-cultes-9275004. Accessed December 8, 2023.

compliance with health measures. About this dialogue that took place, it is interesting to stress that the minister of justice limited his meetings to representatives of recognised religious and non-confessional organisations, even though the Council of State ruling did not specify that these meetings should be limited to them.

This experience shows that the scope of "consultation" and "dialogue" between the public authorities and religious and non-confessional organisations need to be clarified. It seems that guidelines should be put in place, including identification of the parties concerned. Indeed, the question remains whether those organisations need to be recognised to access the dialogue but also whether or not this "dialogue" needs to be institutionalised, as is the case under European Union law under Article 17 of the TFEU and, if so, in what form, with what frequency, how often, etc.

11.3.5 Ritual Slaughter and Animal Welfare[33]

It is impossible to discuss recent developments in Belgian case law on relations between the State and religions – especially Judaism and Islam – without analysing the issue of ritual slaughter and animal welfare. Insofar as a contribution to the present work is devoted in its entirety to this issue,[34] we will limit our comments to the central elements that should be retained from this case.

33 About this issue in Belgian law, see also L.-L. Christians, "Bien-être animal et protection des minorités religieuses en Belgique. Le test de l'abattage rituel entre écarts régionaux et attente constitutionnelle", *Revue du droit des religions* no. 12 (2021): 79–99. https://doi.org/10.4000/rdr.1704; S. Wattier, "Ritual slaughter case: The Court of Justice and the Belgian Constitutional Court put animal welfare first", *European Constitutional Law Review* vol. 1, no. 2 (2022): 264–285. https://doi.org/10.1017/S1574019622000189; A. Deting, "Entre contrainte et ressource: la régionalisation du bien-être animal comme opportunité politique", *Revue interdisciplinaire d'études juridiques* (2022): 217–252. https://shs.cairn.info/revue-interdisciplinaire-d-etudes-juridiques-2022-1-page-217?lang=fr. Accessed October 27, 2024; see also M. El Berhoumi, "Abattage rituel: faut-il sacrifier la liberté religieuse sur l'autel du bien-être animal ?", http://www.justice-en-ligne.be/rubrique366.html. Accessed December 8, 2023; M.C. Foblets, J. Velaers, "Rituele slachtingen: recente ontwikkelingen in het debate". In: D. De Ruysscher, P. De Hert, M. De Metsenaere (eds.), *Een leven van inzet. Liber amicorum Michel Magits* (Mechelen: Kluwer, 2012): 375–402; M.C. Foblets, J. Velaers, "In Search of the Right Balance. Recent Discussions in Belgium and the Netherlands on Religious Freedom and the Slaughter of Animals without Prior Stunning". In: B. Schinkele, R. Kuppe, S. Schima (eds.), *Recht Religion Kultur. Festschrift für Richard Potzzum 70. Geburtstag* (Wien: facultas.wuv, 2014): 67–85; D. Plas, J. Petersen, R.O. Karpiel, M. Leloup, C. Jenart, "Het verbod op onverdoofd slachten gered van de slachtbank?", *Rechtskundig Weekblad* vol. 85, no. 34 (2022): 1330–1343. https://hdl.handle.net/10067/1875840151162165141. Accessed October 27, 2024; G. van der Schyff, S. Sottiaux, "Debating Ritual Slaughter in Belgium: A Multilevel Fundamental Rights Perspective". In: K. Lemmens, S. Parmentier, L. Reyntjens (eds.), *Human Rights with a Human Touch: Liber Amicorum Paul Lemmens*, (Cambridge: Intersentia, 2019): 715–735.

34 See G. van der Schyff, "Ritual Slaughter and Religious Freedom: A Critical Analysis of the 2020 CJEU Judgment Regarding the Belgian Preliminary Reference". In: this book.

As is well-known, the issue of ritual slaughter is particularly sensitive, as it requires balancing the protection of animal welfare on the one hand and freedom of religion on the other. It mostly concerns Judaism and Islam, which, respectively, require the food to be ***kosher*** and *ḥalāl*. The central problem remains in relation to the requirement of consciousness of the animal at the time of its death. While it seems relatively clear that the animal must be conscious at the time of slaughter in the Jewish religion[35], it is less clear for Islam. More precisely,

> there are essentially two main interpretations dealing with industrial halal slaughter, with two groups of opinions about the licitness, or acceptability, of meat in relation to the mode of slaughter. The first is based on a verse of the Koran (5:5) that considers Christian and Jewish traditions of industrialised countries are adequate to render their slaughter methods acceptable to Muslims. [...] [T]he second interpretation considers that meat has a status peculiar to Islam. Meat and meat products are recognised as licit for Muslims only under certain conditions specified by Islamic sources. This interpretation is based on a verse in the Koran that explicitly forbids the consumption of meat deriving from an animal slaughtered in the name of any other being than God.[36]

As regards national legislations, the decision to ban or allow ritual slaughter has highly challenged most European policymakers in recent years.[37] In Belgium, the situation is even more complex, as animal welfare has been a

35 For more details, see F. Bergeaud-Blackler (ed.), *Les sens du Halal: Une norme dans un marché mondial* (Paris: CNRS editions, 2015).

36 F. Bergeaud-Blackler, "New Challenges for Islamic Ritual Slaughter: A European Perspective", *Journal of Ethnic and Migration Studies* vol. 33 no. 6 (2007): 972–973. https://doi.org/10.1080/13691830701432871; see also: M. Hodkin, "When Ritual Slaughter Isn't Kosher: An Examination of Shechita and the Humane Methods of Slaughter Act", *Journal of Animal Law* no. 1 (2005): 134.

37 G. van der Schyff, "Reviewing the Recent Ban on Ritual Slaughter in Flanders", Recht, Religie en Samenleving (2017): 5. In that sense, see among others: J.A. Rovinsky, "The Cutting Edge: The Debate Over Regulation of Ritual Slaughter in the Western World", *California Western International Law Journal* vol. 45 (2014): 79 ff; C.E. Haupt, "Free Exercise of Religion and Animal Protection: A Comparative Perspective on Ritual Slaughter", *Georg Washington International Law Review* vol. 39 (2007): 839 ff; M. Valenta, "Pluralist Democracy or Scientistic Monocracy: Debating Ritual Slaughter", *Erasmus Law Review* vol. 5, no. 1 (2012): 27. https://www.doi.org/10.5553/ELR221026712012005001003; G. van der Schyff, "Ritual Slaughter and Religious Freedom in a Multilevel Europe: The Wider Importance of the Dutch Case", *Oxford Journal of Law and Religion* vol. 3 no. 1 (2014): 76 ff. https://doi.org/10.1093/ojlr/rwt046; P. Lerner, A.M. Rabello, "The Prohibition of Ritual Slaughtering (Kosher Shechita and Halal) and Freedom of Religion of Minorities", *Journal of Law and Religion* (2006) vol. 22, no. 1: 1–62; E. Howard, "Ritual Slaughter and Religious Freedom: Liga van Moskeen", *Common Market Law Review* vol. 56, no. 3 (2019): 803–824.

regional matter since 2014 (sixth reform of the state) and as regionalisation is "almost concomitant"[38] with the evolution of European law in this area.

Since 2018, the Walloon and Flemish legislations have been identical: they prohibit any slaughter of animals without prior stunning, which means even when it is a religious slaughter. Both legislations have been the subject of an annulment appeal to the Constitutional Court, which first referred a preliminary question to the Court of Justice of the European Union. The Brussels Region, which has the largest Muslim population in Belgium, has not yet legislated on the matter: ritual slaughter without stunning is therefore still allowed in slaughterhouses.

The preparatory work of the Flemish decree explains how the legislator has tried to find a balance between animal welfare and religious freedom, especially as regards the Jewish and Islamic requirements:

> Flanders attaches great importance to animal welfare. The objective is, therefore, to eliminate all avoidable animal suffering in Flanders. The slaughter of animals without stunning is incompatible with that principle. [...] The gap between eliminating animal suffering, on the one hand, and slaughtering without prior stunning, on the other, will always be very considerable, even if less radical measures were taken to minimise the impairment of animal welfare. Nevertheless, a balance must be sought between the protection of animal welfare and freedom of religion. Both Jewish and Islamic religious rites require the animal to be drained of as much of its blood as possible. Scientific research has shown that the fear that stunning would adversely affect bleeding out is unfounded. Furthermore, both rites require that the animal be intact and healthy at the time of slaughter and that it die from bleeding [...]. Electronarcosis is a reversible (non-lethal) method of stunning in which the animal, if it has not had its throat cut in the meantime, regains consciousness after a short period and does not feel any negative effects of stunning.[39]

If reversible stunning is in accordance with some Muslim authorities – but not all of them – who accept that the animal is stunned just before its throat is slit, it is more complex within the Jewish religion, whose requirements for the slaughter of the animal are much stricter.[40] Besides, under religious rules, any devout Muslim can slaughter an animal, which is not the case in Judaism, where the slaughter must be carried out by a devout and technically qualified

38 L.-L. Christians, "Bien-être animal et protection des minorités religieuses en Belgique": 82 (free translation).

39 *Centraal Israëlitisch Consistorie van België and Others v. Vlaamse Regering*, C-336/19 [2020] § 13.

40 About the precise differences between *kosher* and *halal* meat, see J. Zurek, M. Rudy, M. Kachel, S. Rudy, "Conventional Versus Ritual Slaughter–Ethical Aspects and Meat Quality", *Processes* no. 9 (2021): 1–18.

man, the *shohet*.[41] As consequence, an action for annulment of both decrees was lodged with the Constitutional Court by Muslim and Jewish religious communities and by the representative body of Muslims in Belgium.[42] In its judgement 53/2019, the Constitutional Court decided to refer three questions on the ban on slaughter without stunning to the Court of Justice of the European Union for a preliminary ruling. The judgement of the Court of Justice is the subject of a commentary in this book, to which the reader is referred.[43] In its judgement *Centraal Israëlitisch Consistorie van België and Others* of December 17, 2020, the Court of Luxembourg considers that the ban on ritual slaughter without prior stunning complies with European Union law – contrary to what was suggested by the advocate-general[44] – and therefore, after a careful balancing of the interests involved, gives priority to the promotion of animal welfare over religious freedom.

None of the violations claimed by the applicant were retained by the Constitutional Court, which validated the compliance of the Walloon and Flemish decrees with the European Regulation 1099/2009 on the protection of animals at the time of killing, with freedom of religion,[45] with the principle of the separation of church and state, with the right to work and the free choice of a profession, the freedom of enterprise and the free movement of freedom of enterprise, and the free movement of goods and services, and with the principle of equality and non-discrimination.

The Muslim and Jewish applicants to the Belgian Constitutional Court have then decided to lodge an appeal with the European Court of Human Rights, which has just handed down its ruling – *Executief van de Moslims van België and others v. Belgique* – on February 13, 2024.[46] The judgement, which will certainly be commented on by many authors, concludes that Belgium did not violate Articles 9 and 14 of the Convention. The Court explained that the case was different from the only precedent it had had to deal with in the area of ritual slaughter (namely, *Cha'are Shalom Ve Tsedek v. France* of 2000), which concerned the granting of authorisations to bodies

41 C. Sägesser, "Les débats autour de l'interdiction de l'abattage rituel", *Courrier hebdomadaire du Crisp* no. 2385 (2018): 6.

42 In Belgium "the Constitutional Court is competent to review legislative acts. By legislative acts are meant both substantive and formal rules adopted by the federal parliament (statutes) and by the parliaments of the communities and regions (decrees and ordinances). All other regulations, such as Royal Decrees, decrees of governments of communities and regions, ministerial decrees, regulations and decrees of provinces and municipalities, and court decisions fall outside the jurisdiction of the Court" (see "Jurisdiction of the Constitutional Court. Jurisdiction of the Constitutional Court". https://www.const-court.be/en/court/presentation/jurisdiction. Accessed October 27, 2024).

43 See G. van der Schyff, "Ritual Slaughter and Religious Freedom".

44 Opinion of Advocate General Hogan in case *Centraal Israëlitisch Consistorie van België and Others v. Vlaamse Regering*, C-336/19 [2020].

45 Council Regulation (EC) No 1099/2009 of September 24, 2009, on the protection of animals at the time of killing (text with EEA relevance) [2009] OJ L 303.

46 *Executief van de Moslims van België and others v. Belgique*, 16760/22 et al. [2024], ECLI:CE:ECHR:2024:0213JUD001676022.

authorised to carry out the killing of animals, whereas in the present case, the measure at issue had the effect of prohibiting ritual slaughter not preceded by stunning of the animal. Unlike the *Cha'are Shalom Ve Tsedek* judgement, in which the Court had found that there had been no interference with the applicants' freedom of religion, the Court held that the ban on slaughter without stunning did constitute an interference, which was provided for by law, in this case by the Walloon and Flemish decrees (§ 89). As regards the question of legitimate aim, the Court emphasised that this was the first time that it had had to rule on the question of whether the protection of animal welfare constituted a legitimate aim within the meaning of Article 9 § 2. The Court pointed out in that regard that the list of exceptions to that freedom contained in the second paragraph of Article 9 was exhaustive and that the definition of those exceptions was restrictive (§ 91). More specifically, the Court had to determine whether the protection of animal welfare could be linked to one of the aims referred to in paragraph 2. The Court emphasised at the outset that, unlike European Union law, which elevates animal welfare to the rank of an objective of general interest, Article 9 of the Convention does not refer to it. However, "the Court has already recognised on several occasions that the protection of animals is a matter of general interest protected by Article 10 of the Convention".[47] It stated that "the protection of public morals, to which Article 9 § 2 of the Convention refers, cannot be understood as aiming solely at the protection of human dignity in relations between individuals".[48] The High Court stressed that "public morality" is an evolving concept and reiterated its doctrine of the living instrument, emphasising that a practice that may have been accepted in the past may no longer be accepted in the future. It noted that, according to the Belgian Constitutional Court, promoting the protection and welfare of animals as sentient beings can be considered a moral value shared by many people in the Flemish and Walloon Regions and underlines that the decrees were adopted by a very large majority in the two regional parliaments. In this sense, the Court "considers that the protection of animal welfare can be linked to the concept of 'public morals', which constitutes a legitimate aim within the meaning of Paragraph 2 of Article 9 of the Convention".[49] In this respect, one may wonder whether the Court did not deliberately avoid the question of the legitimate aim of "protecting the rights and freedoms of others", which could have opened up a "Pandora's box" as to whether or not animals can be considered as subjects of rights.

As regards proportionality, recalling the subsidiary mechanism of the Convention and the importance of the role of the national decision-maker on

47 *Executief van de Moslims van België and others v. Belgique*, 16760/22 et al. [2024] § 94 (free translation).

48 *Executief van de Moslims van België and others v. Belgique*, 16760/22 et al. [2024] § 95 (free translation).

49 *Executief van de Moslims van België and others v. Belgique*, 16760/22 et al. [2024] § 101 (free translation).

issues that may differ widely from one country to another, the Court observed that "the contested prohibition contained in the two decrees at issue stems from a deliberate choice made by the federal legislatures at the end of a carefully considered parliamentary process".[50] It noted that "when animals are slaughtered using special methods required for religious rites, the stunning process applied is reversible and does not result in the death of the animal" and that "based on scientific studies and extensive consultation with interested parties, the parliamentary work concluded that no less radical measure could sufficiently achieve the objective of reducing the harm to animal welfare at the time of slaughter".[51] As regards the argument that it was impossible for the applicants to obtain meat in accordance with their religious requirements, the Court emphasised that the Flemish and Walloon Regions did not prohibit the consumption of meat from elsewhere and that the applicants had not shown before the Court that access to meat slaughtered in accordance with their religious convictions had become more difficult following the entry into force of the contested decrees. Although not expressly referred to, this position is similar to that adopted by the Court in the *Cha'are Shalom Ve Tsedek* decision. Considering the analysed elements, the Court concluded that there had been no violation of Article 9 of the Convention.

As regards the alleged violation of Articles 9 and 14 combined, the Strasbourg Court held, in line with the Court of Justice of the European Union, that "since ritual slaughter is carried out on farmed animals, their killing takes place in a context distinct from that of wild animals slaughtered in the context of hunting and recreational fishing" and that "the same cannot be said of the fishing of farmed fish, which takes place in an aquatic environment that is fundamentally different from slaughterhouses".[52] The Court concluded that the applicants were not in a situation comparable to that of hunters and fishermen and that there had therefore been no violation of Articles 9 and 14 of the Convention.

The position adopted by the European Court of Human Rights in favour of animal welfare will therefore have an important impact on the rights of Islamic and Jewish religious minorities. The Court's rulings apply to all 46 member states of the Council of Europe, and animal welfare is a growing concern in Europe. In Belgium, some political parties are even talking about the possibility of recognising in the Constitution that animals are sentient. Furthermore, the pre-electoral context in Belgium in spring 2024 was marked by the debate on the ban on slaughter without stunning in Brussels,[53] which is

50 *Executief van de Moslims van België and others v. Belgique*, 16760/22 et al. [2024] § 105 (free translation).

51 *Executief van de Moslims van België and others v. Belgique*, 16760/22 et al. [2024] § 118 (free translation).

52 *Executief van de Moslims van België and others v. Belgique*, 16760/22 et al. [2024] § 118 (free translation).

53 See among others in the press: J. Thomas, "A Bruxelles, l'abattage rituel plane sur la campagne électorale". https://www.lesoir.be/576343/article/2024-03-22/bruxelles-labattage-rituel-plane-sur-la-campagne-electorale. Accessed October 27, 2024.

currently the only one of the three regions where the ban does not apply. In the end, the ban was not voted through, probably due to the context of the forthcoming elections[54] and the large Muslim population living in Brussels. In the Brussels-Capital Region, slaughter without stunning remains authorised for the time being, and the Strasbourg Court emphasised in its judgement that the fact that

> the Brussels-Capital Region has not, at the date of adoption of the present judgment, abolished or limited the exception provided for the ritual slaughter of animals, and thus differs from the Flemish and Walloon Regions [...] cannot call into question the importance attached to animal welfare in Belgium.

It remains to be seen whether, under the new legislature (2024–2029), the members of the Brussels Parliament will decide to ban ritual slaughter without stunning.

11.4 To Conclude

The large number of judgements handed down by Belgian courts concerning relations between the State and religions does not allow us to offer a systematic analysis. By focusing on the major decisions handed down in this area, a slightly clearer picture can already be presented. While Belgium continues its secularisation process, like many of its European neighbours, religious issues are paradoxically at the heart of an increasing number of major rulings. There are a number of noteworthy developments in this context: the Constitutional Court's, and then the European Court of Human Rights', validation of the ban on wearing the full veil in the public space; the fact that religious education has been made optional in the French Community's official education system; the ban on slaughtering animals without stunning, including as part of a religious rite; etc., as analysed in this chapter.

These various significant elements also show that the religious phenomenon is increasingly regulated by the Belgian legislator, whether at the federal or federated entity level. This illustrates how difficult it is for the public authorities to define a space in which the religious freedom and beliefs of everyone can coexist with the other fundamental values of our democratic societies.

In this contribution, the choice was made to focus on decisions handed down by the Belgian supreme court. However, by way of conclusion, it is also important to report on a major judgement handed down by the European Court of Human Rights condemning Belgium. The appeal concerned a Brussels ordinance of 2017 stipulating that, from now on, exemption from property tax (which has been a regional tax since the fifth reform of the State) would only be granted to religious communities that belong to a recognised

54 The European, federal and regional elections took place in Belgium on June 9, 2024.

religion. As the applicant religious congregations are Jehovah's Witnesses, they could no longer benefit from exemption from property tax because they are not recognised by the Belgian legislator. They therefore brought an action for annulment of the ordinance before the Constitutional Court, but the Court, in judgement no. 178/2019 of November 14, 2019, found no discrimination and held that the recognition criterion was "objective" and "relevant".[55] Unlike the Constitutional Court, the European Court of Human Rights ruled that the Brussels ordinance created a discrimination. More specifically, in its judgement *Assemblée chrétienne des Témoins de Jéhovah d'Anderlecht and others v. Belgium* of April 5, 2022,[56] the Strasbourg Court ruled that Belgium's system for recognising and funding religions violates Articles 9 (freedom of religion) and 14 (equality and non-discrimination) of the European Convention on Human Rights. According to the Court, "neither the criteria for recognition nor the procedure leading to recognition of a religious denomination by the federal authority were laid down in an instrument satisfying the requirements of accessibility and foreseeability" (§ 51). This judgement confirms that the Belgian system for recognising religions has largely run its course and that the historical legacy[57] is no longer sufficient to maintain it as it is.[58] A coherent and in-depth reform has become necessary in order to make the system more objective, more transparent, and more respectful of the principle of equality and non-discrimination.

55 Belgian Constitutional Court, 178/2019 [2019] (unofficial translation).

56 About this judgment, see S. Wattier, "La Cour de Strasbourg remet en cause tout le système belge de reconnaissance des cultes (obs. sous Cour eur. dr. h., arrêt Assemblée chrétienne des Témoins de Jéhovah d'Anderlecht et autres c. Belgique, 5 avril 2022)", *Revue trimestrielle des droits de l'homme* vol. 133, no. 1 (2023): 265–283; S. Van Drooghenbroeck, B. Garcia Da Silva, "La reconnaissance des cultes: une copie constitutionnelle (de plus) à revoir", *Journal des Tribunaux* no. 6916 (2022): 681–687.

57 On this subject, see C. Sägesser, *Le temporel des cultes dans la Belgique du XIXème siècle: législation, réglementation, jurisprudence et pratiques*, PhD thesis (Brussels, Université libre de Bruxelles, 2013).

58 The idea of reforming the public funding of religious and non-confessional organisations in Belgium has been analysed by a number of authors since the late 1990s. Among others, see C. Sägesser, V. De Coorebyter, "Cultes et laïcité en Belgique", *Dossier du Crisp* no 51 (2020)" 1–36. https://dipot.ulb.ac.be/dspace/bitstream/2013/108611/3/Dossier_51_Cultes_et_laicite.pdf&ved=2ahUKEwi-0qDqq6-JAxXMKRAIHaLUKisQFnoECBgQAQ&usg=AOvVaw00F4z8Ew03TUW1SLXdys_H. Accessed October 27, 2024; J.-F. Husson, "Un autre mode de financement des cultes et de la laïcité est-il possible?". In: J.-F. Husson (ed.), *Le financement des cultes et de la laïcité: comparaisons internationales et perspectives* (Namur: Editions Namuroises, 2005): 183 ff. http://hdl.handle.net/2078.1/139686. Accessed October, 27, 2024; M.-F. Rigaux, F. Mortier, J. Drijkoningen, J.-F. Husson, K. Leus, N. Smets, *Le financement par l'Etat fédéral des ministres des cultes et des délégués du Conseil central laïque*, Rapport de la Commission des Sages à la demande de la ministre de la Justice Laurette Onkelinx (Bruxelles: Commission des sages, 2006); L.-L. Christians, M. Magits, C. Sägesser, L. de Fleurquin, *La réforme de la législation sur les cultes et les organisations philosophiques non confessionnelles*, Rapport du Groupe interuniversitaire à la demande du ministre de la Justice Stefaan De Clerck (Bruxelles: Groupe de travail, 2011); S. Wattier, *Le financement public des cultes et des organisations philosophiques non confessionnelles. Analyse de constitutionnalité et de conventionnalité* (Bruxelles: Bruylant, 2016).

12 Lethargy in the UK

How Not to Accommodate Religion or Belief

Russell Sandberg

Abstract

This chapter explores the main trends in the constitutional and legal protection of religion or belief in the United Kingdom (UK). Recognising the divergent religion-State approaches in the various nations of the UK, it is argued that the regulation of religion remains shaped more by historical happenstance than the sociological reality. The absence of a written constitutional document and civil or criminal codes means that the law relating to religious freedom is dispersed, and, although there are some 21st-century laws on the matter conceptualising freedom of religion or belief as a human right and protecting against discrimination on grounds of religion or belief, many laws are archaic and reflect a much more socially and culturally religious country than the UK is today. This is epitomised by the existence of a State Church: the established Church of England. However, the prevalence and influence of religion is not only found at the constitutional level. It can also be found, for instance, in laws on education and marriage that continue to favour the established Church of England in particular and Christianity in general, giving little protection to and often excluding non-religious beliefs. This is not compatible with human rights expectations and 21st-century social norms, and so this chapter argues that the UK now provides a good example of how not to accommodate freedom of religion or belief. This ineptness, it is contended, is largely accidental and is the result of the UK Government not focusing on matters of social justice due to an obsession with ideological financial austerity and the exiting of the European Union, which has perpetuated hostility towards the very notion of human rights.

Keywords

constitutional protection; religion; belief; discrimination; human rights; social justice

DOI: 10.4324/9781003423294-17

12.1 Introduction

On an early Friday evening in March 2024, when for most people the working week had ended, the then Prime Minister of the United Kingdom (UK) Rishi Sunak decided to address the nation from outside Ten Downing Street for only the second time in his (admittedly short) premiership. Sunak was motivated by what he referred to as the "shocking increase in extremist disruption and criminality" that he said had occurred in "recent weeks and months", which he said had "gone on long enough and demands a response not just from government, but from all of us".[1] Sunak's response amounted largely to sermonising followed by a reassertion of the importance of public order laws. The then Prime Minister identified "Islamic extremists and the far right" as the "forces here at home trying to tear us apart". He proclaimed that these groups were spreading a "poison" of "extremism" that "aims to drain us of our confidence in ourselves as a people, and in our shared future. They want us to doubt ourselves, to doubt each other, to doubt our country's history and achievements". Speaking of these achievements, Sunak sought to reassure the nation that

> Britain is a patriotic, liberal, democratic society with a proud past and a bright future. We are a reasonable country and a decent people. Our story is one of progress, of great achievements and enduring values. Immigrants who have come here have integrated and contributed. They have helped write the latest chapter in our island story. They have done this without being required to give up their identity. You can be a practising Hindu and a proud Briton as I am. Or a devout Muslim and a patriotic citizen as so many are. Or a committed Jewish person and the heart of your local community. And all underpinned by the tolerance of our established, Christian church. We are a country where we love our neighbours. And we are building Britain together.[2]

Many commentators deemed Sunak's sermonising tone hypocritical for a Government that had stoked the culture wars, demonised immigrants and frequently undermined the rule of law (by illegally proroguing Parliament, being fined for flagrantly breaching its own Covid lockdown laws and attacking the legal profession as a means of trying to undermine the then Leader of the Opposition). Others pointed out the emptiness of the content of the speech juxtaposed by the apparent urgency shown by its setting

1 PM address on extremism: March 1, 2024. Prime Minister Rishi Sunak made a statement outside Downing Street on extremism. https://www.gov.uk/government/speeches/pm-address-on-extremism-1-march-2024. Accessed November 17, 2024.

2 PM address on extremism: March 1, 2024.

and timing. However, perhaps the most noteworthy aspect of the speech is its historical and religious illiteracy.

The mistaken notion of the "story […] of progress" is endemic through British culture. The legal historian Robert Gordon referred to "evolutionary functionalism" – the idea of linear progress – as being the "set of background assumptions […] about the course of western History, that American legal scholars tended to take for granted".[3] It is not only Americans and not only legal scholars who unquestionably accept evolutionary functionalism; it is the prevalent unthinking backdrop most of the time: the expectation of linear progress is entrenched. It is, however, nonsense. The reality is that social, political, cultural, religious changes do not occur in a linear line; they ebb and flow. They do not move in one direction. Often, it is one step forward, two steps back; or some variation thereof. Even if we could identify and agree on what "progress" is, it is something only identified in hindsight based on a simplistic, presentist, and arrogant view of history. It supposes the present is superior to the past and that there is a pre-set path to an even better future that is closely aligned to the values held by those who are powerful today.

This historical illiterate account is even more dominant in relation to religion. Sunak's account whereby this progress narrative is "all underpinned by the tolerance of our established, Christian church" is laughable in its naivety, to take the most generous interpretation. The geographical illiteracy here is staggering: as its name suggests, the Church of England is only the established church for one nation of the UK: England. However, Sunak's account also misrepresented even that Church's role in the development of what he refers to as "our island story". Contrary to Sunak's sermonising, English religious history *is* characterised by people "being required to give up their identity". The British tradition is one of discrimination and intolerance of those who are not the religious majority - and this is not consigned to the history books. Although recent laws are framed in terms of religious freedom, older laws that remain active continue to produce discriminatory outcomes. The legal position on religion is characterised by contradictions, complexity, and chaos. Despite Sunak's praising of the status quo, the position of successive Right-Wing Governments is characterised by indifference. Religious groups are only of interest where they can provide services that the State no longer provides or where there are voters to lure. This chapter seeks to attempt to correct the historical illiteracy epitomised but sadly not limited to Sunak's speech by particular reference to the laws on marriage and the teaching of religion in schools.

12.2 The Trouble with History

There is not one history of the interaction between religion and the law in England and Wales. Rather, there are competing, contradictory histories.

3 R.W. Gordon, *Taming the Past: Essays on Law in History and History in Law* (Cambridge: Cambridge University Press, 2017): 221.

As Rebecca Riedel has argued, conventional accounts tend to underplay religious radicalisation.[4] Legal histories generally tend to take a State-centric approach and ignore the roles played by non-State actors such as pressure groups. The work of Sharon Thompson underlines how such groups may have an important influence upon law reform even where their attempts to shape the law are unsuccessful.[5] The value of legal history lies in showing the paths not taken, the alternative arguments and solutions, and seeing the status quo as being created, contingent and changeable. As Frederic Maitland once wrote, done well, legal history teaches the "lesson that each generation has an enormous power of shaping its own law" by showing that "they have free hands".[6]

Even working out where to begin is a complex task. Most century-spanning accounts of English legal history tend to follow Maitland to begin at around 1066 exploring the position immediately before the Battle of Hastings.[7] The importance of the Anglo-Saxon period and the effect of the Norman Conquest is a matter of debate amongst legal historians, and this starting point is especially odd when looking at the history of the interaction between law and religion. The common law or any notion of the State did not exist at this time, and there was also not a national religion: the Church was part of the Catholic Church based in Rome. The year 1066 was not a turning point in terms of the regulation of religion. Christianity had originally come to England when it had eventually become accepted by the Roman Empire, but when the Roman troops left Britain in 410, pagan religion once again asserted its supremacy. The following centuries witnessed the slow re-emergence of Christianity and after the Synod of Whitby in 663, England became fully a part of the world-wide Catholic Church. It could be said that the starting point should be well before 1066 or even afterwards. The impact of 1066 upon church law was also minimal. One innovation under the Normans was the separation of the ecclesiastical courts from the courts of land, the shire courts and the hundred courts.[8]

Moreover, such a starting point invariably treats as homogenous the whole of the medieval period. The period from the Norman Conquest to the Reformation is simplified as one period with tensions between Church and State being seen as exceptional. This is shown by the focus on the dispute

4 R. Riedel, *A Critical Legal Study of the Prevent Duty: The Religious Dimension*, PhD Thesis (Cardiff: Cardiff University, 2023).

5 S. Thompson, *Quiet Revolutionaries: The Married Women's Association and Family Law* (Oxford: Hart, 2022).

6 F.W. Maitland, Letter from Maitland to AV Dicey, c. July 1896, quoted in: C.H.S. Fifoot, *Frederic William Maitland* (Harvard: Harvard University Press, 1971): 143.

7 F. Pollock, F.W. Maitland, *The History of English Law*, vol 1 (Cambridge: Cambridge University Press, 1968). For discussion see R. Sandberg, *A Historical Introduction to English Law: Genesis of the Common Law* (Cambridge: Cambridge University Press, 2023): 45–64.

8 See F. Pollock, F.W. Maitland, *The History of English Law*, vol 1. For discussion see R. Sandberg, *A Historical Introduction to English Law* 68.

between Henry II (1154–1189) and Becket, the Archbishop of Canterbury, over whether clergy who had broken the king's peace should be tried in the king's court, as well as the church courts. This normalises the growing centralisation of the State in a narrative that covers up subservience. The story being told is a typical "top-down" narrative of evolutionary functionalism: where the development of a more sophisticated and therefore better legal system is at the forefront of the narrative. It is also a Christian-centric history, as that tends to downplay or even omit the anti-Semitism and ethnic cleaning that culminated in the expulsion of the Jews in 1290.[9]

The emphasis upon the Reformation further reflects a "schoolboy's history", relying upon developments that are ingrained into the national psyche. Unlike with the Norman Conquest, it is clear that the Reformation marked a distinct turning point in the history of law and religion. England moved from being a Catholic country where adherents owed loyalty to the pope to a Protestant country where subjects owed loyalty to the king. Heresy became treason.

Yet, here too, periodisation simplifies and distorts. The focus is on the posture of the State towards religion. A complex and contradictory process led by personalities is simplified. For instance, the re-establishment following the restoration of the monarchy is skimmed over since that did not fit the story being given of the Tudor legacy.[10] The narrative given is that discrimination and intolerance of faiths other than the Church of England reached its peak at the Reformation given the monarch's position as supreme governor of the Church. This allowed a narrative to be given that it remains defiantly one of progress. This narrative suggests that intolerance and discrimination slowly but decisively give way to toleration. The law is seen to be cleansing itself of previous biases. In most accounts of toleration, a number of Acts of Parliament are cited out of context and with no discussion of their rationale let alone the motivations for their enactment. And they are then collectively praised for representing progress. This is furthered by suggestions that the modern law has gone further still and has moved from toleration to an era of religious freedom. This is attributed to the building of the international human rights system after the Second World War buttressed by the juridification of religion in the early 21st century with new laws on human rights and religious discrimination, and the move in criminal law from protecting beliefs to protecting believers. The law is now seen to treat religion as an individual human right. However, this ignores the fact that all religions (let alone all beliefs) are still not equal. The Church of England's established status remains, and many laws still apply that

9 For discussion see F. Pollock, F.W. Maitland, *The History of English Law*, vol 1. For discussion see R. Sandberg, *A Historical Introduction to English Law* 121–123.

10 R. Sandberg, "The Restoration and Re-Establishment: 1660–1701". In: N. Doe, S. Coleman (eds.), *The Legal History of the Church of England* (Oxford: Hart, 2024): 95–114. https://doi.org/10.5040/9781509973156.ch-005.

have clerical fingerprints. The approach remains Christian-centric. Yet, this is forgotten or at least conveniently overlooked in the narrative of religious equality. There is often more than a whiff of presentism to the discussion; a dividing line is being drawn, and all that has previously been discussed is being classified and dismissed as history.

The flaws with the conventional history of the interaction between law and religion in England and Wales matter. The progress narrative fits with and perpetuates a narrative of secularisation. Social functional differentiation is taken as the norm. This is the move from a situation where a few social institutions (most notably the Church) performed several social functions to where a number of social institutions now exists, with each discharging separate and specific social functions. So, education and legal adjudication become the preserve of the educational and legal systems, respectively, rather than roles played by religious authorities. Social functional differentiation frames the way in which the interaction between law and religion is seen. The operation of religious courts, the existence of faith schools, and the general presence of religion in the public sphere offends social functional differentiation. Religion is relegated to the margins since it is regarded as a medieval throwback. The very presence of religion in the public sphere offends our cultural and social mindsets. It is instantly seen as a problem that law ought to fix.

This can be shown by exploring in detail two particular areas – the laws on getting married and on religion in schools[11] – that highlight well the limits of progress narratives and how an alternative understanding can be developed that moves away from the conventional approach that fetishes social functional differentiation and evolutionary functionalism and which highlights the complex and contradictory ways in which religion is regulated in England and Wales.

12.3 Two Case Studies: Education and Marriage Laws

When writers comment on marriage law and education law in England and Wales, they typically embrace the story of progress of secularisation and social functional differentiation. They invariably recount how these laws still show evidence of their Christian past but point out that, although the Christian fingerprints are still visible on the law, they have somewhat faded. The account given is typically an example of what Charles Taylor has called "subtraction stories":[12] accounts of things that the historical churches used to do where their impact has been reduced over time. In most of these subtraction stories, no distinction is made between the different branches of Christianity, let alone of other religions or beliefs. Rather, the perceived declining social and legal

11 On which see further R. Sandberg, *Religion and Marriage Law: The Need for Reform* (Bristol: Bristol University Press, 2021); R. Sandberg, *Religion in Schools: Learning Lessons from Wales* (London: Anthem Press, 2022).

12 C. Taylor, *A Secular Age* (Harvard: Harvard University Press, 2007): 22.

power of the established Church of England is considered to be synonymous with the perceived decline of Christianity. And the underlying assumption is that the Christian hold on such laws will and should weaken further as differentiation and secularisation run their course. The history of English and Welsh law on marriage and education would look very different if the base assumptions of evolutionary functionalism were questioned. Indeed, both areas of law do not follow the conventional narratives.

12.3.1 The Early History of Education and Marriage Law

Neither the Norman Conquest nor the Reformation had little effect on the development of marriage or education law. In relation to marriage, the church courts had exclusive jurisdiction from the mid-12th century over marriage and divorce, applying Roman Catholic canon law. Although there were some minor amendments, chiefly through the enactment of the Canons Ecclesiastical 1603–1604,[13] it was not until the Marriage Act 1753[14] that significant reform occurred. It was that Act that consolidated the monopoly of the Anglican Church – the Reformation statutes had little to do with it. Marriage had developed as something that the churches did. It was not really the concern of the State. The Reformation identified Church and State more explicitly but did not change the practice. This was largely because the practice was, if not in the shadow of the law, at arm's length away from it. The same was true in relation to education. Primary and secondary education grew out of the work of the churches. Literacy was for centuries tied up with the Church. The earliest schools that we know of, dating back to the Anglo-Saxon period, were linked to the Church, as were the universities at Oxford and Cambridge, which were established in the early medieval period.[15] Again, the Reformation changed very little in terms of law – largely because law rarely if at all concerned itself with education. Education, like marriage, was something left to what we would today call the voluntary sector.

12.3.2 The Centuries Following the Reformation

Similarly, marriage and education law does not fit the periodisation of toleration but rather shows that this process was uneven, contradictory and incomplete. The experiences during the centuries following the Reformation were notably different in these two areas, and neither saw a process of toleration. In terms of education, the fusion of Church and State had not led to any form of

13 Constitutions and Canons Ecclesiastical of the Church of England. https://www.anglican.net/doctrines/1604-canon-law/. Accessed November 17, 2024.

14 An Act for the Better Preventing of Clandestine Marriage [1753] 26 Geo. 2. c. 33.

15 However, as E. Jones and W. Roderick pointed out, "it is mistaken to regard late medieval education as the province only of the monasteries and the Church – there was sufficient demand to foster the creation of grammar schools": G.E. Jones, G.W. Roderick, *A History of Education in Wales* (Cardiff: University of Wales Press, 2003): 13.

monopoly on education by the State or the State Church, and so there was nothing to relax. Instead, the demand for education gradually grew in the centuries that followed, but it remained within the voluntary sector. The churches played a crucial role in this, but they did not monopolise it. From the very start, education took various different forms: from guilds that were developed in many trades, to dissenting academies which were unofficially set up following the Reformation to Sunday Schools, and later on to developments that took place under the auspices of the Poor Law. There were a variety of different types of schools. The bulk of educational provision that had been built up before the 19th century "had been built up by charitable endeavour and private initiative".[16] By contrast, "central and local government played no significant role in the running of schools". The motivation for the provision of education "remained religious, a matter for philanthropy rather than the state".[17]

By contrast, in marriage law, the centuries following the Reformation saw the exact opposite of toleration. The Marriage Act 1753 gave the established Church a monopoly. It provided the foundations of the modern law on marriage. It imposed the canon law requirements upon all weddings except for Jews and Quakers: all marriages were to take the form of a public ceremony in the parish church at which a clergyman would officiate according to authorised rites, and it required that the marriage be preceded by banns or licence. Breach of any of these requirements, which had previously made a marriage irregular, would now render it void. Although it was not the first attempt to regularise the performance and registration of marriage, the Marriage Act 1753 is often regarded to be a pivotal moment providing certainty as to who was married and stopping marriages taking place in ways that the State was unaware of. This was problematic, because marital status bestowed certain legal rights and social attitudes at the time saw children born out of wedlock as being illegitimate. Although it has now been questioned whether the Act largely reinforced existing social conventions rather than stamping out a serious and prevalent problem of marriages being conducted in various and unusual ways,[18] nevertheless, the effect of the legislation was clear. The emphasis on marriage taking place in a religious building open to the public continues to underscore the current law. The Act imposed uniformity. The monopolisation of the Church of England over marriage, therefore, was not the result of the Reformation but was only formally consolidated by the 1753 Act.

16 W. Cornish, S. Banks, C. Mitchell, P. Mitchell, R. Probert, *Law and Society in England 1750–1950* (Oxford: Hart, 2019): 411.

17 G.E. Jones, G.W. Roderick, *A History of Education in Wales* 27.

18 R. Probert, *Marriage Law and Practice in the Long Eighteenth Century* (Cambridge: Cambridge University Press, 2009).

12.3.3 The 19th Century

The experiences of marriage and education law also question the narrative that secularisation and the privatisation of religion furthered in the modern era. Significant reforms to both areas of the law took place in the 19th century. On the face of it, there is some evidence of marriage law following this toleration template. The Marriage Act 1836[19] made provision for "civil marriage" permitting marriages to take place in register offices following a civil ceremony in the presence of a registrar and witnesses. That Act also provided that buildings registered as a place of religious worship could be registered for solemnising marriages therein. This was a key component of the piecemeal toleration of other forms of religion. The foundations of the modern law of marriage were now fully laid out. Yet, the picture is more complex than that. Rebecca Probert has argued that there is a need to question the common perceptions about the 1836 Act whereby it is "seen as an important liberalizing measure" and the "story told about it has generally been a positive one in that it has been recognised the religious (and irreligious) diversity of nineteenth-century England and Wales".[20] Probert notes that there is "a tendency in at least some of the scholarship to exaggerate the extent to which the 1836 Act liberalised the law" in that many "imply that it allowed couples to be married in any chapel and by any minister of religion". As she noted, "[T]he exacting criteria for places of worship to be registered for weddings meant that many were not". The Act required a separate building for all but Catholics and 20 householders had to certify that it was their usual place for worship. Furthermore, it was not until the Marriage Act 1898[21] that registered places of worship were permitted to appoint their own "authorised person" in place of a registrar. And even today, "many registered places of worship have not appointed their own authorised person and remain dependent on a registrar attending and registering any weddings that take place there". Probert noted that, above all else, how any given couple could marry depended very much on local factors. She further argued that the category of civil marriage has been misunderstood. The term "civil" was not defined in the Act, and the register office weddings were not envisaged as being the default. Rather, the "option of getting married in a register office was intended for that small subcategory of dissenters who regarded marriage as a civil contract". Moreover, civil was not originally synonymous with being secular. It was not until the Marriage and Registration Act 1856[22] that religious content became prohibited in civil ceremonies. The effect of the Marriage Act 1836 has often been overstated as part of a narrative of progress. It did not sever the monopolistic assumptions that had previously been consolidated by the 1753 Act.

19 Marriage Act 1836, 6 & 7 Will. 4. c. 85.

20 R. Probert, *Tying the Knot: The Formation of Marriage 1836–2020* (Cambridge: Cambridge University Press, 2021).

21 Marriage Act [1898] 62 Vic. No. 1582.

22 Marriage and Registration Act 1856, UK Public General Acts1856 c. 119.

The situation in relation to education law was also messier than talk of toleration and religious autonomy often suggests. Religious rivalry was often a catalyst for change and State involvement increased gradually, usually in a pragmatic way. The turning point came with the Elementary Education Act 1870.[23] The Act established local school boards in areas where there were insufficient voluntary schools. Their function was to build and manage schools to fill up the gaps in the system provided by the denominations and charities to ensure that education was provided up to the age of 13. This proved contentious amongst religious groups: while the Church of England "wished to preserve and even to extend its grip on education; the Non-conformists fiercely opposed any additional financial support for Church schools".[24] The question of religious teaching came to the fore during the passage of the Bill through Parliament. Parliamentarians considered whether the Act should require compulsory religious instruction, whether it should "not be used or directed in favour of or against the distinctive tenets of any religious denomination", and whether there should be a conscience clause allowing a right to withdraw from this.[25] In the end, a compromise was reached by what became known as the "Cowper-Temple clause"[26] that "no religious catechism or religious formulary distinctive of any particular denomination" was to be taught in these new schools.[27] The "Cowper-Temple clause" limited how denominational religious instruction in the new schools could be but did not mean that schools could not teach their religious ethos. The splits caused by these provisions had a significant political effect and were to be far-reaching. The situation was worsened by the fact that the Act only applied to the new elementary schools which were only built where there was no existing sufficient provision and by the fact that a grace period was provided to allow churches to set up new schools before the new system came into effect.[28] As Anthony Howard noted,

> The result, inevitably, was a typically British compromise – or more bluntly, muddle – in which some parents could choose between secular and denominational education while others, mainly in rural villages, had no choice but to send their children to schools in which the dogmas of the Established Church formed a specific part of the curriculum.[29]

These 19th-century developments culminating in the Elementary Education Act 1870[30] saw the State take an interest in education for the first time and

23 Often known as the 'Forster Act' after William Edward Forster who was responsible for education in Gladstone's Government.

24 G.E. Jones, G.W. Roderick, *A History of Education in Wales* 79.

25 See the House of Commons discussion at Committee stage: HC Hansard (30 June 1870) columns 1236–1263.

26 Named after the compromise put forward by Liberal MP W. Cowper-Temple.

27 Elementary Education Act 1870, 33 & 34 Vict. c. 75, sec. 14(2).

28 W. Cornish, S. Banks, C. Mitchell, P. Mitchell, R. Probert, *Law and Society in England* 422.

29 A. Howard, *Rab: The Life of R.A. Butler* (London: Jonathan Cape, 1987): 111.

30 Elementary Education Act 1870, 33 & 34 Vict. c. 75.

attempt to bring it within the purview of State law. It can therefore be compared as the education equivalent of the Reformation legislation or indeed the Marriage Act 1753. However, the Elementary Education Act 1870 did not lead to anything like the monopolisation of the Church of England that occurred under those other two developments. It was also not an act of toleration or of secularisation. Rather, it was an example of the State working alongside the existing provision provided mostly by the churches. Yet, this pragmatic response was never completely stable. Both marriage and education law were the object of significant legislation in the mid-20th century, but while the Marriage Act 1949[31] largely consolidated the existing law, the education legislation was to prove much more controversial. As Howard commented,

> The seeds for the last great battle fought on behalf of the historical forces of Dissent in Britain had been sown. So firmly were they planted that they defied the successive efforts of Governments of differing political complexions over the next seventy years to uproot them.[32]

This battle, however, was completely omitted from the conventional progress narrative. Contrary to the "subtraction stories" often told about the perceived secularisation of the law, education reform actually clarified, consolidated and then reinforced the hold of Christianity.

12.3.4 The 20th Century

There were three major reforms in education law in the 20th century: the Education Act 1902,[33] the Education Act 1944[34] and the Education Reform 1988. The Education Act 1902 is often overlooked but brought about significant structural change. It replaced the school boards with Local Education Authorities (LEAs) and brought the voluntary schools "under the control of the LEAs".[35] These were mainly church schools and mainly associated with the Church of England. Such schools were now supported by the rates, and in return, LEAs appointed a third of the managers/governors of the school.[36] This meant that "in return for a modest surrender of independence they had acquired financial security".[37] The 1902 Act therefore formally recognised the "dual system" whereby "denominational schools run (but no longer wholly paid for) by the Churches lived cheek-by-jowl with schools both administered

31 Marriage Act 1949, 12, 13 & 14 Geo. 6. c. 76.
32 Marriage Act 1949, 12, 13 & 14 Geo. 6. c. 76.
33 Education Act 1902, Edw. 7 c. 42.
34 The Education Act of 1944, 7 & 8 Geo. 6. c. 31. Often known as the "Butler" Act.
35 Some funding had previously been provided under the Voluntary Schools Act 1897, 60 & 61 Vict. c. 5.
36 Education Act 1902 sec. 6(2).
37 W. Cornish, S. Banks, C. Mitchell, P. Mitchell, R. Probert, *Law and Society in England* 450.

and supervised by the State".[38] The passage of the Act witnessed "a great deal of Nonconformist antagonism" in a way that made clear that further reform would be politically controversial. [39] It also led to civil disobedience from some dissenters who refused to pay their rates knowing that they would fund the Church of England school. Parental choice was respected by means of a conscience clause, but the nature of religious instruction remained undefined. The only concession was made in the legislation was the "Kenyon-Slaney clause",[40] section 7(6), which provided that religious education in schools not provided by the State was to be in accordance with the trust deed and was to be under the control of the by the managers/governors of the school unless the trust deed specified differently.

The Education Act 1944 revolutionised both the position of the voluntary church schools that existed alongside the State schools and the teaching of religion in both types of school. Prior to the Act, the ban on teaching by catechism only applied to those schools completely run by local authorities.[41] Moreover, many areas were what the Education Minister Rab Butler called "single-school" areas where the Church of England school was the only school available and "non-conformists naturally regretted sending their children to a school which taught the catechism of the Church of England". Yet, Butler's reforms would strengthen rather than weaken the position of the Church of England. It has been noted that under the Butler Act, "the role of Anglicanism within education was not only secured but enlarged".[42] Butler saw the 1902 Act as having damaged both the Conservative Party and the Church of England, and so the Act that he would be remembered for was "an attempt to bring Church and state back together and reverse the effects of 1870 and 1902 in keeping them apart".[43]

Manoeuvres from religious leaders themselves were to prove influential.

As Butler noted in his memoirs, in Cambridgeshire in 1924, a committee of Anglicans, free churchmen, and teachers met and drew up a syllabus of religious instruction for use in the county's schools.[44] By 1942, the Cambridgeshire syllabus was in use in over 100 LEAs. Butler noted that "because of this, many Anglican managers were willing to hand over their schools to the local authorities in return for Christian teachings on these lines". In meetings with church leaders, Butler seized upon this new potential and stressed "the financial challenge the Church of England would face if it sought to maintain its school

38 A. Howard, *Rab: The Life of R.A. Butler* 112.

39 W. Cornish, S. Banks, C. Mitchell, P. Mitchell, R. Probert, *Law and Society in England* 451.

40 Named after W. Kenyon-Slaney MP.

41 As Butler himself noted in his autobiography, voluntary schools which were mostly run by the churches "gave the religious instruction of the Church to which they belonged, while local authority schools gave religious instruction unconnected with the formulary or beliefs of any particular Church". R.A. Butler, *The Art of the Possible: The Memoirs of Lord Butler* (Harmondsworth: Penguin, 1973) 98.

42 W. Cornish, S. Banks, C. Mitchell, P. Mitchell, R. Probert, *Law and Society in England* 454.

43 W. Cornish, S. Banks, C. Mitchell, P. Mitchell, R. Probert, *Law and Society in England* 455.

44 R.A. Butler, *The Art of the Possible*, 100.

system unimpaired".[45] Moreover, he presented a solution that gave the churches "an offer of two alternatives".[46] The Butler solution was to create two categories of voluntary schools, voluntary controlled schools and voluntary aided schools with the difference between the two being dictated by control and financing. This built upon the existing category of voluntary schools but crucially brought all schools within the system. It was thought that the non-conformist and most Church of England schools would opt for the voluntary aided model with the additional funding outweighing the cost of loss of some control while Catholic schools would go for the aided model, retaining further control but at a cost of providing more finance themselves.

The Education Act 1944 followed the schema that Butler had set and made collective worship and religious instruction statutory obligations.[47] Section 27 stated that in voluntary controlled schools, religious instruction would also be given in accordance with the agreed syllabus unless parents requested that their children receive religious instruction in accordance with the school's trust. Under section 28, the religious instruction given at a voluntary aided school was under the control of the managers or governors of the school and was to be in accordance with the school's trust deed or where provision was not made in the trust deed in accordance with the practice observed in the school. Section 29 provided that LEAs would have the power to "constitute a standing authority council on religious education to advise the authority" known as Standing Advisory Councils for Religious Education (SACRE).[48] Schedule 5 stated that a conference would be convened to prepare any agreed syllabus, and this would consist of four committees: the first of these was to consist of the representatives of religious denominations that the LEA considered ought to be represented "having regard to the circumstances of the area"; the second, in England, was a committee of representatives of the Church of England; the third was to be a committee of teachers; and the fourth of representatives of the local authority". The LEA was to have regard to any unanimous recommendations made to them (Section 29). These provisions further entrenched the position of the Church of England since it meant that the Church had its own committee that had a deciding vote.[49] The Butler Act made no further comment as to the content of religious instruction or worship. The matter had been raised by an amendment in the House of Lords by the Bishop of Chichester.[50] Lord Selborne responded

45 A. Howard, *Rab: The Life of R.A. Butler*, 125.

46 R.A. Butler, *The Art of the Possible*, 102.

47 G. McCulloch, *Educational Reconstruction: The 1944 Education Act and the Twenty-First Century* (Ilford; Essex: Woburn Press, 1994) 39.

48 Such bodies were optional under the Act and there is evidence of similar bodies existing before the Act.

49 W. Cornish, S. Banks, C. Mitchell, P. Mitchell, R. Probert, *Law and Society in England* 454–455.

50 The Education Act of 1944 [1944] House of Lords Hansard vol. 132, c. 362.

that stating it was not necessary to explicitly state this because the Act's provisions on the composition of the SACRE meant that "it will be a syllabus which the Church of England can accept, and the Church of England is not going to accept a syllabus which is not in accordance with the Christian faith". This issue was, however, raised during the passage of what was to become the Education Reform Act 1988.

The 1988 Act proved to be a watershed moment in the history of education presenting a raft of reforms including the introduction of the National Curriculum.[51] The focus of the Thatcher Government was not upon religious matters. However, the Bishop of London successfully tabled amendments to amendments to ensure that, as he saw it, the Bill did not represent a move towards secularism or a move away from traditional Christian values. In the House of Lords debate, he stated that these amendments were based upon five main principles:

> We have sought to provide a framework for worship which, first, maintains the tradition of worship as part of the process of education, giving proper place to the Christian religion; secondly, maintains the contribution of the collective act of worship to the establishment of values within the school community; yet, thirdly, does not impose inappropriate forms of worship on certain groups of pupils; fourthly, does not break the school up into communities based on the various faiths of the parents, especially in that it makes some groups feel that they are not really part of the community being educated in the school; and, lastly, is realisable and workable in practical terms of school accommodation and organisation.[52]

The Bill as amended by the House of Lords reinforced the place of Christianity. It stated that daily collective worship, which could be "a single act of worship for all pupils or separate acts of worship for pupils in different age groups or different school groups" (Section 6), had in a county school to "be wholly or mainly of a broadly Christian character", and this would be satisfied "if it reflects the broad traditions of Christian belief without being distinctive of any particular Christian denomination" (Section 7). However, every act of collective worship did not need to comply with this provision "provided that, taking the school term as a whole, most such acts that take place in the school do comply". Powers were given to SACREs to determine whether it was not appropriate for the rule to "apply in the case of a county school or in the case

51 On the Act generally see, e.g., L. Bash, D. Coulby (eds.), *The Education Reform Act: Competition and Control* (London: Cassell, 1989); D. Lawton (ed.) *The Education Reform Act: Choice and Control* (London: Hodder & Stoughton, 1989) and M. Flude, M. Hammer (eds.), *The Education Reform Act 1988: its Origins and Implications* (London: Falmer Press, 1990).

52 Education Reform Act 1988, House of Lords Hansard [1988] c. 434.

of any class of description of pupil's, at such a school".[53] It was further specified that the agreed syllabus adopted under Schedule 5 of the 1944 Act "shall reflect the fact that the religious traditions in Great Britain are in the main Christian whilst taking account of the teaching and practices of the other principal religions represented in Great Britain" (Section 8). The rationale was to "reinforce" the Butler Act.[54] However, the 1988 Act clearly went beyond the Butler Act.[55] At the very least, the Act made explicit what had previously been implicit – and what may have been implicit and taken for granted in the 1940s was no longer uncontroversial in Thatcher's Britain. This applied not only to the idea that Christianity in general and the Church of England in particular were the norm but also the notion that local areas were largely mono-creedal. The growth of religious diversity and pluralism rendered quaint the idea that each locality could determine their own unique and distinct religious makeup, and so the disconnect between the law and the social reality became a constant theme in the literature.

This disconnect is also observable in marriage law where, by contrast to education law, the 20th century saw comparatively little change. The Marriage Act 1949 consolidated the much older law and did not readjust the legal framework on getting married. It differentiates between marriages solemnised according to the rites of the Church of England / Church in Wales and marriages otherwise solemnised. This second category of marriages otherwise solemnised include civil marriages in a register office or in approved premises, marriages "according to the usages of the Society of Friends", marriages "between a man and a woman professing the Jewish religion according to the usages of the Jews", and marriages in any place of worship registered under the Places of Worship Registration Act 1855 and Section 41 of the Marriage Act 1949. On the surface, therefore, the Act allows for the legal recognition of religious marriages. However, the way in which it deals with religions differently breeds confusion and disadvantage. The fact that three religious groups are specifically named in the legislation has led to some confusion.[56] The problem is not that other religious marriages cannot be legally recognised under the Act. It is rather that the requirements required for such recognition indirectly discriminate against some religions: the requirements that religious weddings (other than Anglican, Jewish, and Quaker ceremonies) must be inside a registered place of worship and that a prescribed choice of words must be used do not fit with some religious traditions. This leads to religious marriages taking place that are not legally recognised, which can prove problematic on relationship breakdown where the redress and support provided by the State for those separating and

53 SACRES were now compulsory.

54 The Education Act of 1944 [1987] House of Commons Hansard vol 124, c. 439W.

55 For a further analysis see E. Cox, J.M. Cairns, *Reforming Religious Education: The Religious Clauses of the 1988 Education Reform Act* (London: Kogan Page, 1989).

56 *Getting Married: A Consultation Paper on Weddings Law* (London: Law Commission, 2020) § 5.25 ff.

divorcing are not available to those who are not legally married. It also poses a problem for weddings conducted by belief organisations which simply cannot be legally binding in their own right. Couples who have such weddings are not married in the eyes of the law unless and until they also undergo a civil ceremony. Accounts of marriage law also tend to present these legal obstacles as being long-standing. Yet, the Marriage Act 1949 simply reflects compromises reached in a previous situation that is more than ripe for readjustment and reform now. As with education law, exploring the development of these areas of law over time debunks any linear account of a secular "progress". Moreover, the picture could and should be complicated further by adjusting the focus away from majority interests. Focusing on non-Christian religions and on non-religious beliefs would cast the historical development of the law and the need for reform in a dramatically different light.

12.3.5 The 21st Century

The current domestic law governing religious observance in schools in England[57] can now be found in the Education Act 1996[58] and the School Standards and Framework Act 1998.[59] These provisions continue to be broadly the same as the settlement reached in 1944, as amended by the 1988 Act. This means that law on religious education in England continues to privilege Christianity and places unrealistic obligations upon schools. This is particularly true in relation to the recognition of non-religious beliefs; something that English law has struggled with generally. This is reflected in a series of unprincipled and contradictory Employment Tribunal decisions on how belief is to be defined for the purpose of employment law. Beliefs in independence for Scotland[60] and veganism[61] have been protected whilst the wearing of a Poppy [62] and vegetarianism[63] have not, for instance.[64] In relation to education and marriage law, the problem is rather different: non-religious belief systems are excluded by the letter of the law that extends protection only to religions. In recent years, this has led to litigation in both education law and marriage law.

57 There has been recent reform of the law on religious education in Wales as documented: R. Sandberg, *Religion in Schools*.

58 Education Act 1996, UK Public General Acts1996, c. 56.

59 School Standards and Framework Act 1998, UK Public General Acts1998, c. 31.

60 *McEleny v. MOD* [2018] UKET 4105347/2017.

61 *Casamitjana v. The League of Cruel Sports* [2020] ET 3331129/2018.

62 *Lisk v. Shield Guardian Co Ltd & Others* [2011] ET 3300873/2011.

63 *Mr G Conisbee v. Crossley Farms Ltd &Ors* [2019] ET 3335357/2018.

64 See R. Sandberg, "Is the National Health Service a Religion?", *Ecclesiastical Law Journal*, vol. 22, no. 3 (2020) 343.

12.3.5.1 Bowen

The outmoded nature of the letter of the law in the education law context is shown by the recent decision in *R (on the Application of Bowen) v. Kent County Council.*[65] This High Court decision makes it clear that local authorities cannot exclude humanist representatives from their SACREs. Although many SACREs already included humanists, and this interpretation has been articulated in soft law, the judgement of Constable J is unambiguous on that point and shows that the letter of education law is now to be interpreted in a flexible, some may say fictitious, manner. Moreover, the judgement also highlights how the protection of non-religious beliefs continues to be controversial and lacking in clarity.

Under section 390(4)(a) of the Education Act 1996, Group A of each SACRE is required to be "a group of persons to represent such Christian denominations and other religions and denominations of such religions as, in the opinion of the authority, will appropriately reflect the principal religious traditions in the area". Kent County Council refused to appoint Mr Bowen to Group A on the basis that as a humanist he did not represent "a religion or a denomination of a religion", and so it would have been unlawful for them to do so (section 390(4)(a) § 2).

Mr Bowen successfully contended that this was discriminatory and in breach of Article 14 ECHR. His argument was that pursuant to section 3 of the Human Rights Act 1998, the words "other religions" should be construed "in much the same way that Warby J construed the phrase 'religious education'" in *R (Fox) v. Education Secretary.*[66]

The decision in *Fox* concerned the new subject content issued for General Certificate of Secondary Education (GCSE) Religious Studies. The High Court held that the statement that the "subject content is consistent with the requirements for the statutory provision of religious education in current legislation" was "a false and misleading statement of law" because complying with the subject content would not necessarily fulfil the religious education obligations since it might not include the study of non-religious views. As Warby J noted,"[T]he complete exclusion of any study of non-religious beliefs for the whole of Key Stage 4, for which the Subject Content would allow, would not [...] be compatible" with the ECHR.[67] *Bowen* took *Fox* to its logical conclusion to underline that to exclude non-religious beliefs from religious education breaches the ECHR. As Constable noted in *Bowen*,

> [I]t is plain from *Fox* that a religious education curriculum must, in order to be compliant with the [Human Rights Act] 1998, cover more than religious faith teaching. The content of religious education teaching

65 *R (on the Application of Bowen) v. Kent County Council* [2023] EWHC 1261 (Admin).

66 *R (on the Application of Fox) v. Secretary of State for Education* [2015] EWHC 3404 (Admin); *R (Fox) v. Education Secretary* [2023] § 3.

67 *R (Fox) v. Secretary of State for Education* [2015] § 74.

> must include, at least to some degree, the teaching of non-religious beliefs (such as humanism).[68]

Constable held that the discriminatory nature of section 390(4) as interpreted by Kent County Council was "manifestly without reasonable foundation and not justifiable": "Indeed, it is antithetical to what the provisions can sensibly be considered as aiming to achieve, when that aim is now to be realised in light of the fact that "religious education" must include some teaching of non-religious beliefs, as confirmed in *Fox*".[69] Constable J made it clear that Parliamentary materials suggesting that the original intent was to protect religious beliefs only would not be of "any relevance".[70] He reasoned that, although historic Parliamentary material showed that "religious education was to be confined to teaching Christianity and other principal faiths", the question of whether that should be the case was

> an entirely different issue from whether once it is recognised [...] that the curriculum must include some elements of non-religious beliefs, a SACRE's constitution should be capable of including representatives of those non-religious beliefs which are appropriate to be included in the curriculum.[71]

The High Court was clear, however, that the judgment extended no further than determining that the basis of Kent County Council's decision was erroneous in law:

> It does not follow that any and every non-religious belief would need to be treated similarly – for example, it may be legitimate to conclude that a particular belief (religious or non-religious) does not attain the requisite level of cogency, seriousness, cohesion and importance to attract protection. Similarly, as I have described, there remains considerable discretion for the local authority when determining who to appoint pursuant to section 390(6) to ensure consistency with the efficient discharge of the group's functions.[72]

Although worth stating, these points are obvious and non-contentious. The more pressing matter is where the line is to be drawn. While this judgment makes it clear that this particular statutory reference to "other religions" is to be construed to include the non-religious, it remains unclear[73] as to how far

68 *R (Fox) v. Education Secretary* [2023] § 68.
69 *R (Fox) v. Education Secretary* [2023] § 9.3.
70 *R (Fox) v. Education Secretary* [2023] § 84.
71 *R (Fox) v. Education Secretary* [2023] § 84.
72 *R (Fox) v. Education Secretary* [2023] § 107.
73 *R (Fox) v. Education Secretary* [2023] § 17–18.

this term extends. Constable J referred briefly to recent reforms in Wales, but there too the issue of how to define belief has been fudged. *Bowen* follows the approach of the Welsh reforms in assuming that the human rights jurisprudence provides a clear steer as to definition. Unfortunately, it does not.

Following Warby J in Fox, Constable J in *Bowen* did not attempt to reformulate the legislation.[74] He made it clear that humanism is clearly included but left wide open the question of where the line is to be drawn:

> Whatever the precise wording that might in due course be adopted by Parliament, should it choose to do so, humanism is self evidently a belief system which is appropriate to be included within a religious education syllabus (not least because it overwhelmingly is already), and would be encompassed within any Convention-compliant interpretation of section 390(4)(a).[75]

This is not the only open-ended question. While *Bowen* makes it clear that the term "other religions" in section 390 is to be read as including humanism, questions remain about other statutory requirements in education law and beyond. As Constable noted, "[T]here are indeed a number of different ways in which Parliament might seek to amend the various religious education related provisions, including section 390, and accept that that may involve policy decisions which are beyond the remit of this Court".[76] *Bowen* is an important milestone in the (regrettably) gradual recognition that freedom of religion or belief protects non-religious beliefs. The High Court judgment is particularly welcome in making clear that a literal interpretation of England's educational laws on this matter is not legally correct, and it debunks many of the objections often given for extending protection in this way. There remains much more to do, and this can be underlined by looking at the position in marriage law and the decision in *R (on Application of Harrison) v. Secretary of State for Justice*.[77]

12.3.5.2 Harrison

A report by an All Party Parliamentary Humanist Group in 2018 suggested that until the 1970s a blind eye had been turned to weddings conducted by belief groups, and they were considered to be legally binding.[78] According to the report, "[S]ome ethical societies performed wedding ceremonies in their

74 *R (Fox) v. Education Secretary* [2023] § 104.
75 *R (Fox) v. Education Secretary* [2023] § 106.
76 *R (Fox) v. Education Secretary* [2023] § 102.
77 *R (on Application of Harrison) v. Secretary of State for Justice* [2020] EWHC 2096 (Admin).
78 All-Party Parliamentary Humanist Group, "Any Lawful Impediment?" A Report of the All-Party Parliamentary Humanist Group's Inquiry into the Legal Recognition of Humanist Marriage in England and Wales(2018) 11. https://humanists.uk/wp-content/uploads/APPHG-report-on-humanist-marriage.pdf. Accessed November 17, 2024.

venues, and relatively lax interpretations of the law at the time meant that these generally had legal recognition. The Report noted that 'this continued until the anomalous position was picked up by Government officials in the 1970s'".Ever since, it has been clear that the reference to religions excluded non-religious beliefs.

In *R (on the Application of Hodkin) v. Registrar General of Births, Deaths and Marriages*,[79] Lord Toulson held that the exclusion of secular belief systems was appropriate because there are other legal provisions which allow for secular wedding services on approved premises.[80] However, this contention rested on the assumption that a civil wedding is an appropriate substitute for humanists. The High Court in *Harrison* disagreed with this analysis.

Just months before a consultation paper on wedding law reform was due to be published by the Law Commission,[81] a challenge was brought before the High Court by six couples – supported by Humanists UK – against the current prohibition on humanist weddings. In a Briefing to Members of Parliament, Humanists UK pointed out that while the Law Commission could "make recommendations on how humanist marriages could be recognised, it can't recommend to the Government if they should be".[82] In the end, the decision in *R (On Application of Harrison) v. Secretary of State for Justice*[83] indicated that the law should change but did not go quite as far as to require immediate change. Ironically, given the stance of the humanist campaign, the High Court held that the only reason that stopped a declaration that the current law was discriminatory and incompatible with human rights was the current and then ongoing work of the Law Commission because the decision to look at the issue within the contest of wider reform was justified.

The Secretary of State maintained that there had been no breach of Convention rights since the law on civil marriage provided a legally recognised, non-religious ceremony that was sufficiently capable of accommodating the claimants' wishes and beliefs. He further considered that even if there had been any difference in treatment between the claimants and their religious comparators, the measures under challenge were "objectively and reasonably justified, not least given ongoing consideration of reform in this area of social policy".[84] Eady disagreed. The evidence was that for many who hold humanist beliefs, "ceremonies that mark significant life events, such as marriage, provide a close and direct link to the beliefs of the participants" would be enough

79 *R (on the Application of Hodkin) v. Registrar General of Births, Deaths and Marriages* [2013] UKSC 77.

80 *R (on the Application of Hodkin) v. Registrar General of Births, Deaths and Marriages* [2013] UKSC 77 § 58–59.

81 *Getting Married.*

82 "Briefing for MPs on humanist marriages in England and Wales". https://humanism.org.uk/briefing-for-mps-on-humanist-marriages-in-england-and-wales. Accessed August 12, 2020.

83 *R (On Application of Harrison) v. Secretary of State for Justice* [2020] EWHC 2096 (Admin).

84 *R (On Application of Harrison) v. Secretary of State for Justice* [2020] EWHC 2096 (Admin) § 4.

for a wish to hold such ceremonies to constitute a manifestation of Article 9.[85] Eady held that there had been a discriminatory difference of treatment between the claimants and religious comparators. The differential treatment in this case was that "unlike their religious comparators, a marriage ceremony according to their humanist beliefs will not be legally recognised absent the supervisory presence of state officials".[86] There is no option for humanist celebrants to take on the role played by the superintendent registrar and registrar in civil weddings.

Eady held that such discrimination could not be justified on grounds of "the special place of marriage and of particular marriage ceremonies to the religions in question" since that would "simply repeat the discrimination of which the claimants complain" and because there was "no rational connection between the way in which English law recognises marriage and the stated objective".[87] Neither could the current position be justified on grounds that creating a new separate category of marriage ceremony for humanists would add further complexity and would introduce new forms of discrimination against non-humanists or non-belief systems: it was "no defence to plead that the system is already discriminatory and no answer to rely on a possible risk of some new, hypothetical discrimination as justification for the very real adverse impact already suffered".[88]

However, the current discrimination was justified by the "legitimate aim not to wish to reform the law in a piecemeal fashion when there are further issues arising in this area of social policy (presently being considered by the Law Commission)" and that the Government and then Parliament should be allowed time to reflect.[89] It was relevant that the Law Commission concurred with the Government's view, that reform was needed on a wholesale, rather than piecemeal, basis. Following its consultation paper, the Law Commission published its final report in July 2022 calling for wholesale reform and a move from regulating buildings to recognising celebrants.[90] The Government's response, which ought to have been made within six months of publication, has yet to be made and there is now no chance of reform this side of the General Election. It would remain to be seen what would happen should a similar case to *Harrison* be considered by the courts now that the Law

85 *R (On Application of Harrison) v. Secretary of State for Justice* [2020] EWHC 2096 (Admin) § 70.

86 *R (On Application of Harrison) v. Secretary of State for Justice* [2020] EWHC 2096 (Admin) § 93.

87 *R (On Application of Harrison) v. Secretary of State for Justice* [2020] EWHC 2096 (Admin) § 93, 105.

88 *R (On Application of Harrison) v. Secretary of State for Justice* [2020] EWHC 2096 (Admin) § 106, 110.

89 *R (On Application of Harrison) v. Secretary of State for Justice* [2020] EWHC 2096 (Admin) § 107.

90 Celebrating Marriage: A New Weddings Law Commission for England and Wales, Report no. 408. https://doi.org/10.1093/lawfam/ebad031.

Commission have reported, and the Government has not acted. A *Bowen*-like decision that results in a change of interpretation would be more problematic in the marriage law context, but the judgment in *Harrison* makes clear that the current law cannot remain for long.

12.3.6 Reflection

It is clear that marriage and education law do not correspond with the conventional progress narratives. Rather, what we have seen is a pragmatic and often chaotic approach whereby law slowly, inelegantly, and often inadequately has tried to regulate aspects of an activity that previously was largely, if not completely, dealt with by the voluntary sector. The picture is not one of the voices of the churches declining but rather of the State attempting – not entirely successfully– to obtain a foothold. This is not the picture that we are usually presented with. That is because social functional differentiation and talk of religious equality is so ingrained. Many accounts assume that the current law is archaic and reflects a historical reality that has been relaxed over time. This is not so. In place of the usual subtraction stories that highlight the perceived decline of influence of the churches, the previous discussion has presented a much less straightforward picture whereby legal change is often the result of pragmatic and unpredictable compromise and whereby the letter of the law often exists in a different reality than the social practice. In so doing, it presents the current law not as a stump of a once magnificent tree that has been chopped away at over time but rather as the product of a historical quirk based on grubby compromises and an unwillingness if not downright refusal to consider comprehensive reform.

The conventional subtraction stories, predicated upon the idea that religious involvement is a historical throwback, are so ingrained and so successful that they frustrate the reform movement. They focus our attention upon the experience of majorities and present the historical foundations of the law as being firmer and older than they are. This conceals the extent to which the legal rules are actually the result of grubby compromises fit for purpose at the time in which they were made but which can now be remodelled to suit today's social situation. The fact that the direction of travel has been far from linear, definitely not inevitable, and absolutely not irreversible highlights the capacity for legal change and highlights that reform can be achieved in a pragmatic basis. Seeing the present law as being the often-accidental consequence of tweaks that were politically possible at particular times, rather than as some received wisdom passed down and "improved" as societies advanced, makes the need for reform not only more compelling but also means that such reform could and should be more radical.

12.4 Conclusion

Sunak's simplistic and some might say opportunistic sermonising illustrates the historical, geographical, and religious literacy that is sadly prevalent. It comes from a place of complacency. The success story being told demands this. The narrative of progress explains away existing inequalities as historical taints rather than seeing, let alone accepting, the rotten core that exists. Moreover, the entrenched inequalities cannot be just attributed to history. They are the result of choices made – often comparatively recently – and perpetuated daily. The continued existence of the status quo is a sign of indifference, of lethargy, and also the result of a political programme under successive Right-Wing Governments that have sought to reduce the welfare State while allocating blame for this and the resultant declining living conditions upon "others". It is notable that many of the laws regulating religious freedom were enacted during the last Labour Government. Since then, Conservative-led Governments with a rotating seat of Prime Ministers have paid little real attention to social justice due to an obsession with ideological financial austerity and the exiting of the European Union, which has perpetuated hostility towards the very notion of human rights as something "foreign". It remains to be seen whether the Labour Government elected in 2024 will redress this or will continue the trend. The background of the new Prime Minister Sir Keir Starmer as a human rights lawyer indicates an end to hostility towards human rights from Number 10 yet the financially prudent course taken to date suggests the revival of austerity and a deprioritisation of social justice in favour of "balancing the books". Historically, the UK has provided a very idiosyncratic and perhaps context-specific way of regulating religion or belief that often had little to recommend itself to others, with the exception perhaps of the flexibility provided by common law fudge. In recent years, however, it is beyond question that the UK approach provides a stunning exemplar: of how *not* to accommodate religion or belief.

13 *Laïcité*, the Legal Framework for the Exercise of Religions in France

François Finck

Abstract

The principle of the French secularism (*Laïcité*) was established to free politics and education from the hegemony of the Catholic Church. This chapter explores its relation to minority religions, especially Judaism and Islam, through the examples of the wearing of conspicuous religious symbols or dress in State schools, male circumcision, and ritual slaughter. This chapter argues that the legal framework analysed guarantees the accommodation of minority religious practices in France.

Keywords

Laïcité; secularism; freedom of conscience; religious symbols; circumcision; ritual slaughter

13.1 Introduction

Secularism (*Laïcité*)[1] is a fundamental principle of the French legal order. It is based on three inseparable values: freedom of conscience, legal equality of spiritual and religious options, and the neutrality of political power. Secularism implies the neutrality of the State: it must not favour any spiritual or religious option. Based on the principle of equality, the secular State does not grant public privileges to any religion, and its relations with them are characterised by legal separation. The freedom to worship allows all religions to express themselves, to associate, and to pursue spiritual goals together.

As a result of a long struggle against Catholic dominance over State and society in France, *Laïcité* was established as a protection of the State against

1 The French *Laïcité* will be used in this text.

DOI: 10.4324/9781003423294-18

religious hegemony, contrary to secularism in the United States, which served as a guarantee of the freedom of religious communities against State interference. The main laws which established Laïcité have been adopted in order to put an end to the monopoly of the Catholic Church in important spheres of public life. Hence, religious minorities were not an issue of political and legal debate. On the contrary, *Laïcité* was largely supported by religious minorities at the time of the adoption of the Separation Act in 1905,[2] because it enshrined and guaranteed their full legal equality.

An analysis of the law and case law reveals a certain paradox: the primary aim of the Separation Act, and of secular principles taken as a whole, is to free the State – and therefore the public sphere – from religious interference. Yet, and this is the apparent contradiction, French law has been somewhat indifferent to religious practices that may raise human rights issues or animal welfare issues. And thus, before getting to the heart of the matter, some basic facts about this principle need to be given, as it is often misunderstood.

13.2 The Principle of *Laïcité*

Laïcité has been a constitutional principle since 1946.[3] The current Constitution of 1958[4] states that

> France is an indivisible, secular (laïque), democratic and social Republic. It ensures that all citizens are equal before the law, regardless of their origin, race or religion. It respects all beliefs.

In addition, the Preamble to the 1946 Constitution, which possess constitutional value, states that "the organisation of free, secular (*laïque*) public education at all levels is a duty of the State".

The Declaration on the Rights of Man and of the Citizen established that "No one may be disturbed on account of his opinions, even religious ones, as long as the manifestation of such opinions does not interfere with the established Law and Order".[5] The phrase "even religious ones" must be understood in the context of the text's adoption: religious expressions other than Catholic were prohibited. It gives religious minorities the right to practice and to express their convictions. Linked with the general principle of liberty enshrined in Article 4, Article 10 guaranteeing freedom of opinion and Article 11 ensuring that the all opinions can be expressed, the Declaration marks the departure

2 Loi du 9 décembre 1905 concernant la séparation des Églises et de l'État. https://www.legifrance.gouv.fr/loda/id/LEGITEXT000006070169. Accessed December 9, 2025.

3 Constitution de 1946, IVe République. https://www.conseil-constitutionnel.fr/les-constitutions-dans-l-histoire/constitution-de-1946-ive-republique. Accessed December 9, 2025.

4 Constitution du 4 octobre 1958. https://www.legifrance.gouv.fr/loda/id/JORFTEXT000000571356/. Accessed December 9, 2025.

5 The Declaration of the Rights of Man and of the Citizen. https://www.elysee.fr/en/french-presidency/the-declaration-of-the-rights-of-man-and-of-the-citizen. Accessed December 9, 2025.

from the traditional principle of Catholicity, in which the legal system rested upon the rights of "Truth", to a legal system based on Laïcité, in which the State does not impose any religious opinion, a system in which the core principle is the principle of liberty.[6]

Public, secular and compulsory education was implemented, at the primary educational level, by the school laws of March 28, 1882, on compulsory primary education[7] and of October 30, 1886, on the organisation of primary education.[8] The creation of a secular public education system, and thus putting an end to the virtual monopoly of the Catholic Church, was one of the most fundamental milestones in the consolidation of the Republic. This was, in fact, also the first significant step towards a secular State.

Under the Concordate,[9] the Catholic Church in France enjoyed many privileges, and was used to wielding political power, but there was a price to be paid: the bishops were appointed by government. Main aim of the 1905 Separation Act was to put an end to century-long domination of the Catholic Church over political life, and to protect the Republic against religious interference. Hence, the law did not deal specifically with religious minorities. Various approaches were put forward by republican politicians, including some overtly anti-clerical proposals. Eventually, the liberal approach prevailed.[10]

The gist of *Laïcité* is expressed by the first two articles of the 1905 law:

> The Republic ensures freedom of conscience. It guarantees the free exercise of religious worship subject only to the restrictions set out below in the interests of public order.
>
> The Republic shall not recognise, nor pay the salaries of or subsidise any religion.

The 1905 Law was a watershed moment. It affirmed the neutrality of the State. Just as it does not defend religious dogma, the secular State does not promote atheistic or agnostic beliefs. As a consequence, the principle is the neutrality of the State, and public services have been secured. The administration, subject to political power, not only provides all the guarantees of neutrality but also itself acts in a way that can leave no doubt as to its neutrality.

6 P. Raynaud, *La laïcité, Histoire d'une singularité française* (Paris: Gallimard, 2019): 39.

7 Jules Ferry Education Act of March 28, 1882. In: D.N. Baker, P.J. Harrigan, *The Making of Frenchmen: Current Directions in the History of Education in France*, 1679–1979 (Ontario: Historical Reflections Press, 1980): 143–205.

8 Loi du 30 octobre 1886 portant sur l'organisation de l'enseignement primaire. https://www.legifrance.gouv.fr/loda/id/LEGITEXT000006070886. Accessed December 9, 2025.

9 The Concordat, September 10, 1801-April 8, 1802. https://www.napoleon-series.org/research/government/diplomatic/c_concordat.html. Accessed December 9, 2025.

10 See article Briand (Loi de séparation des Églises et de l'État de 1905, and courants de la *laïcité*.

In the same way, religious individuals and communities must refrain from any hold on the State and renounce their political dimension. Secularism is incompatible with any conception of religion that would seek to govern the social system or political order in the name of its principles.

The law guarantees freedom of conscience (and thus not only freedom of religion). Freedom of conscience is broader, as it extends to atheists and agnostics, and it includes freedom of belief. And it goes much further. Above all, it is an individual freedom and implies the freedom to change one's religion or belief or not to have one. It is both a consequence of and a guarantee of the equality of all before the law, believers and non-believers, adherents of the majority religion or of a minority religion.[11]

Freedom of conscience includes freedom of worship. In legal terms, secularism has not been an instrument for restricting spiritual choices to the detriment of religions but rather the affirmation of freedom of religious and philosophical conscience for all. It is a question of reconciling the principles of the separation of Church and State with the protection of freedom of opinion, "even religious opinion", as set out in the Declaration of the Rights of Man and of the Citizen.

The "Stasi report" drafted by the Commission for reflection on the application of the principle of secularism in the Republic, named after its chair, Bernard Stasi, then the French Ombudsman, encapsulates the expression of the philosophy behind French secularism:

> The secular framework can be the place where the dual requirement of forging unity while respecting the diversity of society can be reconciled. It must provide the means for individuals who do not share the same convictions to coexist within the same territory, rather than juxtaposing them in a mosaic of closed and mutually exclusive communities.[12]

Moreover, as the Republic guarantees freedom of conscience and the free exercise of religion, it has also taken on several accompanying obligations, like the one concerning the creation of a service of chaplaincy in closed institutions, such as prisons and the army, on the grounds that inmates or soldiers (in barracks or on a mission abroad) are not free to go to religious office. Paradoxically, it favours established religions (Catholic, Protestant, Jewish, Muslim) over other religions and over secular humanists, as the latter are not recognised and do not possess their own chaplaincy (as opposed to Belgium, for example, where the *Laïcité organisée* is recognised by the State).

11 See C. Kintzler, "Laïcité et philosophie", *Archives de Philosophie du Droit* vol. 48 (2024): 43–56 on the philosophical analysis of the principle of *Laïcité*.

12 Commission de réflexion sur l'application du principe de laïcité dans la République: rapport au Président de la République (Paris: Présidence de la République, 2003).

It should be stressed that the 1905 Law not only recognises the right to freedom of conscience and of religious worship, which is based on the 1789 Declaration, but it guarantees these liberties. It imposes positive obligations on the State. Circumcision and ritual slaughter are religious rites; hence, their exercise is protected: they are considered within the realm of religious practice, whose free exercise is guaranteed by law.[13]

At the same time, in the last decades we have witnessed development in children's rights in international law, and the rise of concern for animal welfare. Three issues will be analysed in the following sections.

13.3 Wearing Religious Symbols at Schools

The ban of religious and political symbols in the State administration and public services is a direct consequence of the principle of State's neutrality and stemming from the principle of secularism. It also imposes religious and political neutrality on its employees.[14]

In 2004, a law[15] was adopted that prohibited the "wearing of signs or dress by which pupils ostensibly manifest a religious affiliation" in State primary and secondary schools. Even though the law has been heavily criticised by some authors, it was needed as a response to the privileged place given to schools in the French republican concept.[16] This special role of schools in France is best summed up in the report of the Commission[17] which formed the basis for the law's adoption:

> The schools of the French Republic are not just places where students go to school, but places where they are destined to become enlightened citizens.
>
> School is thus a fundamental institution of the Republic, catering mainly for minors subject to compulsory education, who are called upon to live together beyond their differences.
>
> It is a specific space, subject to specific rules, so that the transmission of knowledge can take place in peace. Schools must not be sheltered from the world, but pupils must be protected from the 'fury of the

13 On the French approach to public liberties / rights and *Laïcité*, see M. Troper, "French Secularism, or Laïcité", *Cardozo Law Review* vol. 21 (2000): 1267–1284.

14 See *Ebrahimian v. France*, 64846/11 [2015] IHRL 3950; *OP v. Commune d'Ans*, C-148/22 [2023] ECLI identifier: ECLI:EU:C:2023:924.

15 Law No. 2004-228 of March 15, 2004, governing, in application of the principle of secularism, the wearing of signs or clothing demonstrating religious affiliation in public schools, colleges, and high schools. https://www.legifrance.gouv.fr/eli/loi/2004/3/15/2004-228/jo/texte. Accessed December 9, 2025.

16 P. Weil, "Why the French Laïcité Is Liberal", *Cardozo Law Review* vol. 30, no. 5 (2009): 2699–2714.

17 P. Weil, "Why the French Laďcité Is Liberal" 2703.

world': they are certainly not a sanctuary, but they must help to distance pupils from the real world so that they can learn about it.

This concept of schools as a sanctuary dedicated to learning, the development of critical thinking, and self-fulfilment, reaches back to the Enlightenment, and was also laid out by the main intellectual figure of *Laïcité* in the late 19th century, Ferdinand Buisson. In 1936, socialist Education Minister Jean Zay issued directives to headmasters of public schools. prohibiting political propaganda in and around schools "which must remain an inviolable refuge where the quarrels of men do not enter".[18] A later directive stressed,

It is also necessary to protect public education at all levels from political propaganda. It goes without saying that the same prescriptions apply to religious propaganda. Public education is secular. No form of proselytising is permitted in schools.[19]

The 2004 law was not adopted in the name of neutrality, which is not imposed on pupils (users of the public service), but only on the public service and its employees; its aim is to defend pupils' freedom of conscience. To quote the Stasi Report again, adopted in the framework of the preparation of the law,

> The secular State, guarantor of freedom of conscience, in addition to freedom of worship or expression, protects the individual; it freely allows everyone to choose, or not, a spiritual or religious option, to change or renounce it. It ensures that no group or community can impose a religious affiliation or identity on anyone, particularly because of their origins. It protects everyone against any physical or moral pressure exerted under the guise of a particular spiritual or religious prescription. The defence of individual freedom of conscience against any proselytising now complements the concepts of separation and neutrality central to the 1905 law [...] This requirement applies first and foremost to schools. Pupils must be able to learn and develop in a calm environment, so that they can make their own independent judgements. The State must prevent their minds from being harassed by the violence and fury of society: without being a sterile chamber, schools must not become an echo chamber for the passions of the world, otherwise they will fail in their educational mission.

18 Circulaire du Ministre de l'Éducation nationale du 31 décembre 1936. In: O. Loubes, "L'interdiction des propagandes politique et confessionnelle dans les établissements scolaires", *Vingtième Siècle. Revue d'histoire* no. 81 (2004): 135. https://shs.cairn.info/article/VING_081_0131/pdf?lang=fr. Accessed November 14, 2024.

19 Circulaire du Ministre de l'Éducation nationale du 15 mai 1937. In: O. Loubes, "L'interdiction des propagandes politique et confessionnelle dans les établissements scolaires", *Vingtième Siècle. Revue d'histoire* no. 81 (2004): 136.

Importantly, the issue of the rights of girls to be free from community social pressure has played an important role in the argumentation of the Stasi Commission and explains cross-party support for the law in the French Parliament.[20]

13.4 Ritual Circumcision: A Legal Framework Laid Out by Case Law

There is no specific legislation on the issue of ritual circumcision in France. It is thus allowed in the framework of the general legal provisions. This issue is not analysed by courts under the framework of *Laïcité*, but as a matter of parental prerogative to their children's education in general, and religious education in particular.

13.4.1 Circumcision: Not a Matter of Laïcité

The principle of the inviolability of the human body has since long been a fundamental principle of the French law: *Noli me tangere* is "the oldest normative principle in the field".[21]

Article 16-1 of the French Civil Code, adopted in 1994, states that "[e]veryone has the right to respect for their body. The human body is inviolable. The human body, its elements and its products cannot be the subject of a property right".[22] In turn, Article 16-2 of the Civil Code provides that "[t]he judge may prescribe any measures likely to prevent or stop unlawful interference with the human body or unlawful conduct relating to its components or products".

Medical necessity is an exception to the general principle of the inviolability of one's body, generally only with the concerned person's consent:

> The integrity of the human body may only be violated in cases of medical necessity for the individual or, exceptionally, in the therapeutic interests of others.

20 On this approach, see K. Bennoune, "Secularism and Human Rights: A Contextual Analysis of Headscarves, Religious Expression, and Women's Equality Under International Law", *Columbia Journal of Transnational Law* vol. 45, no. 5, (2007): 367; and K. Bennounr, "The Law of the Republic Versus the "Law of the Brothers": A Story of France's Law Banning Religious Symbols in Public Schools". In: D.R. Hurwitz, D.B. Ford (eds.), *Human Rights: Advocacy Stories* (New York: Foundation Press, 2009): 155–190. https://img.slate.com/media/22/CHAP5.Bennoune.Headscarves.pdf. Accessed November 8, 2024.

21 Quoted by V. Fortier, J. Dugne, J. Lelieur, F. Vialla, *La circoncision rituelle au regard du droit français. La circoncision rituelle. Enjeux de droit, enjeux de vérité* (Strasbourg: Presse universitaires de Strasbourg, 2016): 180. https://hal.science/hal-02160720v1/file/view-90.pdf. Accessed November 8, 2024.

22 Loi n°94-653 du 29 juillet 1994. JORF July 30, 1994.

> The consent of the person concerned must be obtained beforehand, except where his or her condition makes necessary a therapeutic intervention to which he or she is not in a position to consent.[23]

The principle of integrity is set aside when two conditions are met: on the one hand, medical necessity (previously therapeutic necessity) and, on the other hand, the consent of the person concerned, provided this does not contravene public order. The protection of the body against any interference not justified by medical necessity applies to both adults and minors.

In this respect, ritual circumcision represents an "exception to the intangibility of the human body, since it constitutes an irreversible attack on the bodily integrity of a boy and, in any event, takes place without his consent".[24] Ritual circumcision is not explicitly regulated by law; it has been incorporated into public acceptance by a long-lasting practice. In the absence of any explicit legal provision, the courts have set conditions to the procedure.[25]

In French law, "for non-therapeutic medical acts, it appears that individual freedom is sufficient to justify the need for the act",[26] as in the case of abortion, for example. Consent is in principle both sufficient and necessary. In this area, the patient's wishes and consent to the procedure are essential. Non-therapeutic medical procedures are subject to a special consent regime. These specific legislative provisions relate to informing patients and obtaining their consent. In the case of non-therapeutic medical procedures, the information provided must be exhaustive so that the patient can make an informed decision. The information thus covers all the possible consequences of the operation and all the risks, including exceptional risks, incurred by the patient.[27] Minors cannot consent to a medical procedure; consent must be given by the parents. However, in the case of non-therapeutic medical procedures, minors benefit from "unprecedented decision-making autonomy"[28] enabling them to give their own consent to the procedure.

However, a distinction must be made between two situations, depending on whether or not the action in question is of an urgent nature. In the case of an urgent medical procedure, one that cannot be delayed until the child reaches the age of majority, the personal freedom of the minor is sufficient to authorise the procedure – for example, in the case of an abortion.

23 Article 16-3 of the Civil Code (transl. G. Rouhette, A. Rouhette-Berton). https://www.fd.ulisboa.pt/wp-content/uploads/2014/12/Codigo-Civil-Frances-French-Civil-Code-english-version.pdf. Accessed November 8, 2024.

24 V. Fortier, J. Dugne, J. Lelieur, F. Vialla, *La circoncision rituelle,* 181–182.

25 See e.g. Aix-en-Provence Court of Appeal, April 23, 1990; Court of Cassation, Mai 30 1991.

26 V. Fortier, J. Dugne, J. Lelieur, F. Vialla, *La circoncision rituelle*, 181–182.

27 V. Fortier, J. Dugne, J. Lelieur, F. Vialla, *La circoncision rituelle*, 187.

28 V. Fortier, J. Dugne, J. Lelieur, F. Vialla, *La circoncision rituelle*, 188–189.

If the procedure is non-urgent, then it must wait until the child reaches the age of majority.

Thus, under general legal provisions, a non-therapeutic medical procedure can be carried out on a minor with the minor's consent in case of urgency. Circumcision does not belong to this category. Moreover, it is usually practiced well before the child is able to give his consent. At this point, the religious nature of the procedure allows for a privileged treatment, as a derogation from general principles. It is considered to be a part of religious education, which, like education in general, is a parental prerogative.

The international human rights standards are also relevant while assessing the legal position of the analysed religious practice in France. Article 14 of the Convention on the Rights of the Child, ratified by France, states that "States Parties shall respect the child's right to freedom of thought, conscience and religion." Under paragraph 2, "States Parties shall respect the rights and duties of the child's parents or, when applicable, legal guardians to provide direction to the child in the exercise of the above-mentioned right in a manner consistent with the evolving capacities of the child."

Thus, the CRC clearly recognises the right to freedom of thought, conscience and religion to children, but parents or legal guardians have the right to provide "direction" to the child in his exercise of this right. For these authors, "in the context of parental authority, the minor is merely the subject of rights and of the law. [...] Certain rights granted to minors under the CRC are difficult to reconcile with parental prerogatives, which makes it possible to doubt their effectiveness"[29] Indeed, in French law, it seems the parental right to guidance and the parental authority trumps children's rights: among other issues, it is up to the parents to choose their child's religious education. However, this prerogative is not unlimited. As a result, holders of parental authority must not endanger the child's health, safety or morality, by conforming with the religious obligations, or put in jeopardy the conditions of their child's education or training through obedience to religious dogmas and practices.[30]

It can be claimed that considerations of health and safety may appear in cases involving circumcisions carried out in unsanitary conditions, endangering the child's health. However, circumcision *per se* is not seen in French case law as endangering the child's health;[31] the intrusion into the child's bodily integrity, while permanent, is considered minor and not entailing significant consequences when done in safe conditions.

29 V. Fortier, J. Dugne, J. Lelieur, F. Vialla, *La circoncision rituelle*, 188–189.

30 Cf. V. Fortier, J. Dugne, J. Lelieur, F. Vialla, *La circoncision rituelle*, 181–182.

31 E.g., S. Wahedi, "The Health Law Implications of Ritual Circumcisions", *Quinnipiac Health Law Journal* vol. 22 (2019): 209–249. http://hdl.handle.net/1765/116606. Accessed November 8, 2024.

It also needs to be stressed that, in legal practice, the child's freedom alone carries little weight.[32] In principle, when both parents agree to circumcision, there is nothing to prevent it. Disputes arise when one of the parents wants to have the child circumcised and the second opposes it, or when one of the parents has already had the child circumcised on his or her own initiative, and the second takes the matter to court.[33] Also, little attention is paid to the child's right to religious freedom. As the authors point out, it is less a question of protecting the child than of protecting the rights of the parents, as they state, "Curiously, the notion of the child's interests is almost never mentioned, at least not explicitly".[34]

13.4.2 An Unusual Act of Parental Authority: Who Can Consent to Circumcision?

The French Civil Code does not define what is meant by usual or non-usual acts of parental authority. Usual acts of parental authority benefit from a presumption of agreement under Article 372-2 of the Civil Code. With regard to acts concerning the child, routine acts of care are certainly "usual acts". However, ritual circumcision seems to be not of this category.

As a consequence of the classification of ritual circumcision as a non-routine act of parental authority, the agreement of both parents is required to circumcise the child. In cases when parents do not agree on circumcision, judges never authorise the procedure to be carried out, as it would mean making a choice of the child's religious education, which they cannot do because of their obligation of religious neutrality stemming from the principle of *Laïcité*. No religious criterion can intervene in the judge's choice. This approach is expressed in many judgements, including an example of the *dictum* by the Lyon Court of Appeal:

> As this involves intervention into the child's physical integrity, this serious decision can only be taken by mutual agreement between the parents and with the consent of the child, aged 11; in the absence of consent from either the mother or the child, who has repeatedly expressed his opposition to such an operation, the application must be rejected.[35]

32 See, e.g., R. Bozarslan, *The removal of male foreskin: Circumcision or Mutilation? A study on the conflict between the right of the parent to freedom of religion vs. the right of the child to freedom of religion and bodily integrity* (Uppsala: Upsala University, 2024): 37–38. http://www.diva-portal.org/smash/get/diva2:1874128/FULLTEXT01.pdf. Accessed November 8, 2024.

33 K. Neutel, *Shedding religious skin: an intersectional analysis of the claim that male circumcision limits religious freedom. The complexity of conversion: intersectional perspectives on religious change in antiquity and beyond* (Sheffield: Equinox Publishing, 2021): 23.

34 V. Fortier, J. Dugne, J. Lelieur, F. Vialla, *La circoncision rituelle* 190.

35 Lyon Court of Appeal, July 25, 2007, JurisData 2007-346158.

In a case that was examined by the Nancy Court of Appeal, judges confirmed that the father was prohibited from circumcising his child, pointing out that

> the protection and education of the child, which must also be understood as religious education, are the raison d'être of parental authority. Given the importance of any decision in religious matters, it is inconceivable that such a decision could be taken without the agreement of both parents who jointly exercise parental authority.[36]

If one parent ignores the other parent's opposition, this will be treated as a serious matter, with a sanction that may go as far as limiting parental authority or withdrawing visiting rights.

In one of the more complex cases, where the father had probably attempted to circumcise the child himself, a significant lesion had affected the child's foreskin, which was also psychologically traumatising. The judges considered that, at the very least, the father's negligence required a review of the arrangements for organising paternal custody rights.[37]

Another case concerned a 3-year-old boy circumcised in Algeria at the sole initiative of the father, even though the mother refused to raise the child in the Muslim religion. On his return to France, the child developed a serious infection. The court found that the father's failure to comply with the rules of joint parental authority was particularly serious and therefore awarded exclusive parental authority to the mother. The ruling prohibited the father from taking the children to a religious community and/or denominational school, prohibited them from leaving the country, and even removed the right to visits and accommodation on Wednesdays insofar as this time spent with children would be used by the father to take the children to a mosque.[38]

On a side note, one should also stress that for the medical staff performing a circumcision without ensuring double consent from both parents, the category "blameworthy thoughtlessness" would be applicable, and legal consequences would follow.[39]

In conclusion, ritual circumcision is not prohibited in France, as long as the aforementioned legal framework is respected. In fact, circumcision will only be prohibited if there is a risk that not all conditions are met. Consequently, as long as both parents agree and the procedure is carried out in conditions respecting the boy's health and safety, circumcision is authorised. Contrary to developments in other European countries, the procedure itself and its conformity with children's

36 Nancy Court of Appeal, October 5, 2009, JurisData 2009-023366.
37 Orléans Court of Appeal, March 14, 2006, JurisData no. 2006-310764.
38 Lyon Court of Appeal, January 10, 2011, also Toulouse Court of Appeal, October 13, 2014.
39 V. Fortier, J. Dugne, J. Lelieur, F. Vialla, *La circoncision rituelle* 180, 196.

rights to bodily integrity and right to freedom of thought, conscience, and religion are barely put in question.

For the authors of an important study on the matter,

> [t]he religious imperative has supplanted the legal imperative. The conflict between religious imperative and legal imperative is resolved in favour of the former. The rite would prevail over the rule of law of public order, which it nonetheless contravenes. In this competition between the two normative orders, a procedural conception of the law is favoured, with the judge verifying whether or not the conditions laid down for the performance of the act have been met.[40]

However, this analysis is not entirely correct. If it's true that this is a purely procedural conception of the law, without taking a stand on the substance, in a secular legal system, the religious imperative in itself does not supersede the legal imperative, but the legal order chooses to regulate the issue in giving precedence to parental authority over considerations of children's rights.

In the absence of a specific law, the rules of ordinary law prevail; the prohibition of interventions into body integrity and the child's right to freedom of conscience and religion, on the one hand, and the parents' right to educate their children, including in religious matters, on the other, are at stake and in judicial assessment, parental prerogatives prevail. It is mostly because of the fact that the parental authority is a well-established, "strong" right in French law, whereas the standards of the rights of the child stem from an international convention that is less well integrated into the legal system and moreover unclear on this point.

Moreover, ritual circumcision is in itself a long-standing and well-established religious practice. Prohibiting circumcision outright would be tantamount to overturning the established practice, which judges are very reluctant to do, in application of the French concept of the separation of powers. Article 5 of the French Civil Code prohibits judges from making general rulings. It thus seems that in order to finally clarify this complex and consequences bearing issue, the decision should be taken by the legislature in a form of a special law.

13.5 Ritual Slaughter: A Derogation to Implement the Principle of *Laïcité*

Unlike circumcision, ritual slaughter is expressly provided for by law, as it is a derogation from general rules on the prohibition of animal abuse and the regulation of slaughter.

40 V. Fortier, J. Dugne, J. Lelieur, F. Vialla, *La circoncision rituelle*, 197.

13.5.1 A Well-Established Legal Foundation and Practice

Legal provisions prohibit the mistreatment of domestic animals or wild animals that have been tamed or kept in captivity.[41] Article 521-1 of the French Criminal Code punishes "[t]he act, whether committed publicly or not, of seriously abusing or committing an act of cruelty against a domestic or tamed animal, or one held in captivity[...]". However, two exceptions are provided.[42] First, the relevant provisions do not apply to "bullfighting where an uninterrupted local tradition can be invoked. Nor do they apply to cockfighting in localities where an uninterrupted tradition can be established". As far as bullfighting is concerned, the case law is well-established and it follows that "local tradition" is understood to mean "a tradition that exists in a demographic grouping determined by a common culture, the same habits, the same aspirations and affinities, the same way of feeling things and of being enthusiastic about them', the same system of collective representations, the same mentalities", to quote the ruling by the criminal chamber of the Court of Cassation (highest civil and criminal court).[43] Secondly, ritual slaughter is only authorised in cases strictly defined by law.[44]

Animals must be stunned before slaughter or killing, except in the situation when such stunning is not compatible with the practice of ritual slaughter. A slaughterhouse may only implement this derogation if it has obtained a prior authorisation from the Ministry of Agriculture. It also must meet strict hygiene conditions, etc. A further provision provides for a system of authorisation of sacrificers "by religious bodies approved, on a proposal from the Minister of the Interior, by the Minister of Agriculture".

The derogation providing for the legality of ritual slaughter have been challenged before administrative courts. The higher administrative court (Conseil d'Etat), ruling on a request by an association promoting animal welfare, requesting the annulment of this exception,[45] stated,

> [W]hile it follows from the principle of *Laïcité* that all citizens are equal before the law without distinction of religion and that all beliefs must be respected, this same principle requires the Republic to guarantee the free

41 Article L. 214-3of the French Rural and Maritime Fishing Code (Code rural et de la pêche maritime. https://www.legifrance.gouv.fr/codes/texte_lc/LEGITEXT000006071367/. Accessed November 8, 2024.

42 A. Fornerod, "L'encadrement de l'abattage rituel en droit français : une irréductible exception", *Revue du droit des religions* no. 12 (2021): 65–78. https://hal.science/hal-03511606. Accessed November 8, 2024.

43 Court of Cassation, February 6, 1992, no 89-84675 which held in this case that "a bullfighting tradition exists in Bordeaux and in the geographical area of which it is the capital" which held in this case that "a bullfighting tradition exists in Bordeaux and in the geographical area of which it is the capital".

44 Article R214-70 of the French Rural and Maritime Fishing Code.

45 Conseil d'État, *Œuvre d'assistance aux bêtes d'abattoirs*, no. 361441 [2013] ECLI:FR:CESSR:2013:361441.20130705.

> exercise of religious worship; as a result, the possibility of derogating from the requirement for stunning for ritual slaughtering does not infringe the principle of *Laïcité*.[46]

Hence, *Laïcité* itself imposes on the State a duty to guarantee the free exercise of religions, and that includes religious rites such as ritual slaughter. As it is a right guaranteed by the State, the State is also competent to set conditions for its exercise. This is a clear application of the fact that *Laïcité* does not only entail the recognition of the right to freedom of worship, but it is a State duty to make sure this right may be effectively exercised.

In another case, a city council has decided to fit out and finance disused premises with an aim of turning them into a temporary local abattoir intended to operate mainly during the three days of the Aïd-el-Kébir religious feast.[47] The City Council's decision had been overturned by the lower administrative court on the grounds that it had been taken in disregard of the law of 9 December 1905 on the separation of Church and State. The lower court pointed especially to the problem of financing a religious activity by public authorities. However, the Conseil d'Etat squashed the judgement, and ruled,

> The 1905 Law does not prevent a local authority [...] from building or acquiring a facility or authorising the use of an existing facility, in order to allow ritual practices falling within the scope of the free exercise of religions, provided that a local public interest, relating in particular to the need for religions to be exercised in conditions that comply with the imperatives of public order, in particular public hygiene and public health, justifies such intervention [...]
>
> and that, in addition, the right to use the equipment is granted under conditions, in particular tariff conditions, that respect the principle of neutrality with regard to religious denominations and the principle of equality and that exclude any donation and, consequently, any aid to a religious denomination.

This ruling exemplifies the pragmatic interpretation of the law favoured by the highest administrative court. In this interpretation, the law does not rule out accommodations made necessary by local circumstances in order to fulfil the obligation of ensuring the free exercise of religious worship.[48]

46 Conseil d'État, *Œuvre d'assistance aux bêtes d'abattoirs*, no. 361441 [2013].

47 Conseil d'État, *Communauté urbaine du Mans*, no 309161 [2011]. https://www.legifrance.gouv.fr/ceta/id/CETATEXT000024390111/. Accessed November 8, 2024.

48 With a similar conclusion, see Conseil d'État, *Association Vigilance Halal*, no. 433067 [2019] ECLI:FR:CECHR:2019:433067.20191227, protection et respect de l'animal et du consommateur/.

Ritual slaughter can only be carried out in equipped premises and by authorised persons. If these conditions are not respected, ritual slaughter may be prosecuted. In a case of slaughter during voodoo ceremonies in a private apartment, several persons, all members of the same family, were prosecuted for "serious abuse or cruelty to a domestic or tame animal or one held in captivity." During voodoo ceremonies, "animal sacrifices were carried out with bare hands or swords by Mrs S... T... Q... who sprinkled the blood over the participants". In its final judgement on the merits of the case,[49] the Court of Cassation stated, "[T]he principle of religious freedom does not imply that the practice of abuse and acts of cruelty, within the meaning of article 521-1 of the Criminal Code, on domestic animals that have been tamed or kept in captivity, which are understood to mean only acts carried out intentionally with the aim of causing their suffering or death, is authorised", nor does it extend the exceptions in Article 521-1 of the Criminal Code. The Court of Cassation ruled that the conviction for maltreatment of animals was justified on the grounds that

> the defendant, with the help of her husband for the large animals, killed hens, pigeons, sheep and goats in the temple located at their home, in breach of the prohibition in article R. 214-73 of the Rural Code on carrying out or having carried out ritual slaughter outside a slaughterhouse [...].[50]

Moreover, "Mr and Mrs Q. did not use any method of sedation before slaughtering a large number of animals", the court rejected the appeal, on the grounds that "no one may rely on his or her religious beliefs to disregard the common rules laid down by criminal law".

13.6 Regulation of Ritual Slaughter and Minority Groups within the Minority

The French context in relation to the issue of ritual slaughter was also present in the European Court of Human Rights. The case *Cha'are Shalom Ve Tsedek v. France* illustrates some controversies that arose in the process of authorisation and regulation of ritual slaughter, and the temptation of State authorities to regulate religious activities to the point of excessive interference.[51]

The association Cha'are Shalom Ve Tsedek represents a minority group among the religious Jews in France, who apply more stringent requirements for ritual slaughter ("glatt" meat) than the interpretation of *Kashrut* by the main body administering Judaism in France (the Jewish Consistorial Association of Paris – Association consistoriale israélite de Paris – the ACIP).

49 Court of Cassation, no. 18-84.554 [2019] ECLI:FR:CCASS:2019:CR00520.

50 Court of Cassation, no. 18-84.554 [2019].

51 *Cha'are Shalom Ve Tsedek v. France*, 27417/95 [2000] § 83, ECLI:CE:ECHR:2000:0627JUD002741795.

The applicant association alleged a violation of Article 9 of the European Convention on account of the French authorities' refusal to grant it the approval necessary for access to slaughterhouses with a view to performing ritual slaughter in accordance with the ultra-orthodox religious prescriptions of its members. Importantly, in 1982, the French government granted the ACIP the exclusive privilege of carrying out Jewish ritual slaughter, in a way no longer satisfying the very strict requirements of the Jewish religion in the interpretation of the applicant. The applicant claimed that

> by refusing it the approval necessary for it to authorise its own ritual slaughterers to perform ritual slaughter, in accordance with the religious prescriptions of its members, and by granting such approval to the ACIP alone, the French authorities had infringed in a discriminatory way the applicant's right to manifest its religion through observance of the rites of the Jewish religion. It relied on Article 9 of the Convention, taken alone and in conjunction with Article 14.[52]

But the ECtHR majority ruled,

> Since it has not been established that Jews belonging to the applicant association cannot obtain "glatt" meat, or that the applicant association could not supply them with it by reaching an agreement with the ACIP, in order to be able to engage in ritual slaughter under the approval granted to the ACIP, the Court considers that the refusal of approval did not constitute an interference with the applicant association's right to the freedom to manifest its religion.[53]

However, several judges expressed their disagreement in a joint dissenting opinion: "[T]he mere fact that approval has already been granted to one religious body does not absolve the State authorities from the obligation to give careful consideration to any later application made by other religious bodies professing the same religion". [54]

The policy of French authorities in this case can be perceived as a tendency of the French authorities to favour one centralised religious institution for each faith group, or to put it differently: to have only one interlocutor for each religion. Another example of this approach was the effort of successive French governments to establish a central Muslim representative authority, an "official Muslim institution", such as the CFCM (French Council of the Muslim Faith).

52 *Cha'are Shalom Ve Tsedek v. France*, 27417/95 [2000] § 58.
53 *Cha'are Shalom Ve Tsedek v. France*, 27417/95 [2000] § 83.
54 *Cha'are Shalom Ve Tsedek v. France*, 27417/95 [2000] § 83.

Governments seek to have a centralised, structured body speaking in the name of each religion, trying thus to mould all religions on the model of the Catholic Church, which is characterised by being centralised and organised along a clear hierarchy.

In a liberal interpretation of the principle of *Laïcité*, that should not be the role or the aim of the State. Religious organisations should be free to organise themselves autonomously, according to their own tradition. In *Cha'are*, the State's answer to the orthodox Jewish association was, in short, that they should reach an agreement with the Central Consistory. But in so doing, authorities favoured the mainstream institution and a centralising tendency in a way that limits smaller and/or dissident groups of the same religious tradition. Authorities thus end up favouring conservatism and conformism. In this particular case, it hindered the rights and freedoms of a more traditionalist and conservative religious group.

13.7 Conclusion

The cases analysed in the present chapter illustrate the nature, and the complexity of the principle of the French *Laïcité*. Its philosophy, concentrated on individual freedom, explains the prohibition of ostensible religious symbols in public schools: it aims at developing individual autonomy and freedom of choice by avoiding religious pressure and proselytism on pupils. In turn, the lack of implicit legal regulation of ritual circumcision shows the wariness of public authorities to regulate issues pertaining to parental choices over their children. Lastly, the French legal regulation of ritual slaughter is a good illustration of an often-overlooked aspect of *Laïcité*: the State duty to guarantee the free exercise of religious worship enshrined in the 1905 Law. And thus, the principle of *Laïcité* is not as an anti-religious construct, even though it does reflect an acute awareness of the oppressive potential of religions, and hence the need to regulate their free exercise. The principle of *Laïcité* is a framework seeking to allow the exercise of the right of every person to freedom of thought, conscience, and belief.

Epilogue: The *Amicus Curiae* Opinion of the International Association for Jewish Lawyers and Jurists of the CJEU *Shechita* Case

Court of Justice of the European Union *Amicus Curiae* Brief

Written by Professor Joseph H. H. Weiler and Meir Linzen

Submitted on behalf of the International Association of Jewish Lawyers and Jurists in case C-336/19 *Centraal Israëlitisch Consistorie van België and Others*

A Background

1 The IJL is an international non-governmental organisation ("NGO") comprising legal practitioners and academic jurists in more than 15 countries. Among its founders were Israeli Supreme Court Justice Haim Cohn of Israel, US Supreme Court Justice and US ambassador to the United Nations Arthur Goldberg, and Nobel Peace Prize laureate René Cassin of France, the main author of the Universal Declaration of Human Rights.

2 The IJL has Category II Status as an NGO at the United Nations, enabling it to participate in the deliberations of various UN bodies, including the Human Rights Council, which assesses compliance with international standards for human rights protection across UN Member States. The IJL presents opinions on international legal matters that are critical to protecting the rights and freedoms of individuals.

3 In this capacity, the IJL concentrates on a wide range of issues related to human rights protection, with particular emphasis on fighting anti-Semitism by law, promoting peace and preventing genocide and war crimes, in addition to international cooperation based on the rule of law and democracy.

DOI: 10.4324/9781003423294-19

B Introduction

4 In the interest of animal welfare, some jurisdictions require that prior to slaughtering for the purpose of human consumption of certain animals (e.g. cattle, sheep, swine) they be 'stunned'. Stunning is performed in a variety of ways including electric shock or shooting of a metal bolt through the brain of the beast. Said stunning renders the animal insensate before knife is put to flesh and the actual butchering takes place. The stunning procedure itself causes pain to the animal but it is of a very short duration.

5 Jewish (and Muslim)[1] religious law prohibit such stunning prior to the actual act of slaughtering. The animal to be slaughtered must be alive, whole and without blemish. Stunning prior to the slaughter would compromise all three requirements. An animal which is not slaughtered in the required manner may not be consumed. The slaughtering, which must be performed by a person specifically trained for such, consists of single incision which severs, inter alia, the carotid arteries. When performed correctly, the massive drainage of blood from the head of the animal also renders it insensate, though this will occur over a longer period of time compared to stunning. Veterinary authorities dispute that period of time with estimates ranging from a few seconds to a few minutes, as well as the degree of suffering caused as a result, compared to the degree of suffering caused as result of stunning.

6 Applying by law the pre-stunning requirement would, thus, violate the strictures of Jewish and Islamic law and amount to a *de jure* and *de facto* outlawing of religiously permitted slaughtering. It would have the collateral effect of a measure of forced vegetarianism[2] (fish may still be consumed) on these communities of faith, and may force these communities to eventually emigrate, leading to the end of Jewish life in Member States which will impose such ban.

7 It will have a secondary collateral effect of publicly branding Judaism and Islam as inhumane. This secondary effect is not to be trivialised given, first, the history of such bans oftentimes driven by overtly Anti-Semitic motives and, second, the current rise in Antisemitism (and Islamophobia) in Europe. The Court should not lightly approve such.

8 Freedom of religion is a fundamental human right guaranteed by all European constitutions as well as the principal European instruments

1 Throughout this Brief we refer mostly to Jewish law though most of the considerations presented would apply, mutatis mutandis, to Islamic law too.

2 Meeting this argument by claiming that such communities could import their meat from countries without such a ban, is no more than another instance of hypocritical 'moral dumping' onto other societies, long denounced in the context of, say, environmental policy. 'We will ban coal burning in our society, but import our electricity from countries which allow such'. Furthermore, there are no adequate solutions for the importation of fresh meat to all Jewish (and Muslim) communities.

such as the Charter of Fundamental Rights of the European Union and the Convention for the Protection of Human Rights and Fundamental Freedoms. To forbid a community of faith to prepare their food in accordance with their religious obligations is thus a prima facie violation of such.

9 In addition, the requirement of pre-stunning, is discriminatory in nature. Though formulated as addressed to all slaughtering regardless of its nature, it is clearly directed at these two communities of faith thus raising the specter of direct discrimination. Even if one accepts that the aim was not to target Jews (and Muslims), but indeed driven by a genuine concern for animal welfare, it is beyond dispute that it produces a disparate impact on these two communities and thus, constitutes a classical case of indirect discrimination, a per se additional violation of human rights as well as an additional hurdle in justifying the primary violation of freedom of religion. The fact that the indirect discrimination affects minority groups requires particular vigilance by the Court. One of the foundations of the empowerment of courts in democratic societies to review the constitutionality even of parliamentary legislation is precisely to protect, where appropriate, minorities against dictates or whims of majorities.

10 Council Regulation 1099/2009 capaciously and comprehensively regulates the protection of animals at the time of killing and thus preempts individual Member State action in this field. The Regulation is binding in its entirety and directly applicable in all Member States. Specifically, it provides in Article 4(4) an exemption for ritual slaughtering and sets out a single condition for such. The Regulation as a whole as well as Article 4(4) are clear, precise and unconditional thus producing direct effect. Member State measures in conflict with the Regulation violate, thus, also the principles of Direct Effect and 3 Council Regulation 1099/2009 of 24 September 2009 on the Protection of Animals at the Time of Killing, 2009 O.J. (L 303) 1. Supremacy of Union Law threatening the uniform application of Union Law in all Member States. Any change to this condition may only be effected by the Union itself.

11 The fact that we have here a prima facie case of violation of freedom of religion and of the non-discrimination principle, both enshrined in the abovementioned constitutional and international instruments, combined with a Union Regulation directly applicable and binding in its entirety providing for the specific exception for slaughter prescribed by religious rites, mandates finding that applying the pre-stunning requirement in the context of religious slaughter cannot survive judicial review.

12 However, even if one is of the view that the pre-stunning requirement is not, in and of itself, irredeemably illegal and unconstitutional, a careful analysis of the competing considerations will lead to the same conclusion.

13 Few human rights, if any, are absolute in nature and this applies, too, to freedom of religion. It is a common place that there can be compelling public reasons which may permit the compromising of fundamental human rights.

14 The point of departure, however, is that every effort must be made by society to honor fundamental rights such as freedom of religion and non-discrimination as fully and capaciously as possible, and the corresponding legal presumption is that violation of such is absent justification unconstitutional. Often times, as in the case of, say, offensive speech, the exercise of such right may provoke popular indignation. We do not need to protect speech we like. We protect speech we do not like. It is for this reason that we empower our courts, the independence of which is at the heart of the Rule of Law, removed from the pressures of popular and populist electoral pressures, to ensure that only under the most compelling of circumstances, fundamental human rights, including freedom of religion, be compromised. The onus of proof must be on the public authority which seeks to compromise such rights. And the burden of proof must be high. Fundamental human rights may not be compromised lightly.

15 Under what conditions may the banning of Jewish (and Muslim) slaughtering in accordance with religious strictures be allowed? (If one does not accept our argument that due to the unique regulatory framework, such banning should not be allowed at all). One must follow here the well-trodden proportionality analysis applied in cases of fundamental human rights.

16 In the first case, the Court would have to be satisfied that the effective ban of religious slaughtering by insisting on pre stunning is enacted in the general interest and is in pursuit of a legitimate public policy.

17 Even should this be the case, it would then have to be satisfied that, within the limits of reasonable practice, said measure is the least restrictive to the exercise of freedom of religion in pursuing the legitimate public policy and that the discriminatory effect is unavoidable.

18 Finally, it would have to decide, in what is sometimes termed as 'balancing' or 'proportionality strictu sensu', whether the values enshrined in the public policy, in this case animal welfare, outweigh the values enshrined in the protected fundamental right, in this case freedom of religion.

19 One further consideration is germane in applying the last stage of the analysis. When the measure in question – in this case the ban on religiously mandated slaughtering – results in discrimination, as is the case here, the scales in the balancing act should be tilted even further on the side of protecting the fundamental human right.

C Applying the Method of Analysis to Ritual Slaughtering

20 Is the *de jure* and *de facto* outlawing of Jewish (and Muslim) ritual slaughtering in pursuit of a legitimate public policy? The answer to this must be affirmative. Even without entering into the jurisprudentially complex issue of 'animal rights', a concern for animal welfare in the raising and the slaughtering of animals intended for human consumption is widespread

and entirely legitimate, as evidenced by an array of laws in many States and in legislation of the European Union itself. Given that pre-stunning reduces the length of suffering in the slaughtering of animals, such a requirement would fall naturally within such a policy.

21 However, there is empirical difficulty in comparing the suffering of the animal under the two methods of slaughtering, since it is undisputed that the animal still suffers even with pre-stunning. Hence, even enforcement of a full ban on slaughtering without pre-stunning will not eliminate concerns for animal welfare.

22 On the other hand, the assessment of the offense to religious liberty by instituting such a ban may not be obvious and clear to everyone. Sometimes the importance of the religious ritual is not self-evident. For non-Catholics, the sacrament of the Eucharist might appear to be a baffling ritual. For a Catholic, its spiritual significance, the possibility of feeling the real presence of the Divine, cannot be overstated.

23 The religious law governing ritual slaughter, including the prohibition on pre stunning, is an inseparable part of the broad and elaborate matrix of Jewish 'Table Law' – governing *Kosher* and Non-*Kosher* foods (and *Halal*) which to the observant Jew or Jewess (and Muslim) has a similarly deep spiritual and religious meaning and in accordance with such law may only be compromised to save human life.

24 While not every legal norm carries the same weight, the legal norm with respect to slaughter is of the highest importance: no observant Jew will eat non-*Kosher* meat, unless, as just noted, it is a matter of life or death of a human subject.

25 And yet, it is precisely that part of Judaism and Islam which appears the least comprehendible, the most baffling, and the one most destitute of any spiritual religious meaning to outside observers. Why, one might almost naturally think, should an animal be made to suffer even one minute more, to honor such ritualistic 'mumbo jumbo'?

26 More generally, whereas Jewish moral law, the Ten Commandments, Love Thy Neighbor and the like, which are similar to Christian moral law, are seen as compelling and profound, the entire corpus of ritual law, of which *Kosher* law is a central part, appear as a black box at best and worthy of derision at worst. And yet the religious significance of ritual slaughtering consists in being part and parcel, inseparable, from the general matrix of that black box of ritual law, as shall be explained below.

27 That the dense matrix of ritual law should be incomprehensible is not surprising in Western civilization. A massive civilisational force – the Christian tradition which defined the West for close to two millennia – conditioned contemporary sensibilities on these issues. One central feature of the Christian Revolution was the teaching (in the Sermon on the Mount, for example) that the Law was accomplished and that the nature of the Covenant between God and (Wo)man had eternally changed. That the function of the prior law was now accomplished through Jesus

Christ. To give but one emblematic example, it was not important what man put into his mouth, but rather the words that came out of a man's mouth. Few teachings of Jesus resonate to Western ears, whether religious or secular, more powerfully than these. And with that, the intricate matrix of rituals which was and remains one central feature of Jewish law, its Nomos, was consigned to the dustbin of Christian religious understanding and practice as a relic of an earlier and more primitive stage in God's world.

28 A normative judgment was associated with this feature of the Christian Revolution, Ritualistic Nomos was the peel. The core of the religious fruit was the interior of the human subject. You do not circumcise your penis, as do Jews and Muslims, but your heart. This normative judgment was (and is) often accompanied by contempt for the primitiveness of those aspects of Islam and Judaism and, even as contempt dissipated – or at least as we learnt to conceal it – a total incomprehension of the profound spiritual significance of Nomos set in.

29 And yet, in order successfully to balance the competing values of religious freedom manifest in ritual slaughtering on the one hand and the concern for animal welfare on the other, the Court simply must fully understand the religious significance of the set of *Kosher* norms of which the rules on ritual slaughter are an integral and inseparable part.

30 What then is this significance? For this purpose, one cannot avoid a brief theological excursus.

D A Theological Excursus – The Religious Significance of *Kosher* Observance

31 The point of departure in answering this question is that there is no intrinsic functional explanation for *Kosher* observance – and this is of considerable significance.

32 *Kosher* food is not healthier, nor did it develop from ancient considerations of physical wellbeing. And this is true not only for the overall complex system of *Kosher* observance but also to the specificities of its internal intricate rules. Shellfish, as manifest in Japanese cuisine, are among the most nutritious and healthy elements of a diet. They are non-*Kosher*. There have, of course, been many attempts to rationalise the rules of *Kosher* observance in such material functional ways – they are not simply unconvincing and forced, but in some ways negate the deeper meanings of such observance.

33 For most, the meaning of the Monotheistic Revolution introduced by the Abrahamic religions was the move from polytheism, the belief in many gods, to the belief in one God only, the Holy One Blessed be He. But for the initiated, Monotheism signifies much more than the oneness of the Lord. It is his transcendent nature. Belief in the Sun as the one and only God is monotheistic. It is not transcendent – and thus idolatrous in the

eyes of Abrahamic Monotheism. The Transcendent God is neither a stone nor a river, neither the sun nor the moon. She or He or It are not of this world. When we try to describe such a God with human, material imagery and allusion, a limitation of our human condition, we inevitably compromise the transcendence of The Transcendent God.

34 The problem transcendence creates is immediately apparent. The Abrahamic God is also the God of Love – a love that flows in both directions between God and humanity. How can one experience a fully transcendent God, let alone love Him? How can one feel the presence of the fully transcendent God in one's life? There must, therefore, be an immanent dimension to the Abrahamic God. This takes the form of what we call Revelation, whereby the Transcendence is breached and Immanence established. But there is a problem with Revelation: it is a one-off event, the knowledge of which might persist for millennia, but not the experience. And religion is not epistemic but experiential. It is not about knowing that there is a God – the God who created the world and did other amazing things thousands of years ago. It is about experiencing such, individually and collectively, from one generation to the next.

35 The revelation of God to the Jews and the enduring manifestation of his immanence was through The Law, Nomos.

36 How does the Law, Nomos, overcome the momentary nature of revelation and constitute a means for an enduring presence in the life of believing Jews and Jewesses? Let us once more dispel one of the most common anti-Semitic tropes – that Jewish law is all about arid rituals, such as circumcision, rules about shaving, head covering for men and women and, yes, *Kosher* observance.

37 The Moral law in both faiths is the same: Love Thy Neighbor is to be found in both Testaments and the Ten Commandments are to be found in the Pentateuch.

38 What differentiates the two traditions, Christian and Jewish, is that the Jewish Nomos retains the dense matrix of ritual law, of which *Kosher* observance is a central part, as normative and binding. And paradoxically, it is the 'arid', mindless, irritating ritualistic part of Nomos which is central to the Jewish approach to solving the Transcendence, the theological dilemma of Monotheism.

39 There are two key features of *Kosher* observance, one so obvious it may escape notice: *Kosher* observance concerns food and eating. We all have to eat, the sine qua non for material survival.

40 There is, of course, much more to food and eating in our culture than merely keeping alive. Cookery books are best sellers, restaurants are more popular than theatres or concert halls, and food and eating and cuisine is ubiquitous in both low, middlebrow and high culture. What to eat, how much to eat, when to eat, where to eat, and with whom to eat are a central part of daily existence.

41 For those Jews who observe *Kosher*, all that patchwork of food practice which imbues our life, from breakfast to that glass of wine before bedtime, is imbued with the thick matrix of *Kosher* practice. Nomos, the immanent manifestation of the transcendent God, is thus omnipresent in one's daily life in every meal, every bite, every invitation. The sacred is part of the most common practice of living, shared by rich and poor, old and young, woman and man.

42 And the very absence of intrinsic functional meaning to *Kosher* rules can suddenly be evaluated differently, as determinative. The homo religious may not kill because so commanded by God in the Ten Commandments. But you do not need that divine command, Nomos, to refrain from killing. But absent Nomos what would connect a Jew in his or her living experience to the presence of the Divine and the moment of Revelation?

43 There is a second dimension which explains the deep significance of *Kosher* observance (alongside Sabbath observance and the ritualistic rules of sex). They are often referred to as the yoke of Nomos. A constant set of restrictions on what may or may not be eaten (the *Kosher* rules) on the world of work and career (the Sabbath rules) and the limitations on sexual practice – covering thus the most fundamental aspects of material human experience. There is a constant temptation to free oneself from the chains of those ritualistic rules, which impinge so dramatically on such important dimensions of the human experience.

44 There is however another side to the freedom coin. But for the rules of *Kosher* eating, a person, in the Jewish view, is but a slave to his natural condition: eating when and what and how much he or she desires – a slave to his or her desires. You may now also consider the way we are enslaved, in this sense of enslavement, to our careers and to our carnal lusts – and get an analogous insight into the ritualistic aspect of Sabbath and sexual ritual laws. They produce the same liberating result.

45 Finally, in this brief excursus one must repeat the non-functional dimension of *Kosher* rules, their apparent arbitrary nature. We are meant to be left wondering. It is clear that no physical or material harm will ensue by disregarding them. But it is precisely this incomprehension and wondering which produces the liberating effect because there is really no earthly reason for the abstention, other than the command of the Divine. That is why the notion that one may dispense with the slaughtering dimension of the *Kosher* rules is fanciful. It is no less or more important than any other of this dense matrix, and abolishing it, for our convenience, including our ethical convenience, undermines the entire religious rationale of such divine rules.

46 It should have become clear that an outright ban on ritual slaughter affects a central and profound dimension of Jewish and Muslim faith – in this respect the logic of Jewish and Islamic law is similar -- and should be allowed only for the most compelling of reasons. It should

also be recalled that apart from the practical consequences of such a ban, the approval of such a ban would amount to public condemnation from the highest judicial authority of the very core of Judaism and Islam as divine Nomos based religions.

E Lesser Restrictive Measures – The Reality of Ritual Slaughtering

47 What, then, may be measures which serve to diminish animal suffering without totally banning ritual slaughter given its religious and spiritual centrality in Judaism and Islam?

48 Even those who oppose ritual slaughtering on grounds of animal welfare would accept that one is debating the length of suffering, and that when executed properly the animal is rendered insensate within a brief period of time. The passion for banning ritual slaughter, if not motivated by Islamophobia and anti-Semitism, latent or overt, is in large measure based (as argued above) on the belief that the ritual ban on pre-stunning is arbitrary and senseless. In which case, there is no reason to allow animal suffering even one second beyond that which is unavoidable. This Brief has attempted to dispel that notion.

49 And yet, the arguments above rest on the proposition that the ritual slaughter is executed properly. Nevertheless, in the reality of industrial, large scale slaughtering (which did not exist when the rules were formulated and consecrated), there may be cases in which the slaughtering is botched resulting in prolonged suffering. The harrowing images one sees in this context are typically the exceptional cases when such occurred.

50 It would be a totally reasonable and proportionate response of public authorities concerned with animal welfare to insist, whilst accepting ritual slaughtering, that guarantees and procedures be put in place to ensure that the slaughtering indeed be conducted as prescribed, avoiding or dramatically minimising the instance of botched cases. This can be achieved, for example, by a regime of State approved veterinary inspectors and inspections to supervise and ensure such, backed by hefty fines in cases of violation.

51 And in fact, this is indeed the approach which was already adopted by the Council Regulations, which allow slaughter prescribed by religious rights, provided that the slaughter takes place in a slaughterhouse, and while allowing Member States to put in place more extensive protection of animals at the time they are slaughtered.

F Conclusion

52 A concern for animal welfare in the process of slaughtering is a legitimate public concern, and policies designed to minimise such are legitimate.

53 An outright ban would constitute an unjustified and unjustifiable grave violation of the religious liberty of Jews and Muslims, and result in addition in an egregious case of indirect discrimination.
54 Such a ban would, additionally, be in violation of directly effective European Union law.
55 In any event, alternative, lesser restrictive measures are available to ameliorate and minimise the suffering of the animal, which is slaughtered in conformity with the religious ritual rules. Once applied, the difference between the pre-stunning process and the ritual slaughtering, properly executed, is reduced to the duration – measured in seconds at best, in minutes at worst – of the animal suffering.
56 Given the centrality of 'dietary rules' (what may or may not be eaten) to the ontology and theology of Judaism and Islam, and the transparent indirect discriminatory effect, an outright ban is a disproportionate outcome in the balancing of religious liberty and non-discrimination, as against the legitimate policy of animal welfare.

Index

Pages followed by "n" refer to notes.

Kolibri 360 GmbH
Ferdinand-Jühlke-Straße 7
99095 Erfurt, Deutschland
produktsicherheit@kolibri360.de